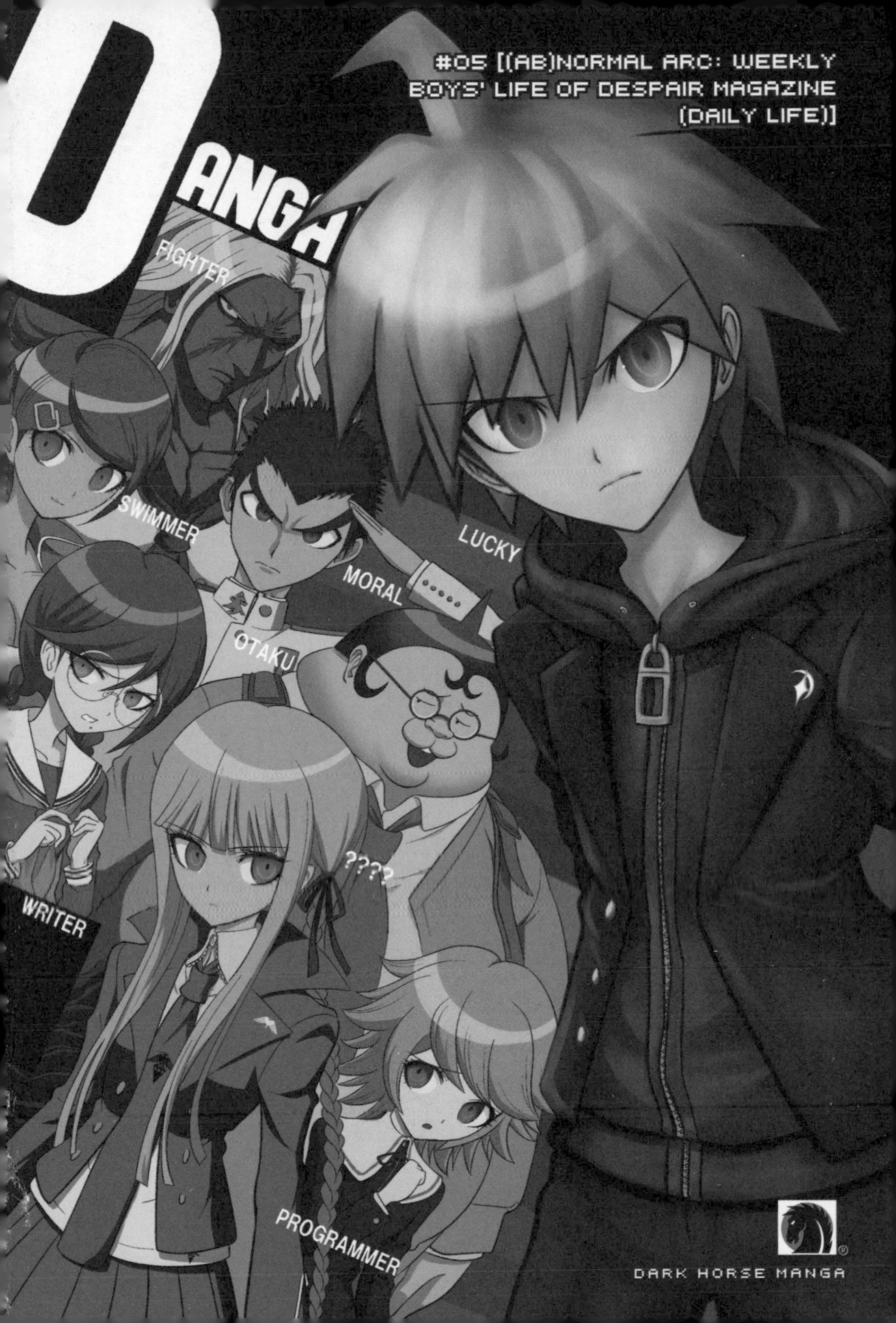

#05 [(AB)NORMAL ARC: WEEKLY
BOYS' LIFE OF DESPAIR MAGAZINE
(DAILY LIFE)]
DANGA
FIGHTER
SWIMMER
LUCKY
MORAL
OTAKU
????
WRITER
PROGRAMMER
DARK HORSE MANGA

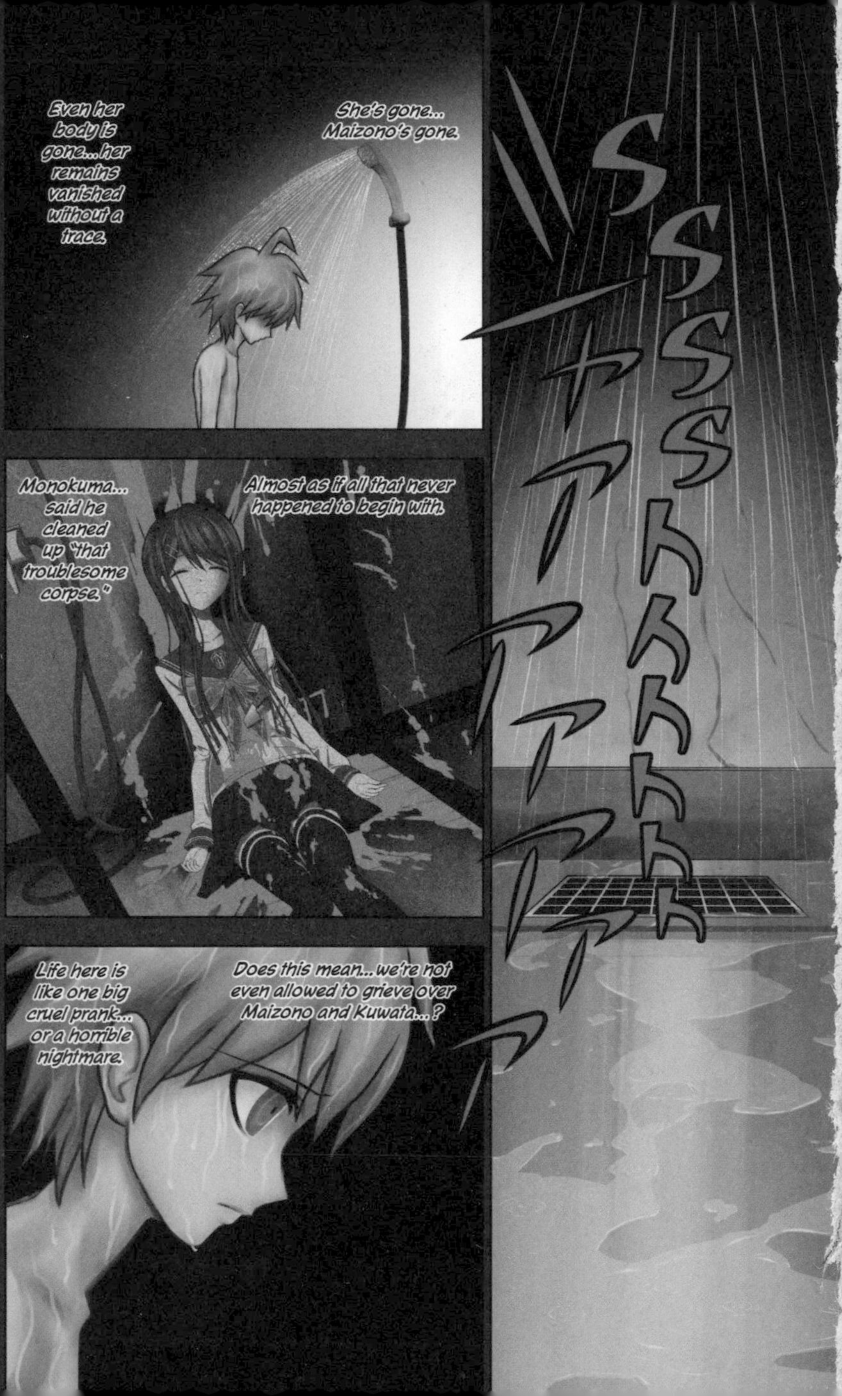
SSSS
She's gone... Maizono's gone.
Even her body is gone...her remains vanished without a trace.
Almost as if all that never happened to begin with.
Monokuma... said he cleaned up "that troublesome corpse."
Does this mean...we're not even allowed to grieve over Maizono and Kuwata...?
Life here is like one big cruel prank... or a horrible nightmare.

Contents

#05 [(AB)NORMAL ARC: WEEKLY BOYS' LIFE OF
DESPAIR MAGAZINE (DAILY LIFE)]
001

#06 [ABNORMAL ARC: WEEKLY BOYS' LIFE OF
DESPAIR MAGAZINE (DEADLY LIFE)]
053

#07 [(AB)NORMAL ARC: THE GALACTIC LEGEND OF
THE NEXT GENERATION RETURNS! STAND TALL,
ARMORED HERO! (DAILY LIFE)]
099

#08 [ABNORMAL ARC: THE GALACTIC LEGEND OF THE
NEXT GENERATION RETURNS! STAND TALL, ARMORED
HERO! (DEADLY LIFE) I]
133

CREATED BY SPIKE CHUNSOFT
MANGA BY TAKASHI TSUKIMI

TRANSLATION BY JACKIE MCCLURE
LETTERING AND TOUCHUP BY JOHN CLARK
EDITED BY CARL GUSTAV HORN
SPECIAL THANKS TO CLARINE HARP,
GIA MANRY, AND SUSIE NIXON AT FUNIMATION

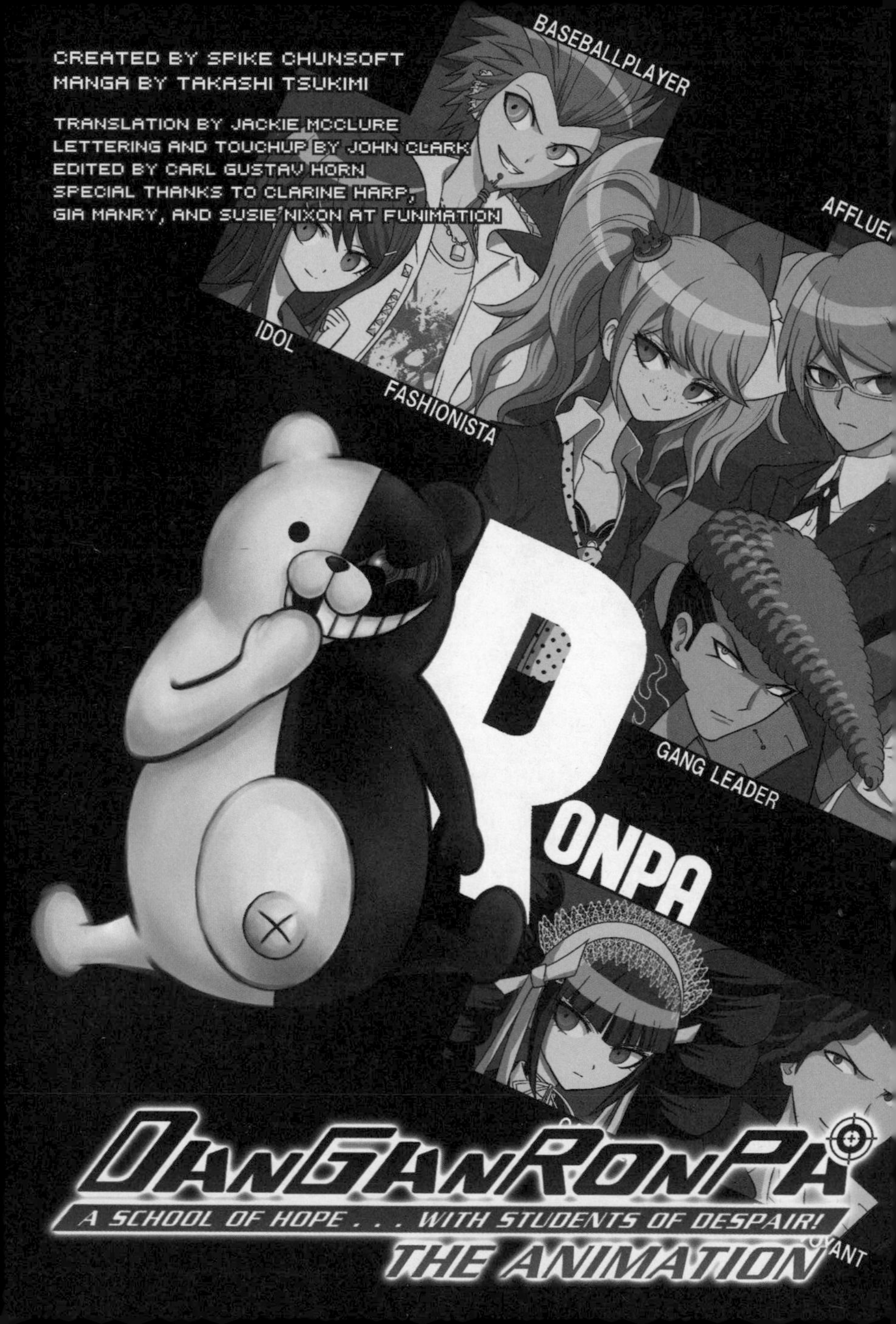
BASEBALLPLAYER
IDOL
FASHIONISTA
GANG LEADER
ONPA
DANGANRONPA
A SCHOOL OF HOPE . . . WITH STUDENTS OF DESPAIR!
THE ANIMATION

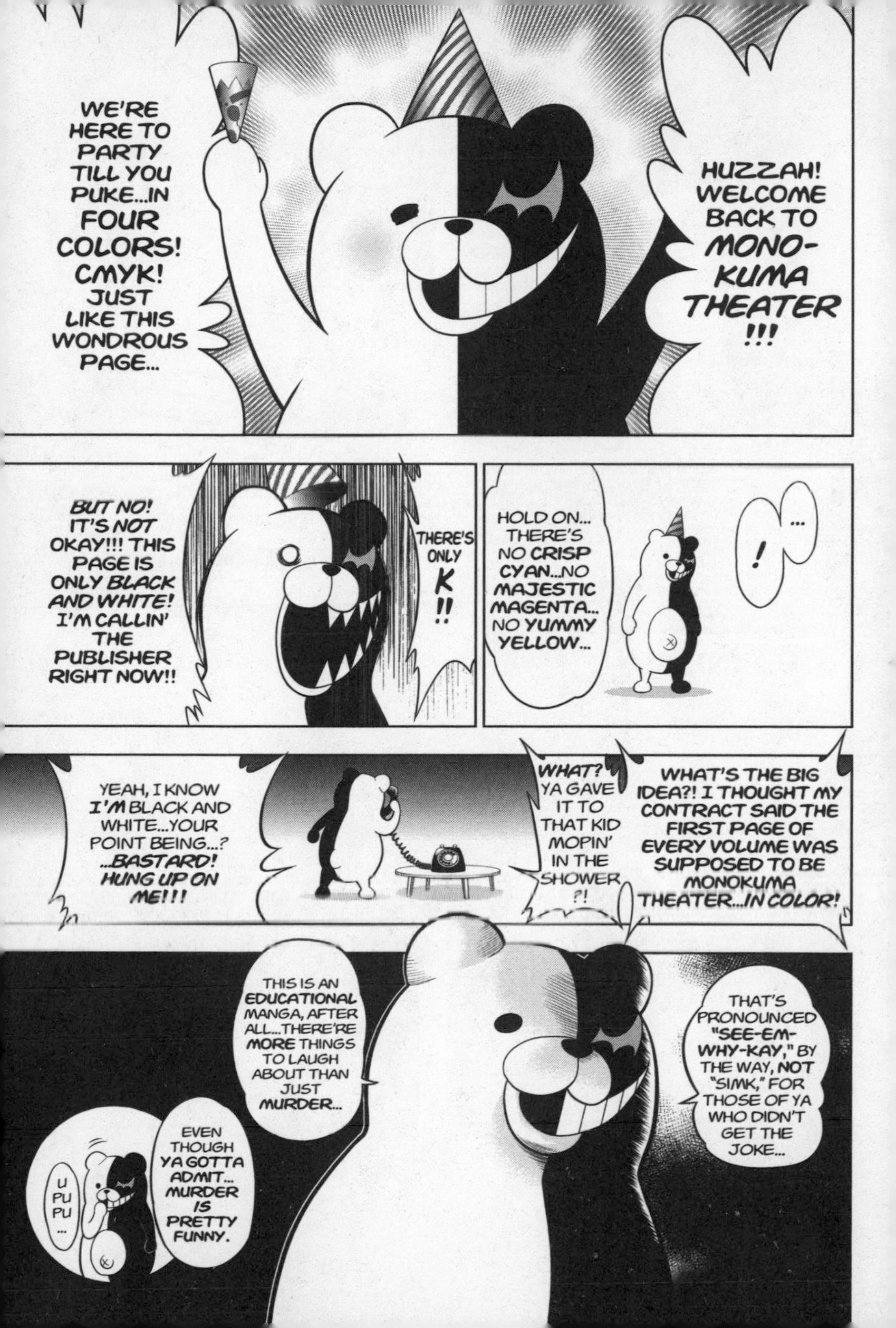
HUZZAH! WELCOME BACK TO MONO-KUMA THEATER!!!
WE'RE HERE TO PARTY TILL YOU PUKE...IN FOUR COLORS! CMYK! JUST LIKE THIS WONDROUS PAGE...
...!
HOLD ON... THERE'S NO CRISP CYAN...NO MAJESTIC MAGENTA... NO YUMMY YELLOW...
THERE'S ONLY K!!
BUT NO! IT'S NOT OKAY!!! THIS PAGE IS ONLY BLACK AND WHITE! I'M CALLIN' THE PUBLISHER RIGHT NOW!!
WHAT'S THE BIG IDEA?! I THOUGHT MY CONTRACT SAID THE FIRST PAGE OF EVERY VOLUME WAS SUPPOSED TO BE MONOKUMA THEATER...IN COLOR!
WHAT? YA GAVE IT TO THAT KID MOPIN' IN THE SHOWER?!
YEAH, I KNOW I'M BLACK AND WHITE...YOUR POINT BEING...? ...BASTARD! HUNG UP ON ME!!!
THAT'S PRONOUNCED "SEE-EM-WHY-KAY," BY THE WAY, NOT "SIMK," FOR THOSE OF YA WHO DIDN'T GET THE JOKE...
THIS IS AN EDUCATIONAL MANGA, AFTER ALL...THERE'RE MORE THINGS TO LAUGH ABOUT THAN JUST MURDER...
EVEN THOUGH YA GOTTA ADMIT... MURDER IS PRETTY FUNNY.
U PU PU ...

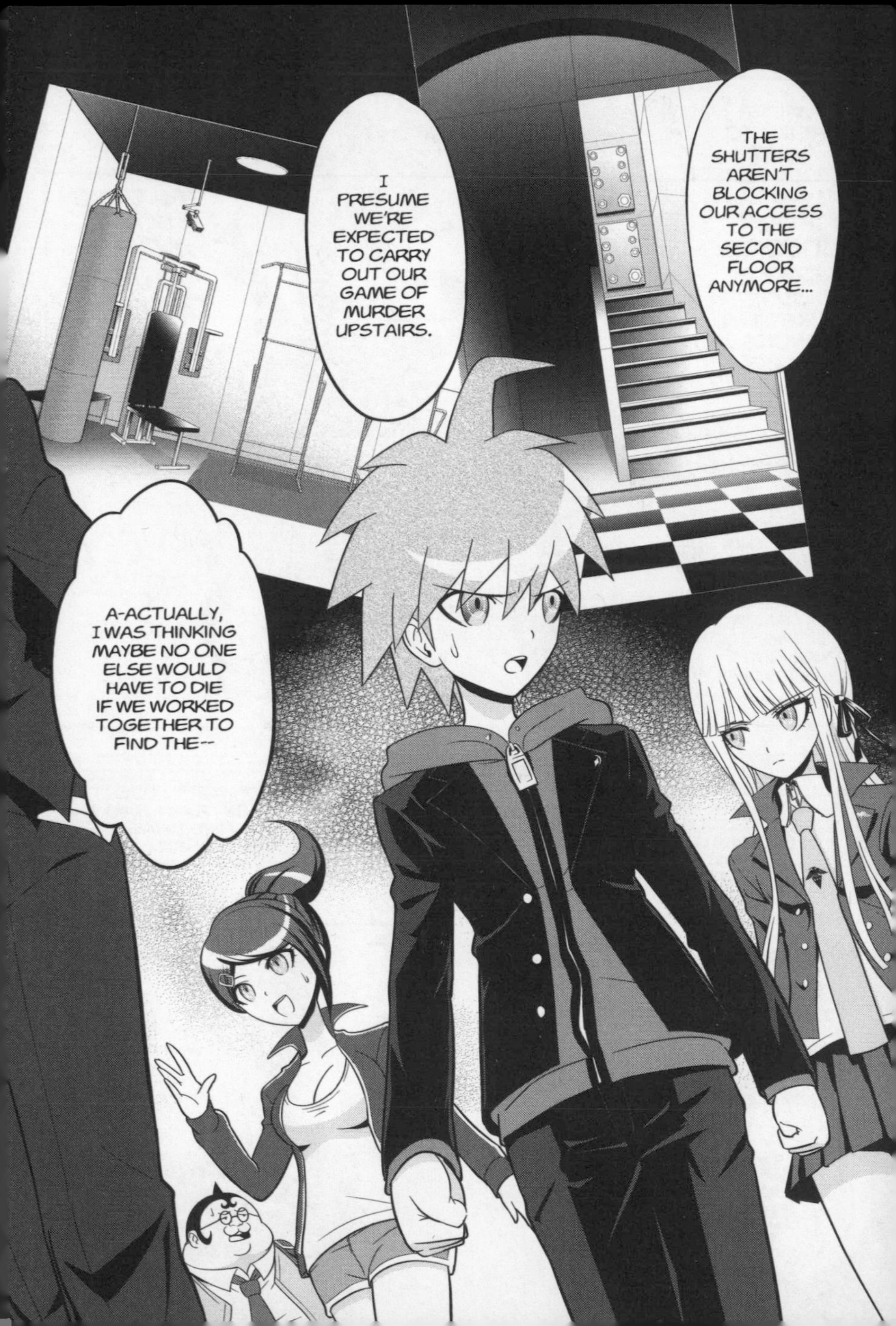
THE SHUTTERS AREN'T BLOCKING OUR ACCESS TO THE SECOND FLOOR ANYMORE...
I PRESUME WE'RE EXPECTED TO CARRY OUT OUR GAME OF MURDER UPSTAIRS.
A-ACTUALLY, I WAS THINKING MAYBE NO ONE ELSE WOULD HAVE TO DIE IF WE WORKED TOGETHER TO FIND THE--

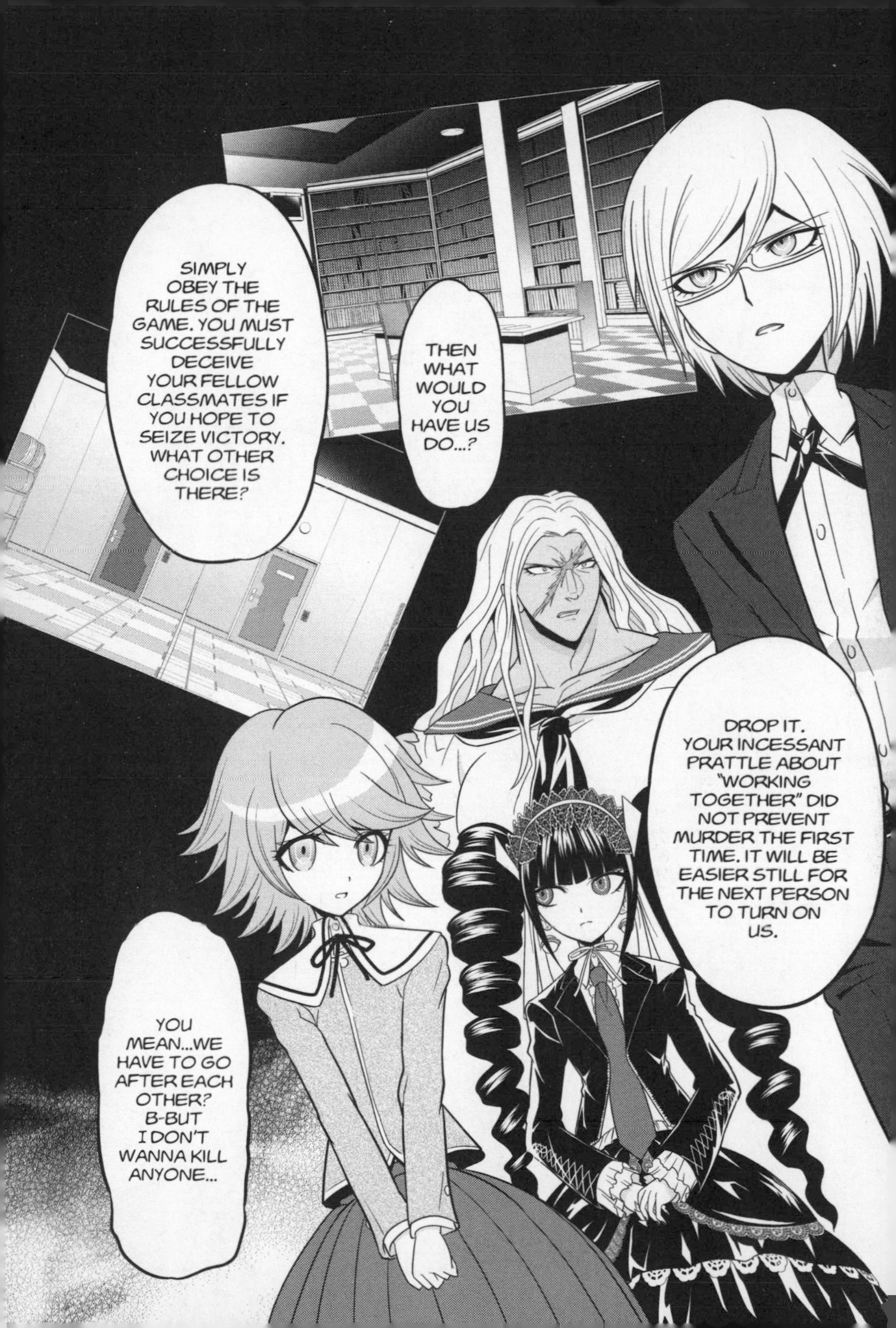
THEN WHAT WOULD YOU HAVE US DO...?
SIMPLY OBEY THE RULES OF THE GAME. YOU MUST SUCCESSFULLY DECEIVE YOUR FELLOW CLASSMATES IF YOU HOPE TO SEIZE VICTORY. WHAT OTHER CHOICE IS THERE?
DROP IT. YOUR INCESSANT PRATTLE ABOUT "WORKING TOGETHER" DID NOT PREVENT MURDER THE FIRST TIME. IT WILL BE EASIER STILL FOR THE NEXT PERSON TO TURN ON US.
YOU MEAN...WE HAVE TO GO AFTER EACH OTHER? B-BUT I DON'T WANNA KILL ANYONE...

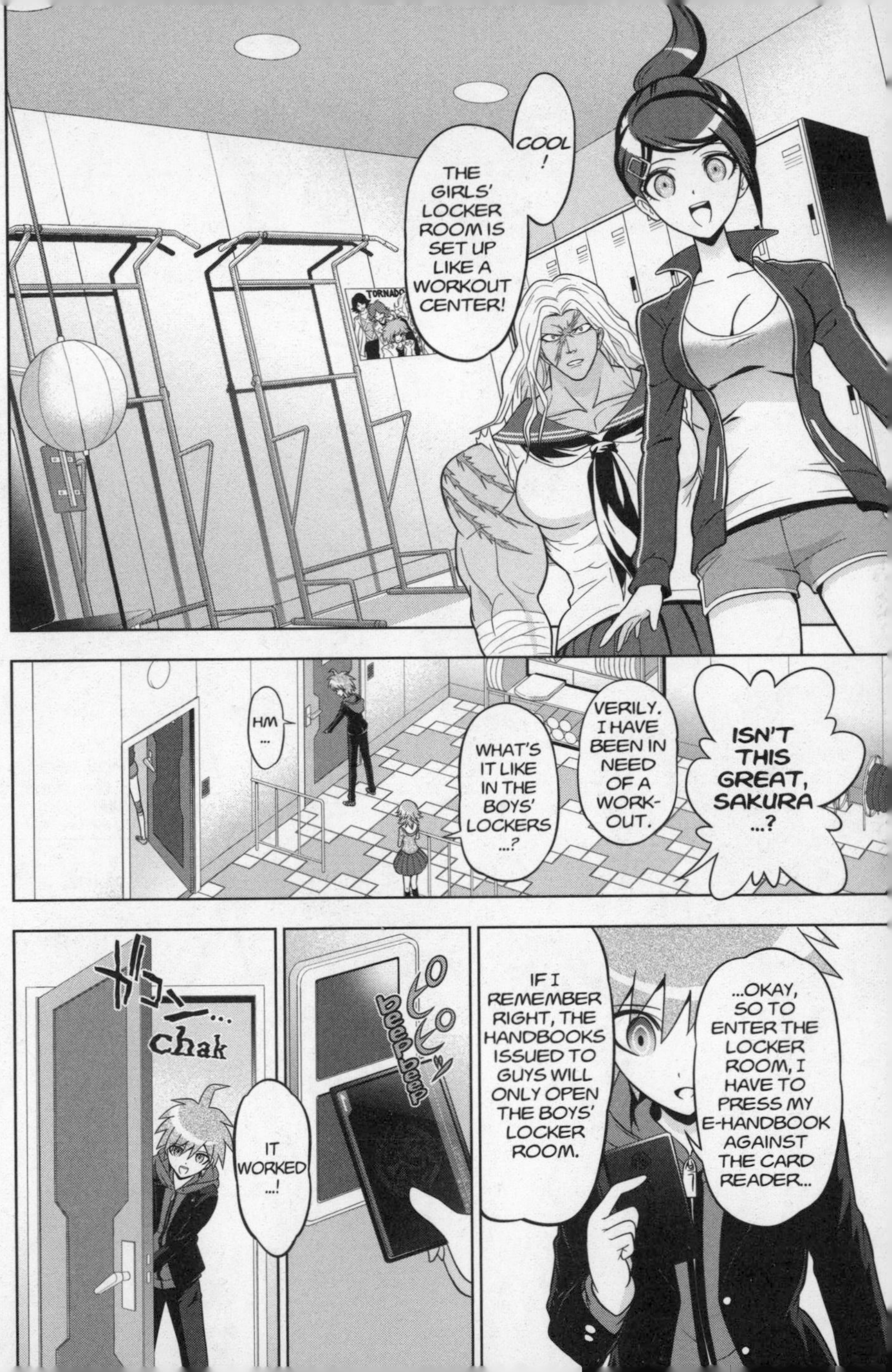
COOL!
THE GIRLS' LOCKER ROOM IS SET UP LIKE A WORKOUT CENTER!
TORNADO
ISN'T THIS GREAT, SAKURA...?
VERILY. I HAVE BEEN IN NEED OF A WORK-OUT.
WHAT'S IT LIKE IN THE BOYS' LOCKERS...?
HM...
...OKAY, SO TO ENTER THE LOCKER ROOM, I HAVE TO PRESS MY E-HANDBOOK AGAINST THE CARD READER...
IF I REMEMBER RIGHT, THE HANDBOOKS ISSUED TO GUYS WILL ONLY OPEN THE BOYS' LOCKER ROOM.
beep beep
chak
IT WORKED...!

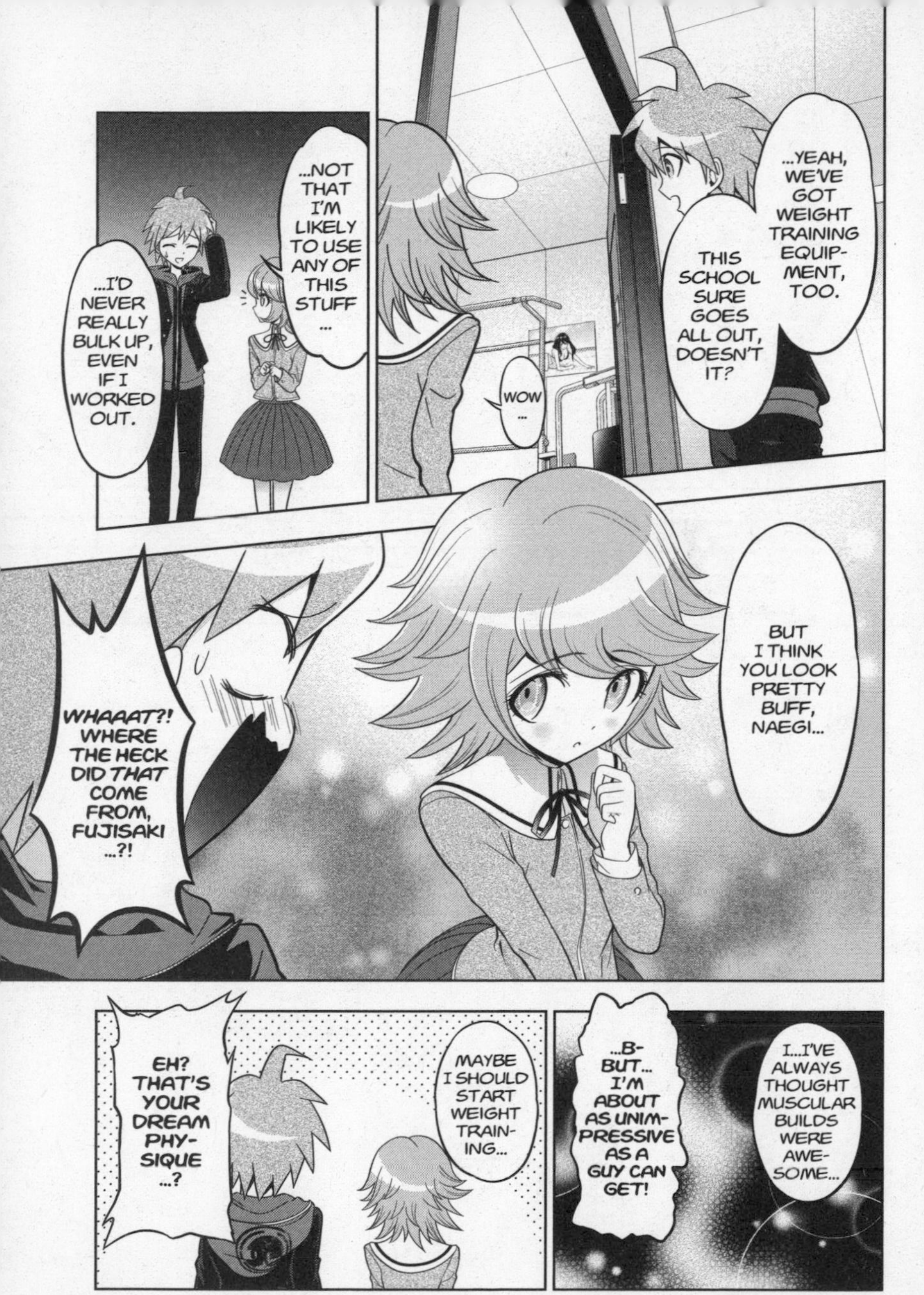
...YEAH, WE'VE GOT WEIGHT TRAINING EQUIP-MENT, TOO.
THIS SCHOOL SURE GOES ALL OUT, DOESN'T IT?
WOW...
...NOT THAT I'M LIKELY TO USE ANY OF THIS STUFF...
...I'D NEVER REALLY BULK UP, EVEN IF I WORKED OUT.
BUT I THINK YOU LOOK PRETTY BUFF, NAEGI...
WHAAAT?! WHERE THE HECK DID *THAT* COME FROM, FUJISAKI...?!
I...I'VE ALWAYS THOUGHT MUSCULAR BUILDS WERE AWE-SOME...
...B-BUT... I'M ABOUT AS UNIM-PRESSIVE AS A GUY CAN GET!
MAYBE I SHOULD START WEIGHT TRAIN-ING...
EH? THAT'S YOUR DREAM PHY-SIQUE...?

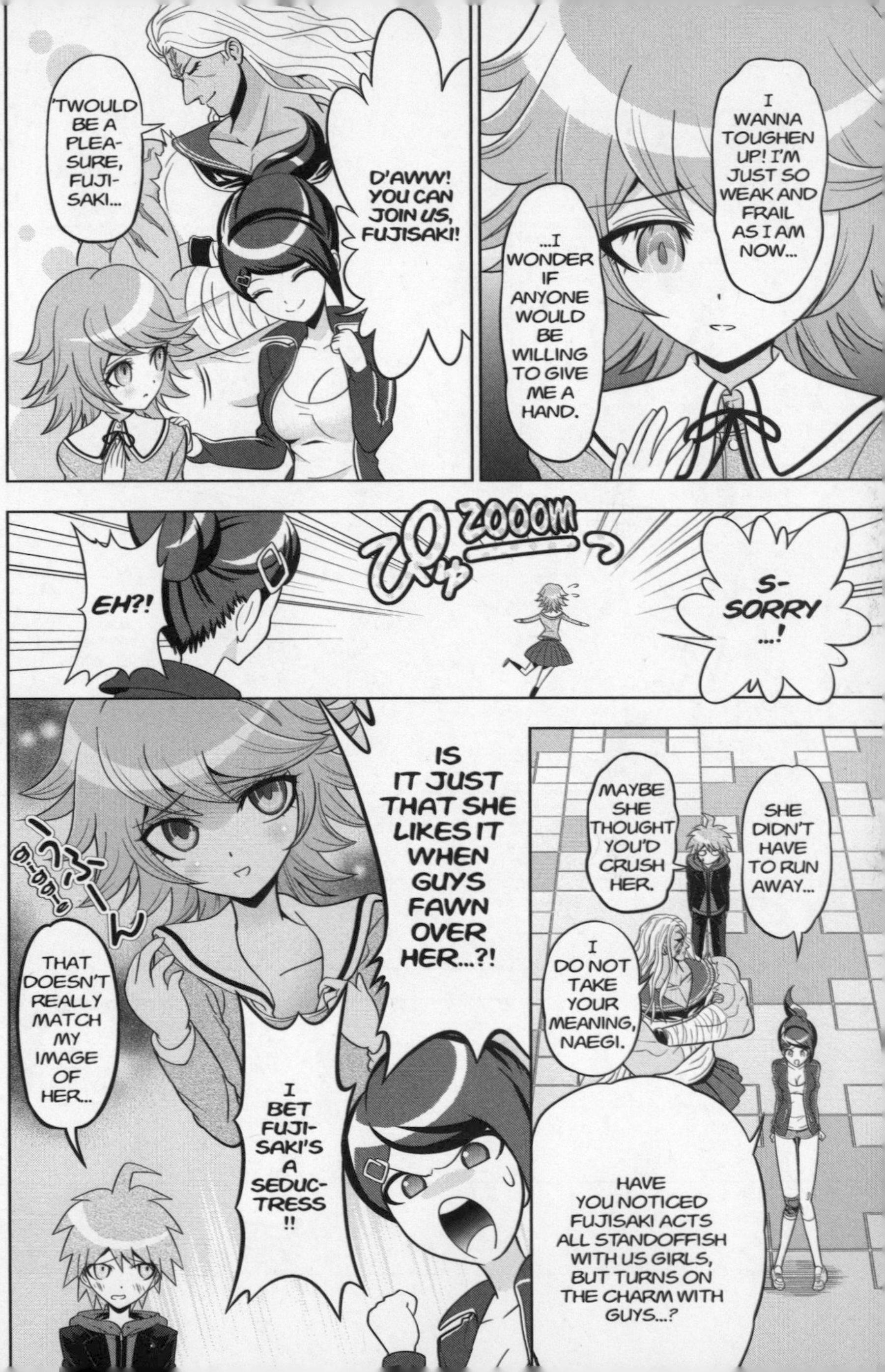
I WANNA TOUGHEN UP! I'M JUST SO WEAK AND FRAIL AS I AM NOW...
...I WONDER IF ANYONE WOULD BE WILLING TO GIVE ME A HAND.
D'AWW! YOU CAN JOIN US, FUJISAKI!
'TWOULD BE A PLEASURE, FUJISAKI...
S-SORRY...!
ZOOOM
EH?!
SHE DIDN'T HAVE TO RUN AWAY...
MAYBE SHE THOUGHT YOU'D CRUSH HER.
I DO NOT TAKE YOUR MEANING, NAEGI.
HAVE YOU NOTICED FUJISAKI ACTS ALL STANDOFFISH WITH US GIRLS, BUT TURNS ON THE CHARM WITH GUYS...?
IS IT JUST THAT SHE LIKES IT WHEN GUYS FAWN OVER HER...?!
I BET FUJISAKI'S A SEDUCTRESS!!
THAT DOESN'T REALLY MATCH MY IMAGE OF HER...

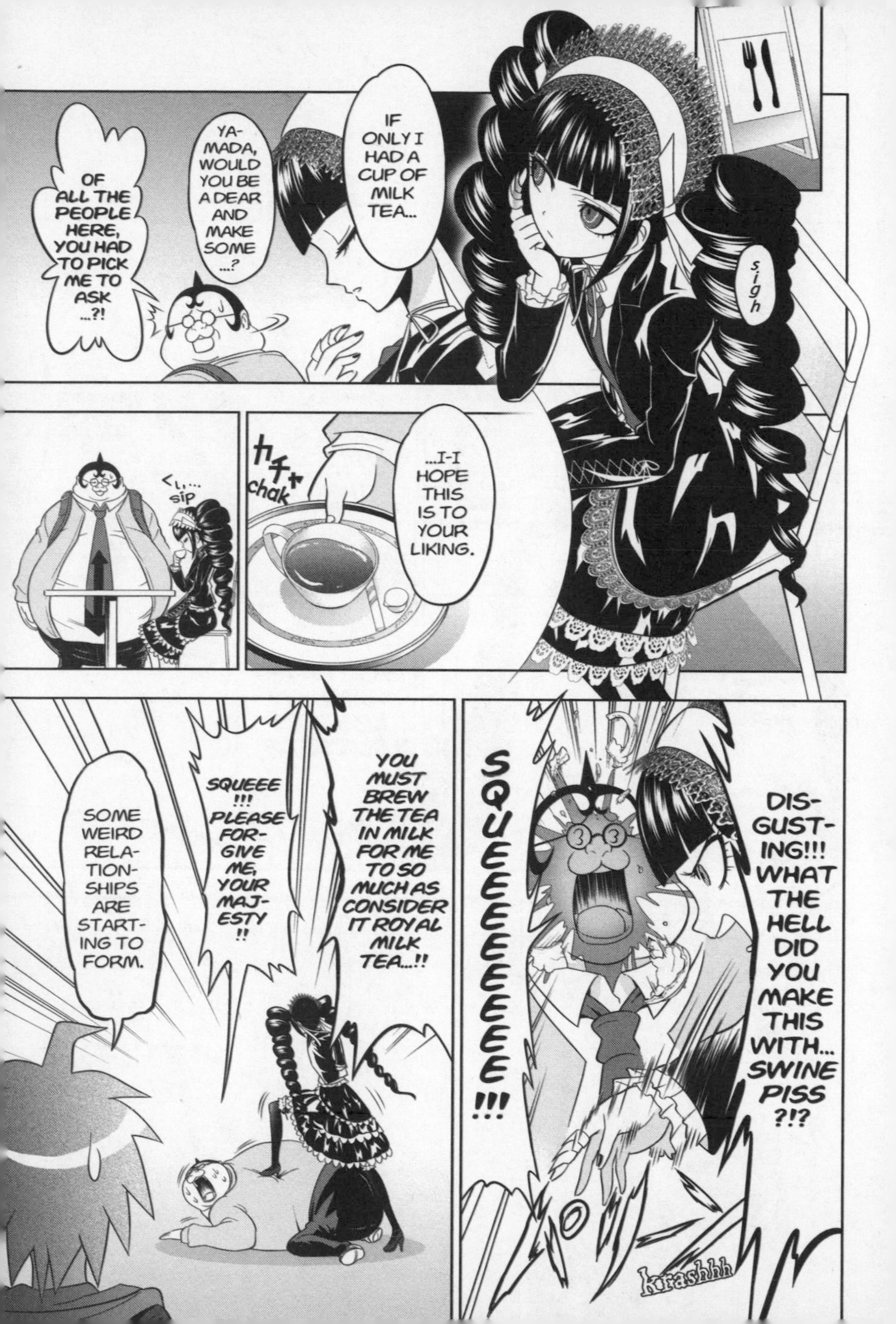
sigh
IF ONLY I HAD A CUP OF MILK TEA...
YA-MADA, WOULD YOU BE A DEAR AND MAKE SOME ...?
OF ALL THE PEOPLE HERE, YOU HAD TO PICK ME TO ASK ...?!
カチャ chak
...I-I HOPE THIS IS TO YOUR LIKING.
sip
DIS-GUST-ING!!! WHAT THE HELL DID YOU MAKE THIS WITH... SWINE PISS ?!?
SQUEEEEEEEEEE!!!
krashhh
YOU MUST BREW THE TEA IN MILK FOR ME TO SO MUCH AS CONSIDER IT ROYAL MILK TEA...!!
SQUEEE!!! PLEASE FOR-GIVE ME, YOUR MAJ-ESTY!!
SOME WEIRD RELA-TION-SHIPS ARE START-ING TO FORM.

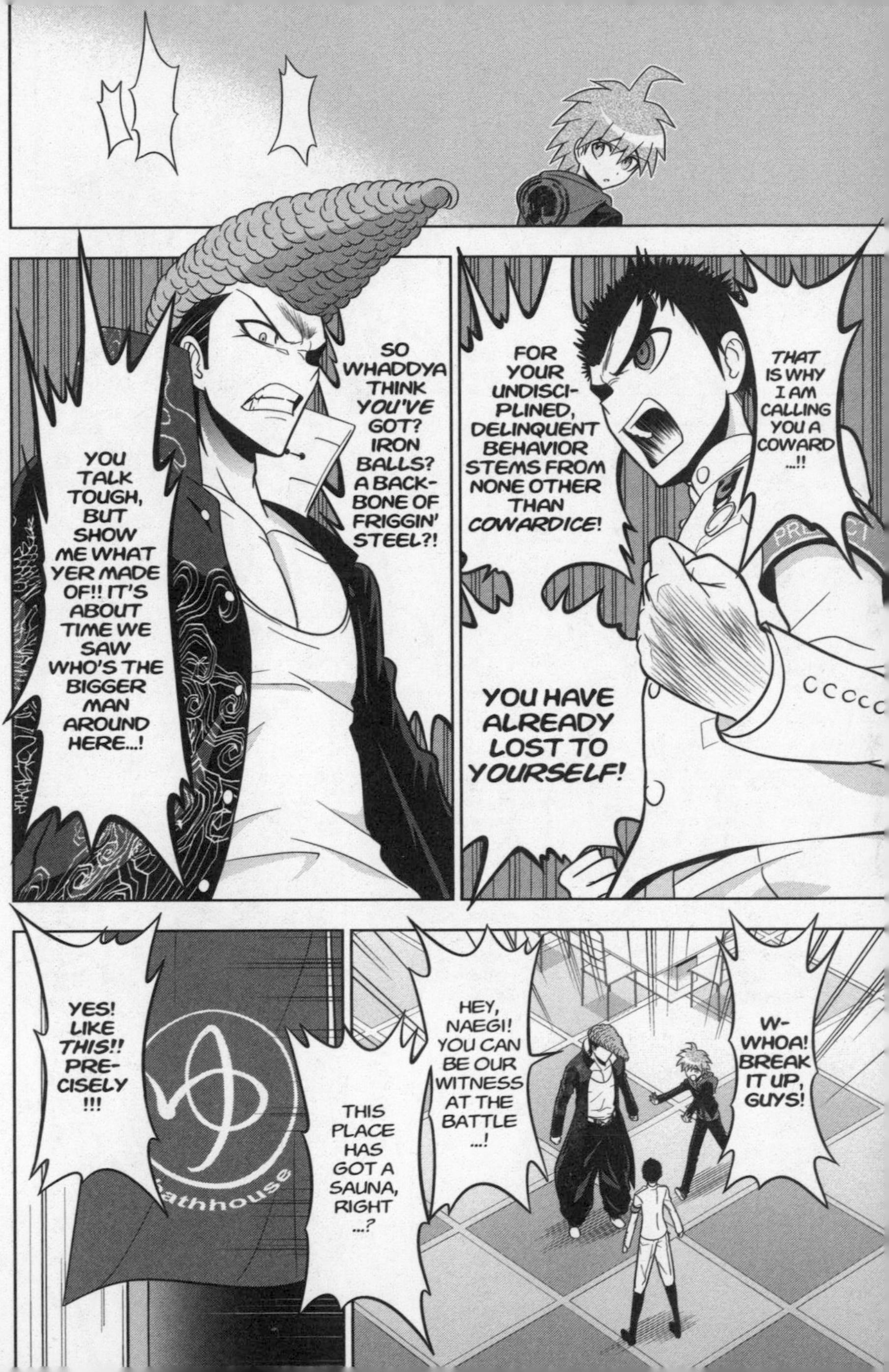
THAT IS WHY I AM CALLING YOU A COWARD ...!!
FOR YOUR UNDISCIPLINED, DELINQUENT BEHAVIOR STEMS FROM NONE OTHER THAN COWARDICE!
YOU HAVE ALREADY LOST TO YOURSELF!
SO WHADDYA THINK YOU'VE GOT? IRON BALLS? A BACKBONE OF FRIGGIN' STEEL?!
YOU TALK TOUGH, BUT SHOW ME WHAT YER MADE OF!! IT'S ABOUT TIME WE SAW WHO'S THE BIGGER MAN AROUND HERE...!
W-WHOA! BREAK IT UP, GUYS!
HEY, NAEGI! YOU CAN BE OUR WITNESS AT THE BATTLE ...!
THIS PLACE HAS GOT A SAUNA, RIGHT ...?
YES! LIKE THIS!! PRECISELY!!!
athhouse

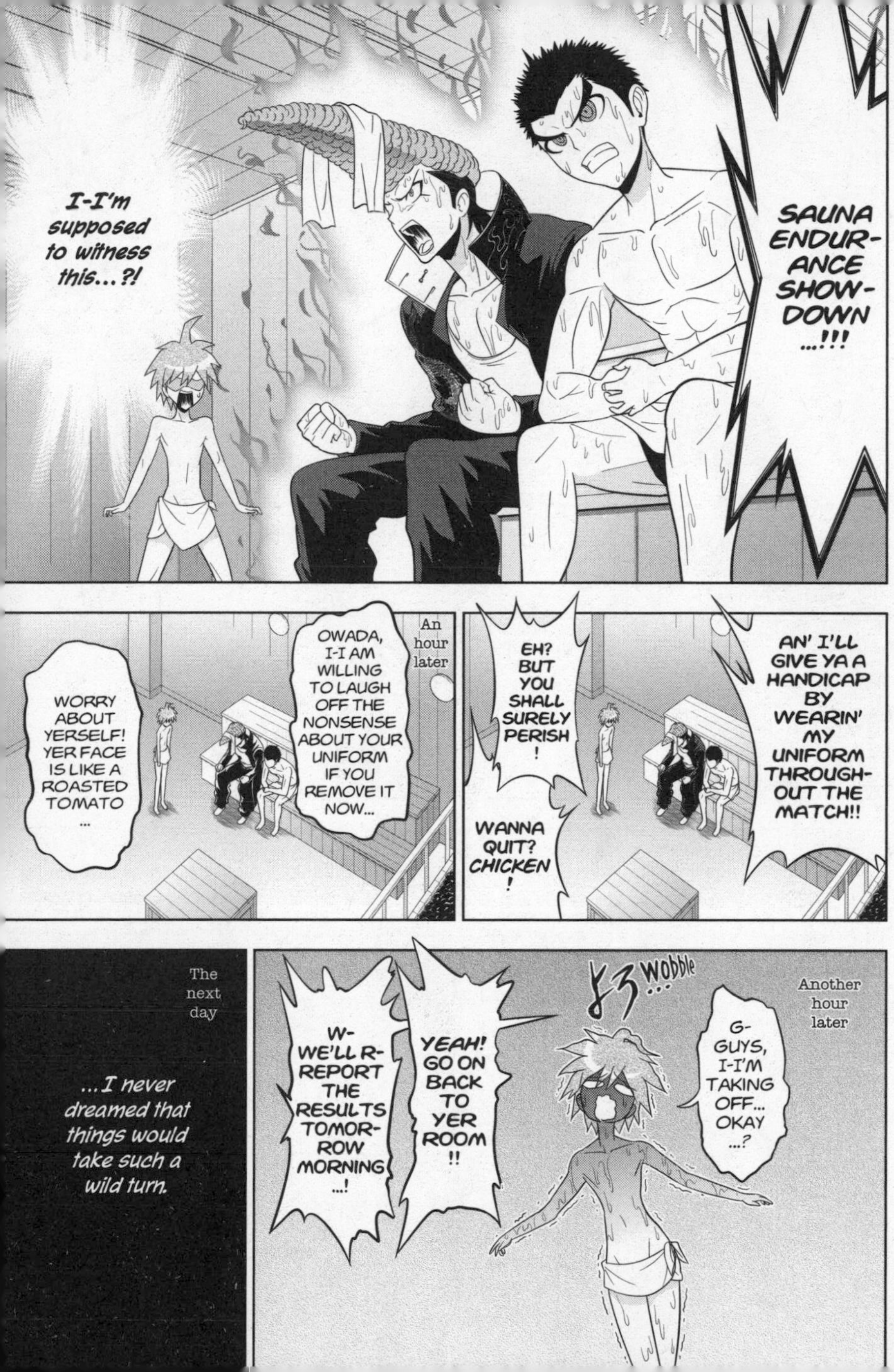
SAUNA ENDURANCE SHOWDOWN...!!!
I-I'm supposed to witness this...?!
AN' I'LL GIVE YA A HANDICAP BY WEARIN' MY UNIFORM THROUGHOUT THE MATCH!!
EH? BUT YOU SHALL SURELY PERISH!
WANNA QUIT? CHICKEN!
An hour later
OWADA, I-I AM WILLING TO LAUGH OFF THE NONSENSE ABOUT YOUR UNIFORM IF YOU REMOVE IT NOW...
WORRY ABOUT YERSELF! YER FACE IS LIKE A ROASTED TOMATO...
Another hour later
G-GUYS, I-I'M TAKING OFF... OKAY...?
よろ wobble...
YEAH! GO ON BACK TO YER ROOM!!
W-WE'LL R-REPORT THE RESULTS TOMORROW MORNING...!
The next day
...I never dreamed that things would take such a wild turn.

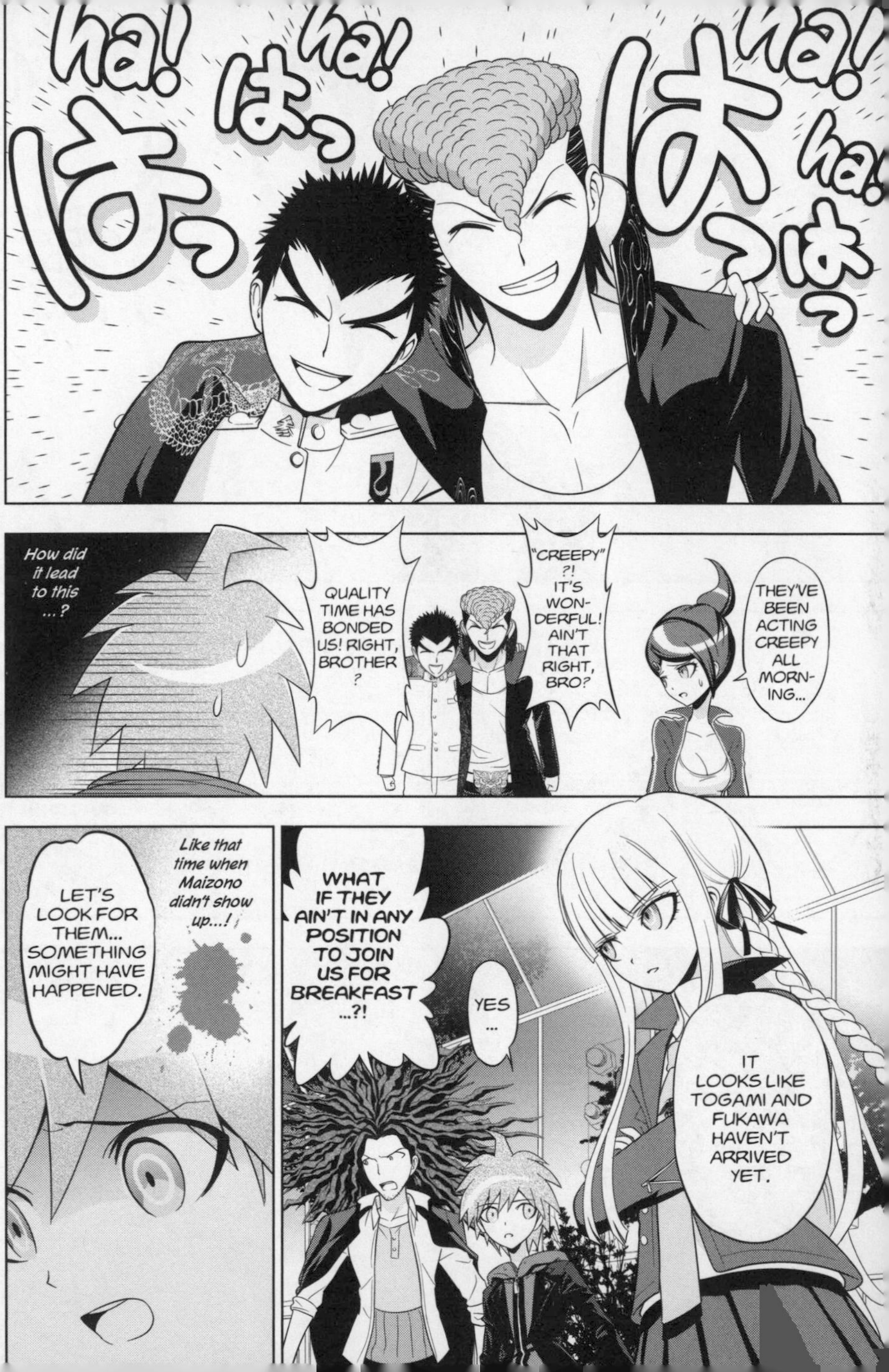

ha!
ha.
はっはっ
ha!
ha!
はっ
ha!
はっ
THEY'VE BEEN ACTING CREEPY ALL MORN-ING...
"CREEPY"?! IT'S WON-DERFUL! AIN'T THAT RIGHT, BRO?
QUALITY TIME HAS BONDED US! RIGHT, BROTHER?
How did it lead to this ...?
IT LOOKS LIKE TOGAMI AND FUKAWA HAVEN'T ARRIVED YET.
YES ...
WHAT IF THEY AIN'T IN ANY POSITION TO JOIN US FOR BREAKFAST ...?!
Like that time when Maizono didn't show up...!
LET'S LOOK FOR THEM... SOMETHING MIGHT HAVE HAPPENED.

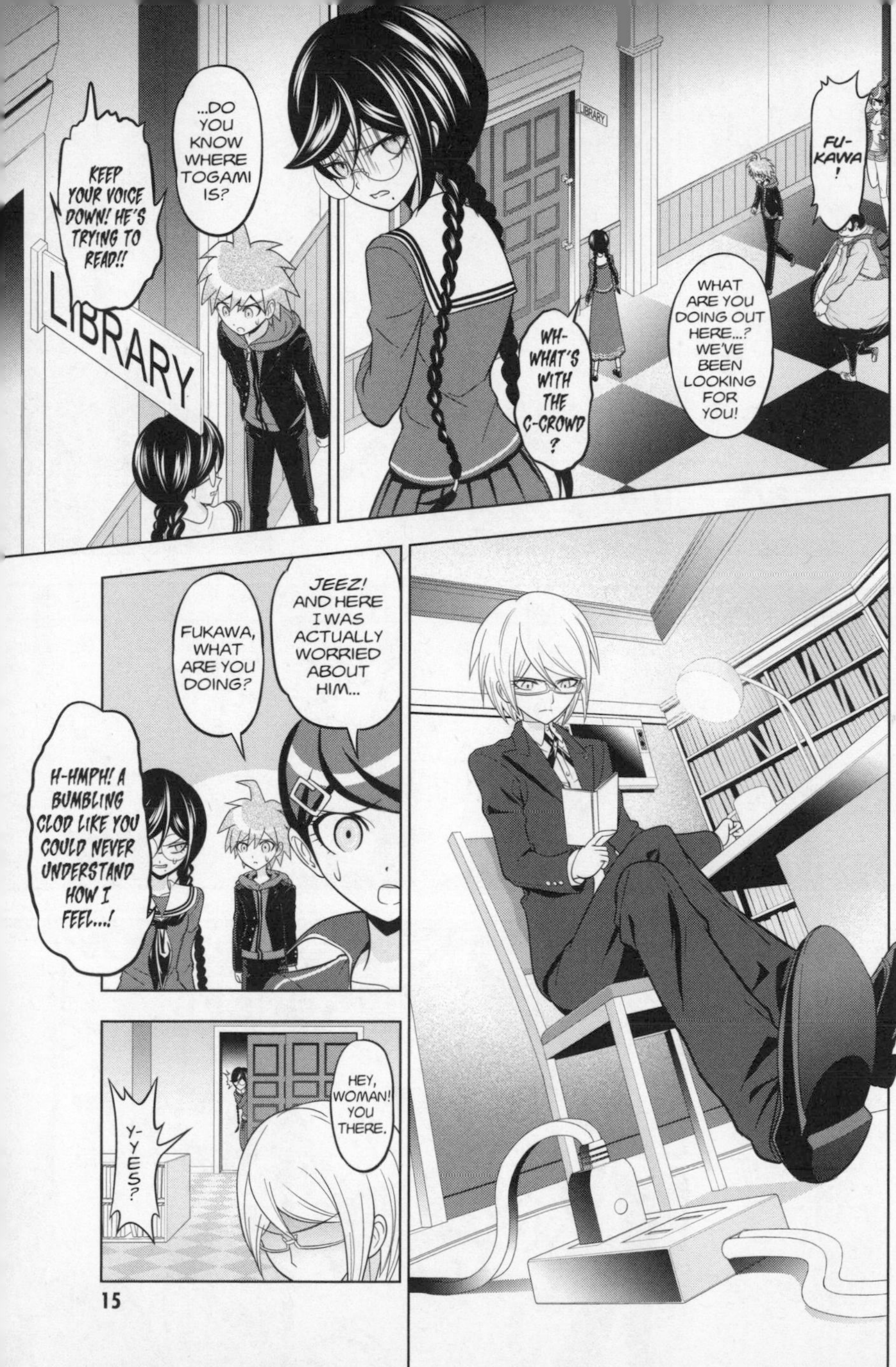
FU-KAWA!
WHAT ARE YOU DOING OUT HERE...? WE'VE BEEN LOOKING FOR YOU!
WH-WHAT'S WITH THE C-CROWD?
...DO YOU KNOW WHERE TOGAMI IS?
KEEP YOUR VOICE DOWN! HE'S TRYING TO READ!!
LIBRARY
JEEZ! AND HERE I WAS ACTUALLY WORRIED ABOUT HIM...
FUKAWA, WHAT ARE YOU DOING?
H-HMPH! A BUMBLING CLOD LIKE YOU COULD NEVER UNDERSTAND HOW I FEEL...!
HEY, WOMAN! YOU THERE.
Y-YES?

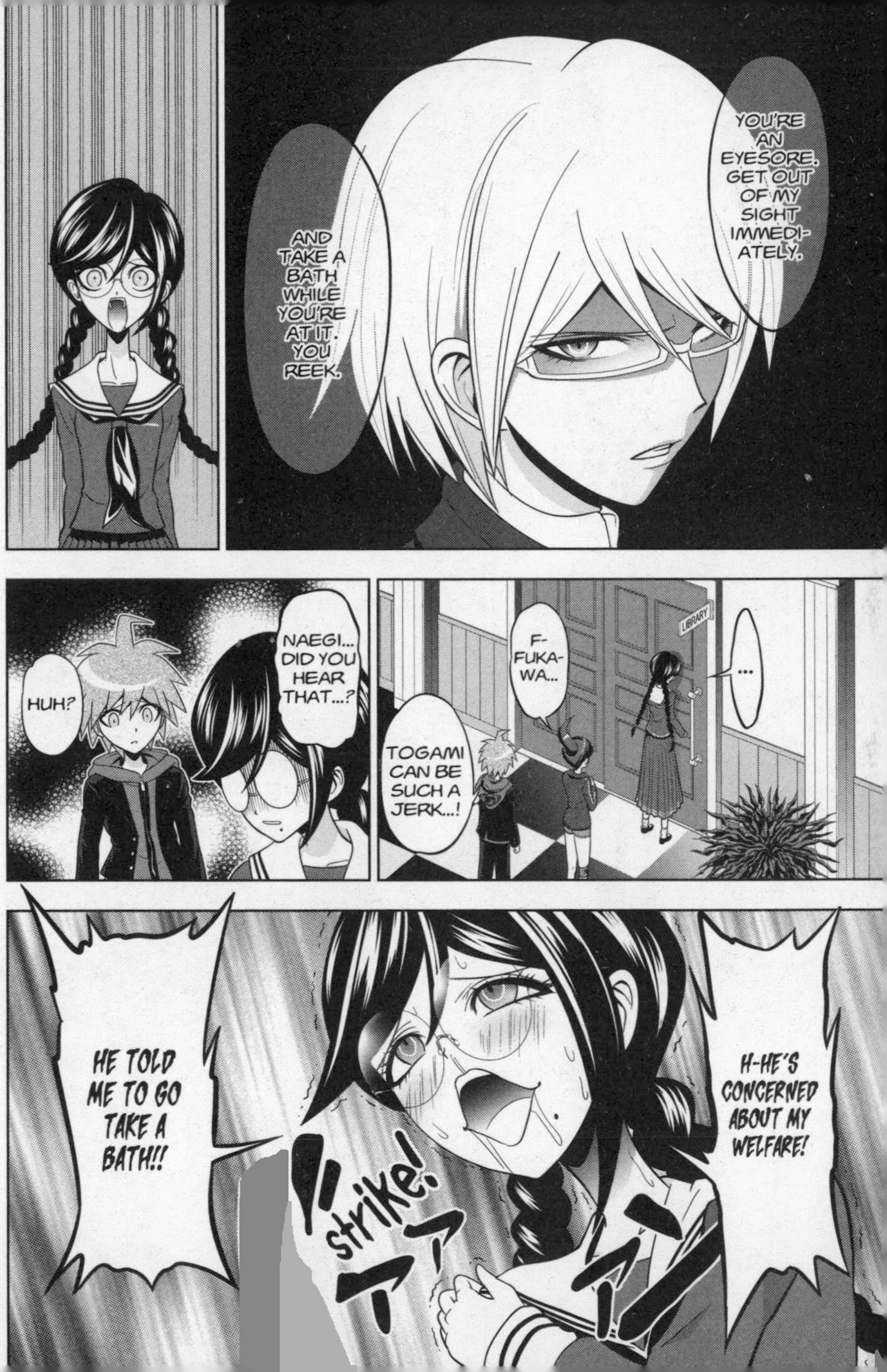

YOU'RE AN EYESORE. GET OUT OF MY SIGHT IMMEDI-ATELY.
AND TAKE A BATH WHILE YOU'RE AT IT. YOU REEK.
LIBRARY
...
F-FUKA-WA...
TOGAMI CAN BE SUCH A JERK...!
NAEGI... DID YOU HEAR THAT...?
HUH?
H-HE'S CONCERNED ABOUT MY WELFARE!
HE TOLD ME TO GO TAKE A BATH!!
strike!

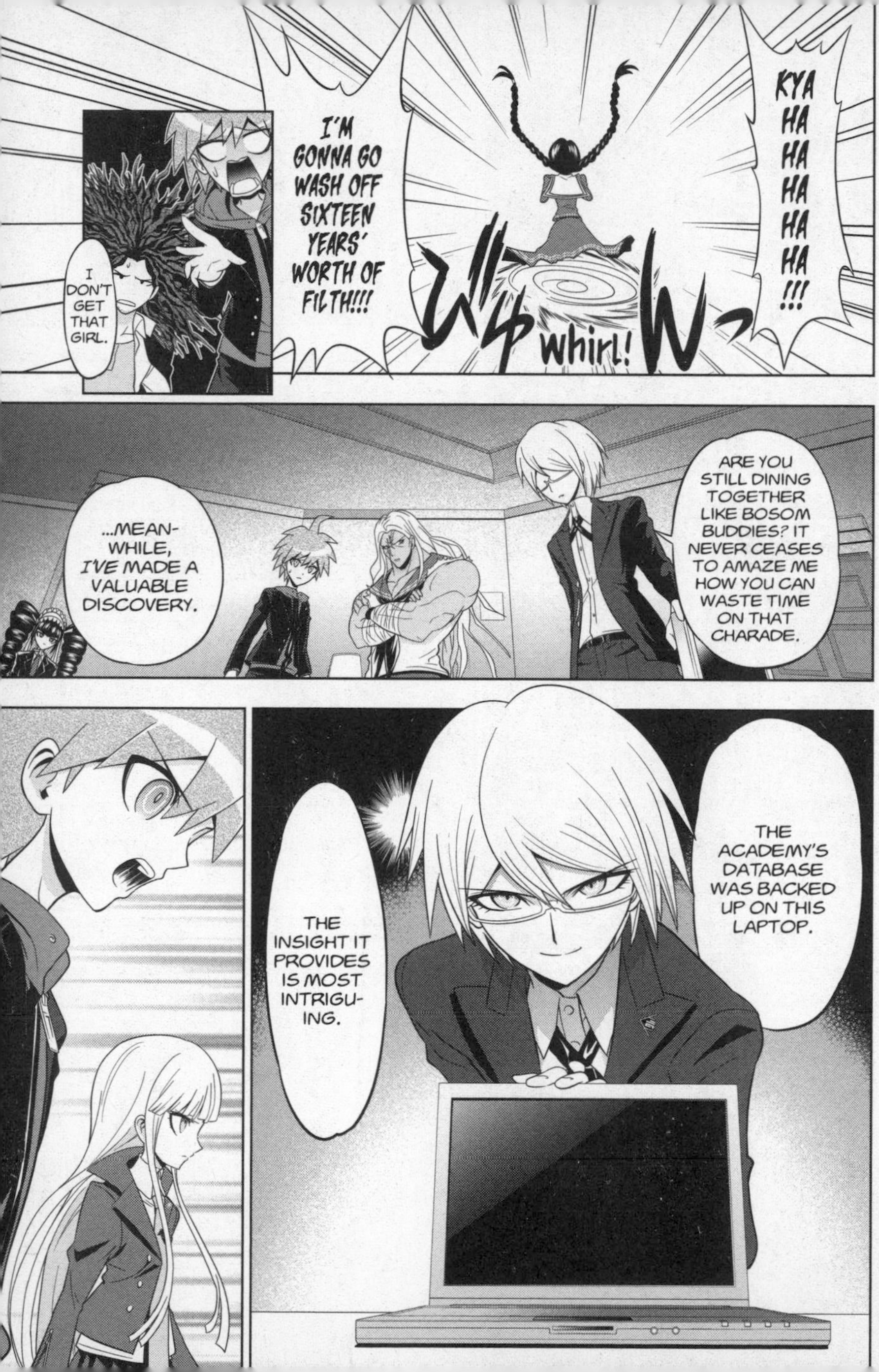
KYA HA HA HA HA HA HA!!!
I'M GONNA GO WASH OFF SIXTEEN YEARS' WORTH OF FILTH!!!
whirl!
I DON'T GET THAT GIRL.
ARE YOU STILL DINING TOGETHER LIKE BOSOM BUDDIES? IT NEVER CEASES TO AMAZE ME HOW YOU CAN WASTE TIME ON THAT CHARADE.
...MEAN-WHILE, *I'VE* MADE A VALUABLE DISCOVERY.
THE ACADEMY'S DATABASE WAS BACKED UP ON THIS LAPTOP.
THE INSIGHT IT PROVIDES IS MOST INTRIGU-ING.

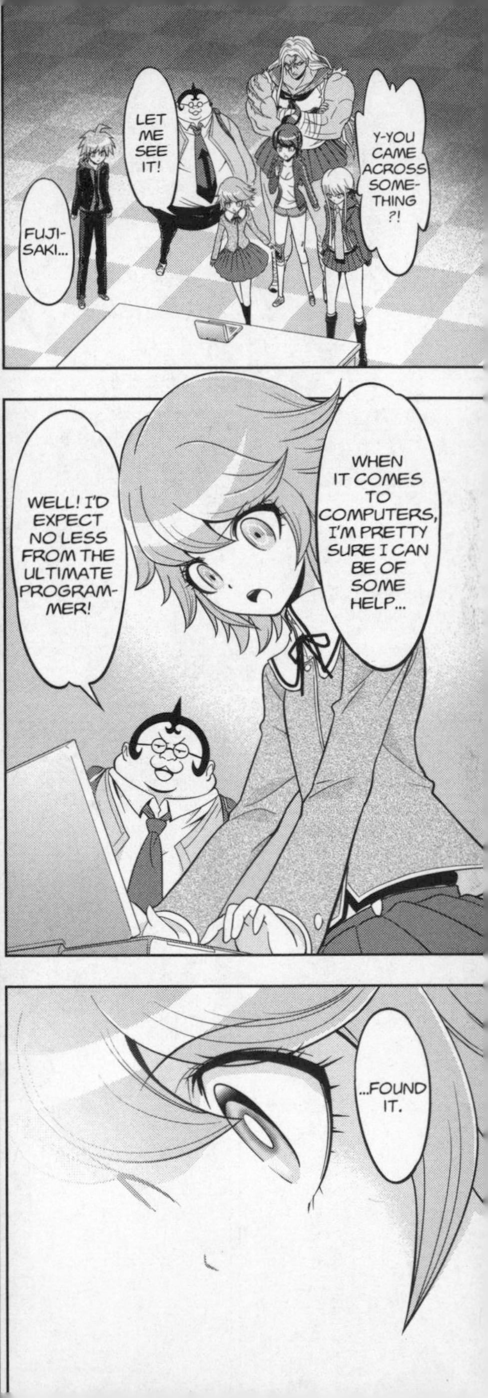
Y-YOU CAME ACROSS SOME-THING?!
LET ME SEE IT!
FUJI-SAKI...
WHEN IT COMES TO COMPUTERS, I'M PRETTY SURE I CAN BE OF SOME HELP...
WELL! I'D EXPECT NO LESS FROM THE ULTIMATE PROGRAM-MER!
...FOUND IT.

NOTICE FROM HOPE'S PEAK ACADEMY: IT HAS BEEN DECIDED TO SHUT DOWN THE SCHOOL. THIS STEP WAS DEEMED NECESSARY AFTER THE "BIGGEST, MOST AWFUL, MOST HOPELESS EVENT IN HUMAN HISTORY" LAST YEAR. THE ACADEMY SHOULD REOPEN IN THE NEAR FUTURE ONCE THE ISSUES ARE RESOLVED.

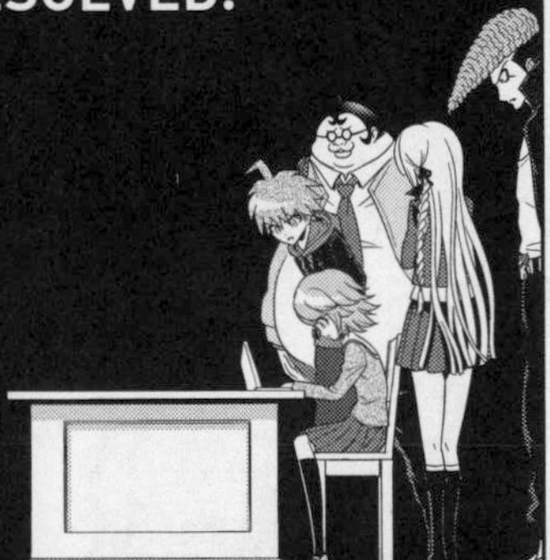

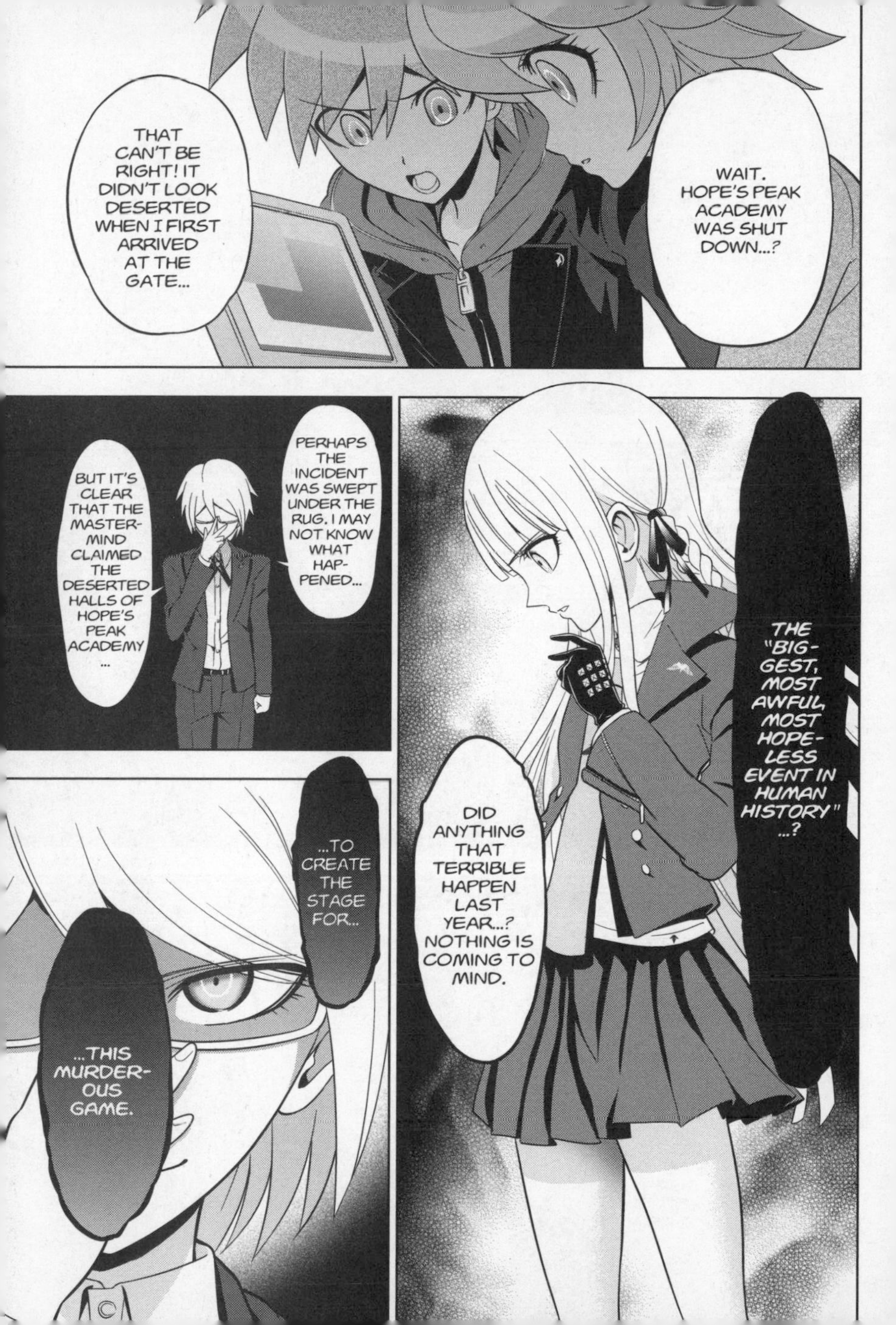
WAIT. HOPE'S PEAK ACADEMY WAS SHUT DOWN...?
THAT CAN'T BE RIGHT! IT DIDN'T LOOK DESERTED WHEN I FIRST ARRIVED AT THE GATE...
THE "BIG-GEST, MOST AWFUL, MOST HOPE-LESS EVENT IN HUMAN HISTORY" ...?
DID ANYTHING THAT TERRIBLE HAPPEN LAST YEAR...? NOTHING IS COMING TO MIND.
PERHAPS THE INCIDENT WAS SWEPT UNDER THE RUG. I MAY NOT KNOW WHAT HAP-PENED...
BUT IT'S CLEAR THAT THE MASTER-MIND CLAIMED THE DESERTED HALLS OF HOPE'S PEAK ACADEMY ...
...TO CREATE THE STAGE FOR...
...THIS MURDER-OUS GAME.

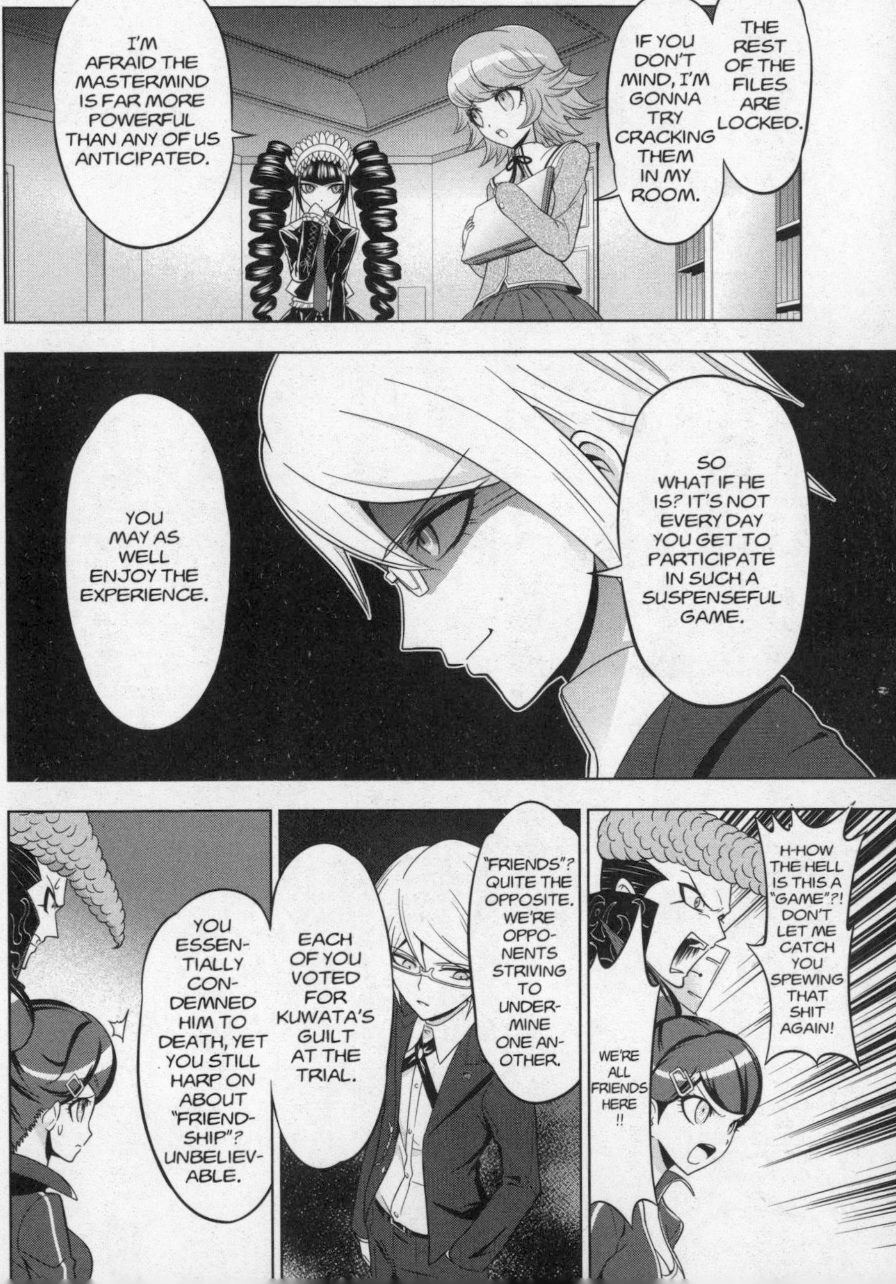
THE REST OF THE FILES ARE LOCKED.
IF YOU DON'T MIND, I'M GONNA TRY CRACKING THEM IN MY ROOM.
I'M AFRAID THE MASTERMIND IS FAR MORE POWERFUL THAN ANY OF US ANTICIPATED.
SO WHAT IF HE IS? IT'S NOT EVERY DAY YOU GET TO PARTICIPATE IN SUCH A SUSPENSEFUL GAME.
YOU MAY AS WELL ENJOY THE EXPERIENCE.
H-HOW THE HELL IS THIS A "GAME"?! DON'T LET ME CATCH YOU SPEWING THAT SHIT AGAIN!
WE'RE ALL FRIENDS HERE!!
"FRIENDS"? QUITE THE OPPOSITE. WE'RE OPPO-NENTS STRIVING TO UNDER-MINE ONE AN-OTHER.
EACH OF YOU VOTED FOR KUWATA'S GUILT AT THE TRIAL.
YOU ESSEN-TIALLY CON-DEMNED HIM TO DEATH, YET YOU STILL HARP ON ABOUT "FRIEND-SHIP"? UNBELIEV-ABLE.

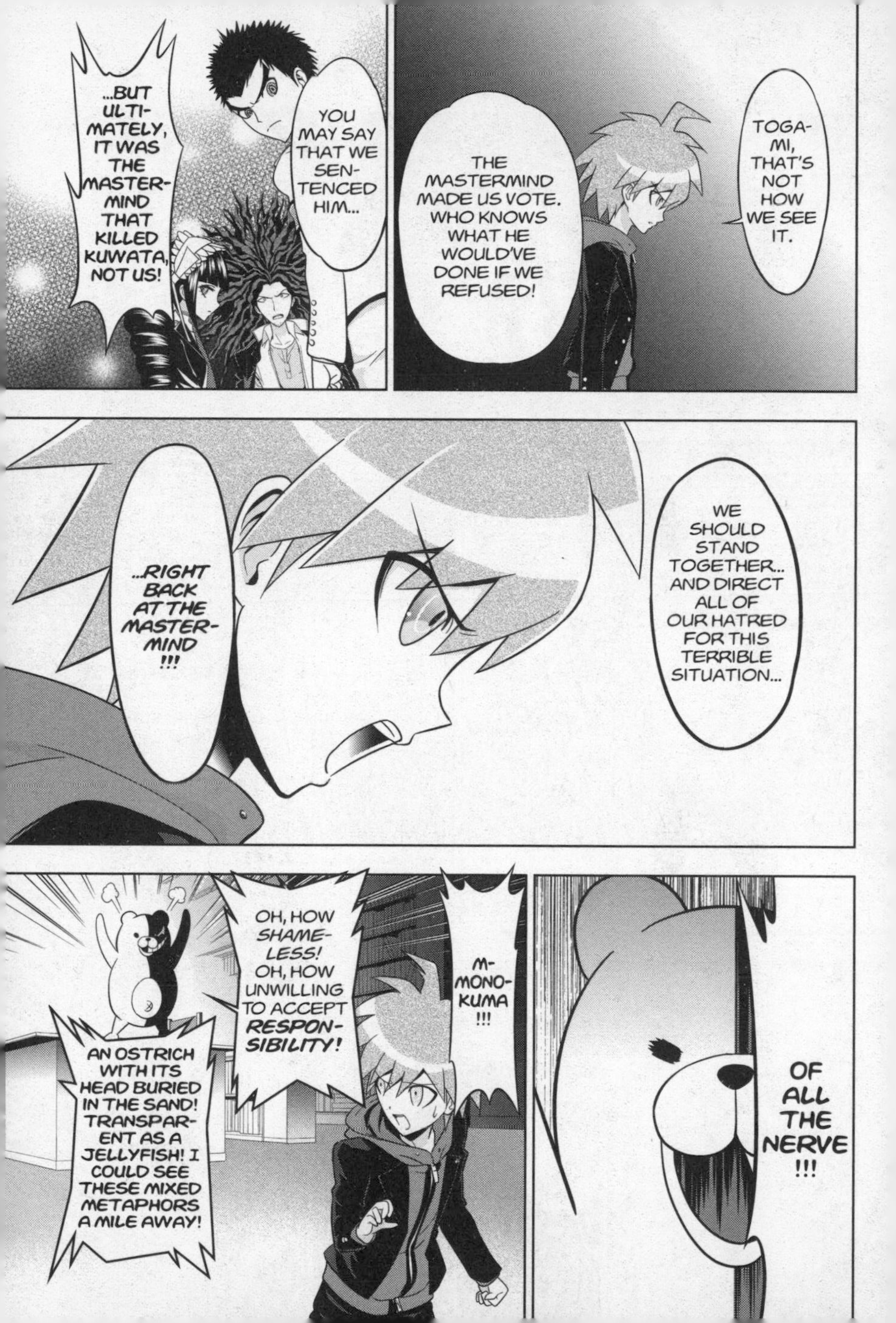
TOGAMI, THAT'S NOT HOW WE SEE IT.
THE MASTERMIND MADE US VOTE. WHO KNOWS WHAT HE WOULD'VE DONE IF WE REFUSED!
YOU MAY SAY THAT WE SENTENCED HIM...
...BUT ULTIMATELY, IT WAS THE MASTERMIND THAT KILLED KUWATA, NOT US!
WE SHOULD STAND TOGETHER... AND DIRECT ALL OF OUR HATRED FOR THIS TERRIBLE SITUATION...
...RIGHT BACK AT THE MASTERMIND!!!
OF ALL THE NERVE!!!
M-MONOKUMA!!!
OH, HOW SHAMELESS! OH, HOW UNWILLING TO ACCEPT RESPONSIBILITY!
AN OSTRICH WITH ITS HEAD BURIED IN THE SAND! TRANSPARENT AS A JELLYFISH! I COULD SEE THESE MIXED METAPHORS A MILE AWAY!

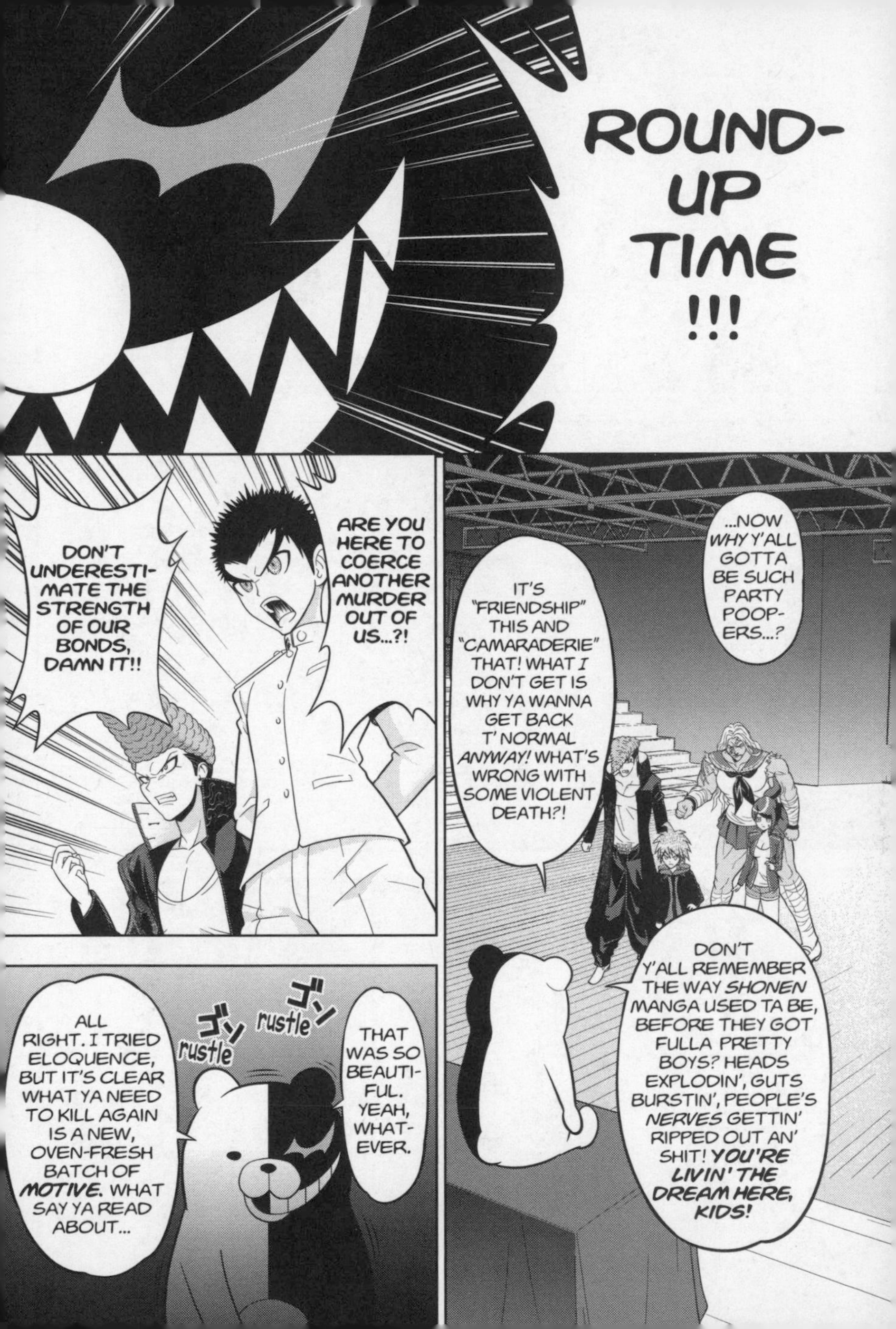
ROUND-UP TIME !!!
...NOW WHY Y'ALL GOTTA BE SUCH PARTY POOPERS...?
IT'S "FRIENDSHIP" THIS AND "CAMARADERIE" THAT! WHAT *I* DON'T GET IS WHY YA WANNA GET BACK T' NORMAL *ANYWAY!* WHAT'S WRONG WITH SOME VIOLENT DEATH?!
DON'T Y'ALL REMEMBER THE WAY *SHONEN* MANGA USED TA BE, BEFORE THEY GOT FULLA PRETTY BOYS? HEADS EXPLODIN', GUTS BURSTIN', PEOPLE'S *NERVES* GETTIN' RIPPED OUT AN' SHIT! ***YOU'RE LIVIN' THE DREAM HERE, KIDS!***
ARE YOU HERE TO COERCE ANOTHER MURDER OUT OF US...?!
DON'T UNDERESTIMATE THE STRENGTH OF OUR BONDS, DAMN IT!!
THAT WAS SO BEAUTIFUL. YEAH, WHATEVER.
ゴソ rustle
ゴソ rustle
ALL RIGHT. I TRIED ELOQUENCE, BUT IT'S CLEAR WHAT YA NEED TO KILL AGAIN IS A NEW, OVEN-FRESH BATCH OF ***MOTIVE.*** WHAT SAY YA READ ABOUT...

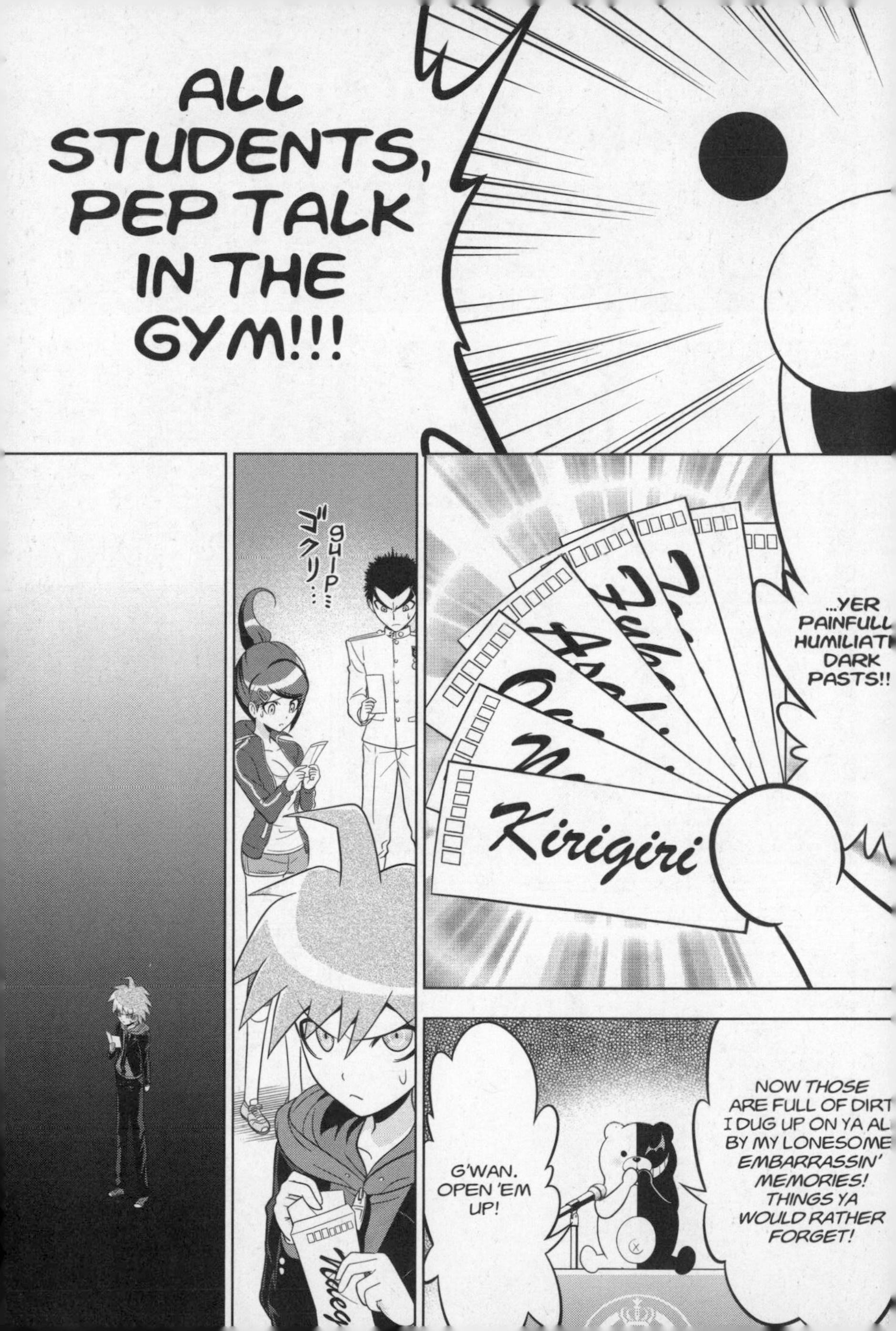
ALL STUDENTS, PEP TALK IN THE GYM!!!
...YER PAINFULL HUMILIATI DARK PASTS!!
Kirigiri
NOW THOSE ARE FULL OF DIRT I DUG UP ON YA AL BY MY LONESOME! EMBARRASSIN' MEMORIES! THINGS YA WOULD RATHER FORGET!
G'WAN. OPEN 'EM UP!
GULP!!
ゴクリ…

Naegi wet the bed clear up until the fifth grade.

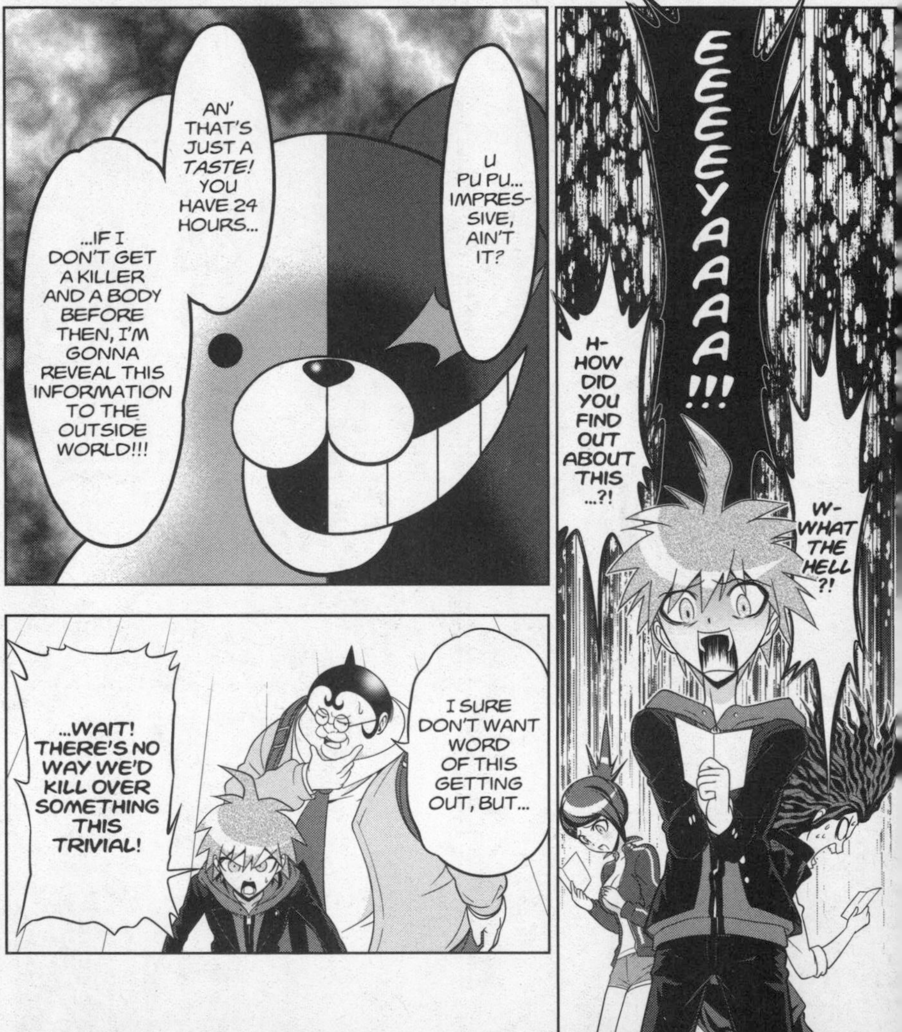
EEEEYAAAAA!!!
H-HOW DID YOU FIND OUT ABOUT THIS ...?!
W-WHAT THE HELL ?!
U PU PU... IMPRESSIVE, AIN'T IT?
AN' THAT'S JUST A *TASTE!* YOU HAVE 24 HOURS...
...IF I DON'T GET A KILLER AND A BODY BEFORE THEN, I'M GONNA REVEAL THIS INFORMATION TO THE OUTSIDE WORLD!!!
I SURE DON'T WANT WORD OF THIS GETTING OUT, BUT...
...WAIT! THERE'S NO WAY WE'D KILL OVER SOMETHING THIS TRIVIAL!

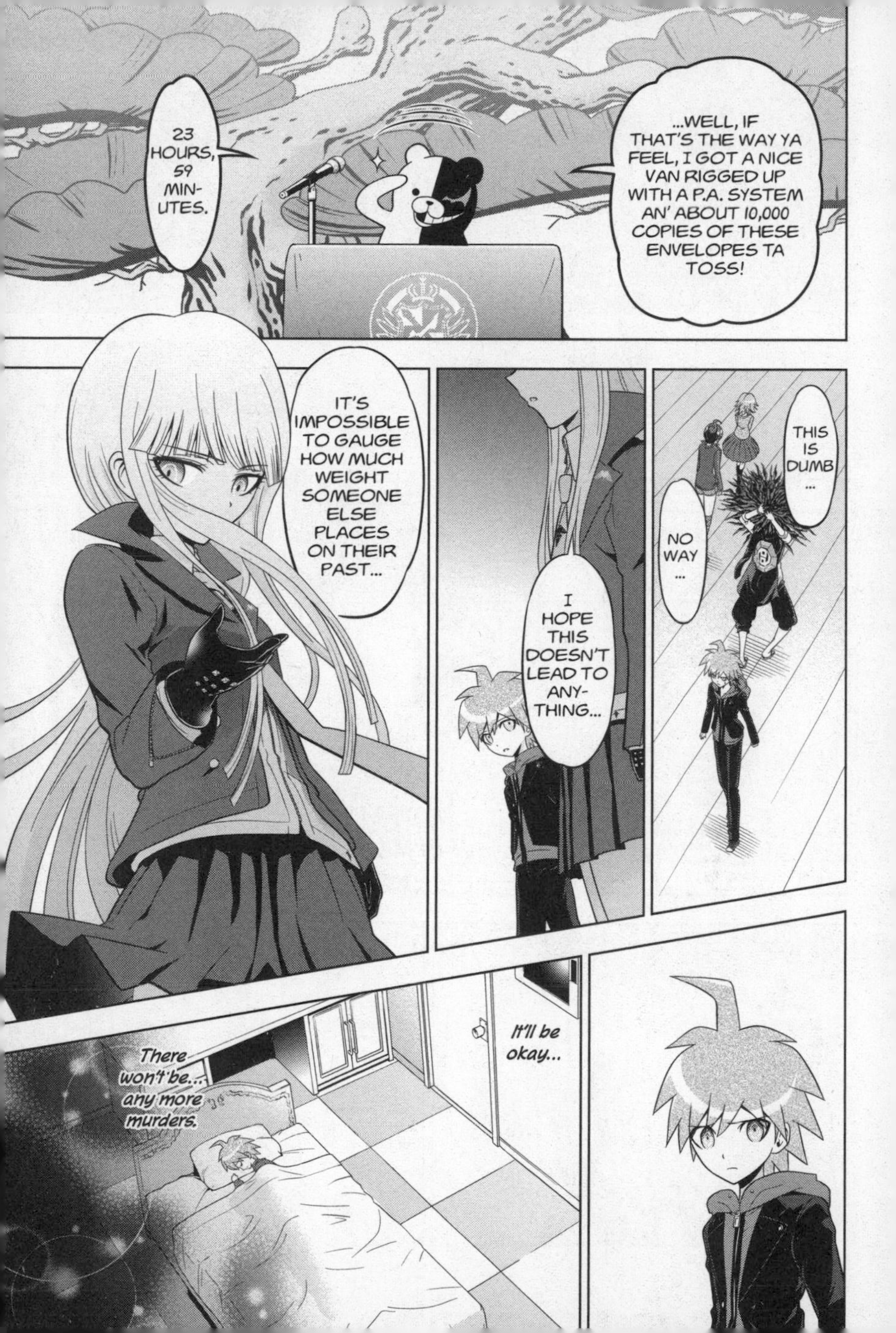
...WELL, IF THAT'S THE WAY YA FEEL, I GOT A NICE VAN RIGGED UP WITH A P.A. SYSTEM AN' ABOUT 10,000 COPIES OF THESE ENVELOPES TA TOSS!
23 HOURS, 59 MIN-UTES.
THIS IS DUMB...
NO WAY...
I HOPE THIS DOESN'T LEAD TO ANY-THING...
IT'S IMPOSSIBLE TO GAUGE HOW MUCH WEIGHT SOMEONE ELSE PLACES ON THEIR PAST...
It'll be okay...
There won't be... any more murders.

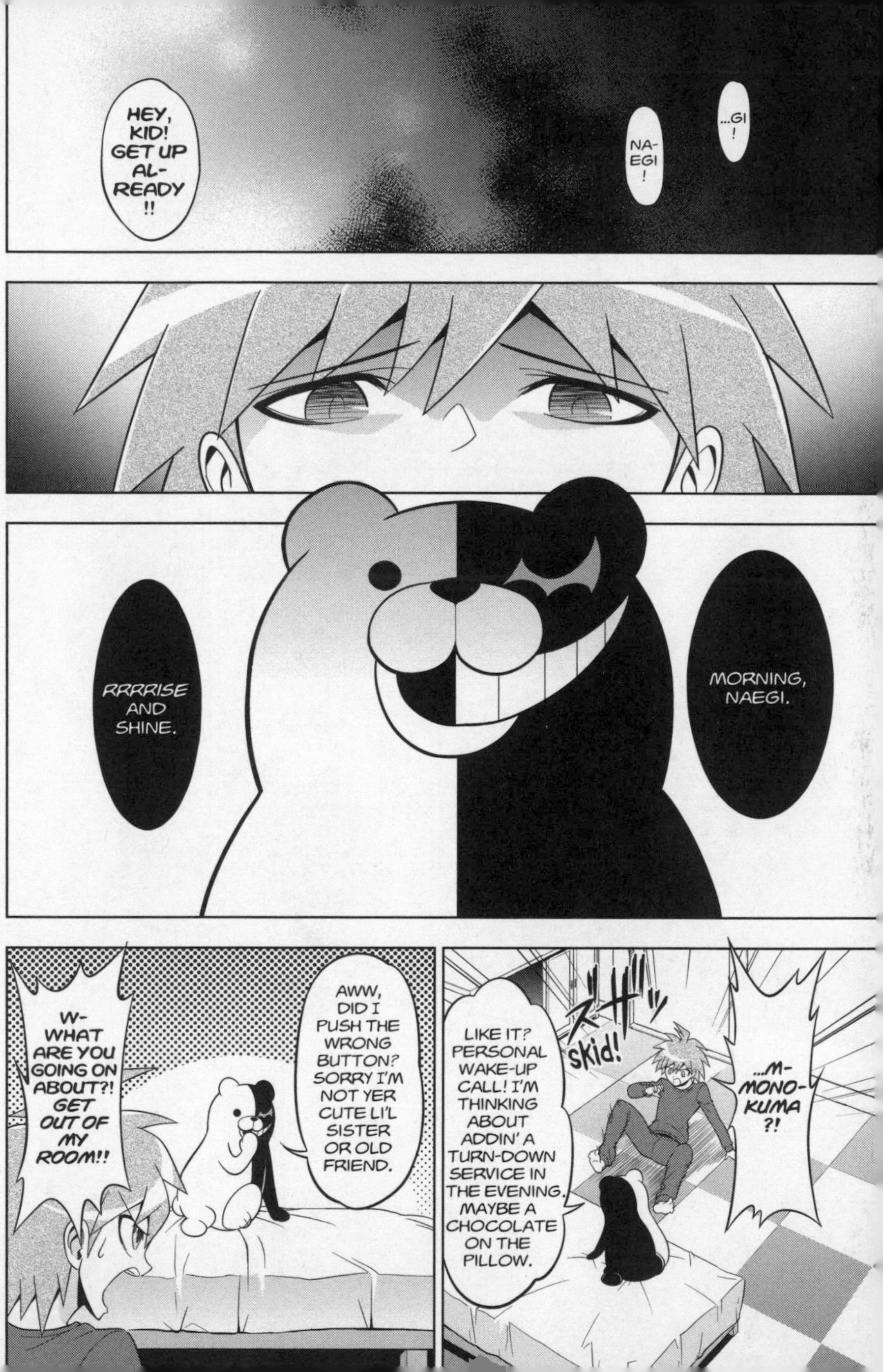
...GI!
NA-EGI!
HEY, KID! GET UP AL-READY!!
MORNING, NAEGI.
RRRRISE AND SHINE.
...M-MONO-KUMA?!
skid!
LIKE IT? PERSONAL WAKE-UP CALL! I'M THINKING ABOUT ADDIN' A TURN-DOWN SERVICE IN THE EVENING. MAYBE A CHOCOLATE ON THE PILLOW.
AWW, DID I PUSH THE WRONG BUTTON? SORRY I'M NOT YER CUTE LI'L SISTER OR OLD FRIEND.
W-WHAT ARE YOU GOING ON ABOUT?! GET OUT OF MY ROOM!!

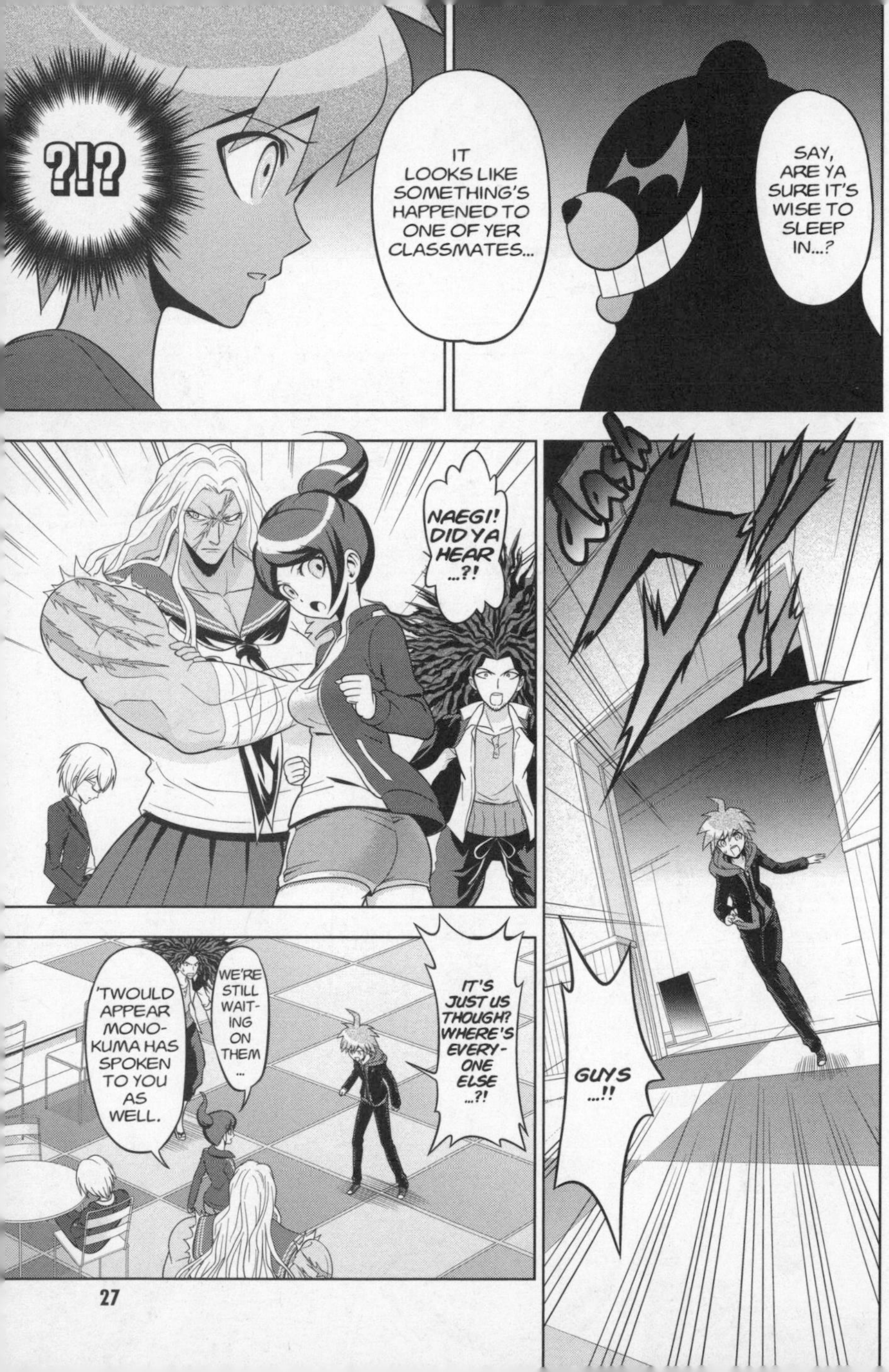
SAY, ARE YA SURE IT'S WISE TO SLEEP IN...?
IT LOOKS LIKE SOMETHING'S HAPPENED TO ONE OF YER CLASSMATES...
?!?
GUYS ...!!
NAEGI! DID YA HEAR ...?!
IT'S JUST US THOUGH? WHERE'S EVERY-ONE ELSE ...?!
WE'RE STILL WAIT-ING ON THEM ...
'TWOULD APPEAR MONO-KUMA HAS SPOKEN TO YOU AS WELL.

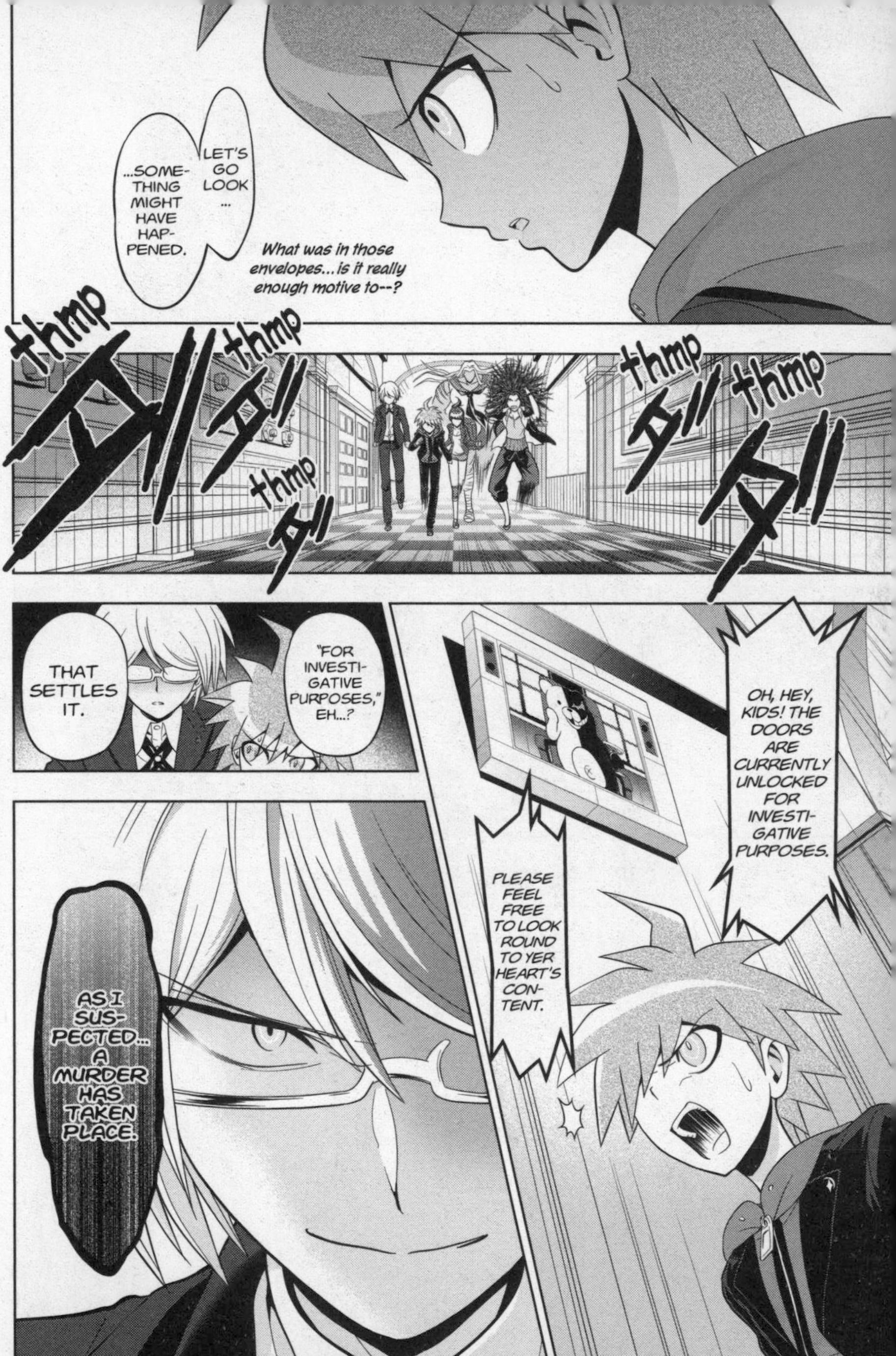
LET'S GO LOOK...
...SOME-THING MIGHT HAVE HAP-PENED.
What was in those envelopes... is it really enough motive to--?
thmp thmp
thmp thmp thmp
OH, HEY, KIDS! THE DOORS ARE CURRENTLY UNLOCKED FOR INVESTI-GATIVE PURPOSES.
PLEASE FEEL FREE TO LOOK ROUND TO YER HEART'S CON-TENT.
"FOR INVESTI-GATIVE PURPOSES," EH...?
THAT SETTLES IT.
AS I SUS-PECTED... A MURDER HAS TAKEN PLACE.

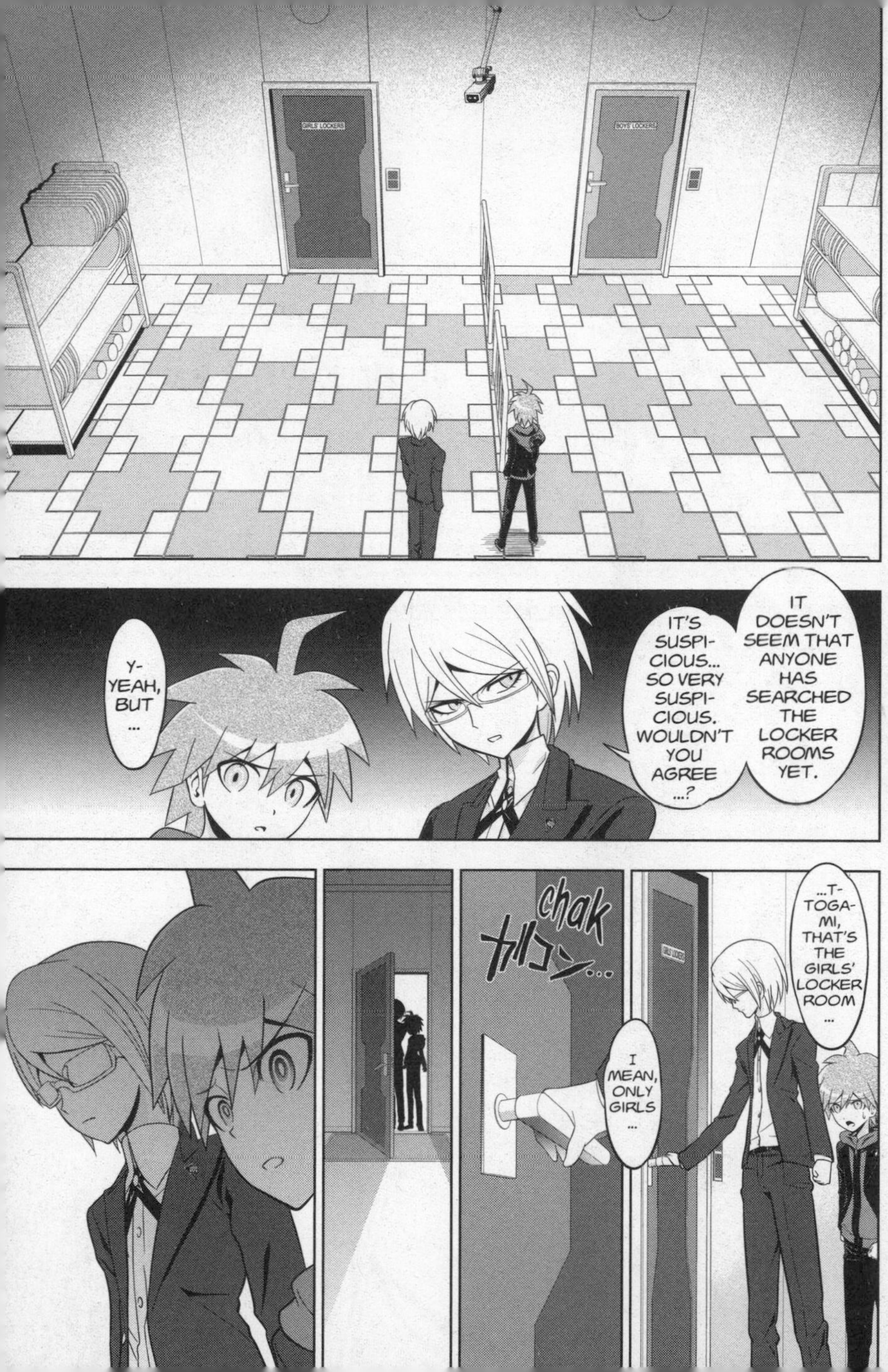
BOYS' LOCKERS
GIRLS' LOCKERS
IT DOESN'T SEEM THAT ANYONE HAS SEARCHED THE LOCKER ROOMS YET.
IT'S SUSPICIOUS... SO VERY SUSPICIOUS. WOULDN'T YOU AGREE ...?
Y-YEAH, BUT ...
...T-TOGAMI, THAT'S THE GIRLS' LOCKER ROOM ...
I MEAN, ONLY GIRLS ...
chak

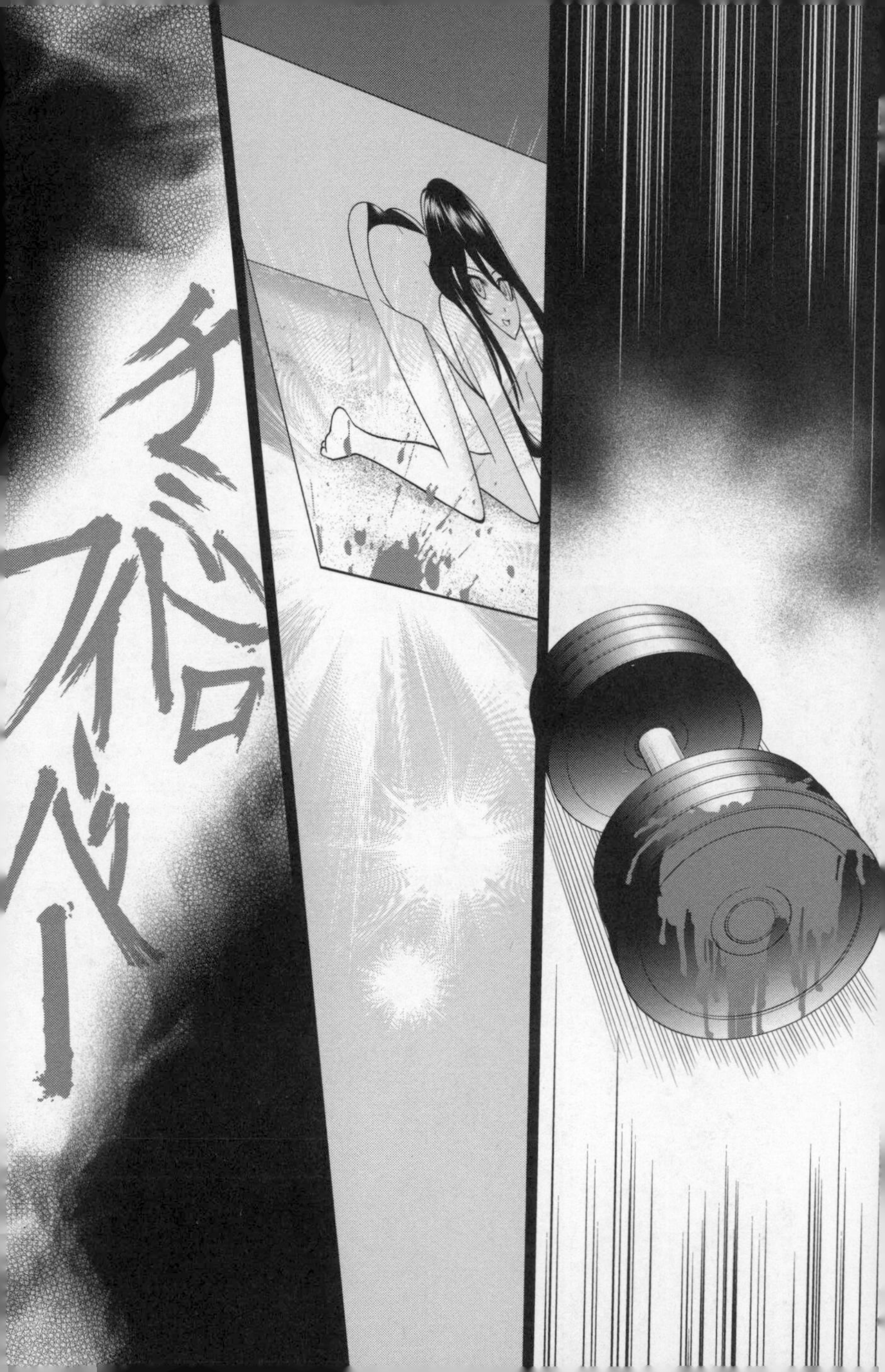
チミドロフィーバー

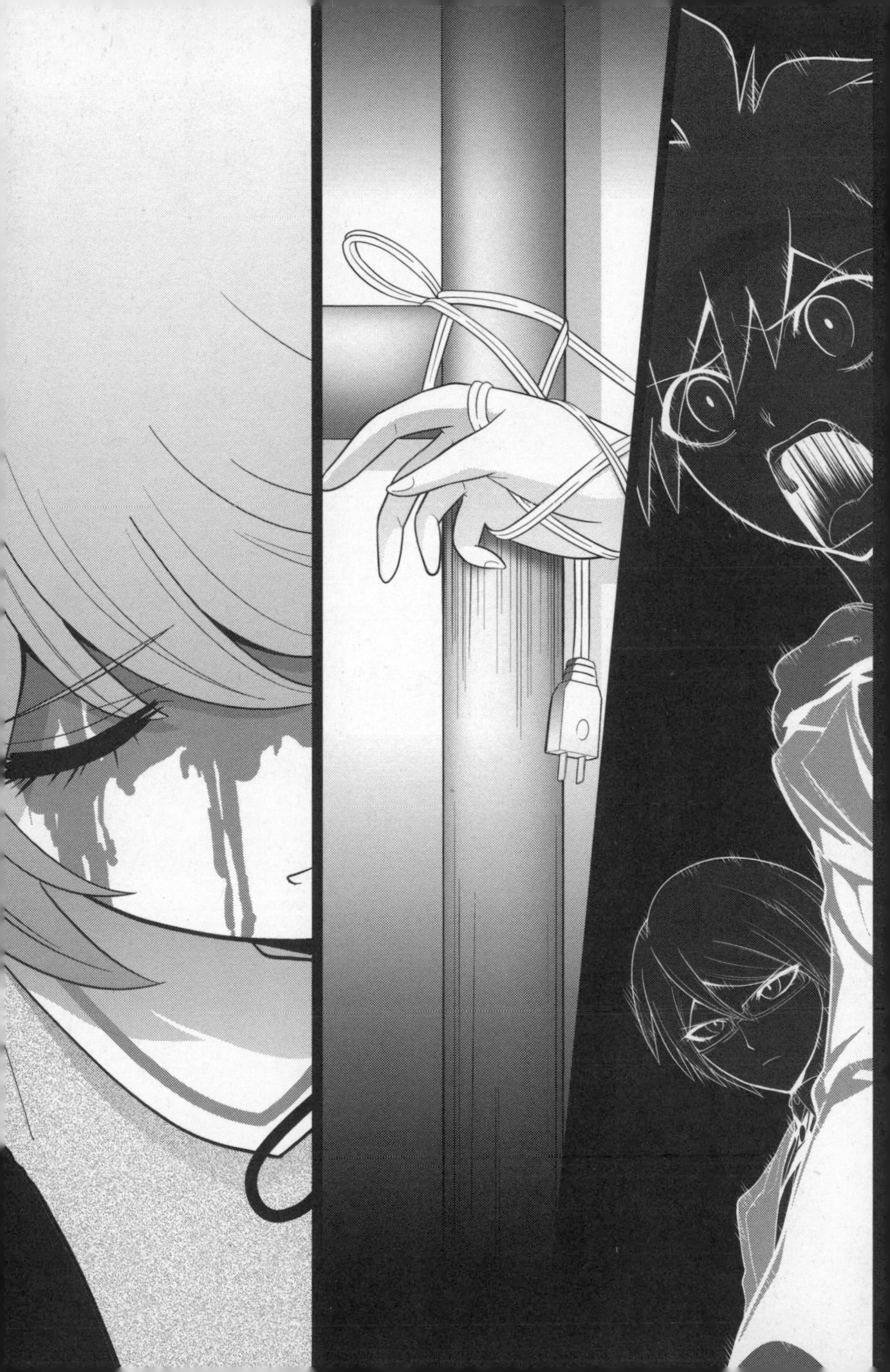

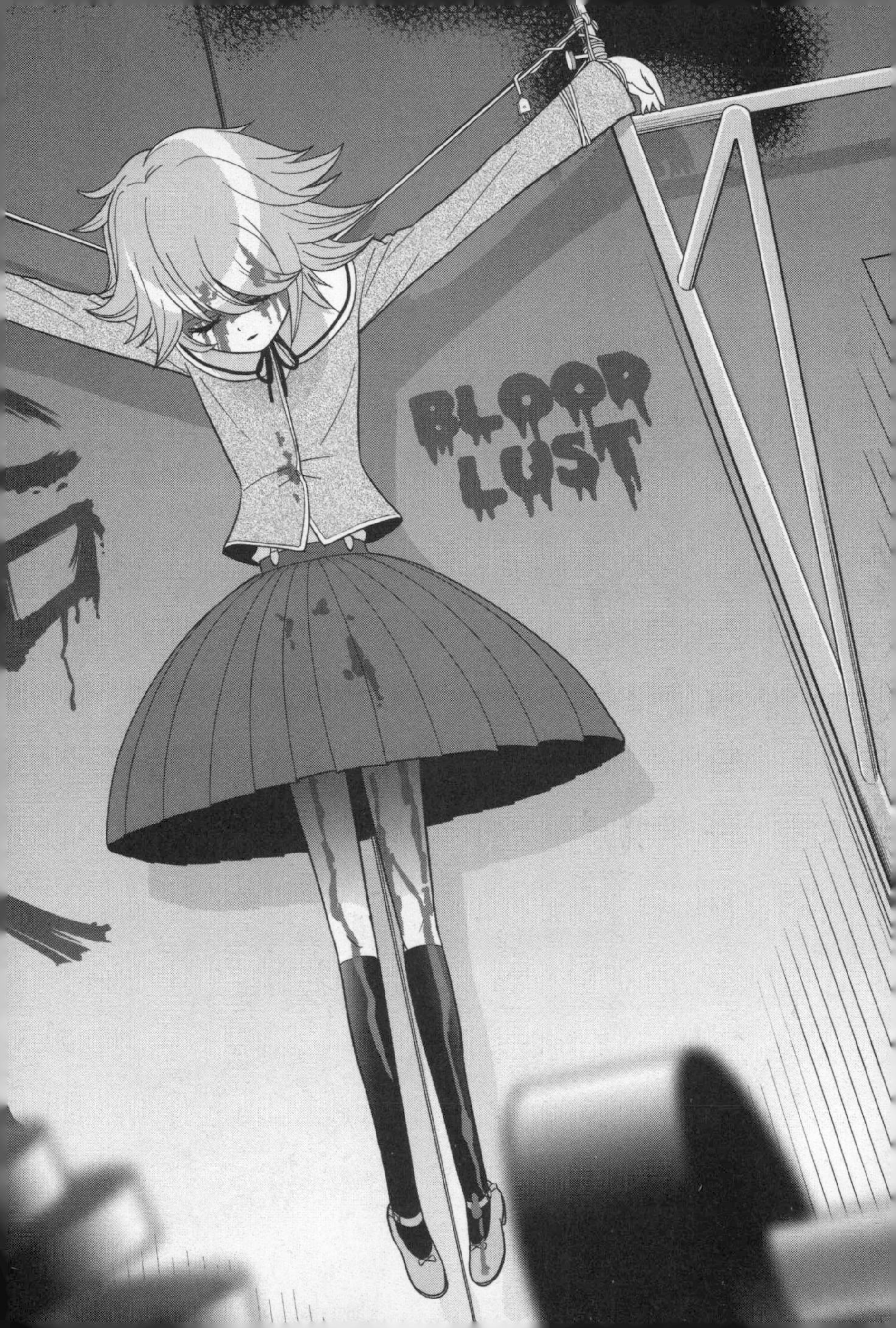
BLOOD LUST

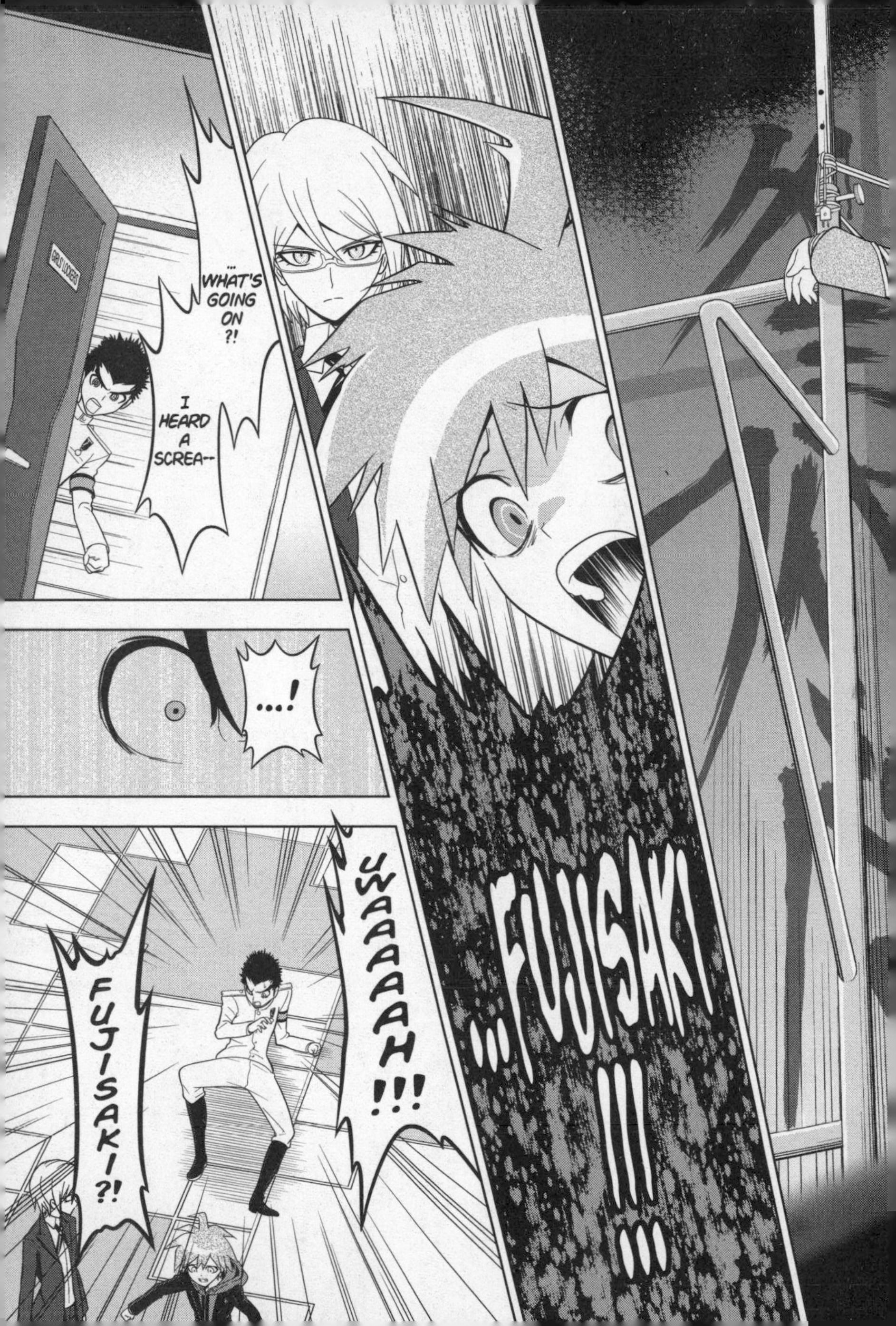

...FUJISAKI!!!...
GIRLS' LOCKERS
...WHAT'S GOING ON?!
I HEARD A SCREA--
...!
UWAAAAAAH!!!
FUJISAKI?!

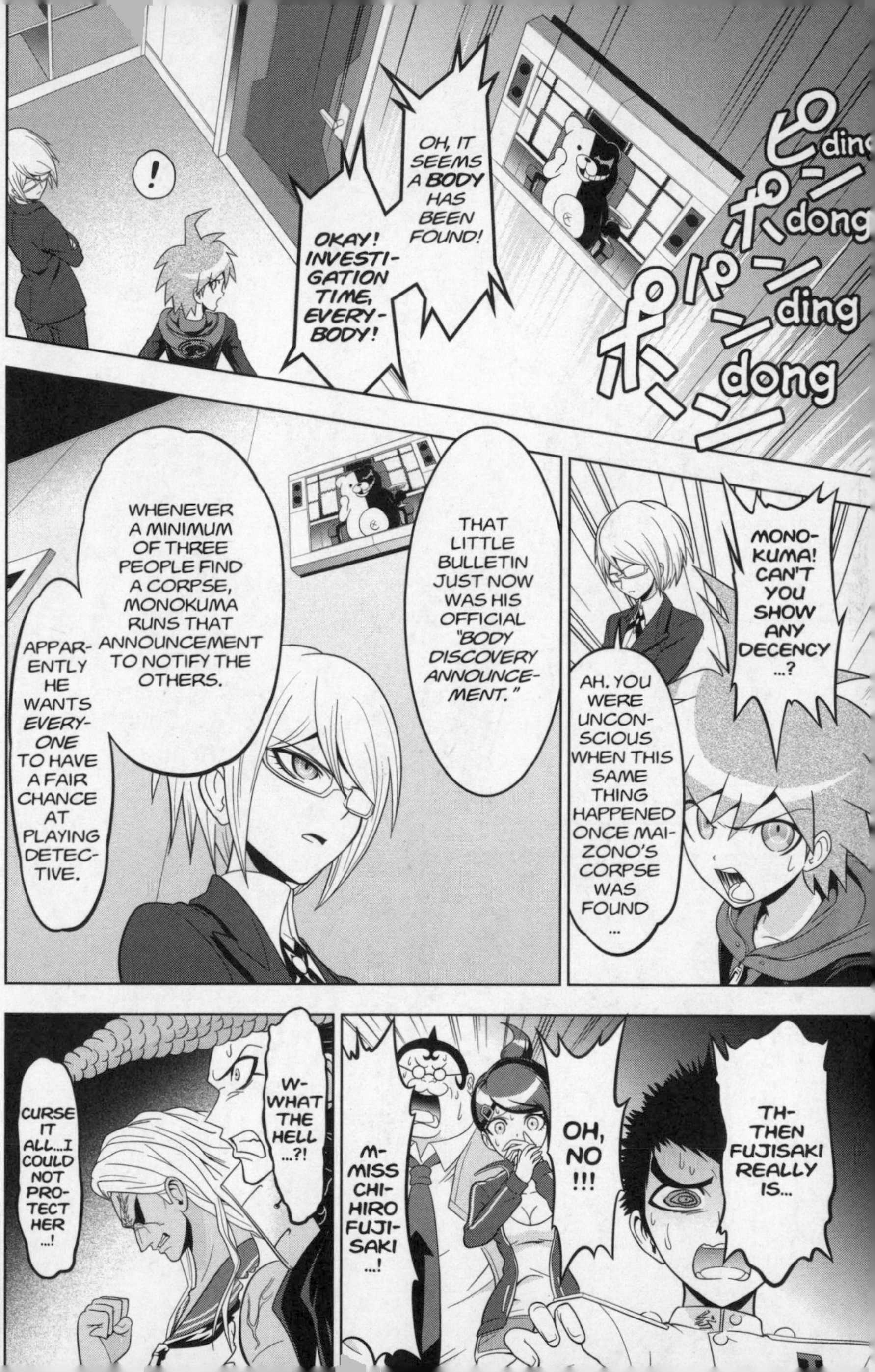
ding dong ding dong
OH, IT SEEMS A BODY HAS BEEN FOUND!
OKAY! INVESTIGATION TIME, EVERYBODY!
MONOKUMA! CAN'T YOU SHOW ANY DECENCY ...?
AH. YOU WERE UNCONSCIOUS WHEN THIS SAME THING HAPPENED ONCE MAIZONO'S CORPSE WAS FOUND ...
THAT LITTLE BULLETIN JUST NOW WAS HIS OFFICIAL "BODY DISCOVERY ANNOUNCEMENT."
WHENEVER A MINIMUM OF THREE PEOPLE FIND A CORPSE, MONOKUMA RUNS THAT ANNOUNCEMENT TO NOTIFY THE OTHERS.
APPARENTLY HE WANTS EVERYONE TO HAVE A FAIR CHANCE AT PLAYING DETECTIVE.
TH-THEN FUJISAKI REALLY IS...
OH, NO !!!
M-MISS CHIHIRO FUJISAKI ...!
W-WHAT THE HELL ...?!
CURSE IT ALL...I COULD NOT PROTECT HER ...!

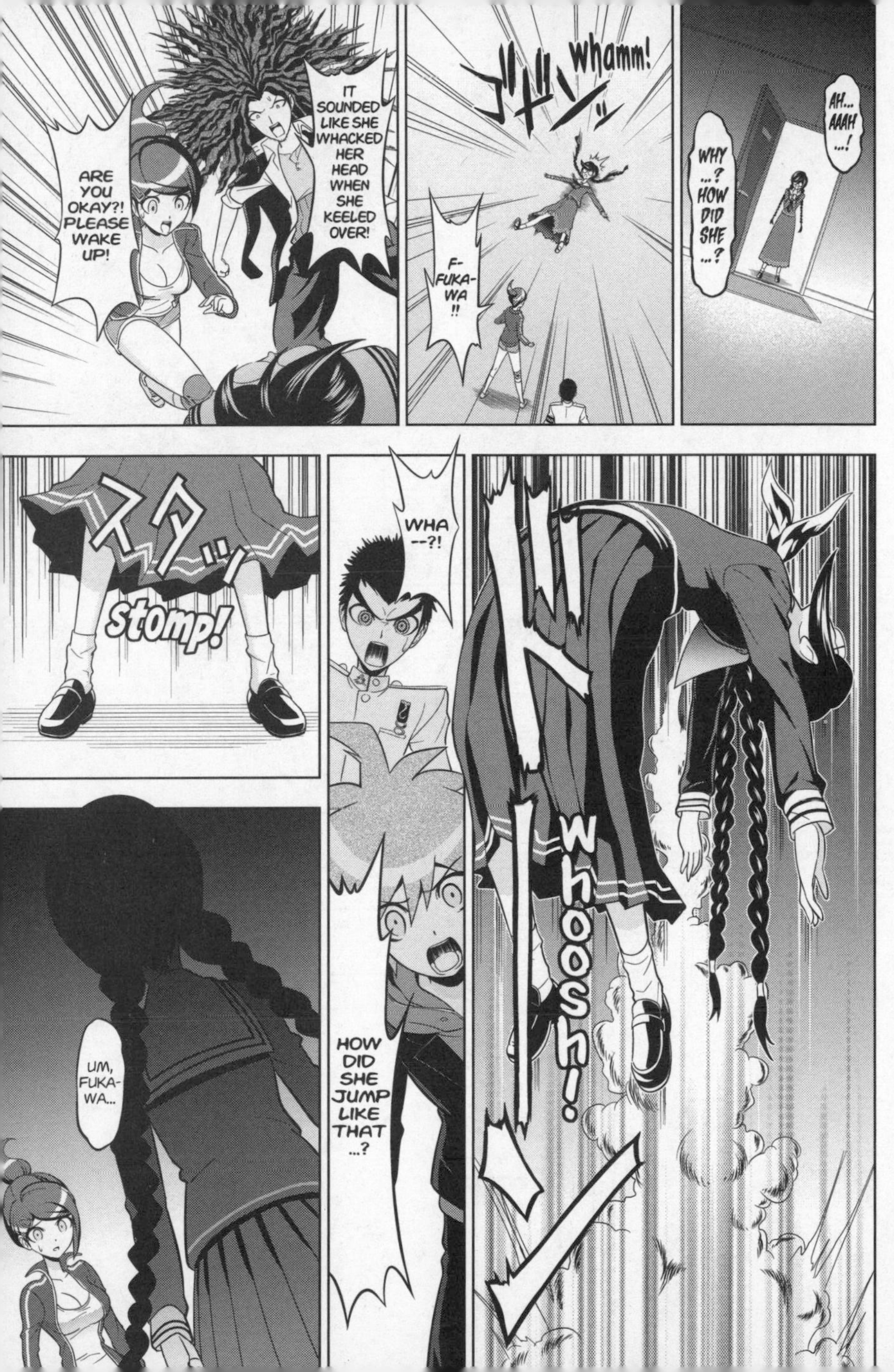
AH... AAAH ...!
WHY ...? HOW DID SHE ...?
whamm!
F-FUKAWA !!
IT SOUNDED LIKE SHE WHACKED HER HEAD WHEN SHE KEELED OVER!
ARE YOU OKAY?! PLEASE WAKE UP!
whoosh!
WHA --?!
HOW DID SHE JUMP LIKE THAT ...?
スタッ
stomp!
UM, FUKAWA...

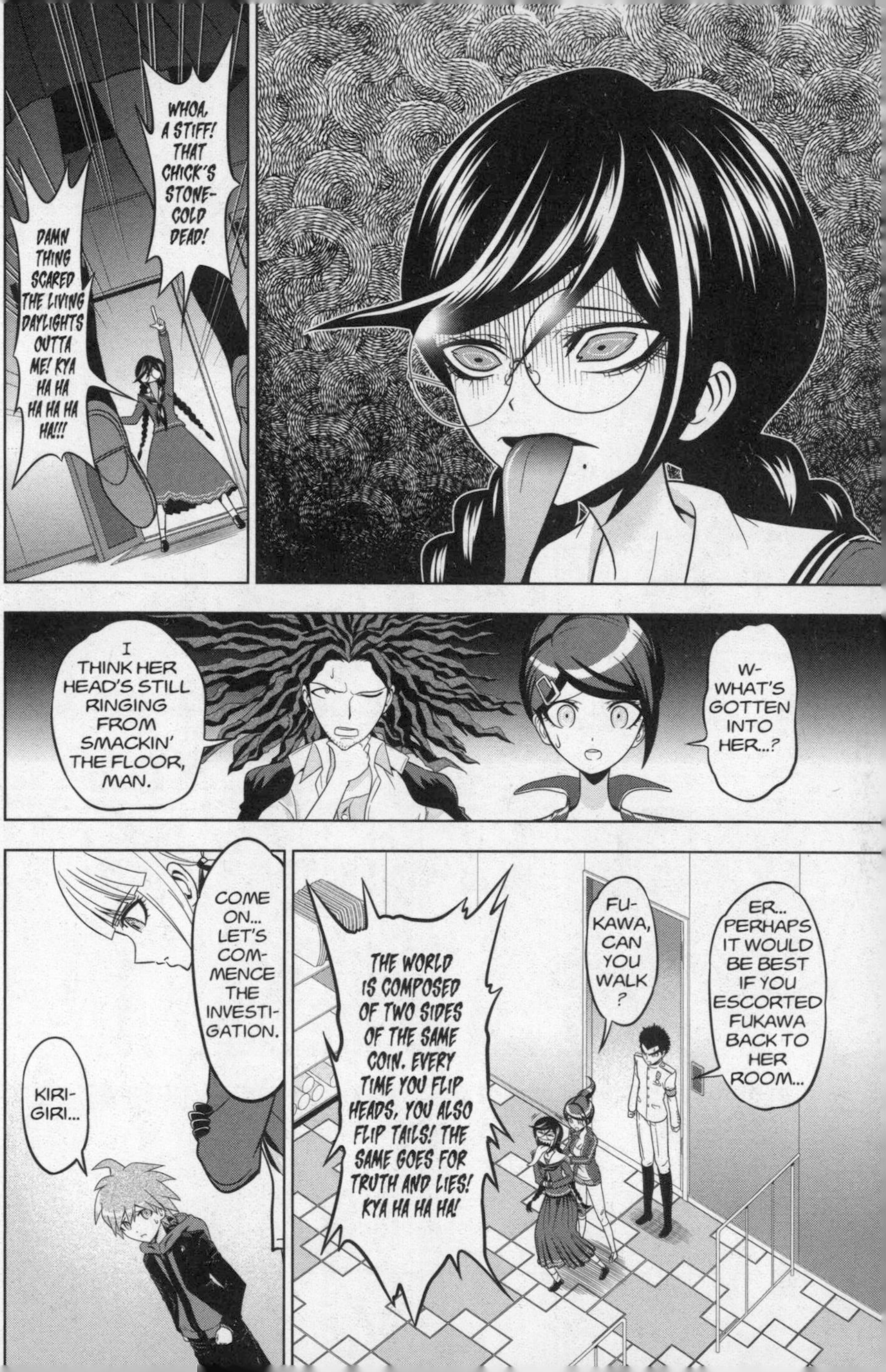
WHOA, A STIFF! THAT CHICK'S STONE-COLD DEAD!
DAMN THING SCARED THE LIVING DAYLIGHTS OUTTA ME! KYA HA HA HA HA HA HA!!!
W-WHAT'S GOTTEN INTO HER...?
I THINK HER HEAD'S STILL RINGING FROM SMACKIN' THE FLOOR, MAN.
ER... PERHAPS IT WOULD BE BEST IF YOU ESCORTED FUKAWA BACK TO HER ROOM...
FU-KAWA, CAN YOU WALK?
THE WORLD IS COMPOSED OF TWO SIDES OF THE SAME COIN. EVERY TIME YOU FLIP HEADS, YOU ALSO FLIP TAILS! THE SAME GOES FOR TRUTH AND LIES! KYA HA HA HA!
COME ON... LET'S COMMENCE THE INVESTIGATION.
KIRI-GIRI...

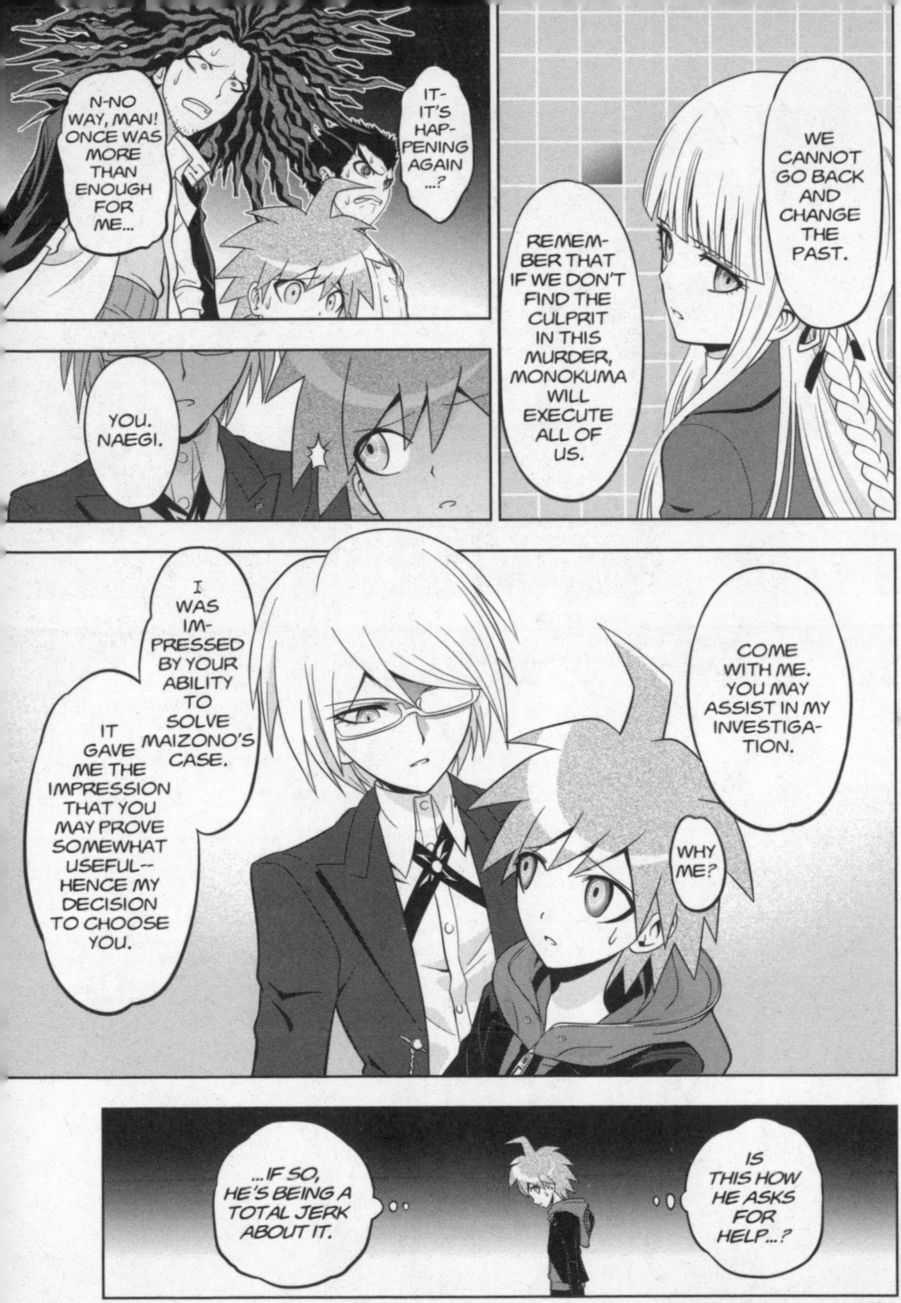
WE CANNOT GO BACK AND CHANGE THE PAST.
REMEMBER THAT IF WE DON'T FIND THE CULPRIT IN THIS MURDER, MONOKUMA WILL EXECUTE ALL OF US.
IT- IT'S HAPPENING AGAIN ...?
N-NO WAY, MAN! ONCE WAS MORE THAN ENOUGH FOR ME...
YOU. NAEGI.
COME WITH ME. YOU MAY ASSIST IN MY INVESTIGATION.
WHY ME?
I WAS IMPRESSED BY YOUR ABILITY TO SOLVE MAIZONO'S CASE.
IT GAVE ME THE IMPRESSION THAT YOU MAY PROVE SOMEWHAT USEFUL-- HENCE MY DECISION TO CHOOSE YOU.
IS THIS HOW HE ASKS FOR HELP...?
...IF SO, HE'S BEING A TOTAL JERK ABOUT IT.

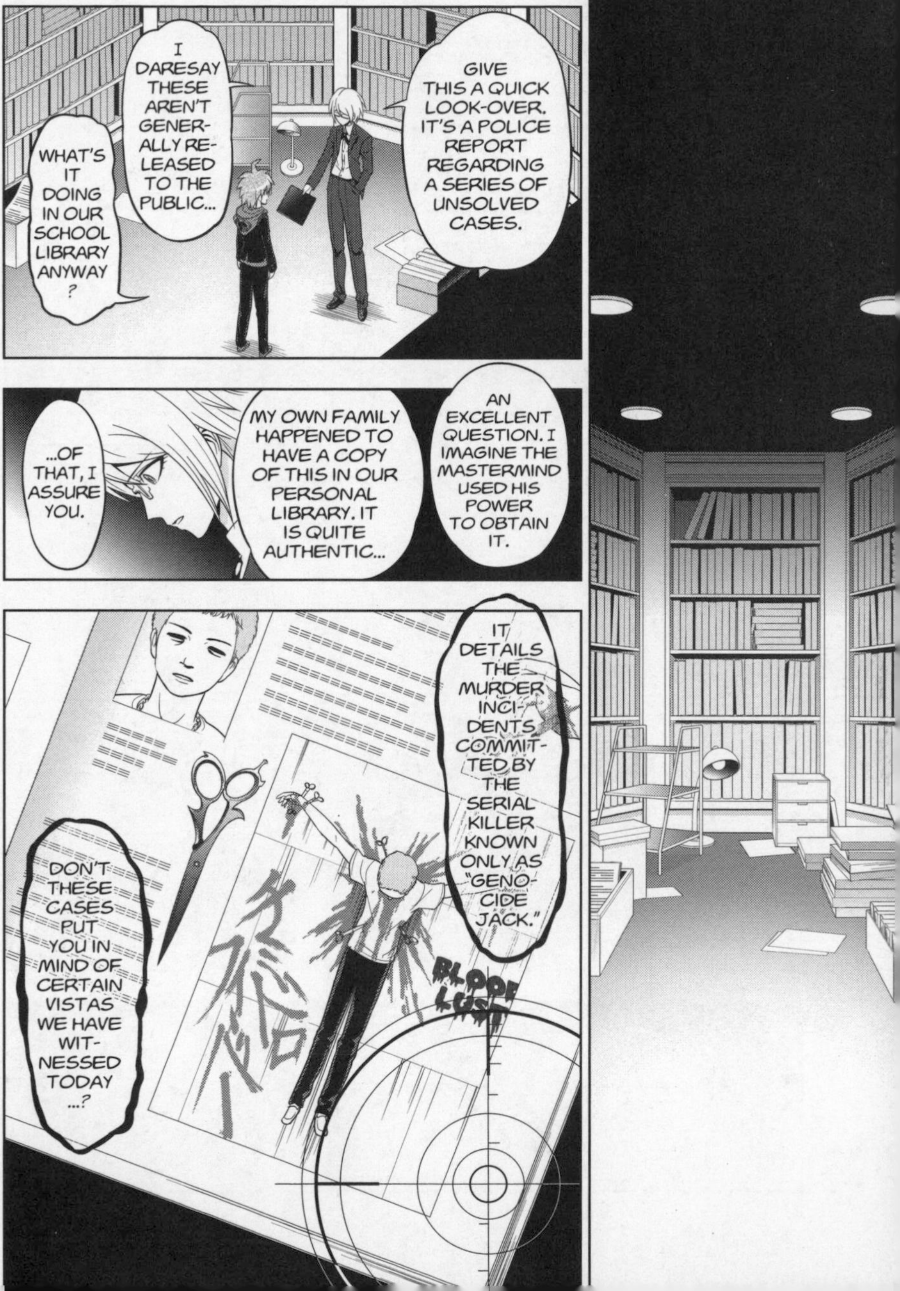

GIVE THIS A QUICK LOOK-OVER. IT'S A POLICE REPORT REGARDING A SERIES OF UNSOLVED CASES.
I DARESAY THESE AREN'T GENER-ALLY RE-LEASED TO THE PUBLIC...
WHAT'S IT DOING IN OUR SCHOOL LIBRARY ANYWAY?
AN EXCELLENT QUESTION. I IMAGINE THE MASTERMIND USED HIS POWER TO OBTAIN IT.
MY OWN FAMILY HAPPENED TO HAVE A COPY OF THIS IN OUR PERSONAL LIBRARY. IT IS QUITE AUTHENTIC...
...OF THAT, I ASSURE YOU.
IT DETAILS THE MURDER INCI-DENTS COMMIT-TED BY THE SERIAL KILLER KNOWN ONLY AS "GENO-CIDE JACK."
DON'T THESE CASES PUT YOU IN MIND OF CERTAIN VISTAS WE HAVE WIT-NESSED TODAY...?

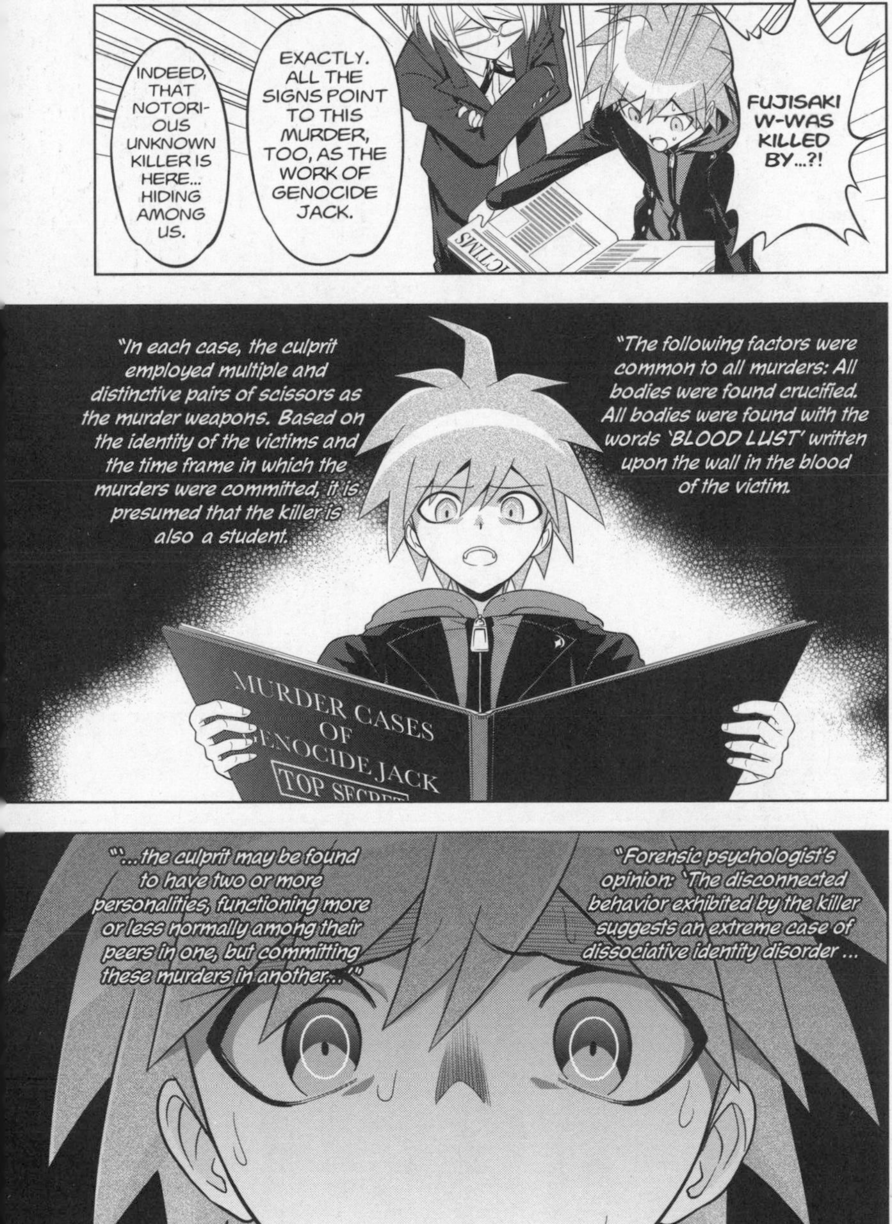
FUJISAKI W-WAS KILLED BY...?!
EXACTLY. ALL THE SIGNS POINT TO THIS MURDER, TOO, AS THE WORK OF GENOCIDE JACK.
INDEED, THAT NOTORIOUS UNKNOWN KILLER IS HERE... HIDING AMONG US.
"The following factors were common to all murders: All bodies were found crucified. All bodies were found with the words 'BLOOD LUST' written upon the wall in the blood of the victim.
"In each case, the culprit employed multiple and distinctive pairs of scissors as the murder weapons. Based on the identity of the victims and the time frame in which the murders were committed, it is presumed that the killer is also a student.
MURDER CASES OF GENOCIDE JACK
"Forensic psychologist's opinion: 'The disconnected behavior exhibited by the killer suggests an extreme case of dissociative identity disorder ...
'...the culprit may be found to have two or more personalities, functioning more or less normally among their peers in one, but committing these murders in another...'"

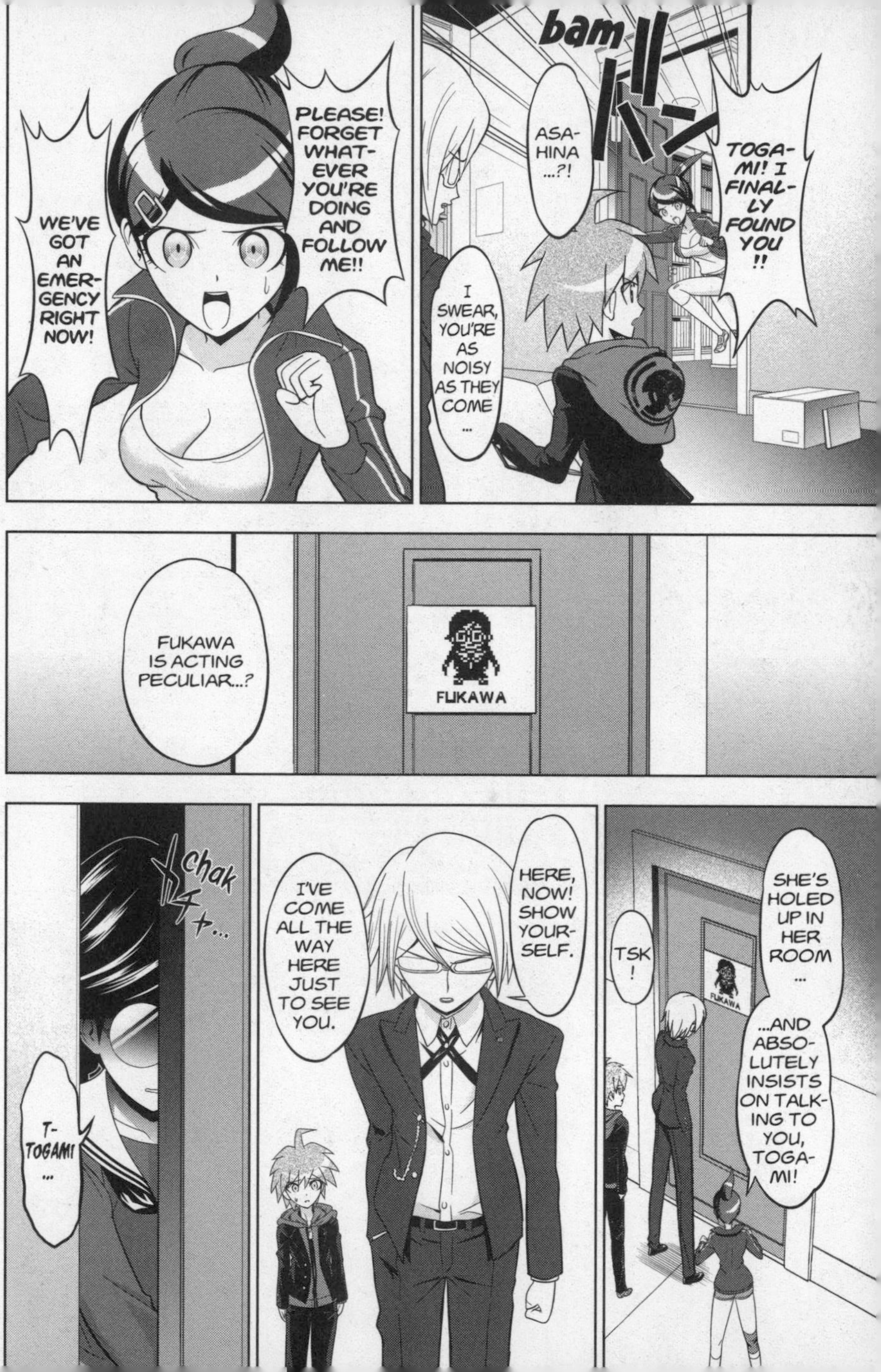
bam
TOGAMI! I FINALLY FOUND YOU!!
ASAHINA ...?!
I SWEAR, YOU'RE AS NOISY AS THEY COME ...
PLEASE! FORGET WHATEVER YOU'RE DOING AND FOLLOW ME!!
WE'VE GOT AN EMERGENCY RIGHT NOW!
FUKAWA
FUKAWA IS ACTING PECULIAR...?
SHE'S HOLED UP IN HER ROOM ...
...AND ABSOLUTELY INSISTS ON TALKING TO YOU, TOGAMI!
FUKAWA
TSK!
HERE, NOW! SHOW YOURSELF.
I'VE COME ALL THE WAY HERE JUST TO SEE YOU.
chak
T-TOGAMI ...

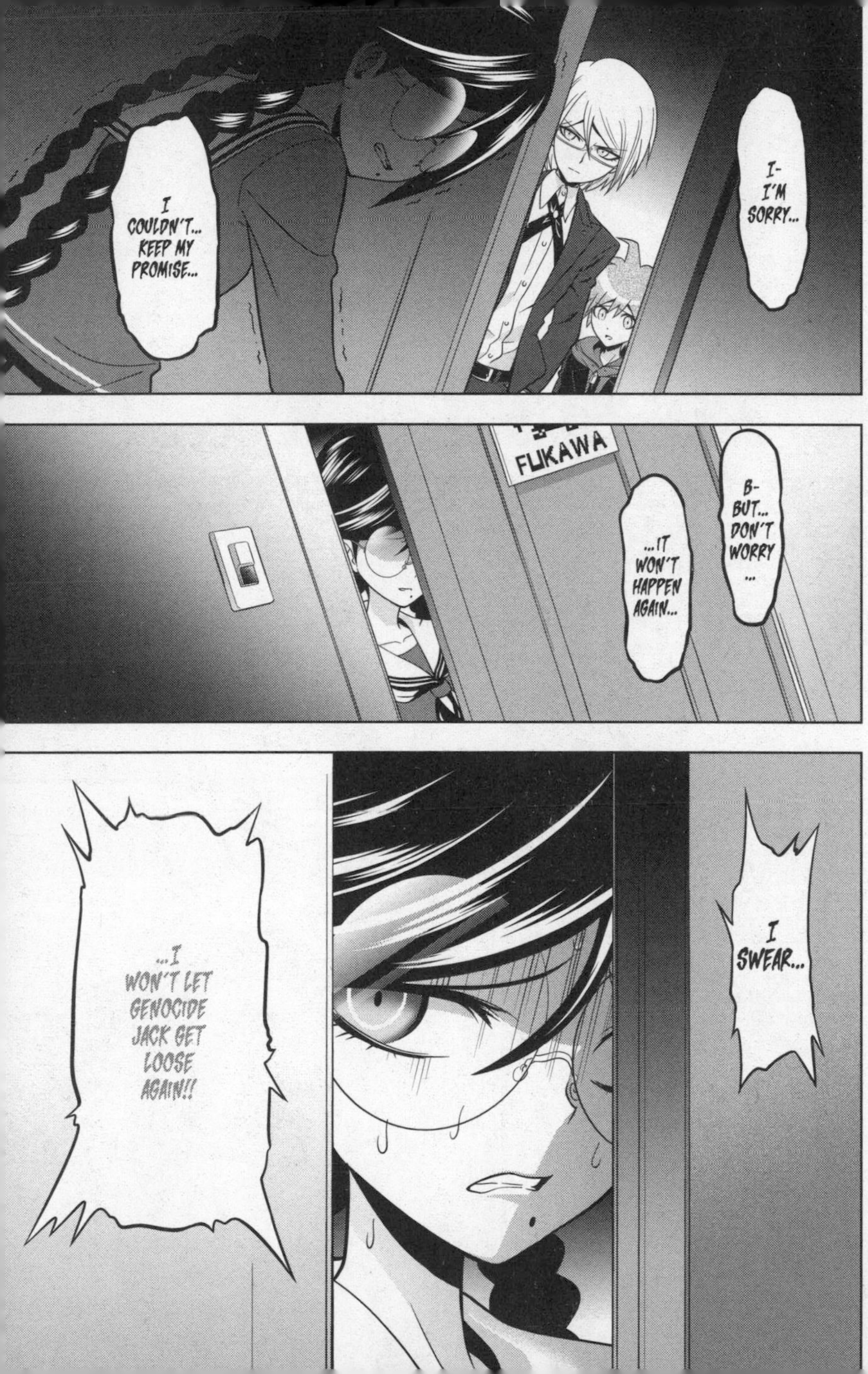
I- I'M SORRY...
I COULDN'T... KEEP MY PROMISE...
FUKAWA
B- BUT... DON'T WORRY ...
...IT WON'T HAPPEN AGAIN...
I SWEAR...
...I WON'T LET GENOCIDE JACK GET LOOSE AGAIN!!

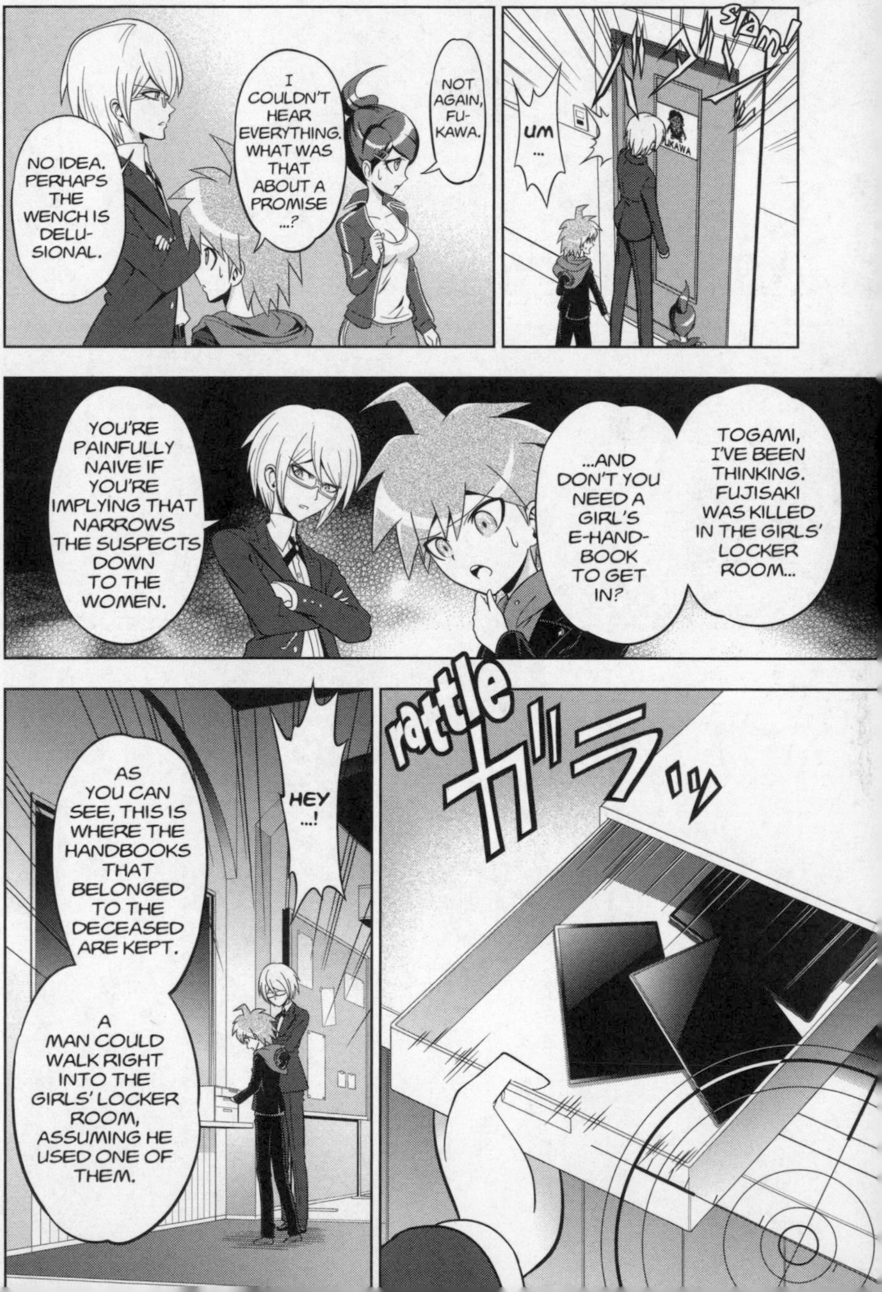
slam!
UM ...
NOT AGAIN, FU-KAWA.
I COULDN'T HEAR EVERYTHING. WHAT WAS THAT ABOUT A PROMISE ...?
NO IDEA. PERHAPS THE WENCH IS DELUSIONAL.
TOGAMI, I'VE BEEN THINKING. FUJISAKI WAS KILLED IN THE GIRLS' LOCKER ROOM...
...AND DON'T YOU NEED A GIRL'S E-HANDBOOK TO GET IN?
YOU'RE PAINFULLY NAIVE IF YOU'RE IMPLYING THAT NARROWS THE SUSPECTS DOWN TO THE WOMEN.
rattle
ガラッ
HEY ...!
AS YOU CAN SEE, THIS IS WHERE THE HANDBOOKS THAT BELONGED TO THE DECEASED ARE KEPT.
A MAN COULD WALK RIGHT INTO THE GIRLS' LOCKER ROOM, ASSUMING HE USED ONE OF THEM.

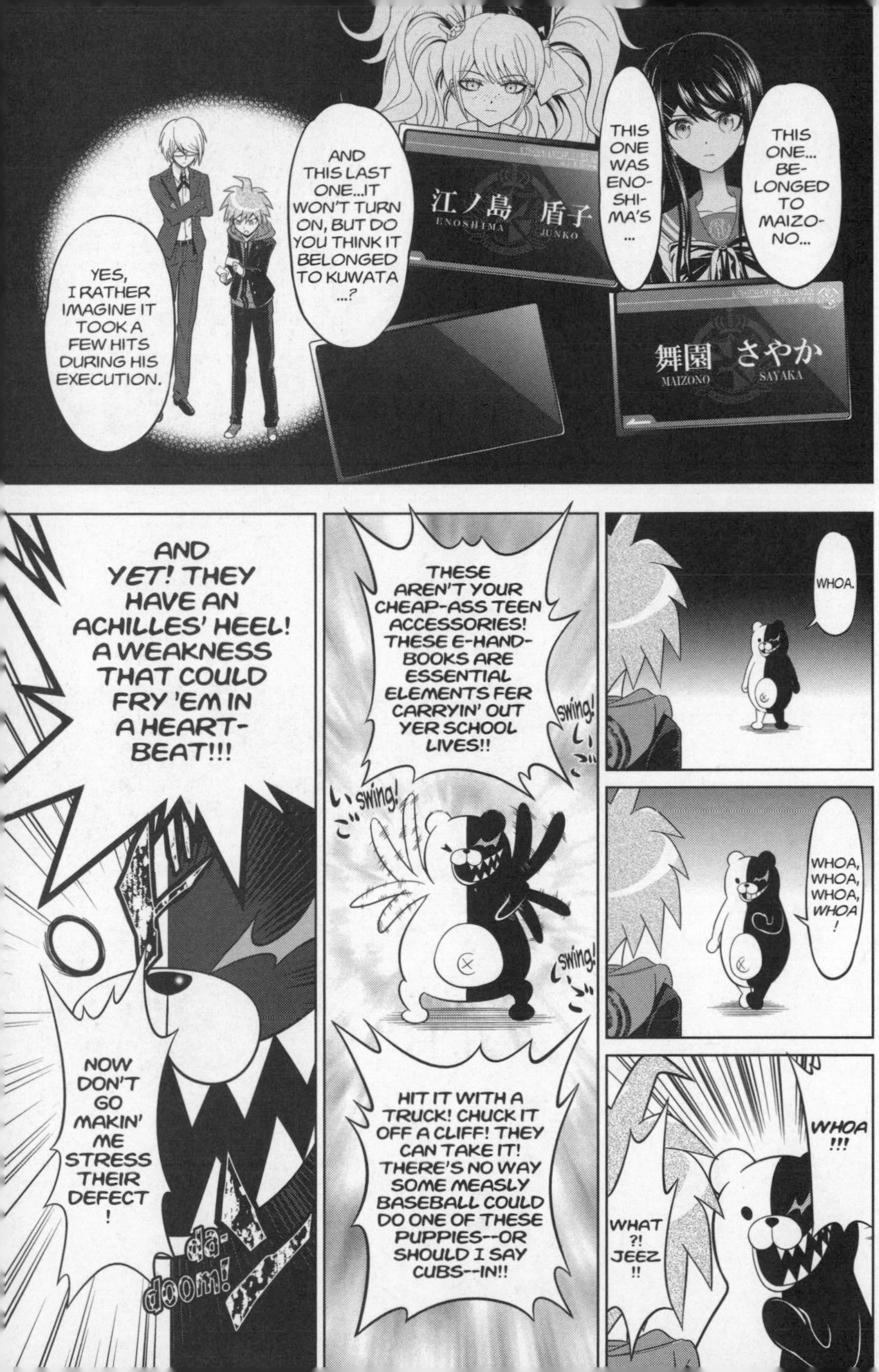
THIS ONE... BE-LONGED TO MAIZO-NO...
舞園 さやか
MAIZONO SAYAKA
THIS ONE WAS ENO-SHI-MA'S ...
江ノ島 盾子
ENOSHIMA JUNKO
AND THIS LAST ONE...IT WON'T TURN ON, BUT DO YOU THINK IT BELONGED TO KUWATA ...?
YES, I RATHER IMAGINE IT TOOK A FEW HITS DURING HIS EXECUTION.
WHOA.
WHOA, WHOA, WHOA, WHOA!
WHOA!!!
WHAT?! JEEZ!!
THESE AREN'T YOUR CHEAP-ASS TEEN ACCESSORIES! THESE E-HAND-BOOKS ARE ESSENTIAL ELEMENTS FER CARRYIN' OUT YER SCHOOL LIVES!!
swing!
swing!
swing!
HIT IT WITH A TRUCK! CHUCK IT OFF A CLIFF! THEY CAN TAKE IT! THERE'S NO WAY SOME MEASLY BASEBALL COULD DO ONE OF THESE PUPPIES--OR SHOULD I SAY CUBS--IN!!
AND YET! THEY HAVE AN ACHILLES' HEEL! A WEAKNESS THAT COULD FRY 'EM IN A HEART-BEAT!!!
NOW DON'T GO MAKIN' ME STRESS THEIR DEFECT!
da-doom!

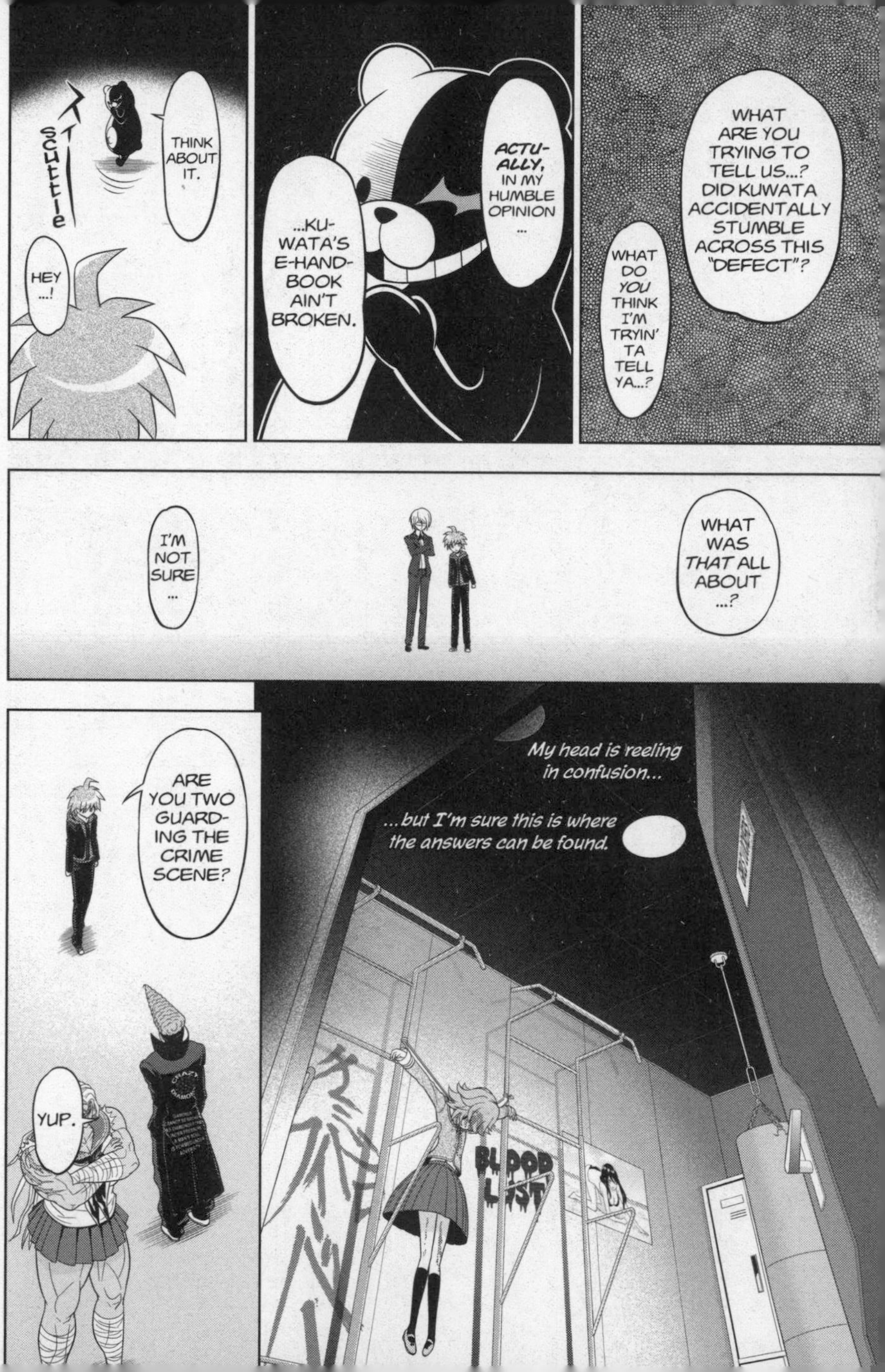
WHAT ARE YOU TRYING TO TELL US...? DID KUWATA ACCIDENTALLY STUMBLE ACROSS THIS "DEFECT"?
WHAT DO YOU THINK I'M TRYIN' TA TELL YA...?
ACTUALLY, IN MY HUMBLE OPINION...
...KUWATA'S E-HANDBOOK AIN'T BROKEN.
THINK ABOUT IT.
Scuttle
HEY...!
WHAT WAS THAT ALL ABOUT...?
I'M NOT SURE...
My head is reeling in confusion...
...but I'm sure this is where the answers can be found.
BLOOD LUST
ARE YOU TWO GUARDING THE CRIME SCENE?
YUP.

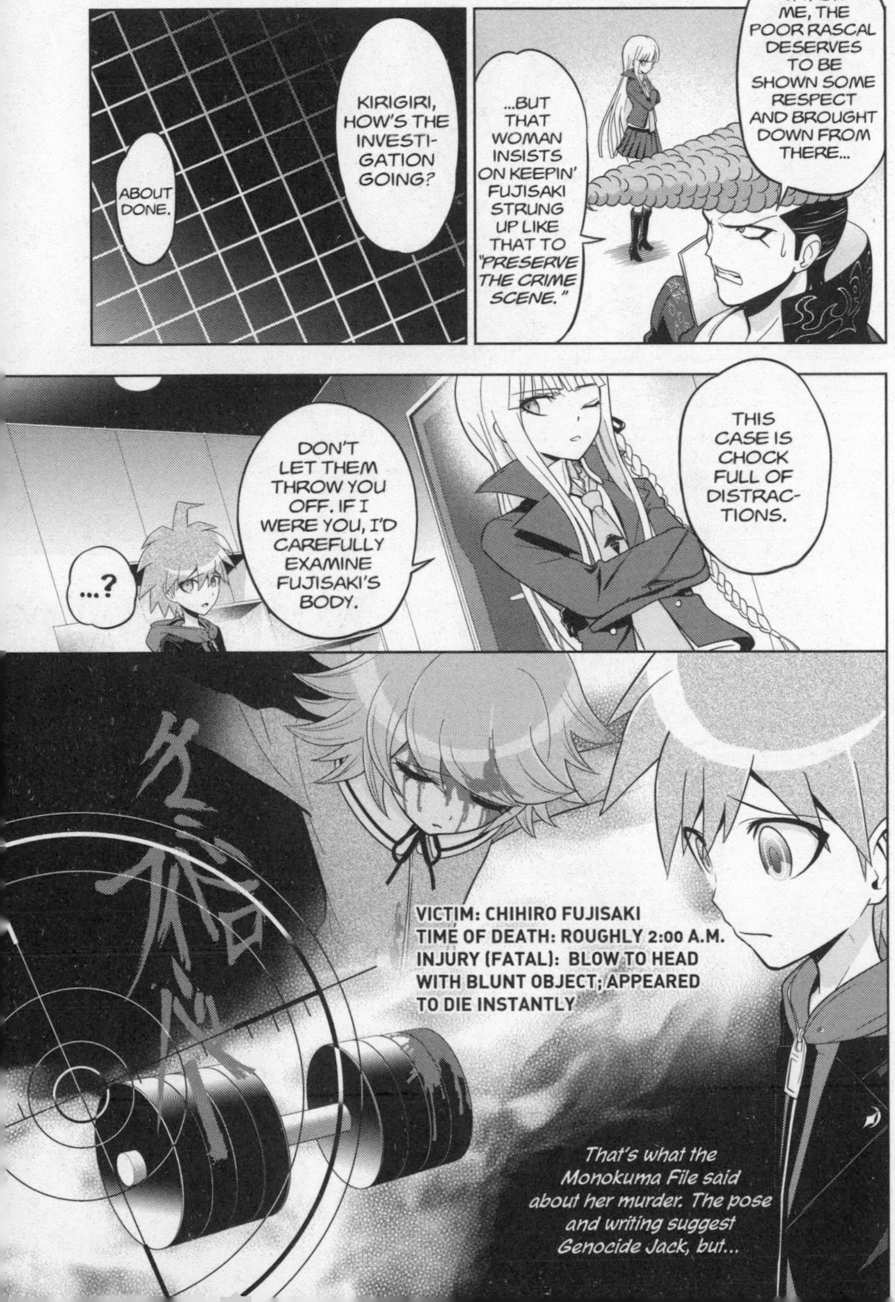
YA ASK ME, THE POOR RASCAL DESERVES TO BE SHOWN SOME RESPECT AND BROUGHT DOWN FROM THERE...
...BUT THAT WOMAN INSISTS ON KEEPIN' FUJISAKI STRUNG UP LIKE THAT TO "PRESERVE THE CRIME SCENE."
KIRIGIRI, HOW'S THE INVESTI-GATION GOING?
ABOUT DONE.
THIS CASE IS CHOCK FULL OF DISTRAC-TIONS.
DON'T LET THEM THROW YOU OFF. IF I WERE YOU, I'D CAREFULLY EXAMINE FUJISAKI'S BODY.
...?
VICTIM: CHIHIRO FUJISAKI
TIME OF DEATH: ROUGHLY 2:00 A.M.
INJURY (FATAL): BLOW TO HEAD WITH BLUNT OBJECT; APPEARED TO DIE INSTANTLY
That's what the Monokuma File said about her murder. The pose and writing suggest Genocide Jack, but...

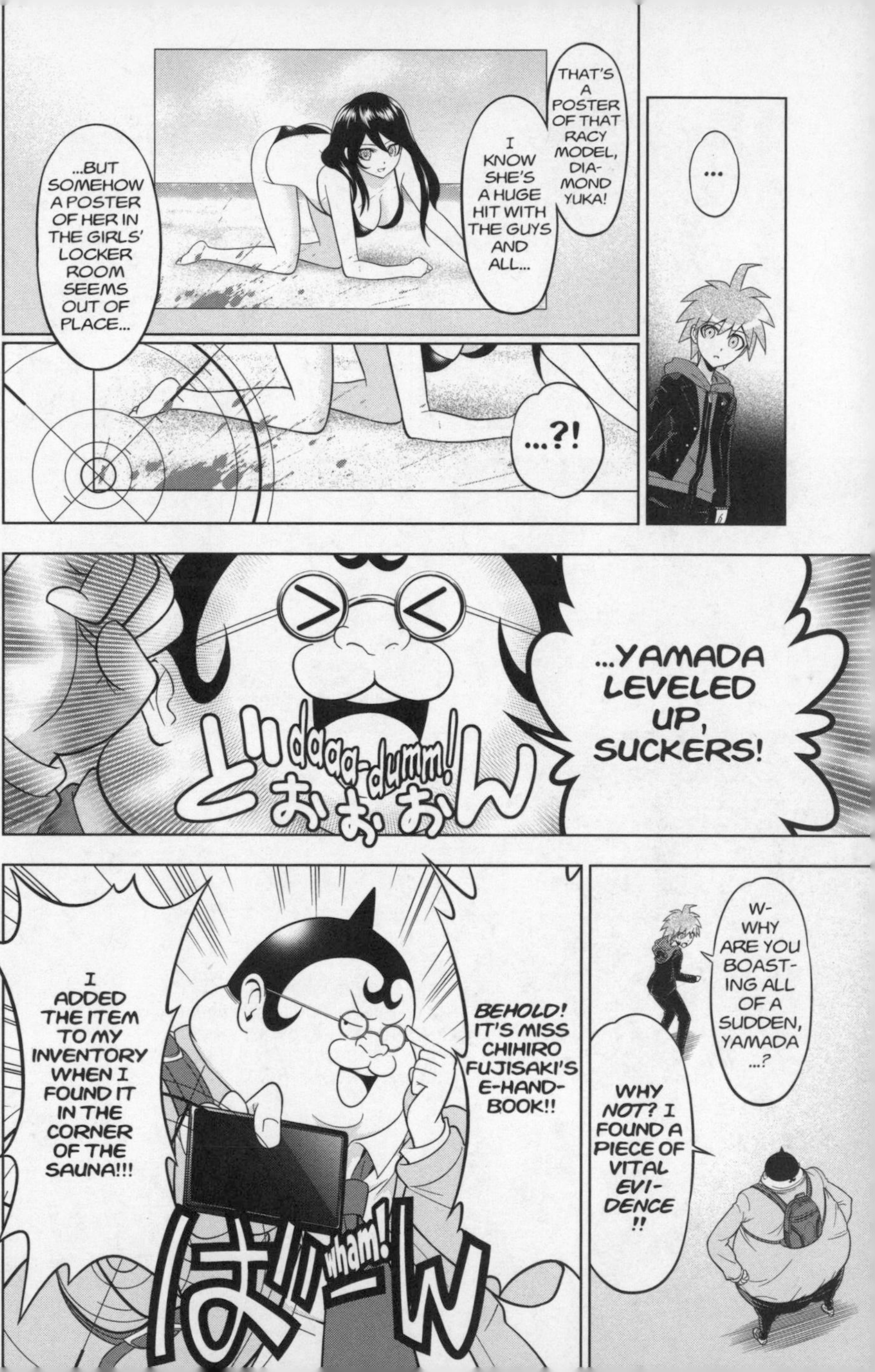
...
THAT'S A POSTER OF THAT RACY MODEL, DIAMOND YUKA!
I KNOW SHE'S A HUGE HIT WITH THE GUYS AND ALL...
...BUT SOMEHOW A POSTER OF HER IN THE GIRLS' LOCKER ROOM SEEMS OUT OF PLACE...
...?!
...YAMADA LEVELED UP, SUCKERS!
どぉぉぉん
daaa-dumm!
W-WHY ARE YOU BOASTING ALL OF A SUDDEN, YAMADA ...?
WHY *NOT*? I FOUND A PIECE OF VITAL *EVIDENCE*!!
BEHOLD! IT'S MISS CHIHIRO FUJISAKI'S E-HANDBOOK!!
I ADDED THE ITEM TO MY INVENTORY WHEN I FOUND IT IN THE CORNER OF THE SAUNA!!!
はーん
wham!

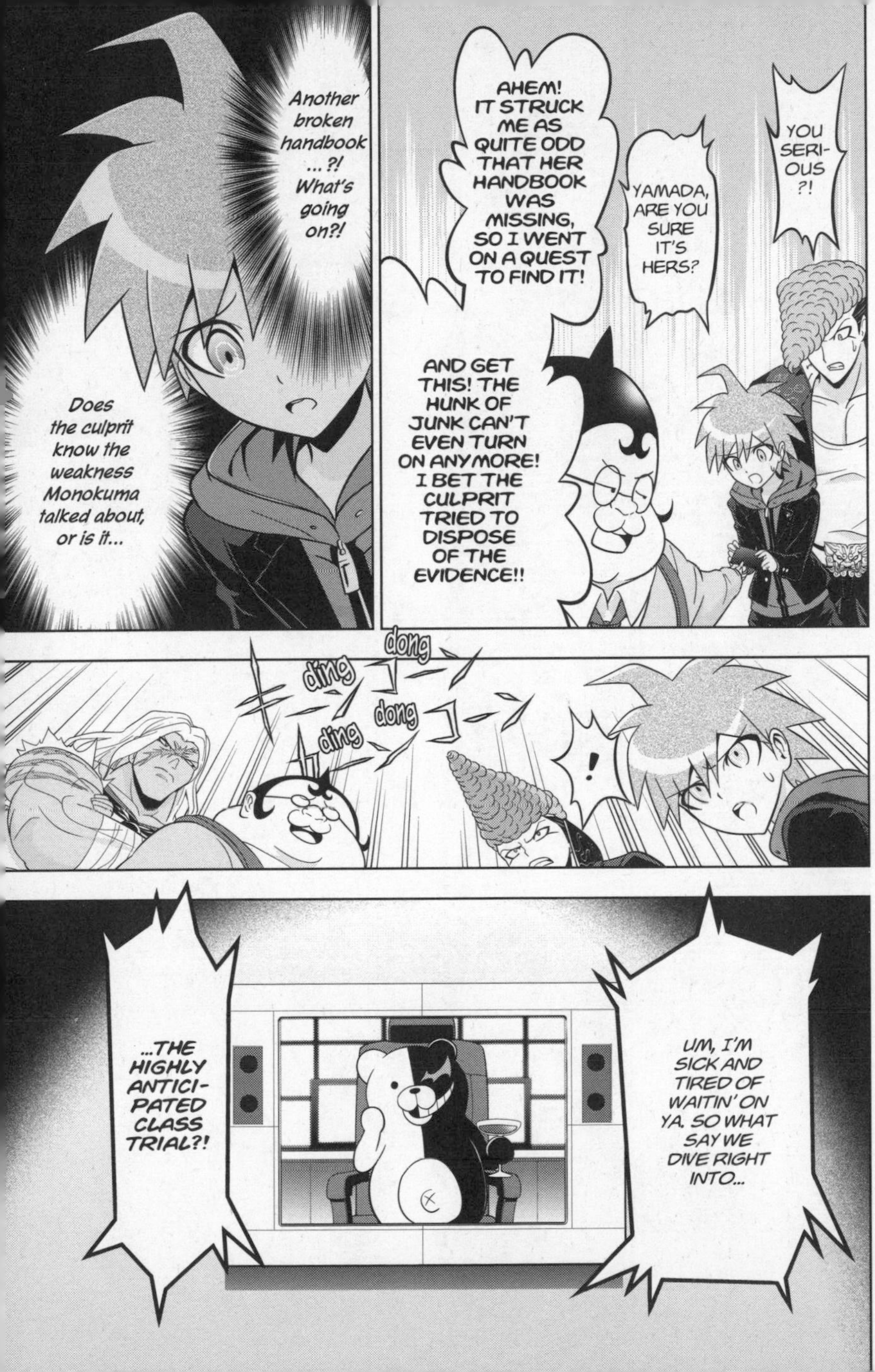
YOU SERIOUS?!
YAMADA, ARE YOU SURE IT'S HERS?
AHEM! IT STRUCK ME AS QUITE ODD THAT HER HANDBOOK WAS MISSING, SO I WENT ON A QUEST TO FIND IT!
AND GET THIS! THE HUNK OF JUNK CAN'T EVEN TURN ON ANYMORE! I BET THE CULPRIT TRIED TO DISPOSE OF THE EVIDENCE!!
Another broken handbook ...?! What's going on?!
Does the culprit know the weakness Monokuma talked about, or is it...
!
dong
ding
dong
ding
UM, I'M SICK AND TIRED OF WAITIN' ON YA. SO WHAT SAY WE DIVE RIGHT INTO...
...THE HIGHLY ANTICIPATED CLASS TRIAL?!

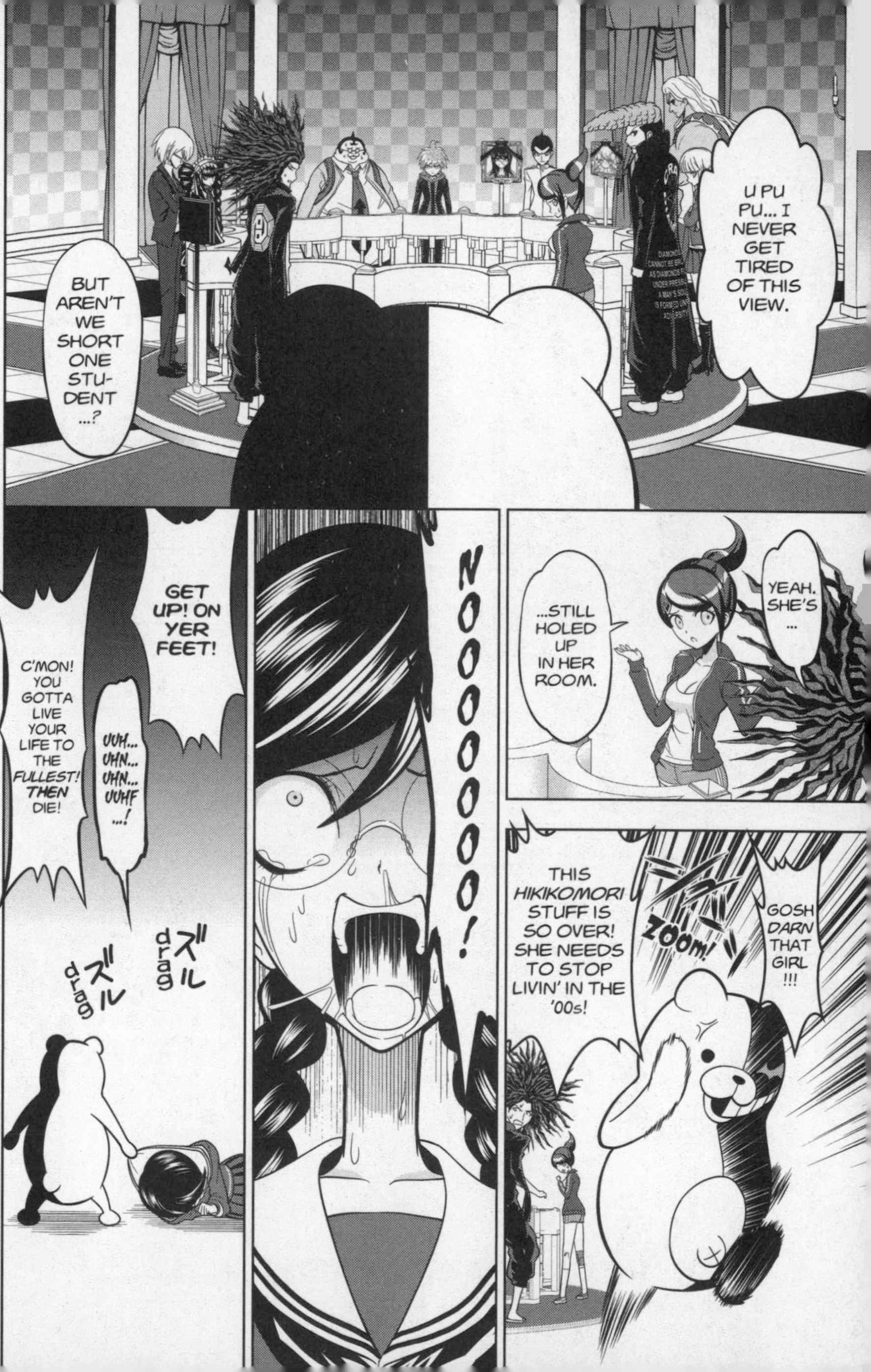

U PU PU... I NEVER GET TIRED OF THIS VIEW.
BUT AREN'T WE SHORT ONE STUDENT ...?
YEAH. SHE'S ...
...STILL HOLED UP IN HER ROOM.
GOSH DARN THAT GIRL !!!
ZOOM!
THIS *HIKIKOMORI* STUFF IS SO OVER! SHE NEEDS TO STOP LIVIN' IN THE '00s!
NOOOOOOOOOO!
GET UP! ON YER FEET!
UUH... UHN... UHN... UUHF ...!
C'MON! YOU GOTTA LIVE YOUR LIFE TO THE *FULLEST!* ***THEN*** DIE!
ズル drag
ズル drag

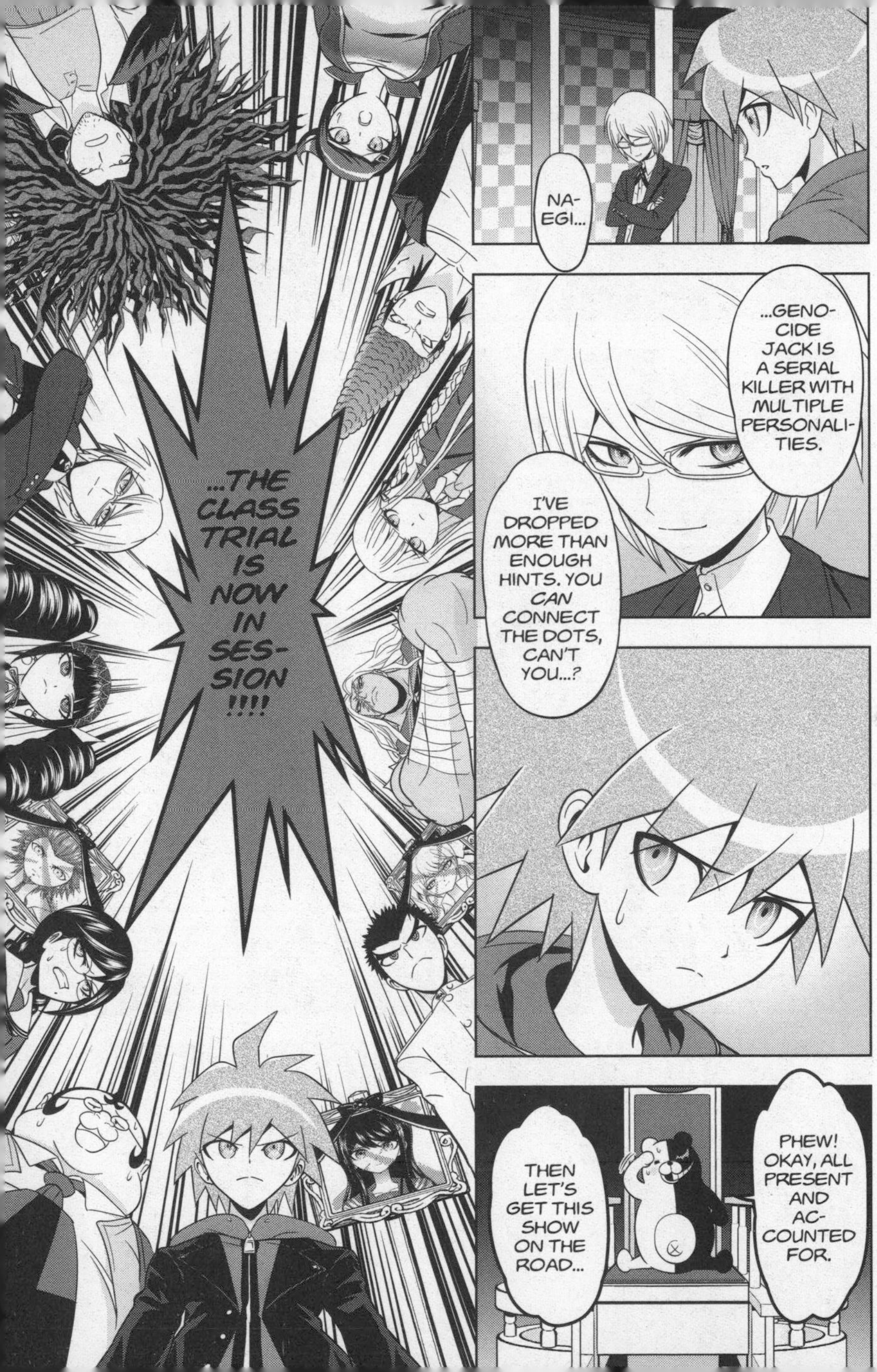
NAEGI...
...GENOCIDE JACK IS A SERIAL KILLER WITH MULTIPLE PERSONALITIES.
I'VE DROPPED MORE THAN ENOUGH HINTS. YOU CAN CONNECT THE DOTS, CAN'T YOU...?
PHEW! OKAY, ALL PRESENT AND ACCOUNTED FOR.
THEN LET'S GET THIS SHOW ON THE ROAD...
...THE CLASS TRIAL IS NOW IN SESSION!!!!

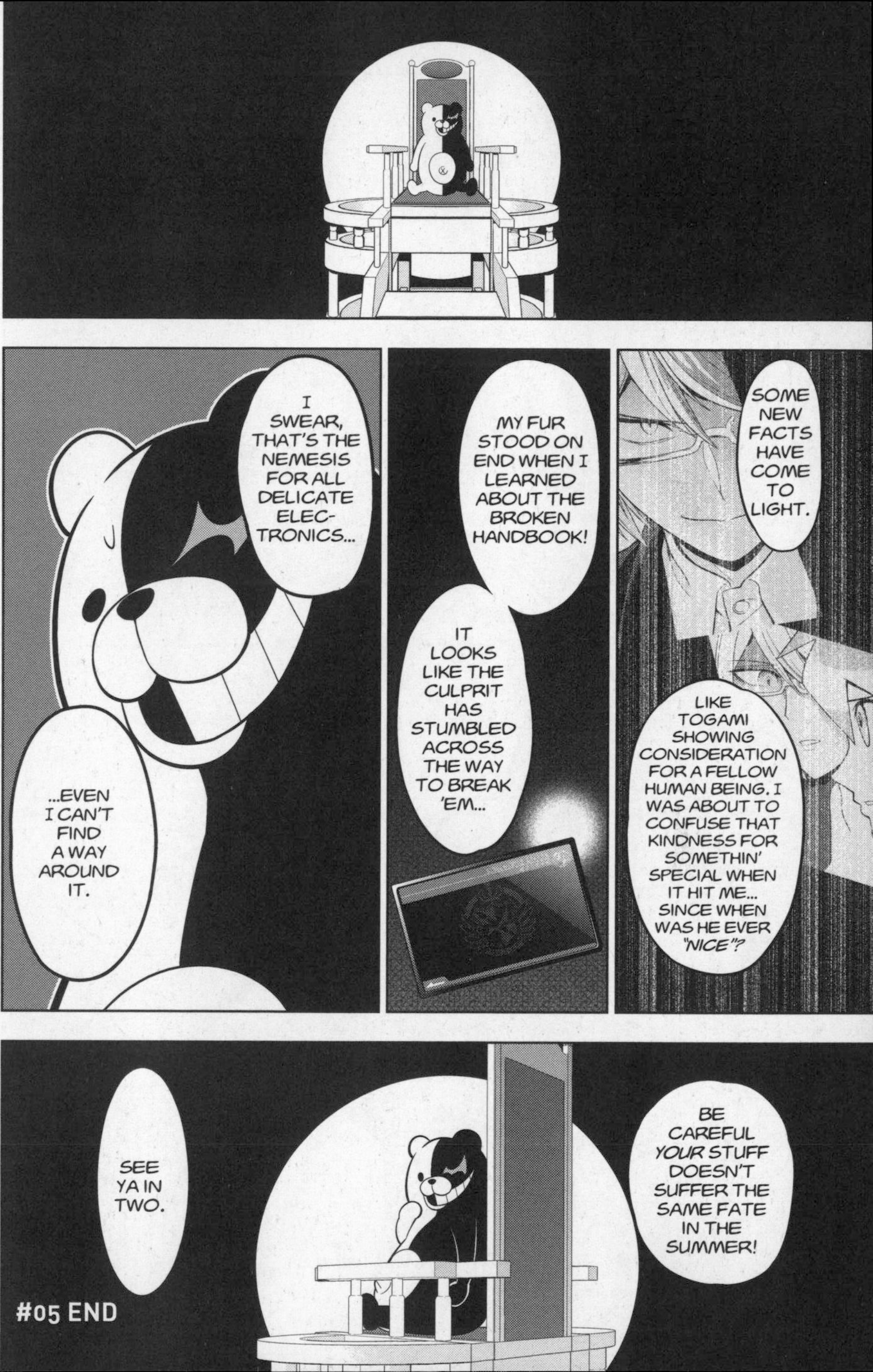
SOME NEW FACTS HAVE COME TO LIGHT.
LIKE TOGAMI SHOWING CONSIDERATION FOR A FELLOW HUMAN BEING. I WAS ABOUT TO CONFUSE THAT KINDNESS FOR SOMETHIN' SPECIAL WHEN IT HIT ME... SINCE WHEN WAS HE EVER *"NICE"*?
MY FUR STOOD ON END WHEN I LEARNED ABOUT THE BROKEN HANDBOOK!
IT LOOKS LIKE THE CULPRIT HAS STUMBLED ACROSS THE WAY TO BREAK 'EM...
I SWEAR, THAT'S THE NEMESIS FOR ALL DELICATE ELEC-TRONICS...
...EVEN I CAN'T FIND A WAY AROUND IT.
BE CAREFUL *YOUR* STUFF DOESN'T SUFFER THE SAME FATE IN THE SUMMER!
SEE YA IN TWO.
#05 END

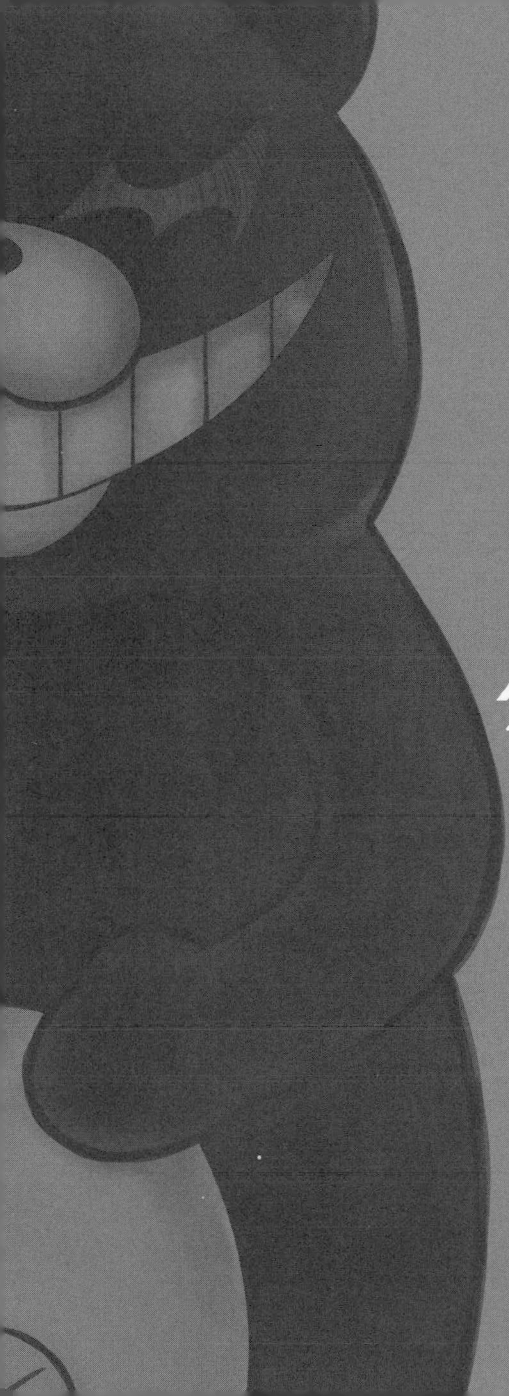

ダンガンロンパ

DANGANRONPA

希望の学園と絶望の高校生

THE ANIMATION

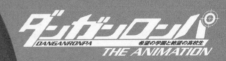

DANGANRONPA

A SCHOOL OF HOPE . . . WITH STUDENTS OF DESPAIR!

THE ANIMATION

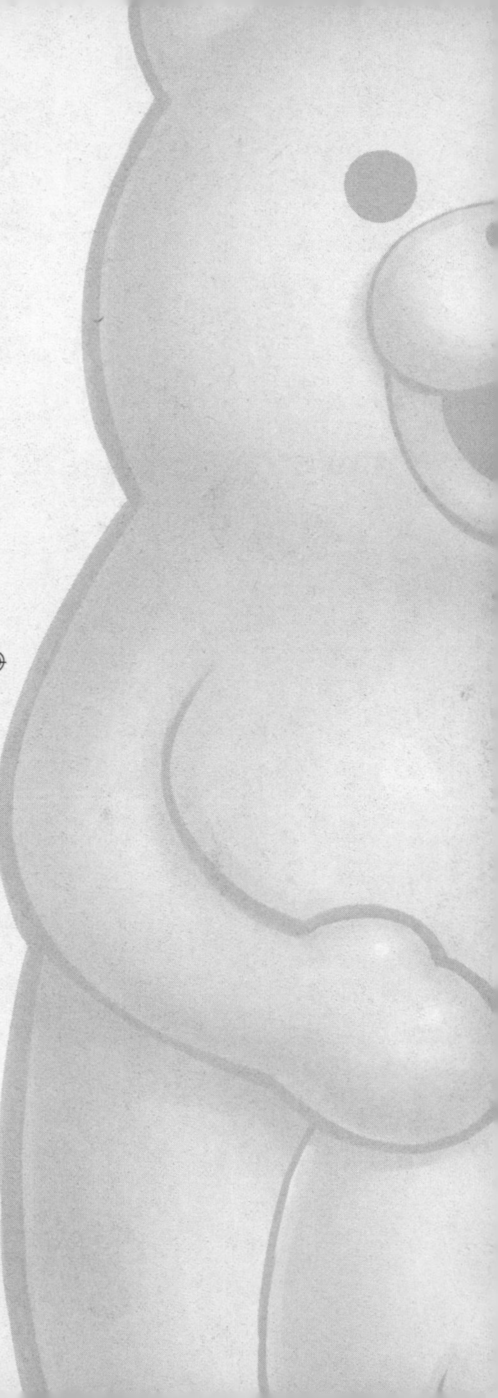

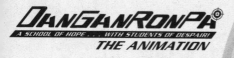

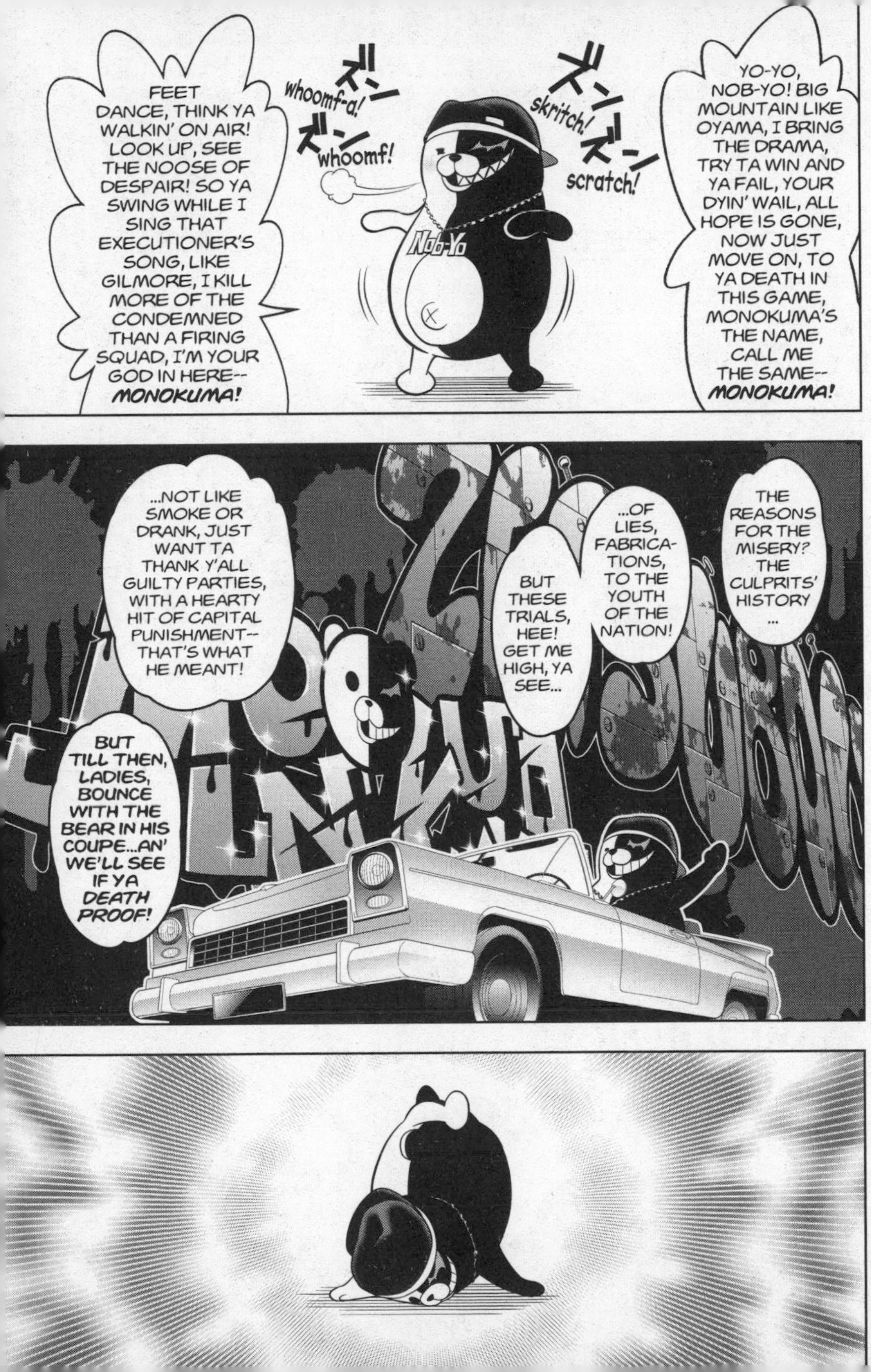
YO-YO, NOB-YO! BIG MOUNTAIN LIKE OYAMA, I BRING THE DRAMA, TRY TA WIN AND YA FAIL, YOUR DYIN' WAIL, ALL HOPE IS GONE, NOW JUST MOVE ON, TO YA DEATH IN THIS GAME, MONOKUMA'S THE NAME, CALL ME THE SAME-- *MONOKUMA!*
ズーン
skritch!
ズーン
scratch!
ズーン
whoomf-a!
ズーン
whoomf!
Nob-Yo
FEET DANCE, THINK YA WALKIN' ON AIR! LOOK UP, SEE THE NOOSE OF DESPAIR! SO YA SWING WHILE I SING THAT EXECUTIONER'S SONG, LIKE GILMORE, I KILL MORE OF THE CONDEMNED THAN A FIRING SQUAD, I'M YOUR GOD IN HERE-- *MONOKUMA!*
THE REASONS FOR THE MISERY? THE CULPRITS' HISTORY ...
...OF LIES, FABRICATIONS, TO THE YOUTH OF THE NATION!
BUT THESE TRIALS, HEE! GET ME HIGH, YA SEE...
...NOT LIKE SMOKE OR DRANK, JUST WANT TA THANK Y'ALL GUILTY PARTIES, WITH A HEARTY HIT OF CAPITAL PUNISHMENT-- THAT'S WHAT HE MEANT!
BUT TILL THEN, LADIES, BOUNCE WITH THE BEAR IN HIS COUPE...AN' WE'LL SEE IF YA *DEATH PROOF!*

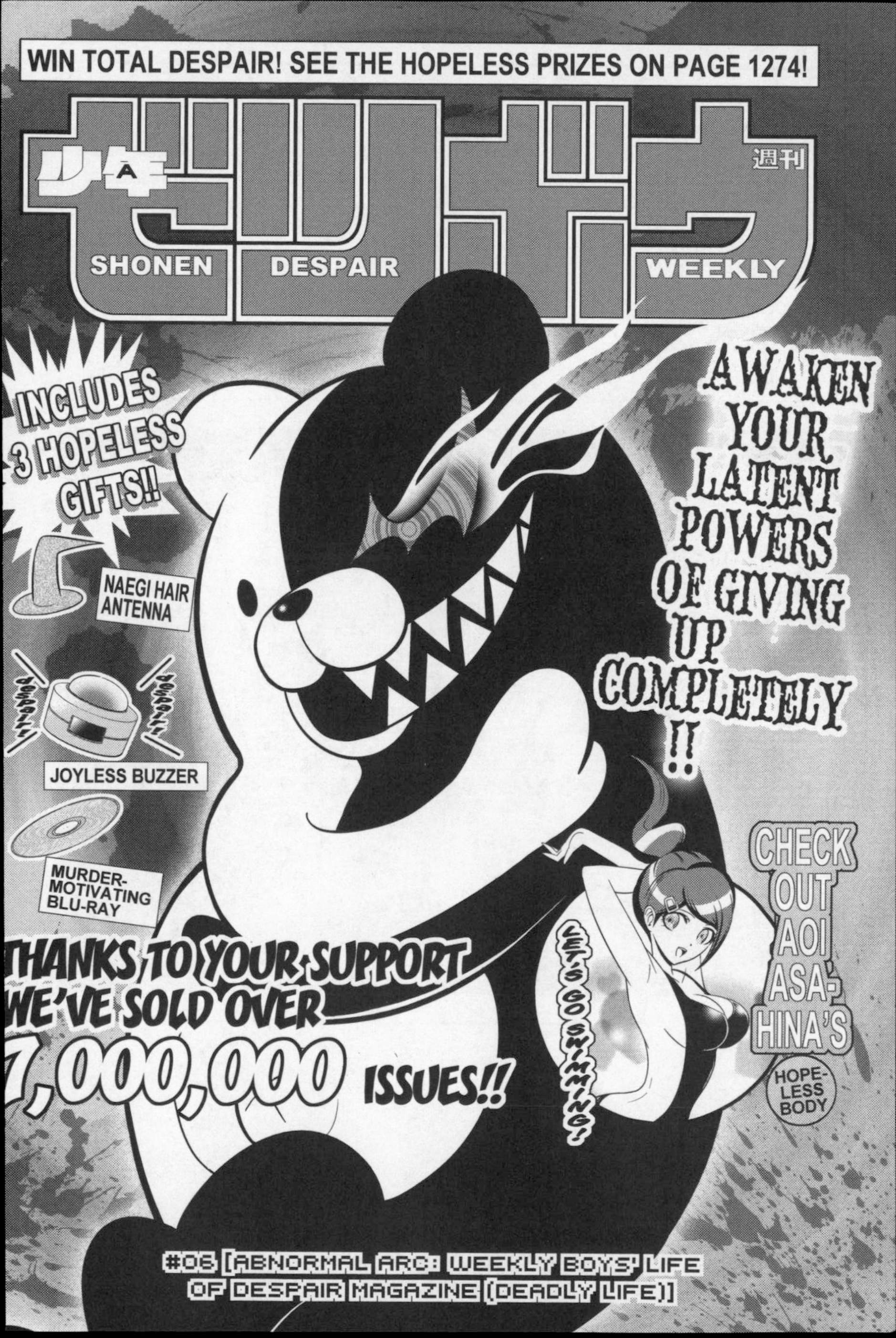
WIN TOTAL DESPAIR! SEE THE HOPELESS PRIZES ON PAGE 1274!
少年
週刊
SHONEN DESPAIR WEEKLY
INCLUDES 3 HOPELESS GIFTS!!
NAEGI HAIR ANTENNA
despair! despair!
JOYLESS BUZZER
MURDER-MOTIVATING BLU-RAY
AWAKEN YOUR LATENT POWERS OF GIVING UP COMPLETELY !!
CHECK OUT AOI ASA-HINA'S
HOPE-LESS BODY
LET'S GO SWIMMING!
THANKS TO YOUR SUPPORT WE'VE SOLD OVER 7,000,000 ISSUES!!
#06 [ABNORMAL ARC: WEEKLY BOYS' LIFE OF DESPAIR MAGAZINE [DEADLY LIFE]]

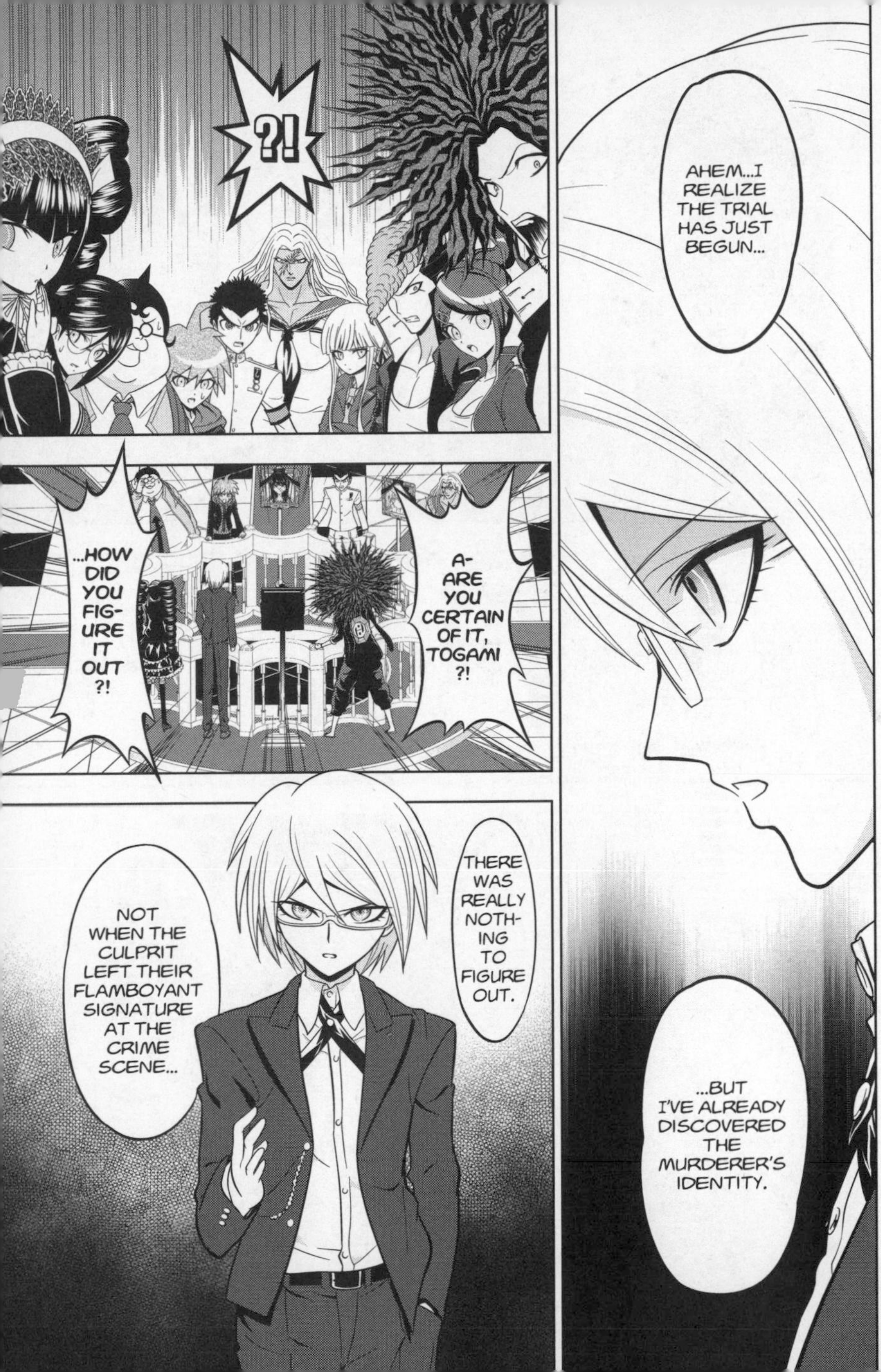
AHEM...I REALIZE THE TRIAL HAS JUST BEGUN...
...BUT I'VE ALREADY DISCOVERED THE MURDERER'S IDENTITY.
?!
A-ARE YOU CERTAIN OF IT, TOGAMI?!
...HOW DID YOU FIGURE IT OUT?!
THERE WAS REALLY NOTHING TO FIGURE OUT.
NOT WHEN THE CULPRIT LEFT THEIR FLAMBOYANT SIGNATURE AT THE CRIME SCENE...

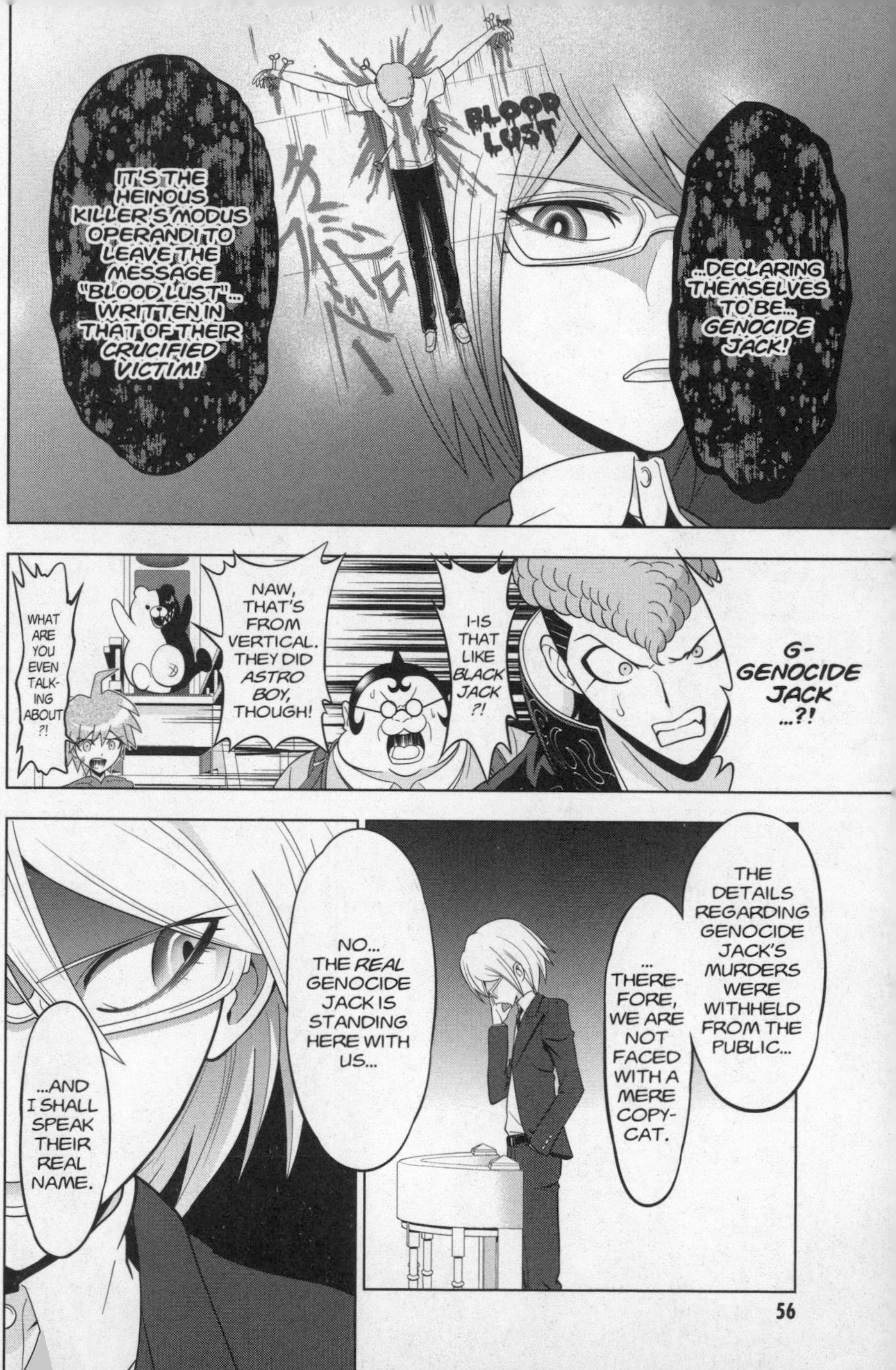
BLOOD LUST
IT'S THE HEINOUS KILLER'S MODUS OPERANDI TO LEAVE THE MESSAGE "BLOOD LUST"... WRITTEN IN THAT OF THEIR CRUCIFIED VICTIM!
...DECLARING THEMSELVES TO BE... GENOCIDE JACK!
G-GENOCIDE JACK...?!
I-IS THAT LIKE BLACK JACK?!
NAW, THAT'S FROM VERTICAL. THEY DID ASTRO BOY, THOUGH!
WHAT ARE YOU EVEN TALKING ABOUT?!
THE DETAILS REGARDING GENOCIDE JACK'S MURDERS WERE WITHHELD FROM THE PUBLIC...
...THEREFORE, WE ARE NOT FACED WITH A MERE COPYCAT.
NO... THE REAL GENOCIDE JACK IS STANDING HERE WITH US...
...AND I SHALL SPEAK THEIR REAL NAME.

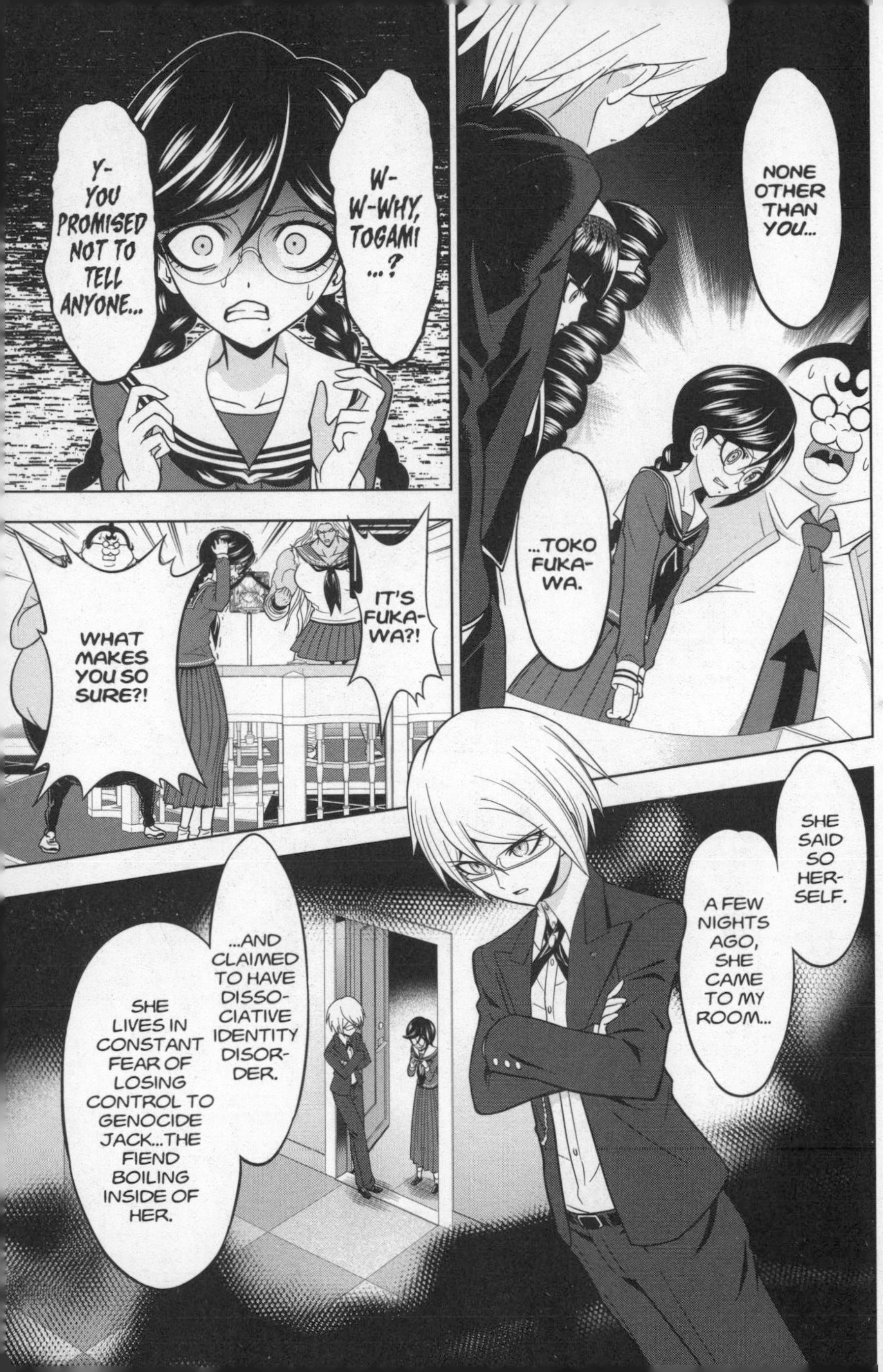
NONE OTHER THAN YOU...
...TOKO FUKAWA.
W-W-WHY, TOGAMI...?
Y-YOU PROMISED NOT TO TELL ANYONE...
IT'S FUKAWA?!
WHAT MAKES YOU SO SURE?!
SHE SAID SO HER-SELF.
A FEW NIGHTS AGO, SHE CAME TO MY ROOM...
...AND CLAIMED TO HAVE DISSO-CIATIVE IDENTITY DISOR-DER.
SHE LIVES IN CONSTANT FEAR OF LOSING CONTROL TO GENOCIDE JACK...THE FIEND BOILING INSIDE OF HER.

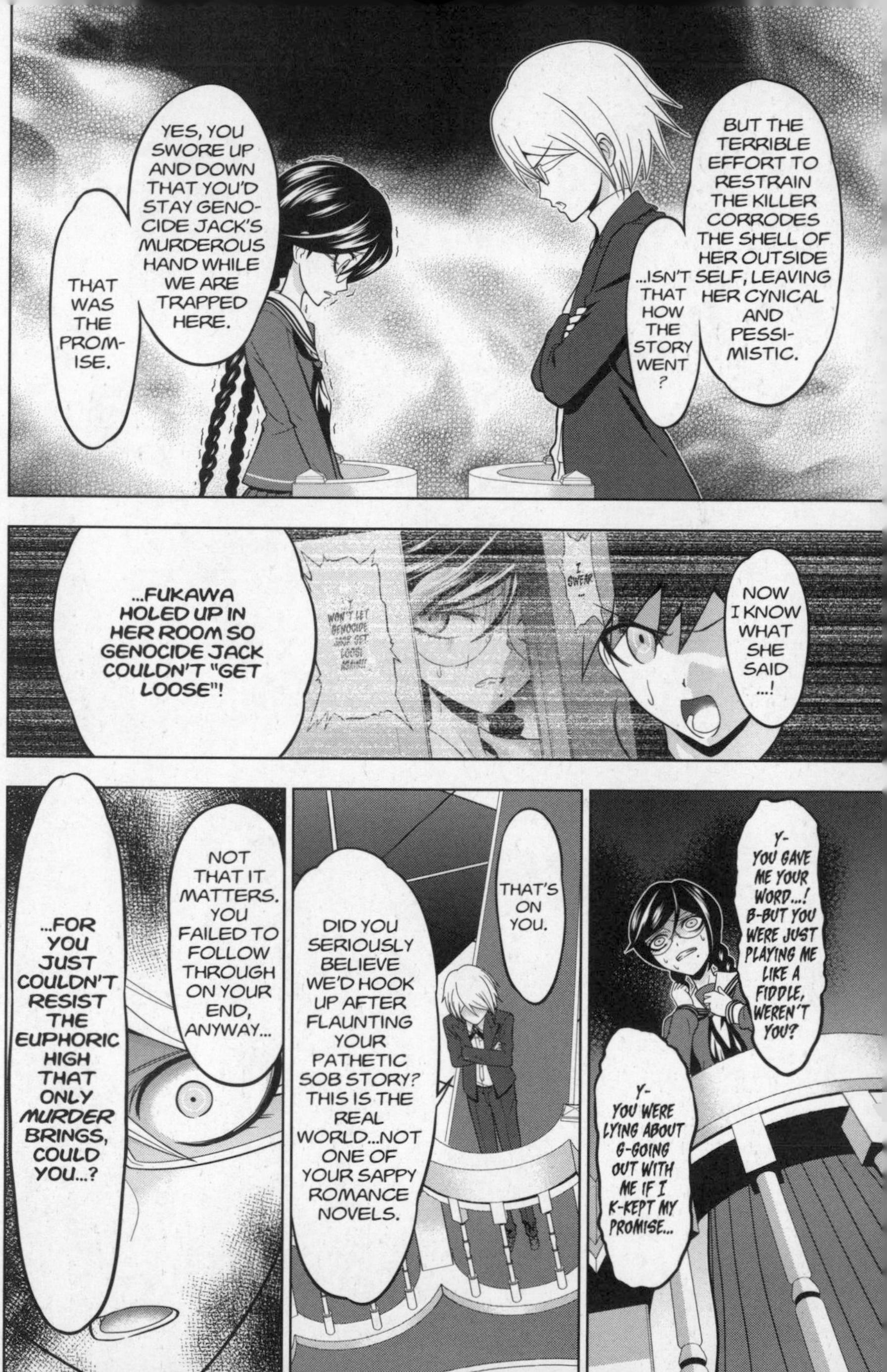
BUT THE TERRIBLE EFFORT TO RESTRAIN THE KILLER CORRODES THE SHELL OF HER OUTSIDE SELF, LEAVING HER CYNICAL AND PESSIMISTIC.
...ISN'T THAT HOW THE STORY WENT?
YES, YOU SWORE UP AND DOWN THAT YOU'D STAY GENOCIDE JACK'S MURDEROUS HAND WHILE WE ARE TRAPPED HERE.
THAT WAS THE PROMISE.
NOW I KNOW WHAT SHE SAID ...!
I SWEAR...
WON'T LET GENOCIDE JACK GET LOOSE AGAIN!!!
...FUKAWA HOLED UP IN HER ROOM SO GENOCIDE JACK COULDN'T "GET LOOSE"!
Y-YOU GAVE ME YOUR WORD...! B-BUT YOU WERE JUST PLAYING ME LIKE A FIDDLE, WEREN'T YOU?
Y-YOU WERE LYING ABOUT G-GOING OUT WITH ME IF I K-KEPT MY PROMISE...
THAT'S ON YOU.
DID YOU SERIOUSLY BELIEVE WE'D HOOK UP AFTER FLAUNTING YOUR PATHETIC SOB STORY? THIS IS THE REAL WORLD...NOT ONE OF YOUR SAPPY ROMANCE NOVELS.
NOT THAT IT MATTERS. YOU FAILED TO FOLLOW THROUGH ON YOUR END, ANYWAY...
...FOR YOU JUST COULDN'T RESIST THE EUPHORIC HIGH THAT ONLY MURDER BRINGS, COULD YOU...?

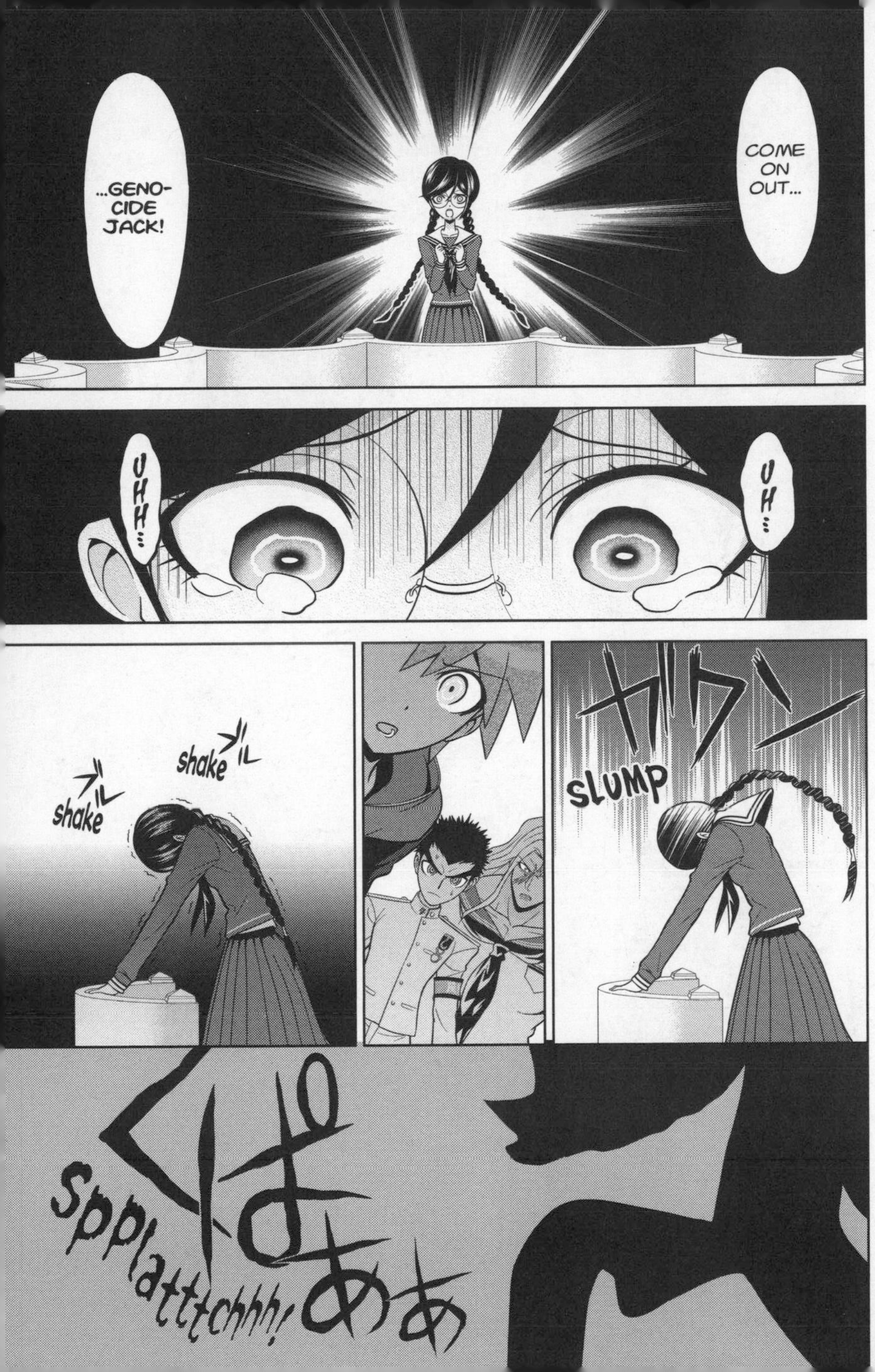
COME ON OUT...
...GENO-CIDE JACK!
UH...
UHH...
SLUMP
shake
shake
Spplatttchhh!

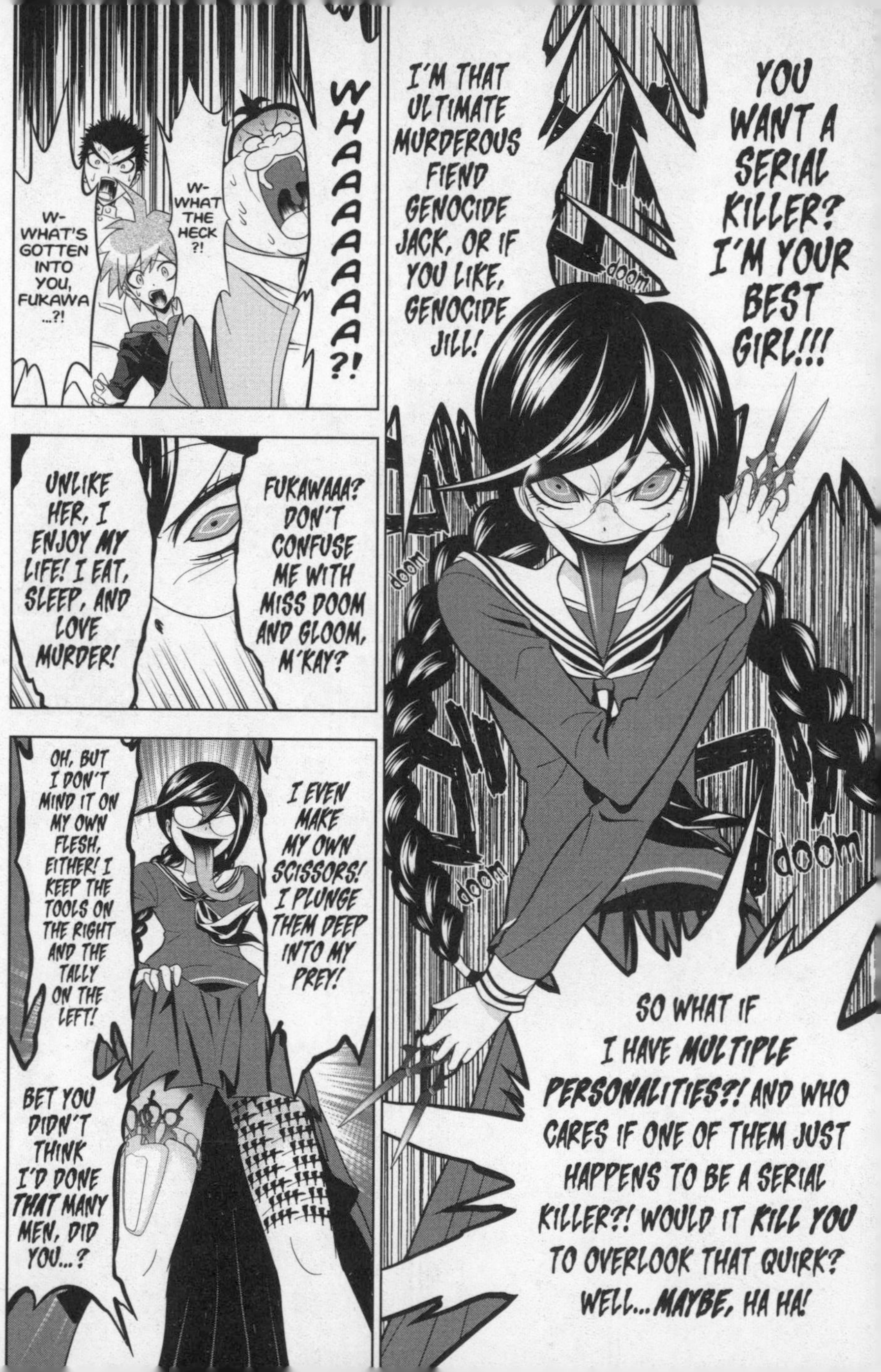

YOU WANT A SERIAL KILLER? I'M YOUR BEST GIRL!!!
I'M THAT ULTIMATE MURDEROUS FIEND GENOCIDE JACK, OR IF YOU LIKE, GENOCIDE JILL!
doom
doom
doom
doom
SO WHAT IF I HAVE MULTIPLE PERSONALITIES?! AND WHO CARES IF ONE OF THEM JUST HAPPENS TO BE A SERIAL KILLER?! WOULD IT KILL YOU TO OVERLOOK THAT QUIRK? WELL...MAYBE, HA HA!
WHAAAAAAAAA?!
W-WHAT THE HECK ?!
W-WHAT'S GOTTEN INTO YOU, FUKAWA ...?!
FUKAWAAA? DON'T CONFUSE ME WITH MISS DOOM AND GLOOM, M'KAY?
UNLIKE HER, I ENJOY MY LIFE! I EAT, SLEEP, AND LOVE MURDER!
I EVEN MAKE MY OWN SCISSORS! I PLUNGE THEM DEEP INTO MY PREY!
OH, BUT I DON'T MIND IT ON MY OWN FLESH, EITHER! I KEEP THE TOOLS ON THE RIGHT AND THE TALLY ON THE LEFT!
BET YOU DIDN'T THINK I'D DONE THAT MANY MEN, DID YOU...?

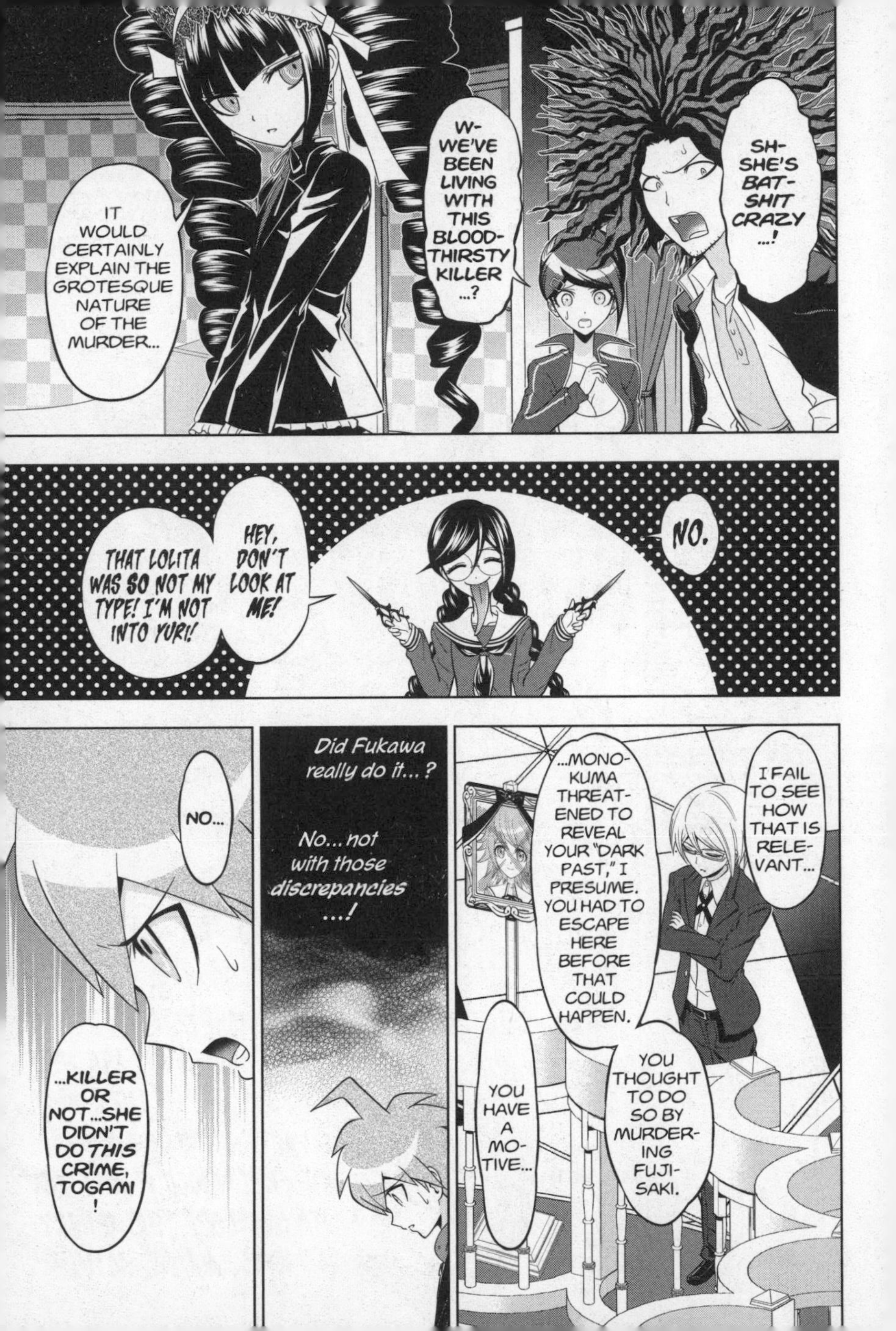
SH-SHE'S BAT-SHIT CRAZY ...!
W-WE'VE BEEN LIVING WITH THIS BLOOD-THIRSTY KILLER ...?
IT WOULD CERTAINLY EXPLAIN THE GROTESQUE NATURE OF THE MURDER...
NO.
HEY, DON'T LOOK AT ME!
THAT LOLITA WAS SO NOT MY TYPE! I'M NOT INTO YURI!
I FAIL TO SEE HOW THAT IS RELE-VANT...
...MONO-KUMA THREAT-ENED TO REVEAL YOUR "DARK PAST," I PRESUME. YOU HAD TO ESCAPE HERE BEFORE THAT COULD HAPPEN.
YOU THOUGHT TO DO SO BY MURDER-ING FUJI-SAKI.
YOU HAVE A MO-TIVE...
Did Fukawa really do it...?
No...not with those discrepancies ...!
NO...
...KILLER OR NOT...SHE DIDN'T DO *THIS* CRIME, TOGAMI !

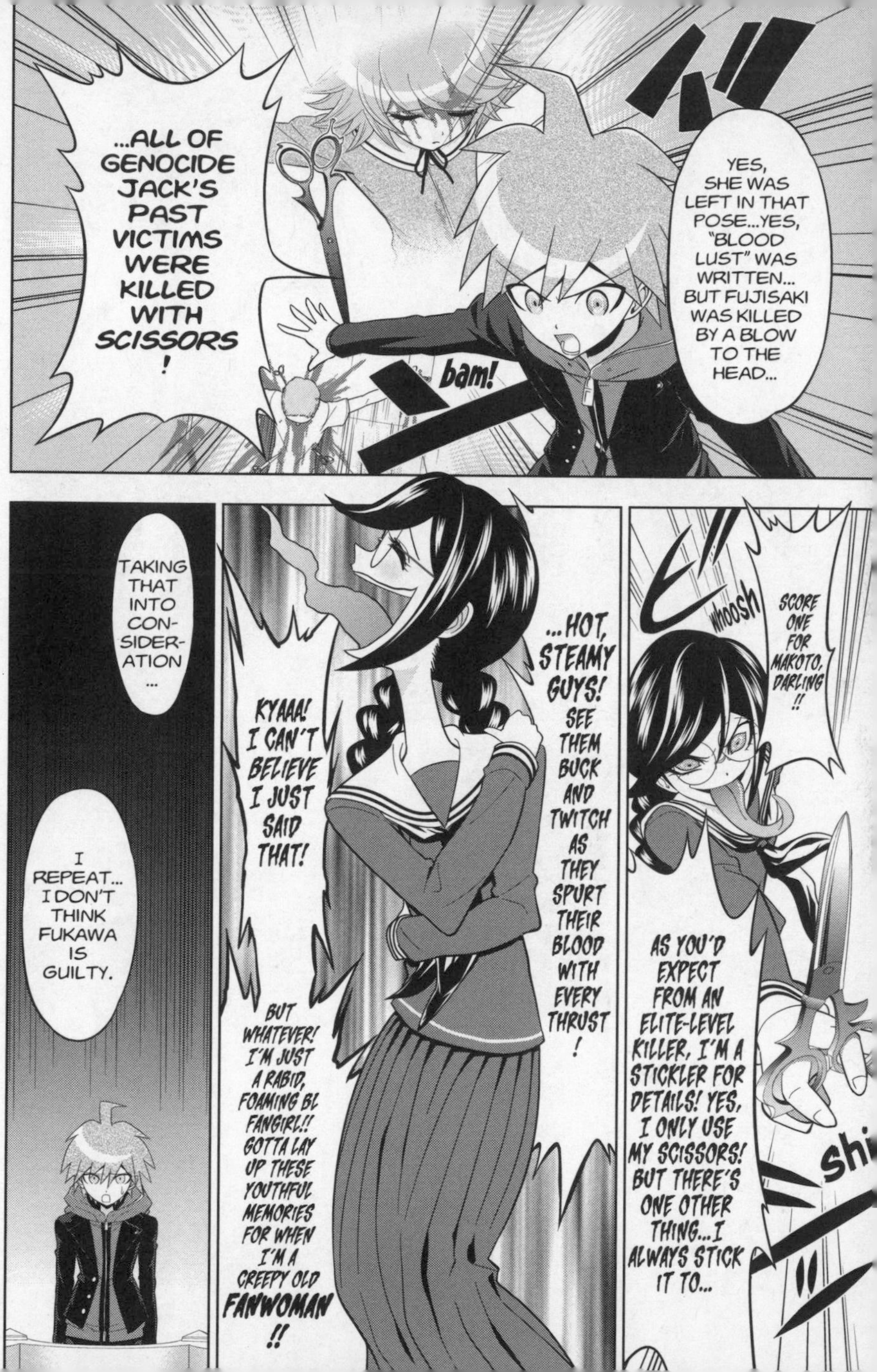
YES, SHE WAS LEFT IN THAT POSE...YES, "BLOOD LUST" WAS WRITTEN... BUT FUJISAKI WAS KILLED BY A BLOW TO THE HEAD...
bam!
...ALL OF GENOCIDE JACK'S PAST VICTIMS WERE KILLED WITH SCISSORS!
whoosh
SCORE ONE FOR MAKOTO, DARLING!!
AS YOU'D EXPECT FROM AN ELITE-LEVEL KILLER, I'M A STICKLER FOR DETAILS! YES, I ONLY USE MY SCISSORS! BUT THERE'S ONE OTHER THING...I ALWAYS STICK IT TO...
Shi
...HOT, STEAMY GUYS! SEE THEM BUCK AND TWITCH AS THEY SPURT THEIR BLOOD WITH EVERY THRUST!
KYAAA! I CAN'T BELIEVE I JUST SAID THAT!
BUT WHATEVER! I'M JUST A RABID, FOAMING BL FANGIRL!! GOTTA LAY UP THESE YOUTHFUL MEMORIES FOR WHEN I'M A CREEPY OLD FANWOMAN!!
TAKING THAT INTO CON-SIDER-ATION...
I REPEAT... I DON'T THINK FUKAWA IS GUILTY.

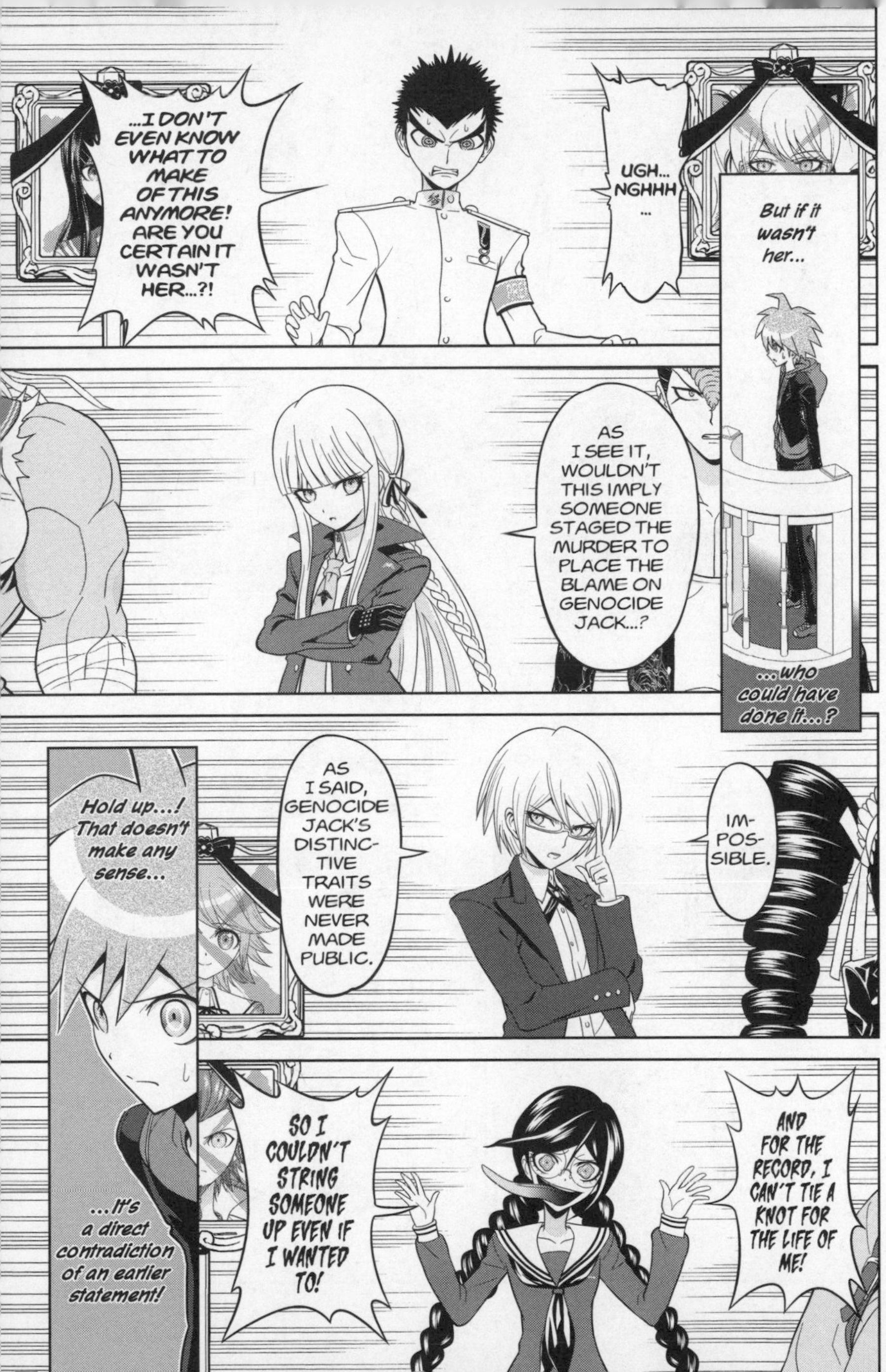
But if it wasn't her...
...who could have done it...?
UGH... NGHHH...
...I DON'T EVEN KNOW WHAT TO MAKE OF THIS ANYMORE! ARE YOU CERTAIN IT WASN'T HER...?!
AS I SEE IT, WOULDN'T THIS IMPLY SOMEONE STAGED THE MURDER TO PLACE THE BLAME ON GENOCIDE JACK...?
IM-POSSIBLE.
AS I SAID, GENOCIDE JACK'S DISTINC-TIVE TRAITS WERE NEVER MADE PUBLIC.
AND FOR THE RECORD, I CAN'T TIE A KNOT FOR THE LIFE OF ME!
SO I COULDN'T STRING SOMEONE UP EVEN IF I WANTED TO!
Hold up...! That doesn't make any sense...
...It's a direct contradiction of an earlier statement!

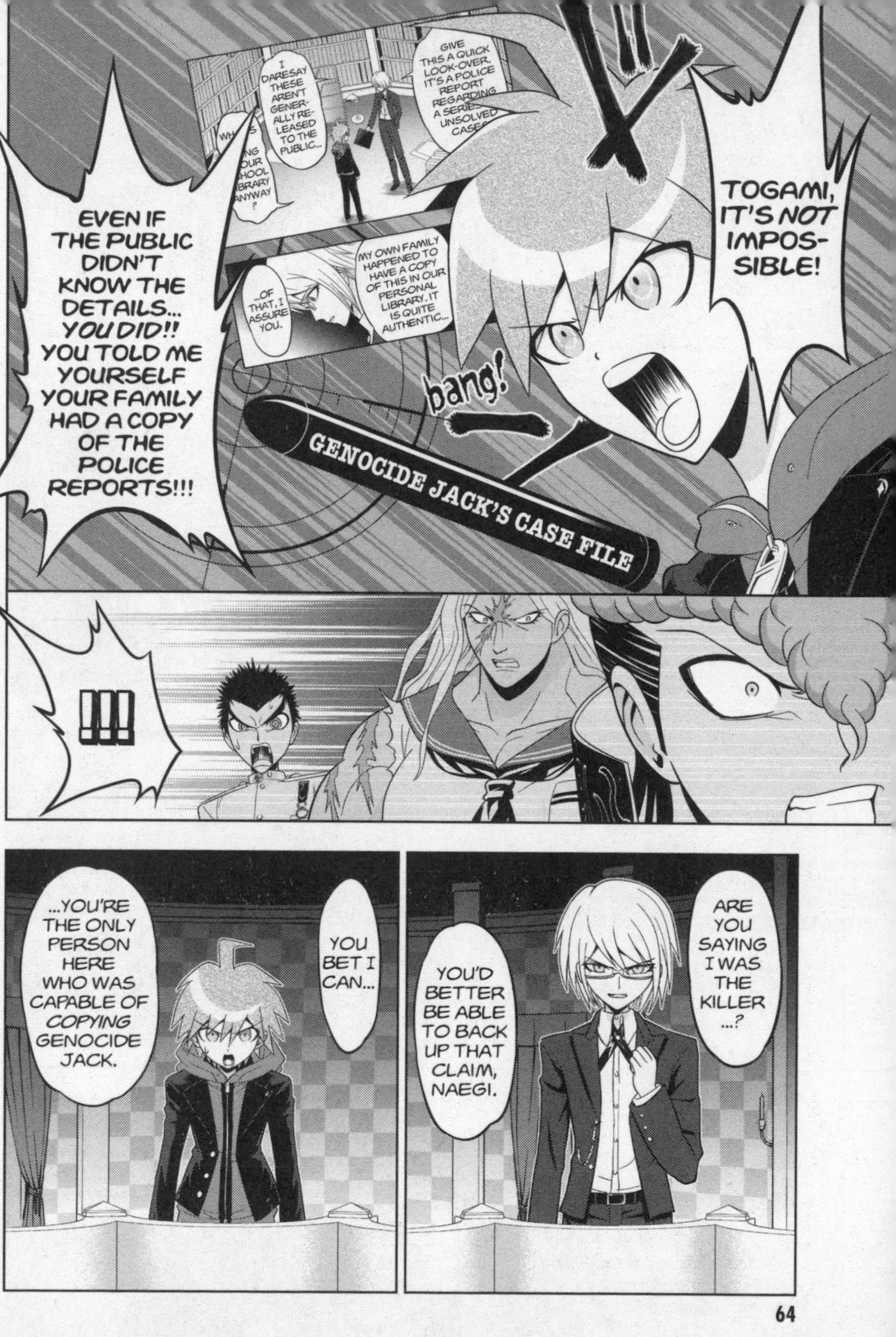

TOGAMI, IT'S NOT IMPOSSIBLE!
GIVE THIS A QUICK LOOK-OVER. IT'S A POLICE REPORT REGARDING A SERIE UNSOLVED CASE
I DARESAY THESE AREN'T GENERALLY RELEASED TO THE PUBLIC...
MY OWN FAMILY HAPPENED TO HAVE A COPY OF THIS IN OUR PERSONAL LIBRARY. IT IS QUITE AUTHENTIC...
...OF THAT, I ASSURE YOU.
bang!
GENOCIDE JACK'S CASE FILE
EVEN IF THE PUBLIC DIDN'T KNOW THE DETAILS... YOU DID!! YOU TOLD ME YOURSELF YOUR FAMILY HAD A COPY OF THE POLICE REPORTS!!!
!!!
ARE YOU SAYING I WAS THE KILLER ...?
YOU'D BETTER BE ABLE TO BACK UP THAT CLAIM, NAEGI.
YOU BET I CAN...
...YOU'RE THE ONLY PERSON HERE WHO WAS CAPABLE OF COPYING GENOCIDE JACK.

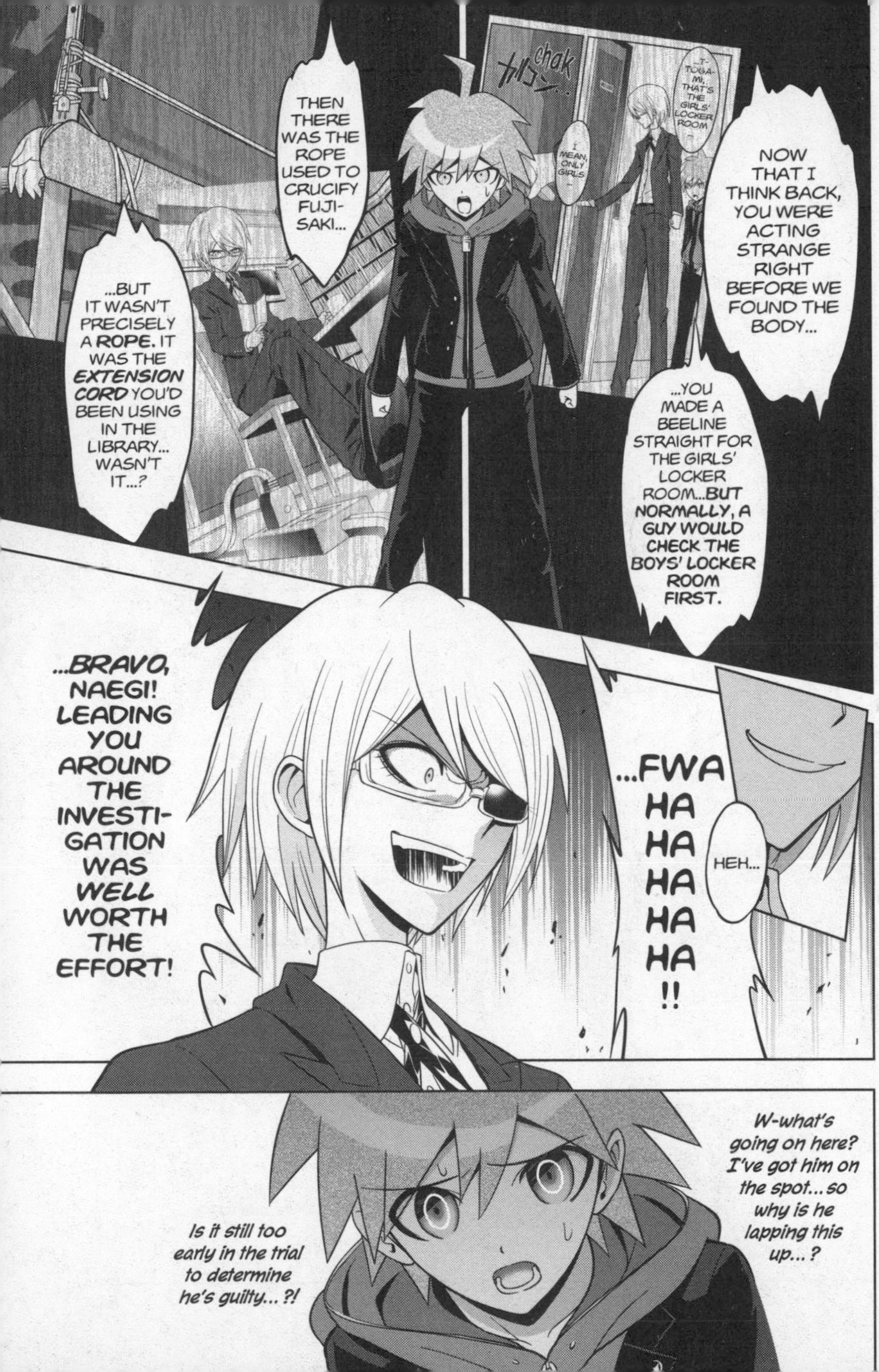
NOW THAT I THINK BACK, YOU WERE ACTING STRANGE RIGHT BEFORE WE FOUND THE BODY...
...T-TOGAMI, THAT'S THE GIRLS' LOCKER ROOM...
I MEAN, ONLY GIRLS.
chak
...YOU MADE A BEELINE STRAIGHT FOR THE GIRLS' LOCKER ROOM...BUT NORMALLY, A GUY WOULD CHECK THE BOYS' LOCKER ROOM FIRST.
THEN THERE WAS THE ROPE USED TO CRUCIFY FUJISAKI...
...BUT IT WASN'T PRECISELY A ROPE. IT WAS THE EXTENSION CORD YOU'D BEEN USING IN THE LIBRARY... WASN'T IT...?
HEH...
...FWA HA HA HA HA HA!!
...BRAVO, NAEGI! LEADING YOU AROUND THE INVESTIGATION WAS WELL WORTH THE EFFORT!
W-what's going on here? I've got him on the spot... so why is he lapping this up...?
Is it still too early in the trial to determine he's guilty...?!

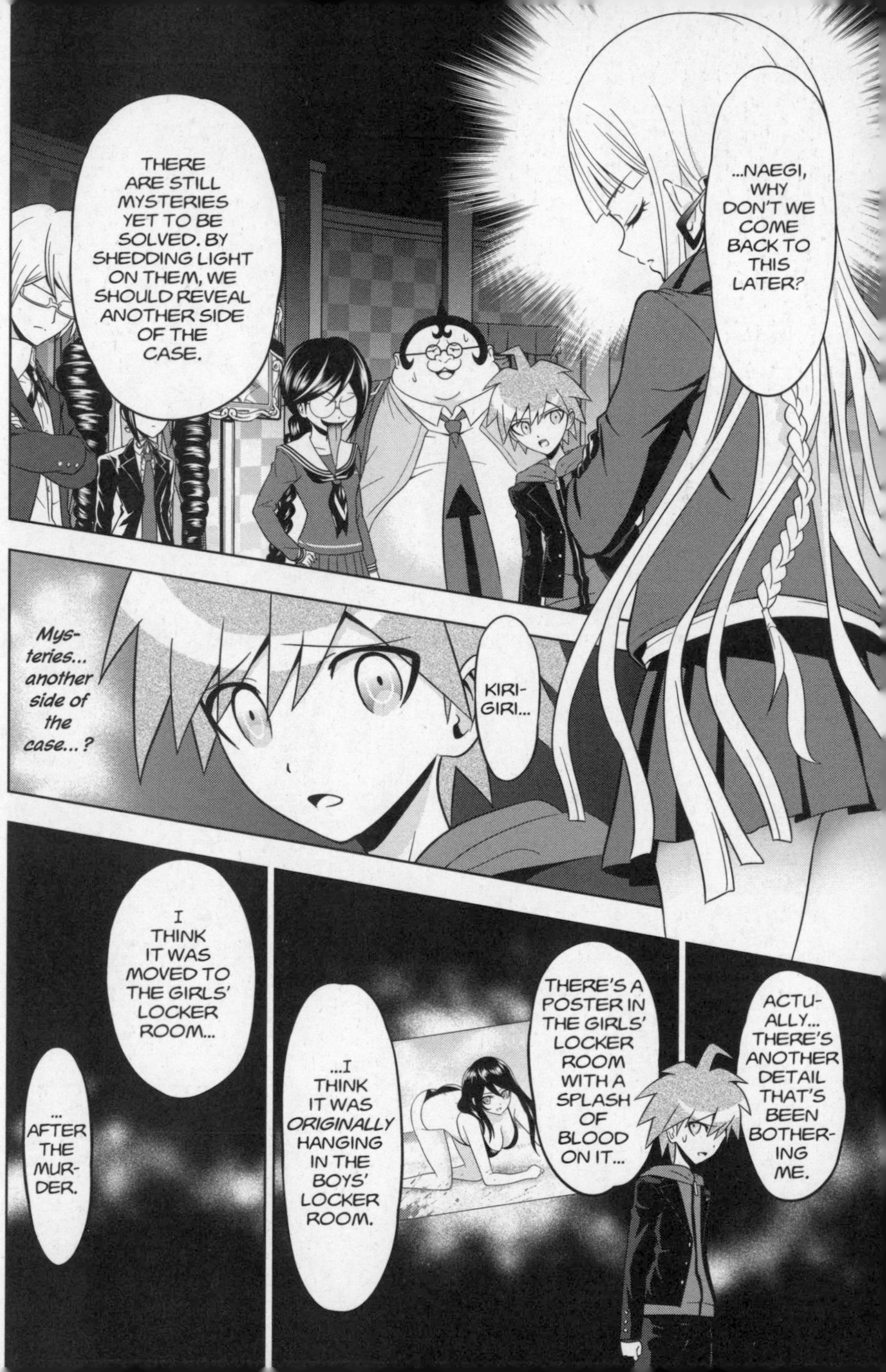
...NAEGI, WHY DON'T WE COME BACK TO THIS LATER?
THERE ARE STILL MYSTERIES YET TO BE SOLVED. BY SHEDDING LIGHT ON THEM, WE SHOULD REVEAL ANOTHER SIDE OF THE CASE.
KIRI-GIRI...
Mys-teries... another side of the case...?
ACTU-ALLY... THERE'S ANOTHER DETAIL THAT'S BEEN BOTHER-ING ME.
THERE'S A POSTER IN THE GIRLS' LOCKER ROOM WITH A SPLASH OF BLOOD ON IT...
...I THINK IT WAS ORIGINALLY HANGING IN THE BOYS' LOCKER ROOM.
I THINK IT WAS MOVED TO THE GIRLS' LOCKER ROOM...
... AFTER THE MUR-DER.

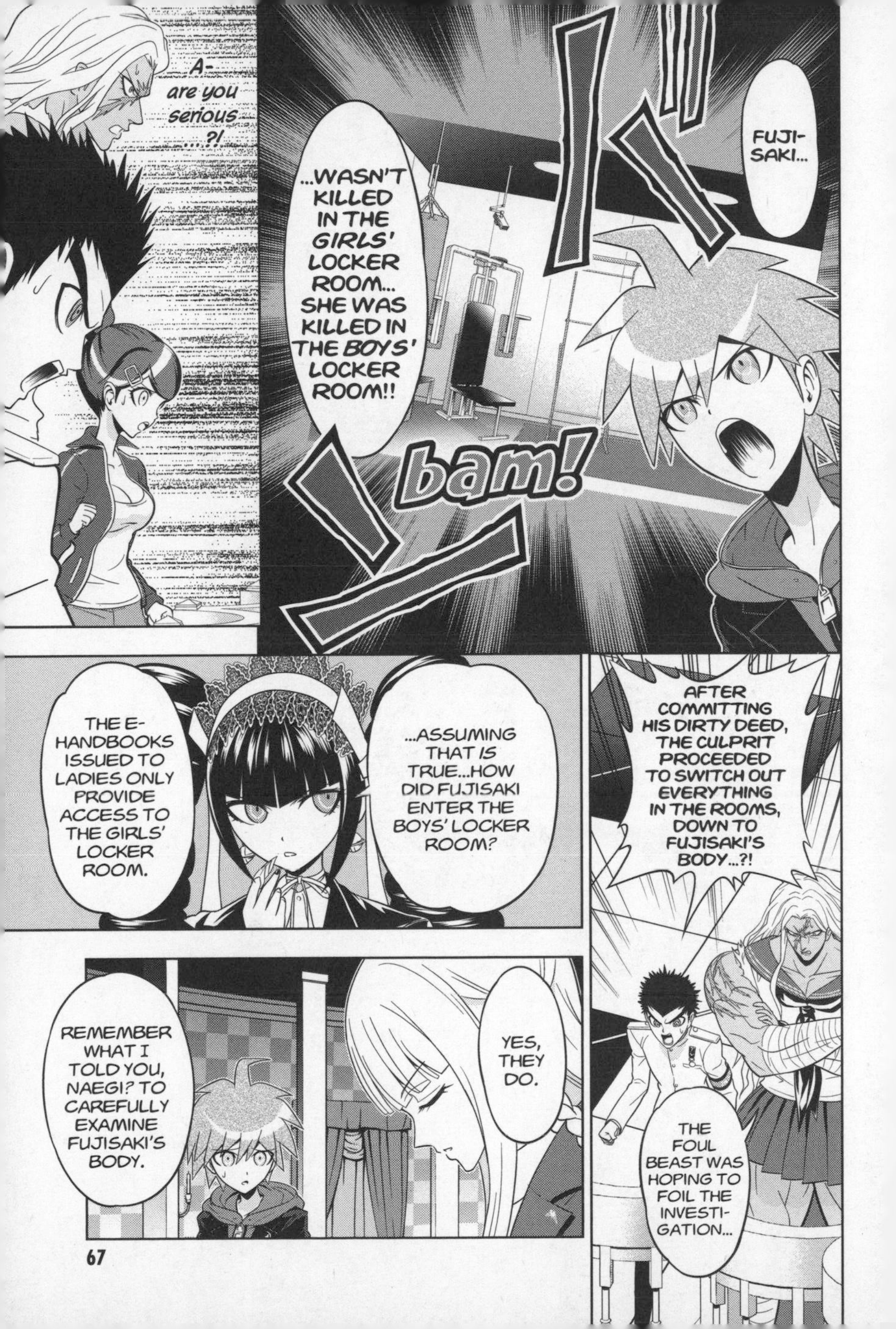
FUJI-SAKI...
...WASN'T KILLED IN THE *GIRLS'* LOCKER ROOM... SHE WAS KILLED IN THE *BOYS'* LOCKER ROOM!!
bam!
A- are you serious ...?!
AFTER COMMITTING HIS DIRTY DEED, THE CULPRIT PROCEEDED TO SWITCH OUT EVERYTHING IN THE ROOMS, DOWN TO FUJISAKI'S BODY...?!
THE FOUL BEAST WAS HOPING TO FOIL THE INVESTI-GATION...
...ASSUMING THAT *IS* TRUE...HOW DID FUJISAKI ENTER THE BOYS' LOCKER ROOM?
THE E-HANDBOOKS ISSUED TO LADIES ONLY PROVIDE ACCESS TO THE GIRLS' LOCKER ROOM.
YES, THEY DO.
REMEMBER WHAT I TOLD YOU, NAEGI? TO CAREFULLY EXAMINE FUJISAKI'S BODY.

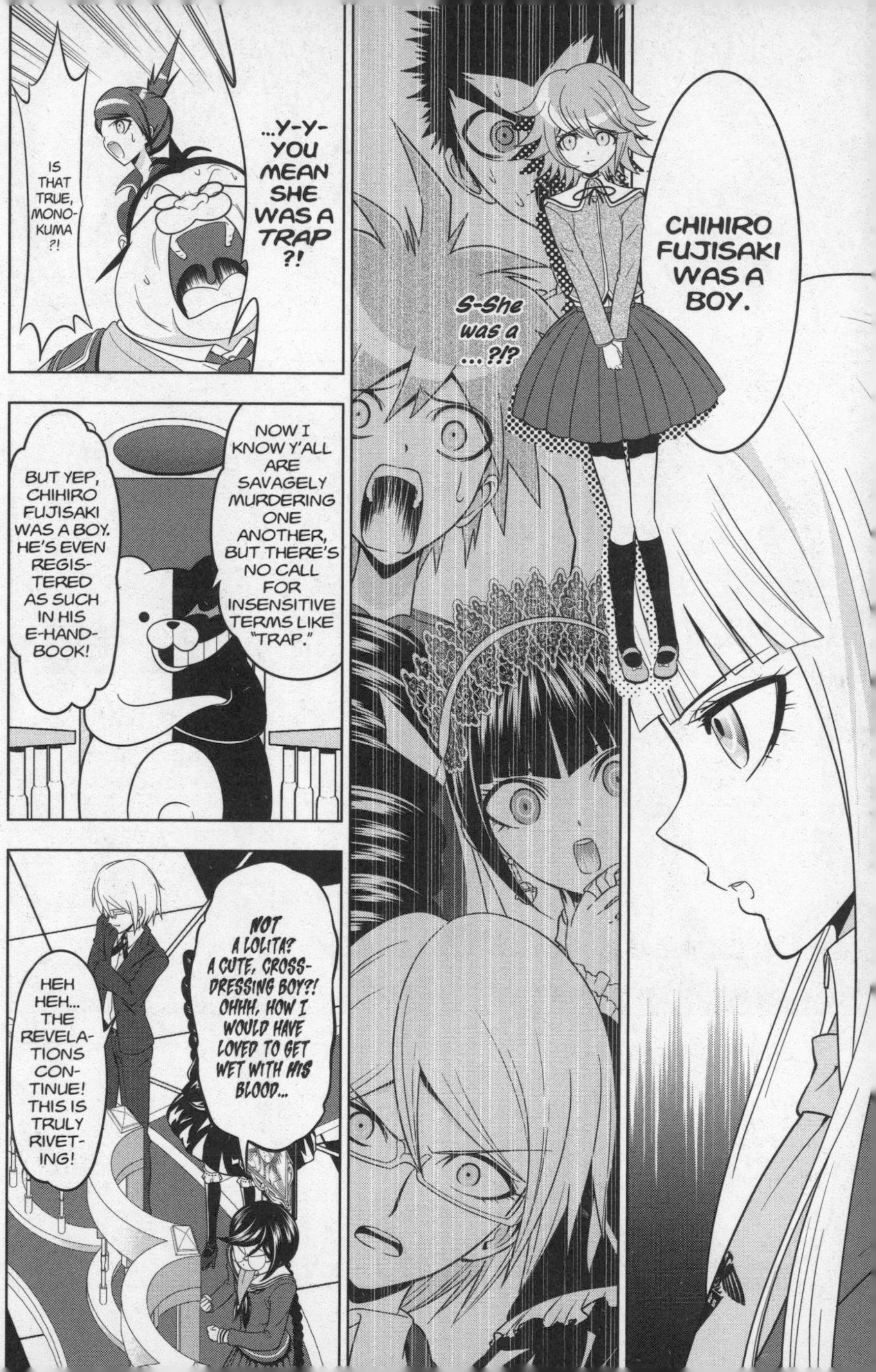
CHIHIRO FUJISAKI WAS A BOY.
S-She was a ...?!?
...Y-Y-YOU MEAN SHE WAS A TRAP?!
IS THAT TRUE, MONOKUMA?!
NOW I KNOW Y'ALL ARE SAVAGELY MURDERING ONE ANOTHER, BUT THERE'S NO CALL FOR INSENSITIVE TERMS LIKE "TRAP."
BUT YEP, CHIHIRO FUJISAKI WAS A BOY. HE'S EVEN REGISTERED AS SUCH IN HIS E-HANDBOOK!
NOT A LOLITA? A CUTE, CROSS-DRESSING BOY?! OHHH, HOW I WOULD HAVE LOVED TO GET WET WITH HIS BLOOD...
HEH HEH... THE REVELATIONS CONTINUE! THIS IS TRULY RIVETING!

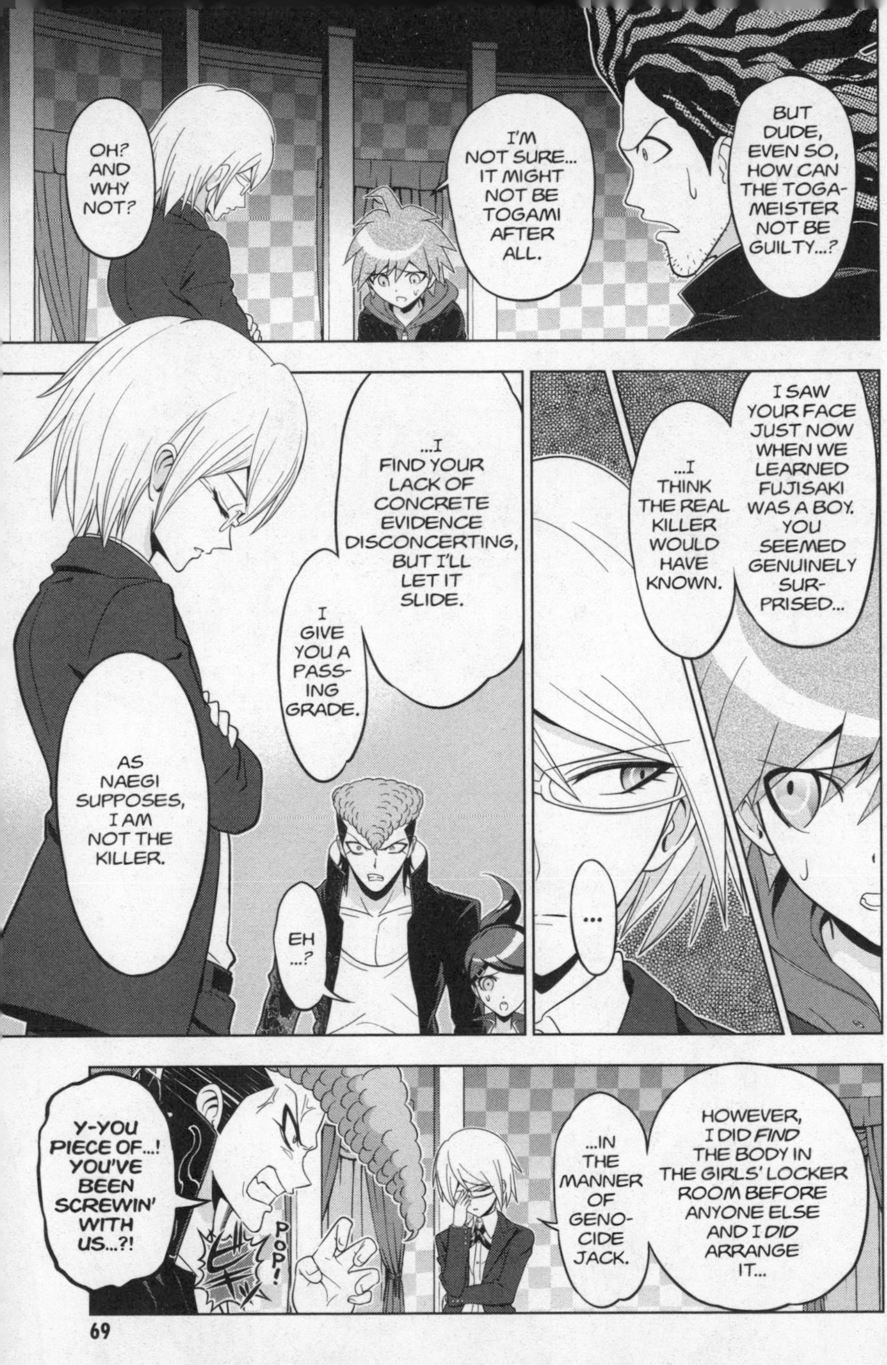
BUT DUDE, EVEN SO, HOW CAN THE TOGA-MEISTER NOT BE GUILTY...?
I'M NOT SURE... IT MIGHT NOT BE TOGAMI AFTER ALL.
OH? AND WHY NOT?
I SAW YOUR FACE JUST NOW WHEN WE LEARNED FUJISAKI WAS A BOY. YOU SEEMED GENUINELY SUR-PRISED...
...I THINK THE REAL KILLER WOULD HAVE KNOWN.
...
...I FIND YOUR LACK OF CONCRETE EVIDENCE DISCONCERTING, BUT I'LL LET IT SLIDE.
I GIVE YOU A PASS-ING GRADE.
AS NAEGI SUPPOSES, I AM NOT THE KILLER.
EH ...?
HOWEVER, I DID *FIND* THE BODY IN THE GIRLS' LOCKER ROOM BEFORE ANYONE ELSE AND I *DID* ARRANGE IT...
...IN THE MANNER OF GENO-CIDE JACK.
POP!
Y-YOU PIECE OF...! YOU'VE BEEN SCREWIN' WITH US...?!

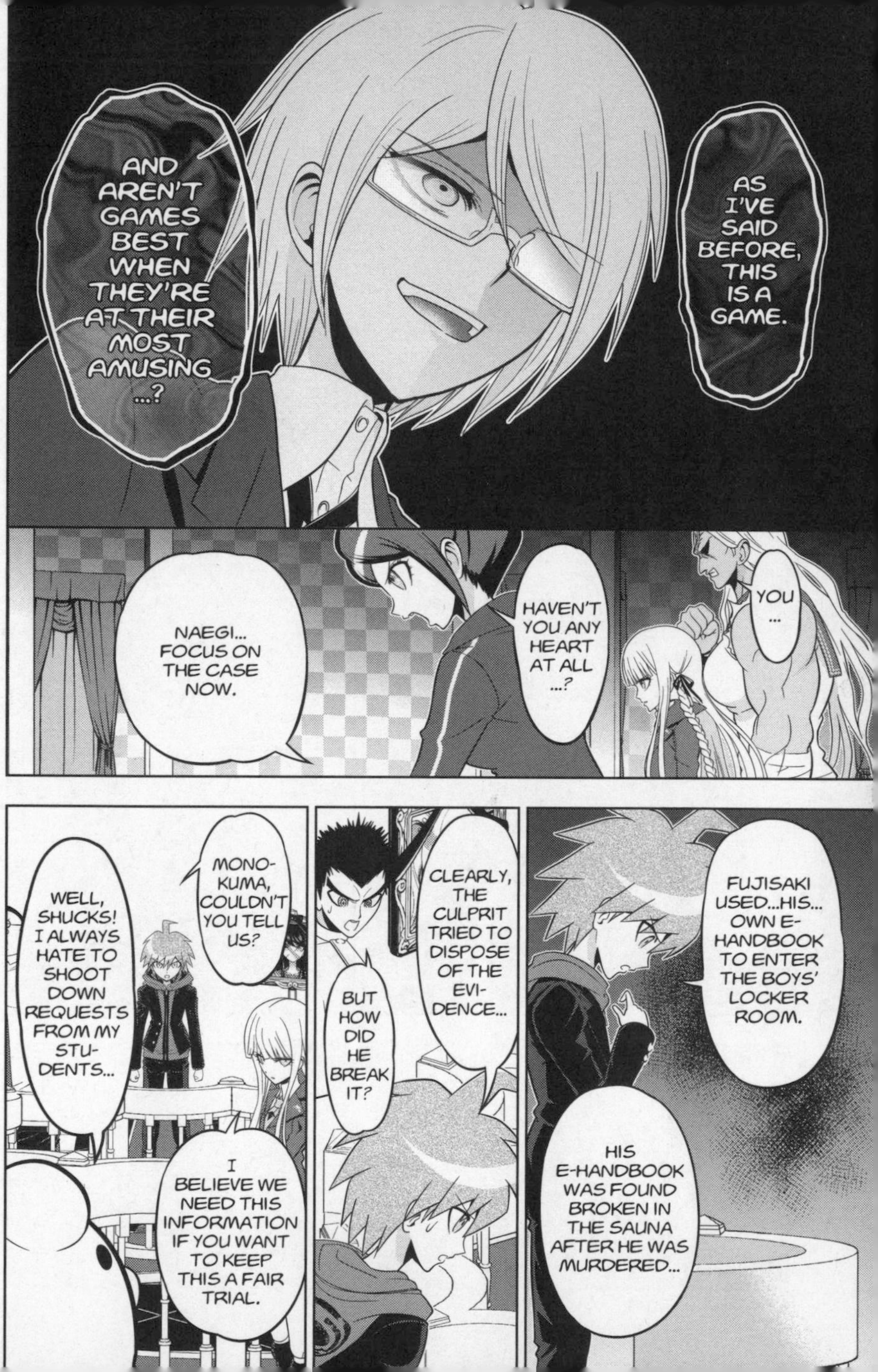
AS I'VE SAID BEFORE, THIS IS A GAME.
AND AREN'T GAMES BEST WHEN THEY'RE AT THEIR MOST AMUSING ...?
YOU ...
HAVEN'T YOU ANY HEART AT ALL ...?
NAEGI... FOCUS ON THE CASE NOW.
FUJISAKI USED...HIS... OWN E-HANDBOOK TO ENTER THE BOYS' LOCKER ROOM.
HIS E-HANDBOOK WAS FOUND BROKEN IN THE SAUNA AFTER HE WAS MURDERED...
CLEARLY, THE CULPRIT TRIED TO DISPOSE OF THE EVI-DENCE...
BUT HOW DID HE BREAK IT?
MONO-KUMA, COULDN'T YOU TELL US?
WELL, SHUCKS! I ALWAYS HATE TO SHOOT DOWN REQUESTS FROM MY STU-DENTS...
I BELIEVE WE NEED THIS INFORMATION IF YOU WANT TO KEEP THIS A FAIR TRIAL.

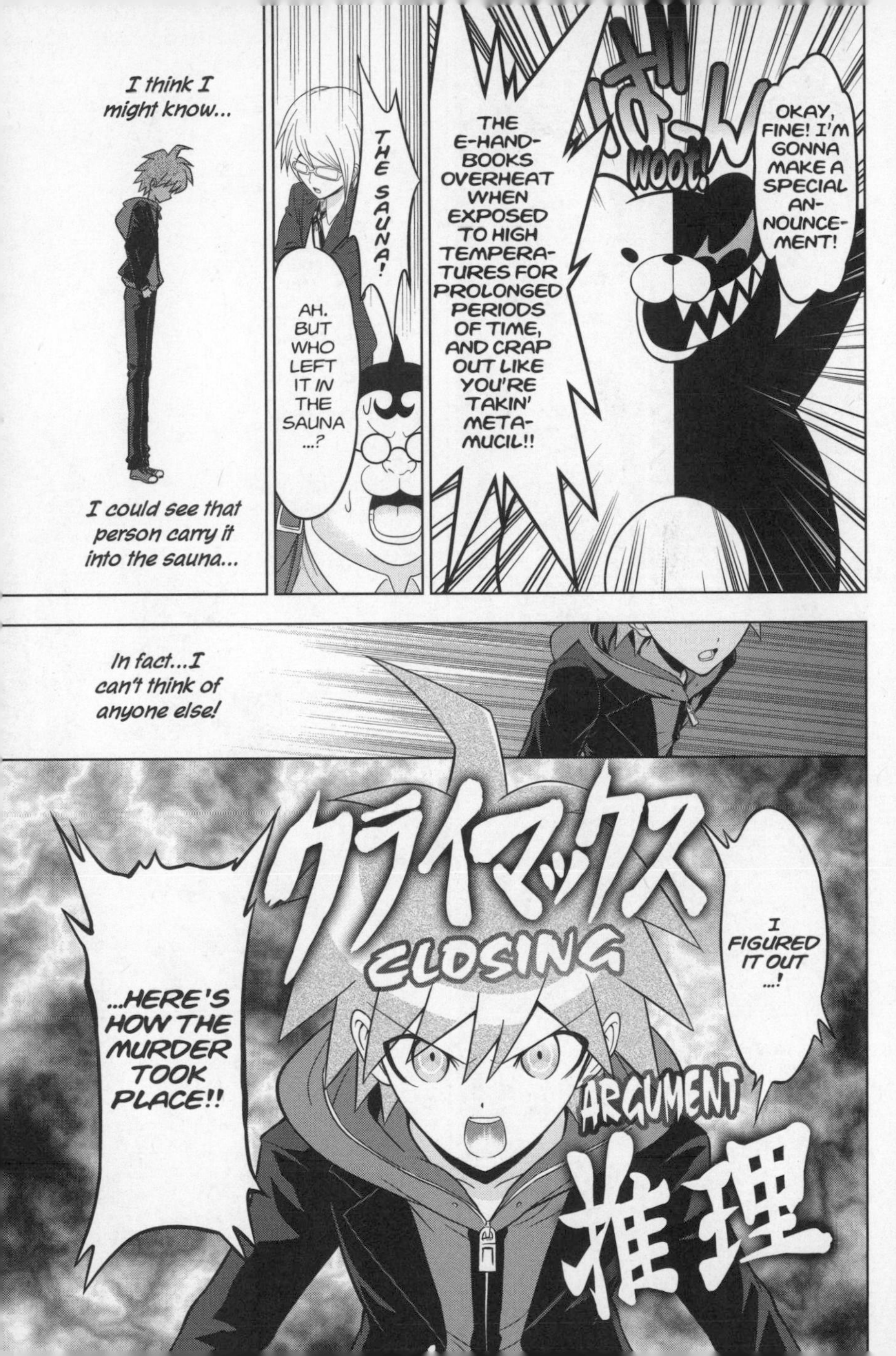
WOOT!
OKAY, FINE! I'M GONNA MAKE A SPECIAL AN-NOUNCE-MENT!
THE E-HAND-BOOKS OVERHEAT WHEN EXPOSED TO HIGH TEMPERA-TURES FOR PROLONGED PERIODS OF TIME, AND CRAP OUT LIKE YOU'RE TAKIN' META-MUCIL!!
THE SAUNA!
AH. BUT WHO LEFT IT IN THE SAUNA ...?
I think I might know...
I could see that person carry it into the sauna...
In fact...I can't think of anyone else!
I FIGURED IT OUT ...!
クライマックス
CLOSING
推理
ARGUMENT
...HERE'S HOW THE MURDER TOOK PLACE!!

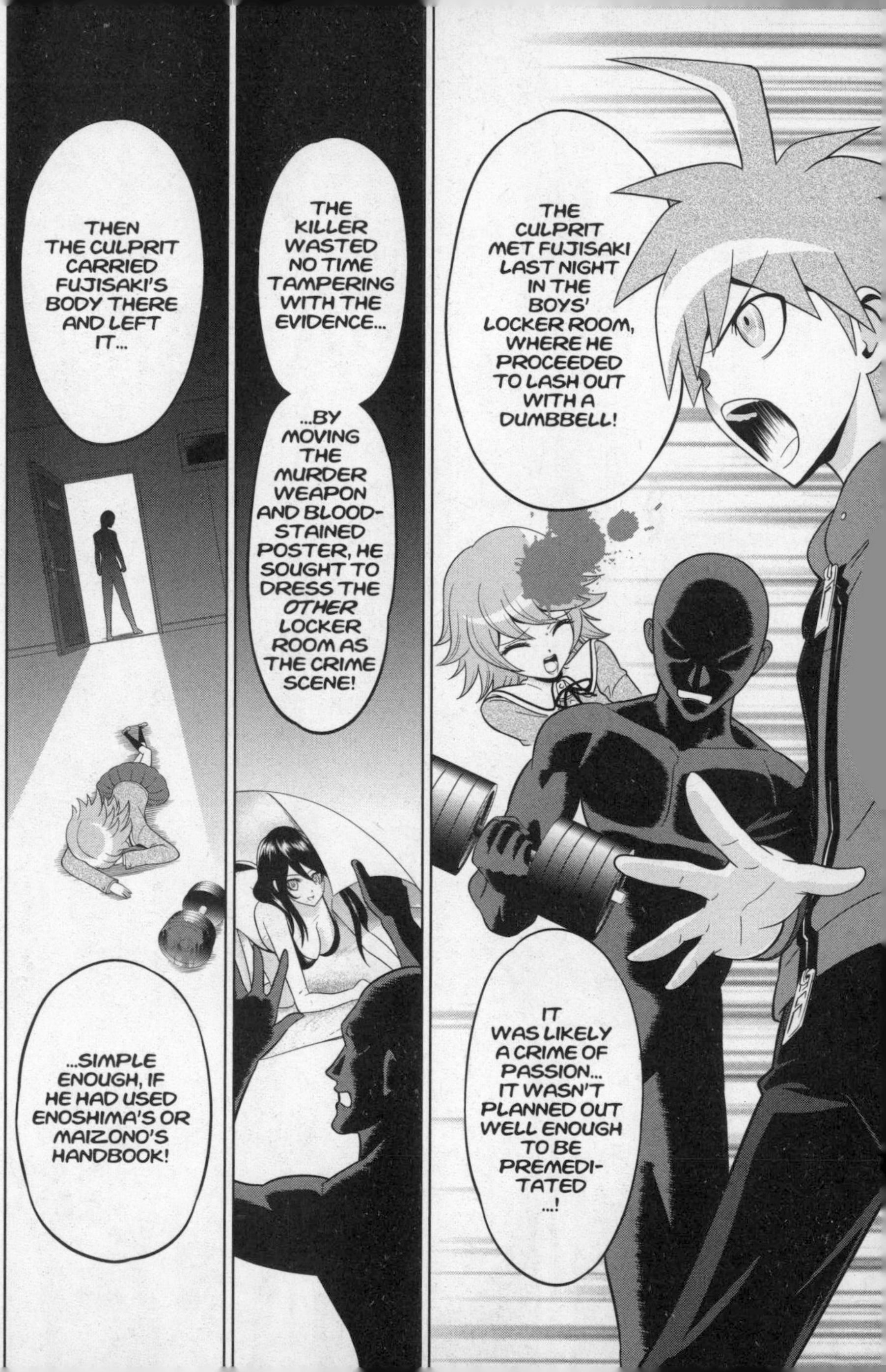
THE CULPRIT MET FUJISAKI LAST NIGHT IN THE BOYS' LOCKER ROOM, WHERE HE PROCEEDED TO LASH OUT WITH A DUMBBELL!
IT WAS LIKELY A CRIME OF PASSION... IT WASN'T PLANNED OUT WELL ENOUGH TO BE PREMEDITATED ...!
THE KILLER WASTED NO TIME TAMPERING WITH THE EVIDENCE...
...BY MOVING THE MURDER WEAPON AND BLOOD-STAINED POSTER, HE SOUGHT TO DRESS THE *OTHER* LOCKER ROOM AS THE CRIME SCENE!
THEN THE CULPRIT CARRIED FUJISAKI'S BODY THERE AND LEFT IT...
...SIMPLE ENOUGH, IF HE HAD USED ENOSHIMA'S OR MAIZONO'S HANDBOOK!

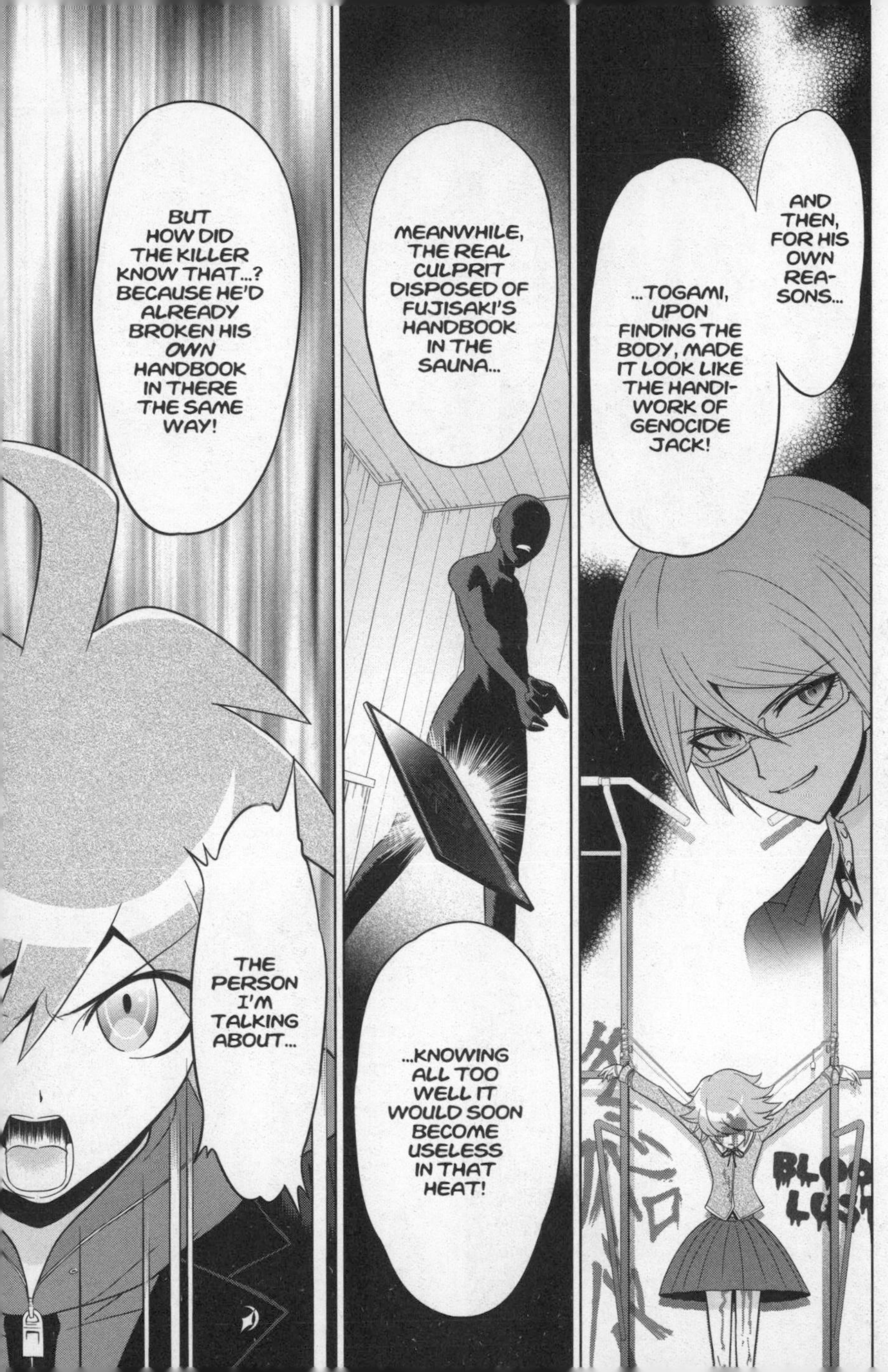
AND THEN, FOR HIS OWN REASONS...
...TOGAMI, UPON FINDING THE BODY, MADE IT LOOK LIKE THE HANDIWORK OF GENOCIDE JACK!
MEANWHILE, THE REAL CULPRIT DISPOSED OF FUJISAKI'S HANDBOOK IN THE SAUNA...
...KNOWING ALL TOO WELL IT WOULD SOON BECOME USELESS IN THAT HEAT!
BUT HOW DID THE KILLER KNOW THAT...? BECAUSE HE'D ALREADY BROKEN HIS OWN HANDBOOK IN THERE THE SAME WAY!
THE PERSON I'M TALKING ABOUT...

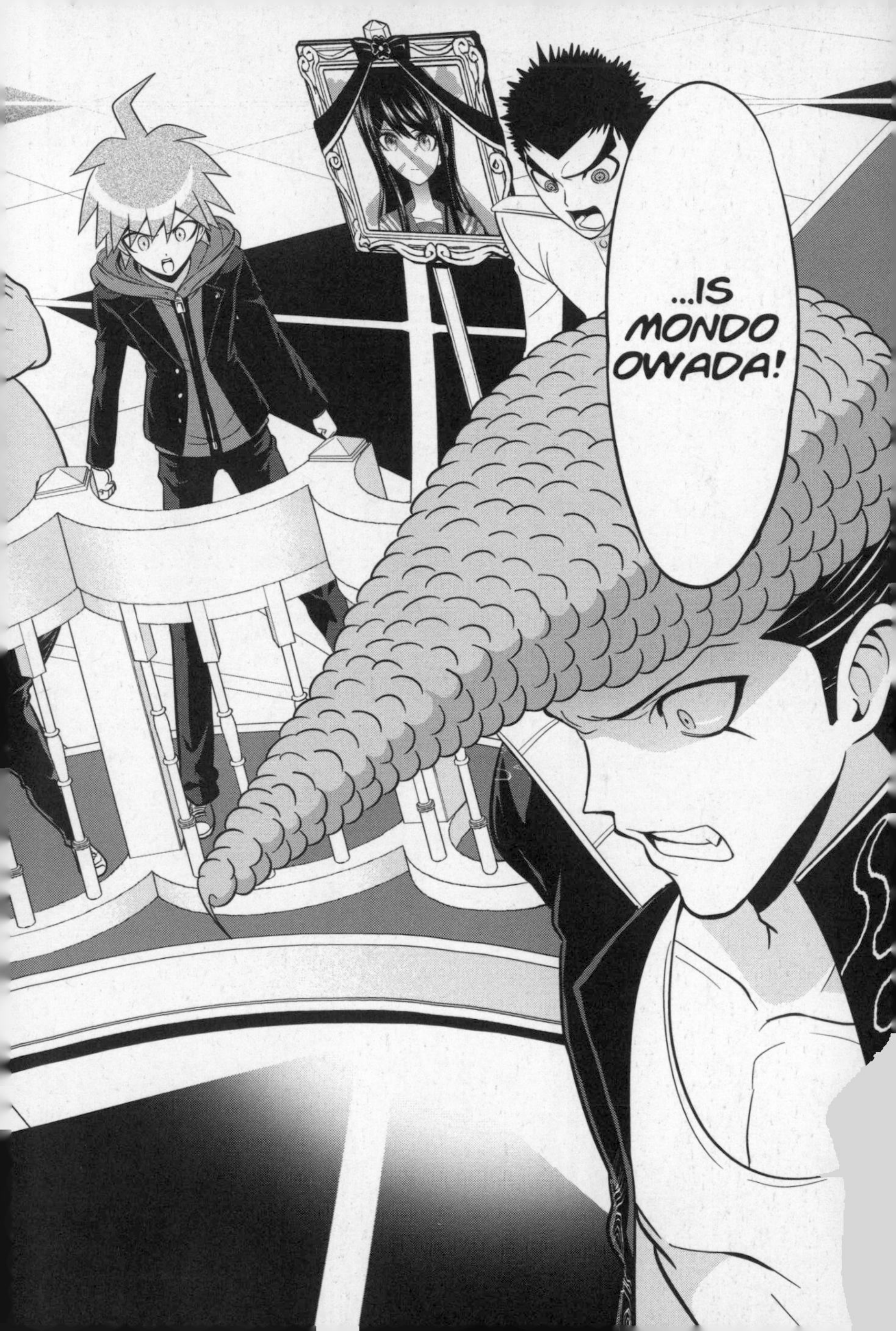
...IS MONDO OWADA!

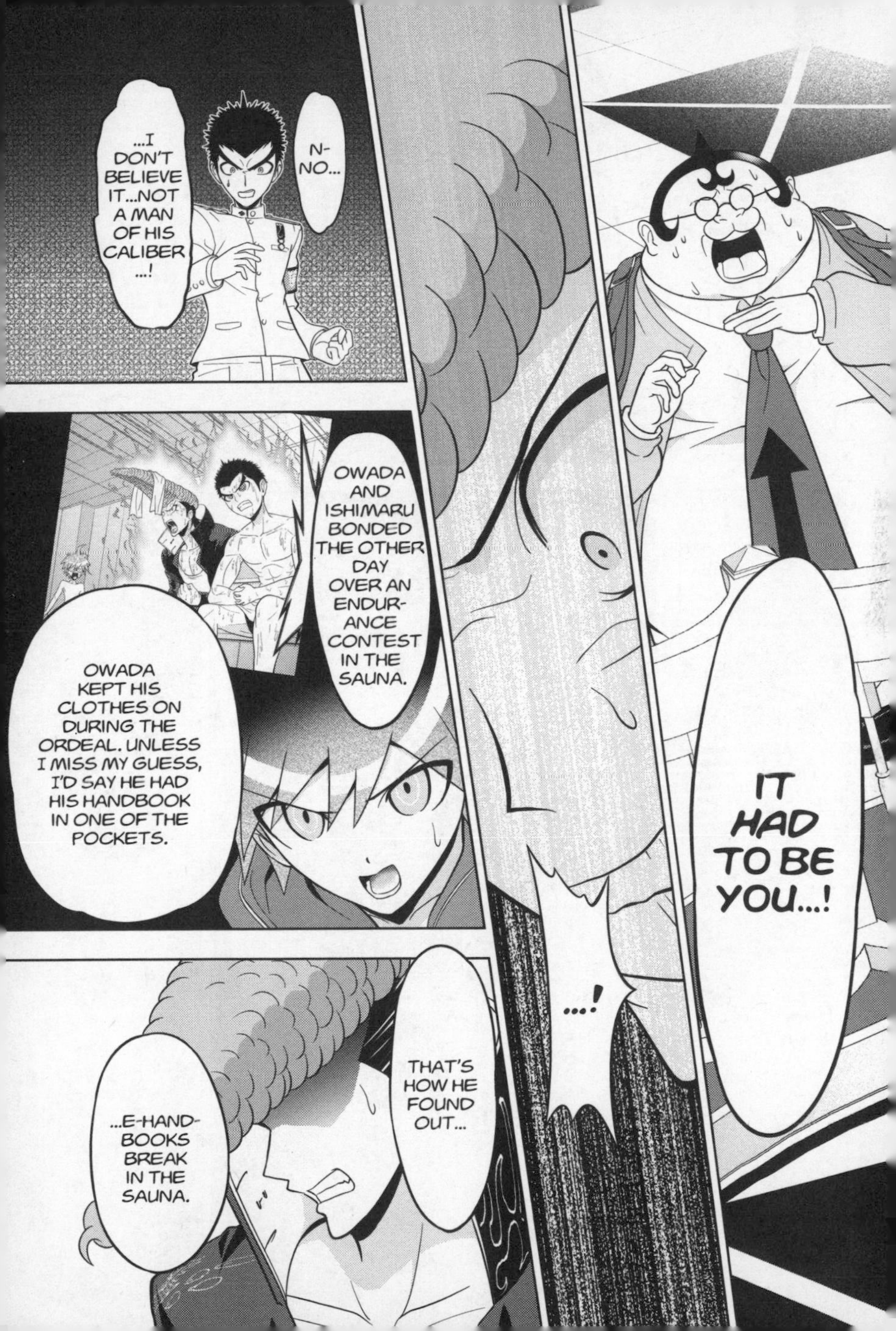
IT HAD TO BE YOU...!
...!
N-NO...
...I DON'T BELIEVE IT...NOT A MAN OF HIS CALIBER ...!
OWADA AND ISHIMARU BONDED THE OTHER DAY OVER AN ENDUR-ANCE CONTEST IN THE SAUNA.
OWADA KEPT HIS CLOTHES ON DURING THE ORDEAL. UNLESS I MISS MY GUESS, I'D SAY HE HAD HIS HANDBOOK IN ONE OF THE POCKETS.
THAT'S HOW HE FOUND OUT...
...E-HAND-BOOKS BREAK IN THE SAUNA.

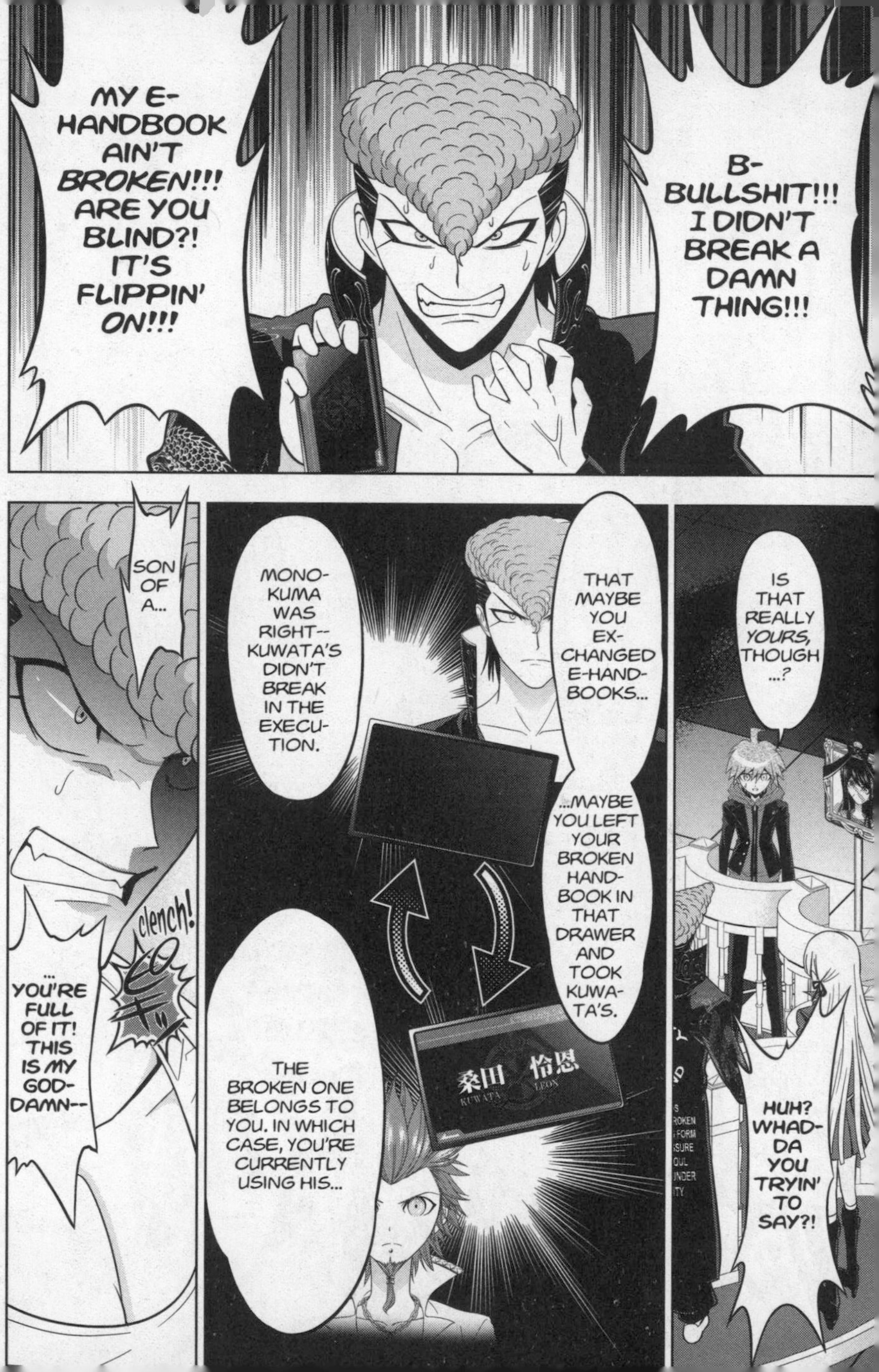
B-BULLSHIT!!! I DIDN'T BREAK A DAMN THING!!!
MY E-HANDBOOK AIN'T BROKEN!!! ARE YOU BLIND?! IT'S FLIPPIN' ON!!!
IS THAT REALLY *YOURS,* THOUGH ...?
HUH? WHADDA YOU TRYIN' TO SAY?!
THAT MAYBE YOU EXCHANGED E-HANDBOOKS...
...MAYBE YOU LEFT YOUR BROKEN HANDBOOK IN THAT DRAWER AND TOOK KUWATA'S.
MONOKUMA WAS RIGHT-- KUWATA'S DIDN'T BREAK IN THE EXECUTION.
桑田 怜恩
KUWATA LEON
THE BROKEN ONE BELONGS TO YOU. IN WHICH CASE, YOU'RE CURRENTLY USING HIS...
SON OF A...
clench!
... YOU'RE FULL OF IT! THIS IS *MY* GODDAMN--

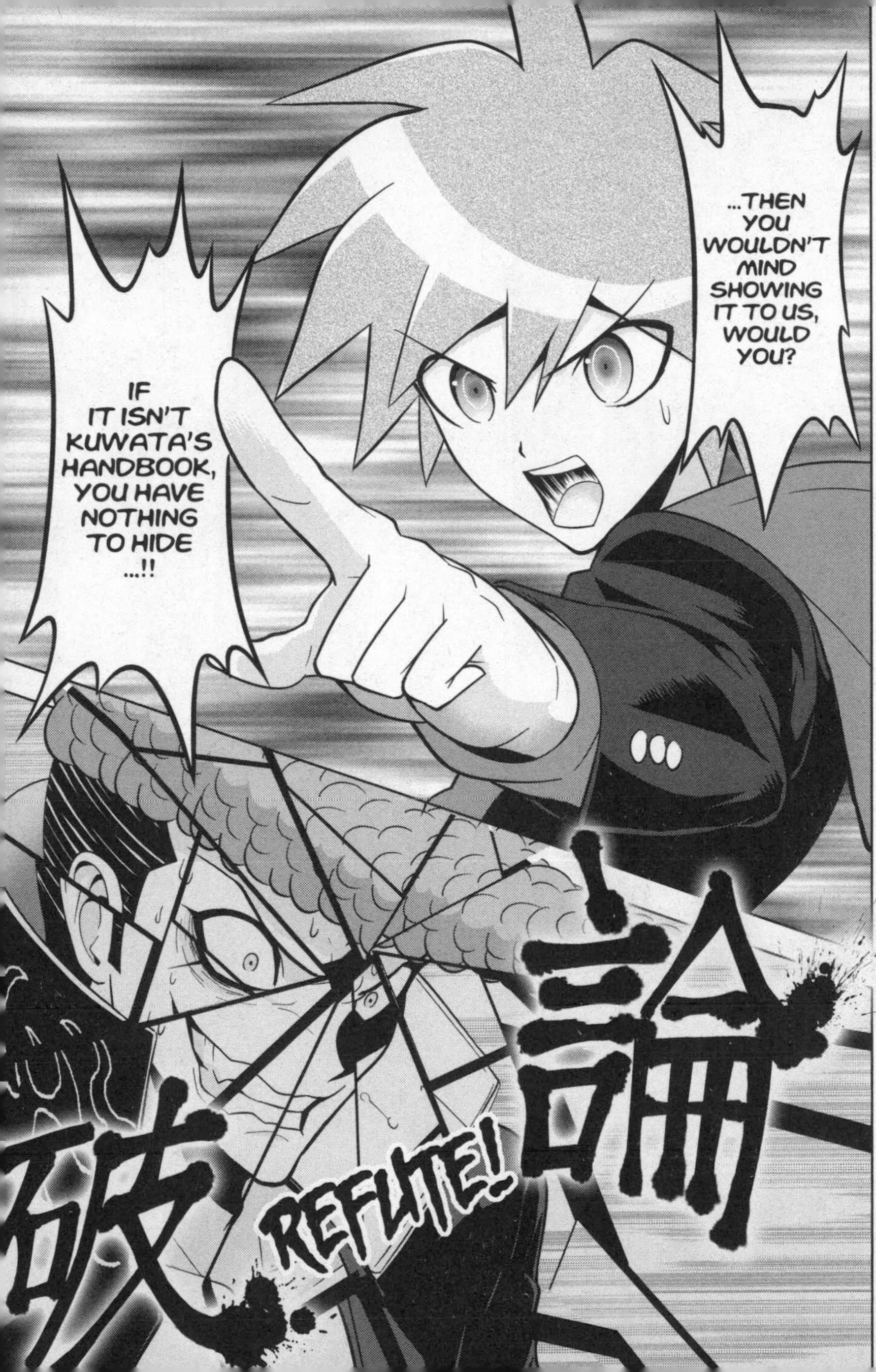
...THEN YOU WOULDN'T MIND SHOWING IT TO US, WOULD YOU?
IF IT ISN'T KUWATA'S HANDBOOK, YOU HAVE NOTHING TO HIDE ...!!
破 REFUTE! 論

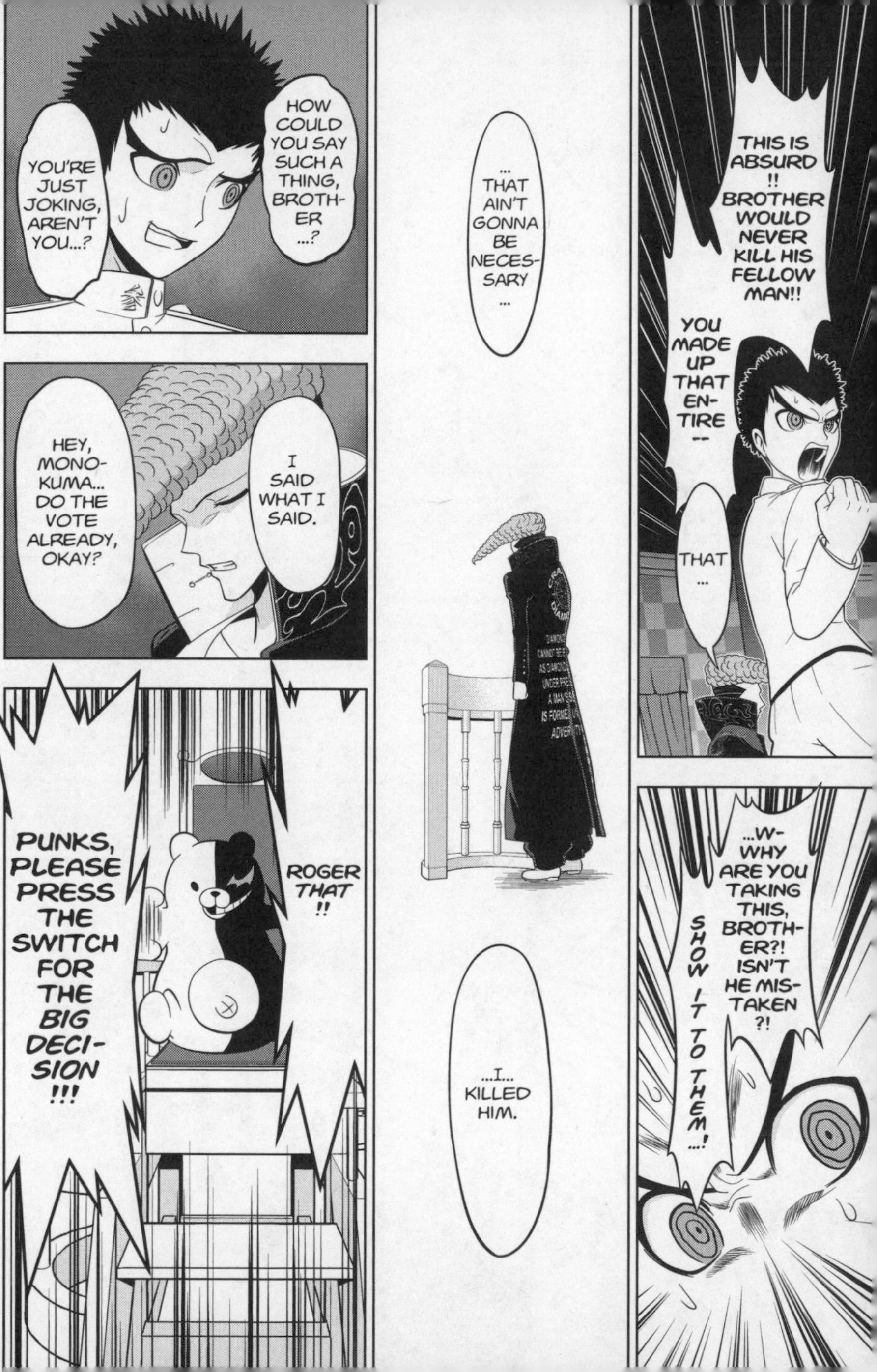
THIS IS ABSURD!! BROTHER WOULD NEVER KILL HIS FELLOW MAN!!
YOU MADE UP THAT EN-TIRE--
THAT...
...W-WHY ARE YOU TAKING THIS, BROTH-ER?! ISN'T HE MIS-TAKEN?!
SHOW IT TO THEM...!
...THAT AIN'T GONNA BE NECES-SARY...
...I... KILLED HIM.
HOW COULD YOU SAY SUCH A THING, BROTH-ER...?
YOU'RE JUST JOKING, AREN'T YOU...?
I SAID WHAT I SAID.
HEY, MONO-KUMA... DO THE VOTE ALREADY, OKAY?
ROGER THAT!!
PUNKS, PLEASE PRESS THE SWITCH FOR THE BIG DECI-SION!!!

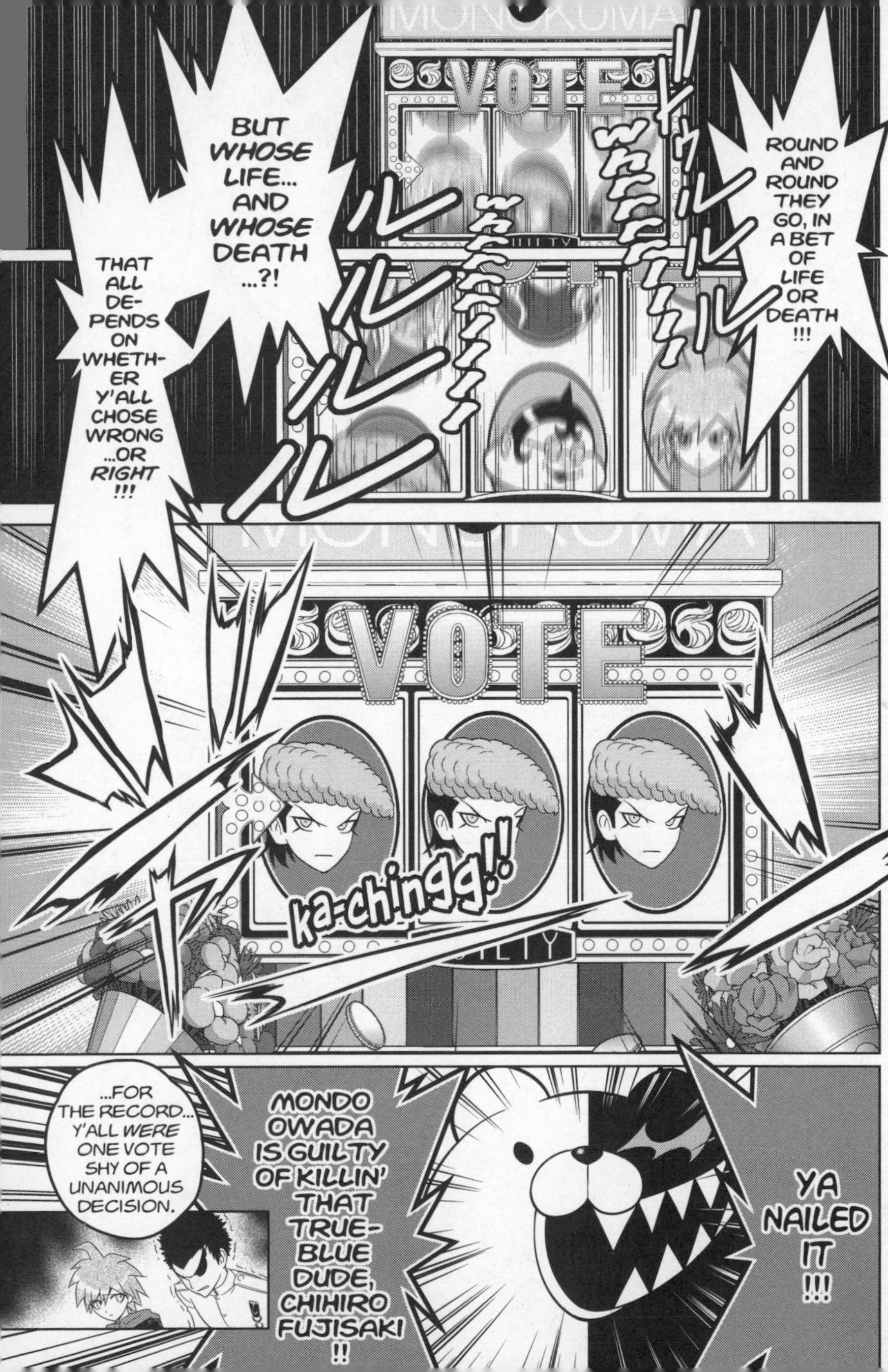
ROUND AND ROUND THEY GO, IN A BET OF LIFE OR DEATH!!!
BUT WHOSE LIFE... AND WHOSE DEATH...?!
THAT ALL DEPENDS ON WHETHER Y'ALL CHOSE WRONG ...OR RIGHT!!!
VOTE
ka-chingg!!
YA NAILED IT!!!
MONDO OWADA IS GUILTY OF KILLIN' THAT TRUE-BLUE DUDE, CHIHIRO FUJISAKI!!
...FOR THE RECORD... Y'ALL WERE ONE VOTE SHY OF A UNANIMOUS DECISION.

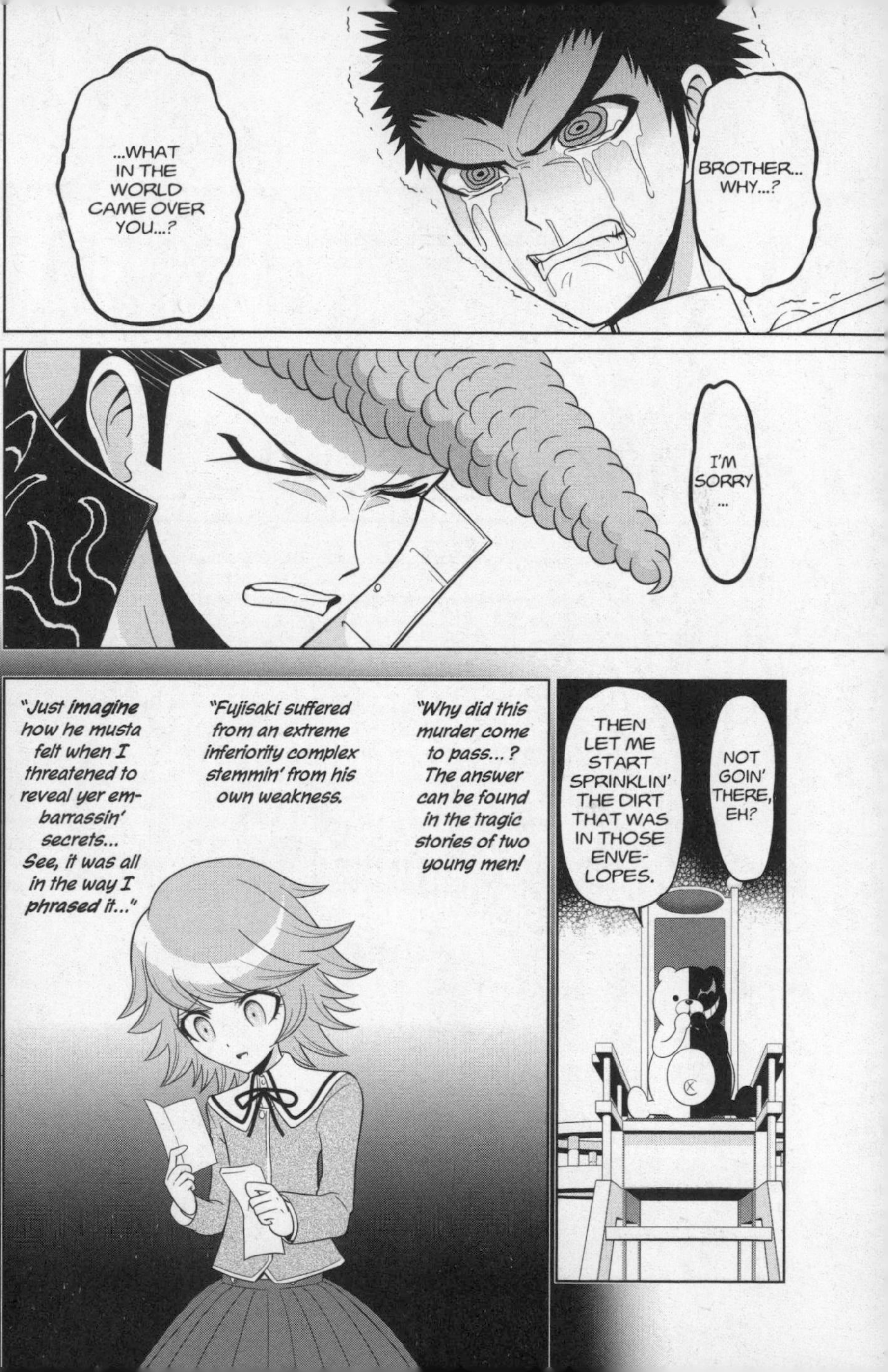
BROTHER... WHY...?
...WHAT IN THE WORLD CAME OVER YOU...?
I'M SORRY ...
NOT GOIN' THERE, EH?
THEN LET ME START SPRINKLIN' THE DIRT THAT WAS IN THOSE ENVELOPES.
"Why did this murder come to pass...? The answer can be found in the tragic stories of two young men!
"Fujisaki suffered from an extreme inferiority complex stemmin' from his own weakness.
"Just imagine how he musta felt when I threatened to reveal yer embarrassin' secrets... See, it was all in the way I phrased it..."

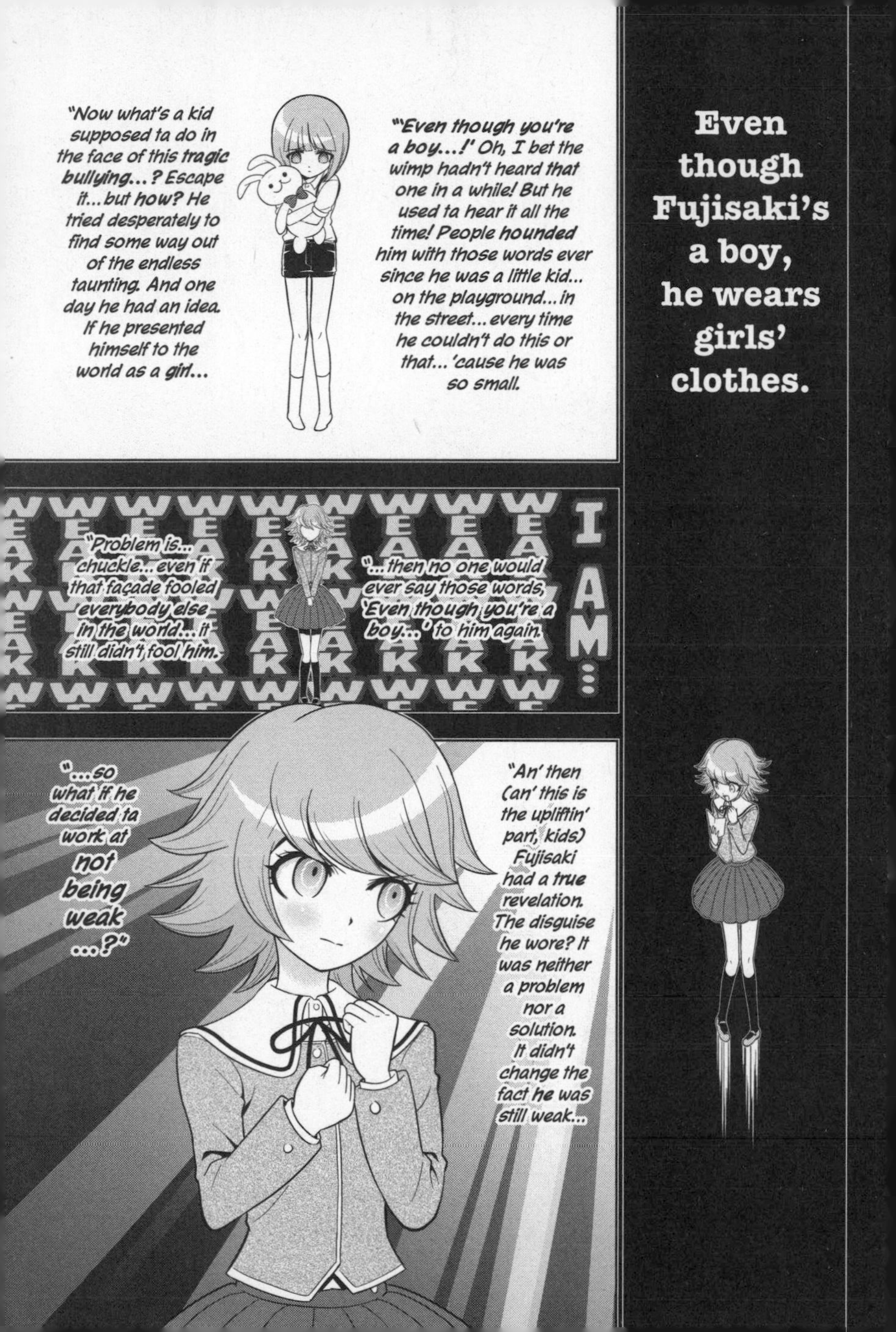
Even though Fujisaki's a boy, he wears girls' clothes.
"'Even though you're a boy...!' Oh, I bet the wimp hadn't heard that one in a while! But he used ta hear it all the time! People hounded him with those words ever since he was a little kid... on the playground... in the street... every time he couldn't do this or that... 'cause he was so small.
"Now what's a kid supposed ta do in the face of this tragic bullying...? Escape it... but how? He tried desperately to find some way out of the endless taunting. And one day he had an idea. If he presented himself to the world as a girl...
I AM...
"...then no one would ever say those words, 'Even though you're a boy...' to him again.
"Problem is... chuckle... even if that façade fooled everybody else in the world... it still didn't fool him.
"An' then (an' this is the upliftin' part, kids) Fujisaki had a true revelation. The disguise he wore? It was neither a problem nor a solution. It didn't change the fact he was still weak...
"...so what if he decided ta work at not being weak...?"

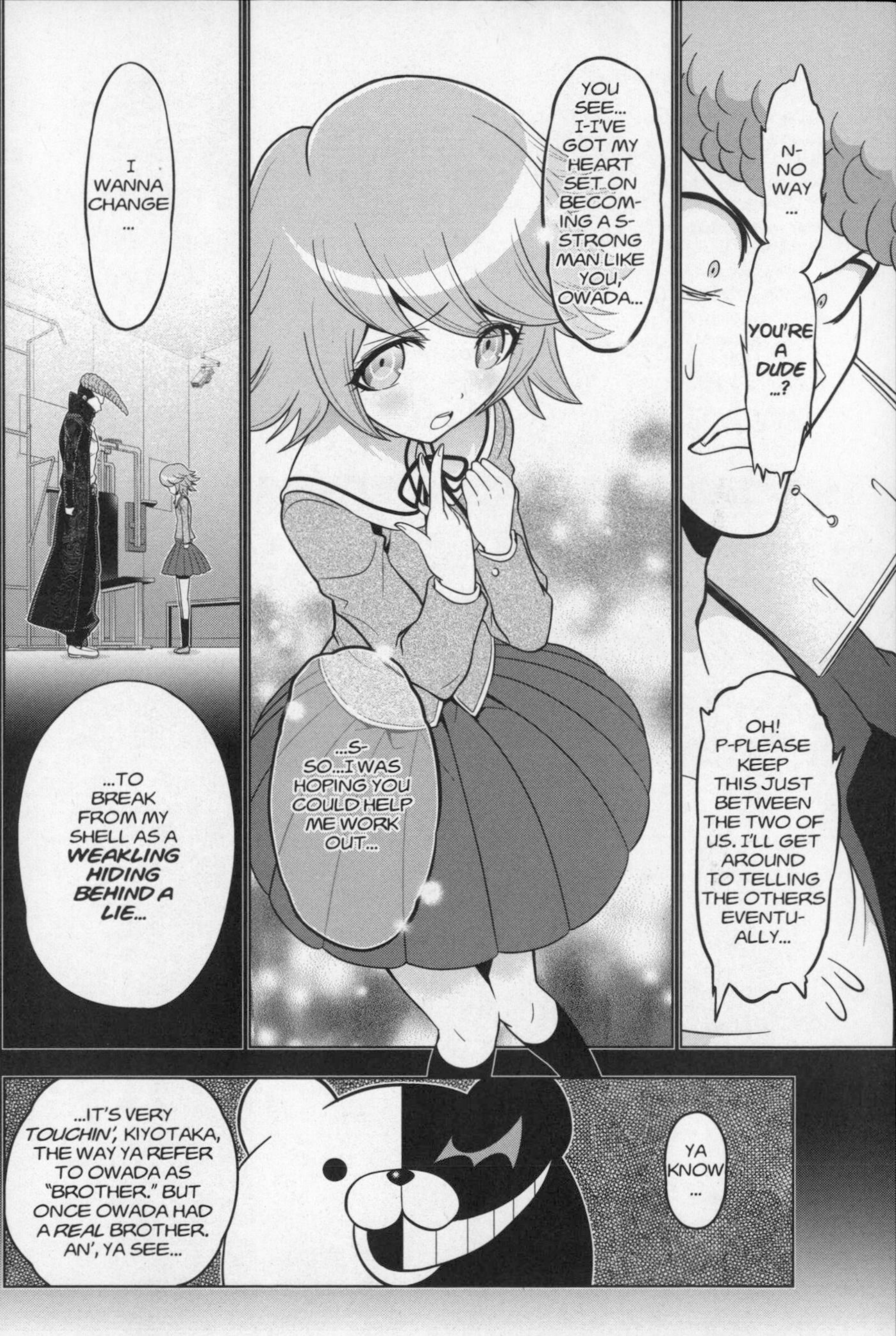
N-NO WAY...
YOU'RE A *DUDE*...?
OH! P-PLEASE KEEP THIS JUST BETWEEN THE TWO OF US. I'LL GET AROUND TO TELLING THE OTHERS EVENTU-ALLY...
YOU SEE... I-I'VE GOT MY HEART SET ON BECOM-ING A S-STRONG MAN LIKE YOU, OWADA...
...S-SO...I WAS HOPING YOU COULD HELP ME WORK OUT...
I WANNA CHANGE...
...TO BREAK FROM MY SHELL AS A ***WEAKLING HIDING BEHIND A LIE...***
YA KNOW...
...IT'S VERY *TOUCHIN'*, KIYOTAKA, THE WAY YA REFER TO OWADA AS "BROTHER." BUT ONCE OWADA HAD A *REAL* BROTHER. AN', YA SEE...

Owada killed his brother.

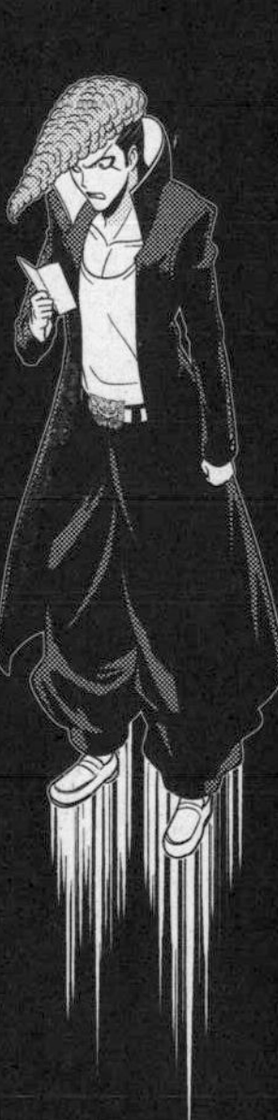

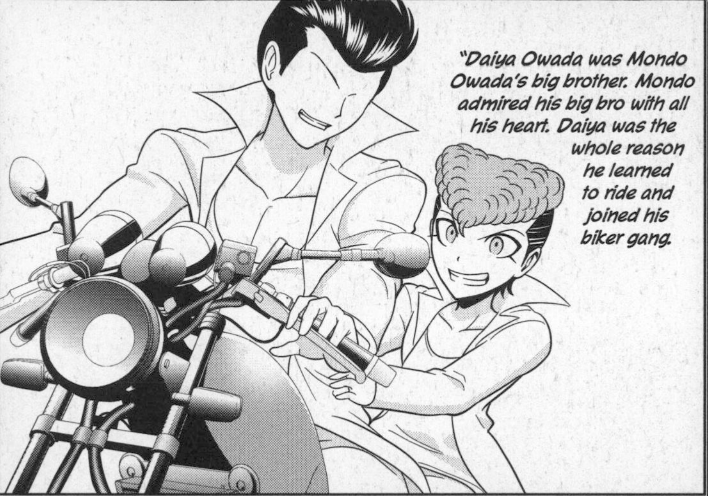
"Daiya Owada was Mondo Owada's big brother. Mondo admired his big bro with all his heart. Daiya was the whole reason he learned to ride and joined his biker gang.

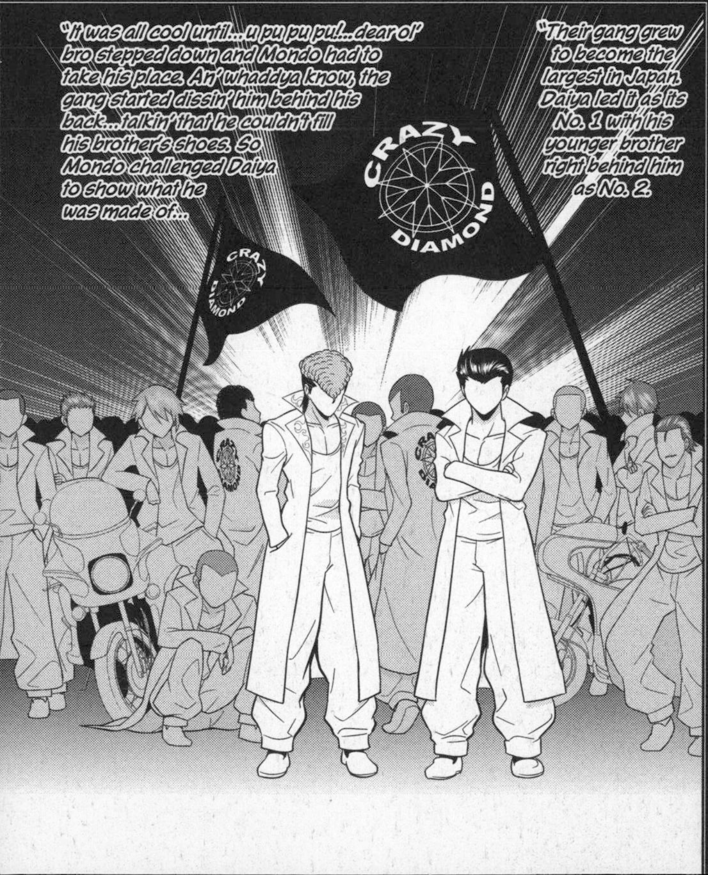
"Their gang grew to become the largest in Japan. Daiya led it as its No. 1 with his younger brother right behind him as No. 2.
"It was all cool until...u pu pu pu!...dear ol' bro stepped down and Mondo had to take his place. An' whaddya know, the gang started dissin' him behind his back...talkin' that he couldn't fill his brother's shoes. So Mondo challenged Daiya to show what he was made of...
CRAZY DIAMOND
CRAZY DIAMOND

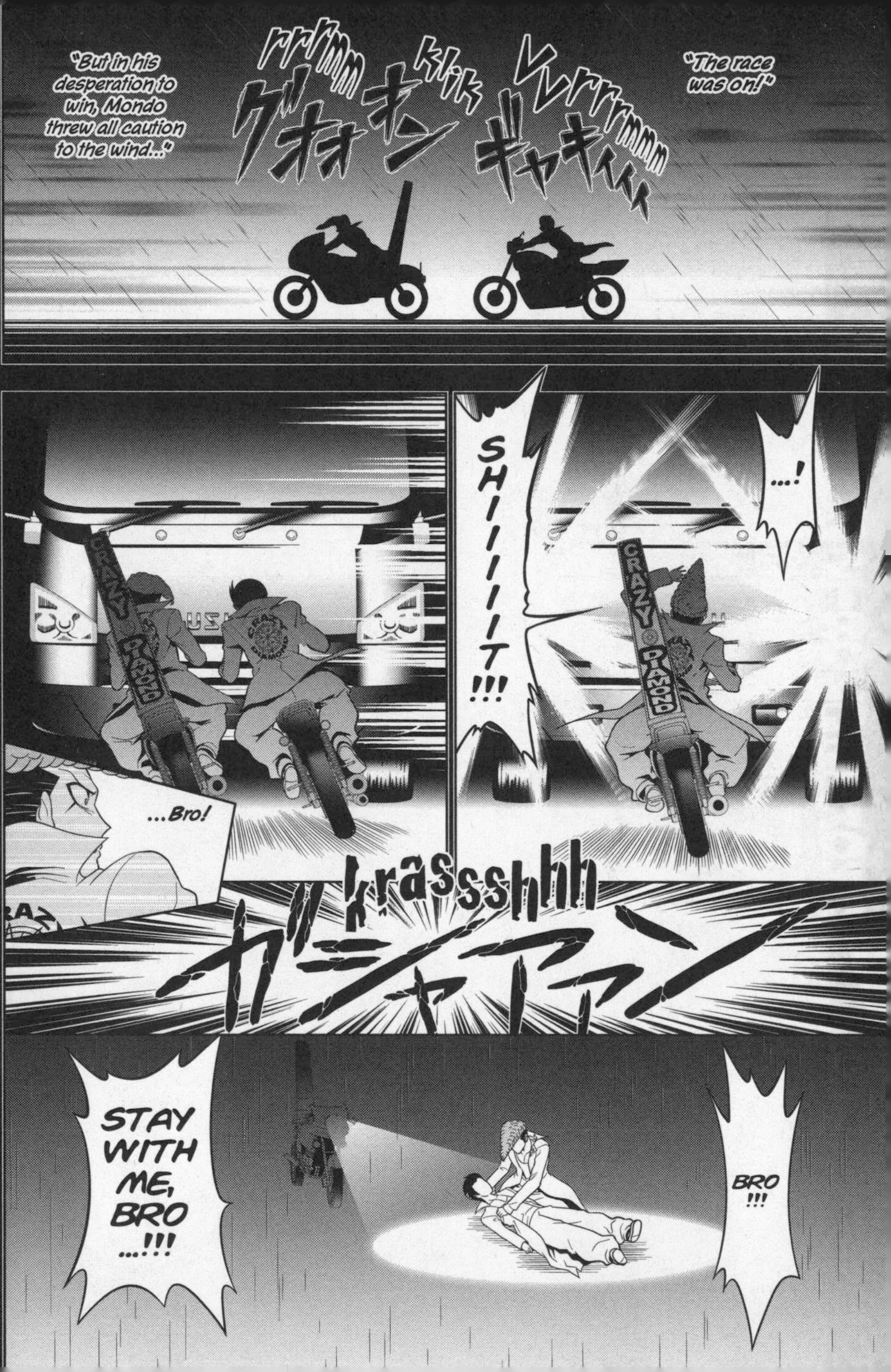
"The race was on!"
vrrrrmmm
ギャキィィィ
klik
rrrmm
グォォオン
"But in his desperation to win, Mondo threw all caution to the wind..."
...!
SHIIIIIIIT!!!
...Bro!
krassshhh
ガシャアァン
BRO!!!
STAY WITH ME, BRO ...!!!

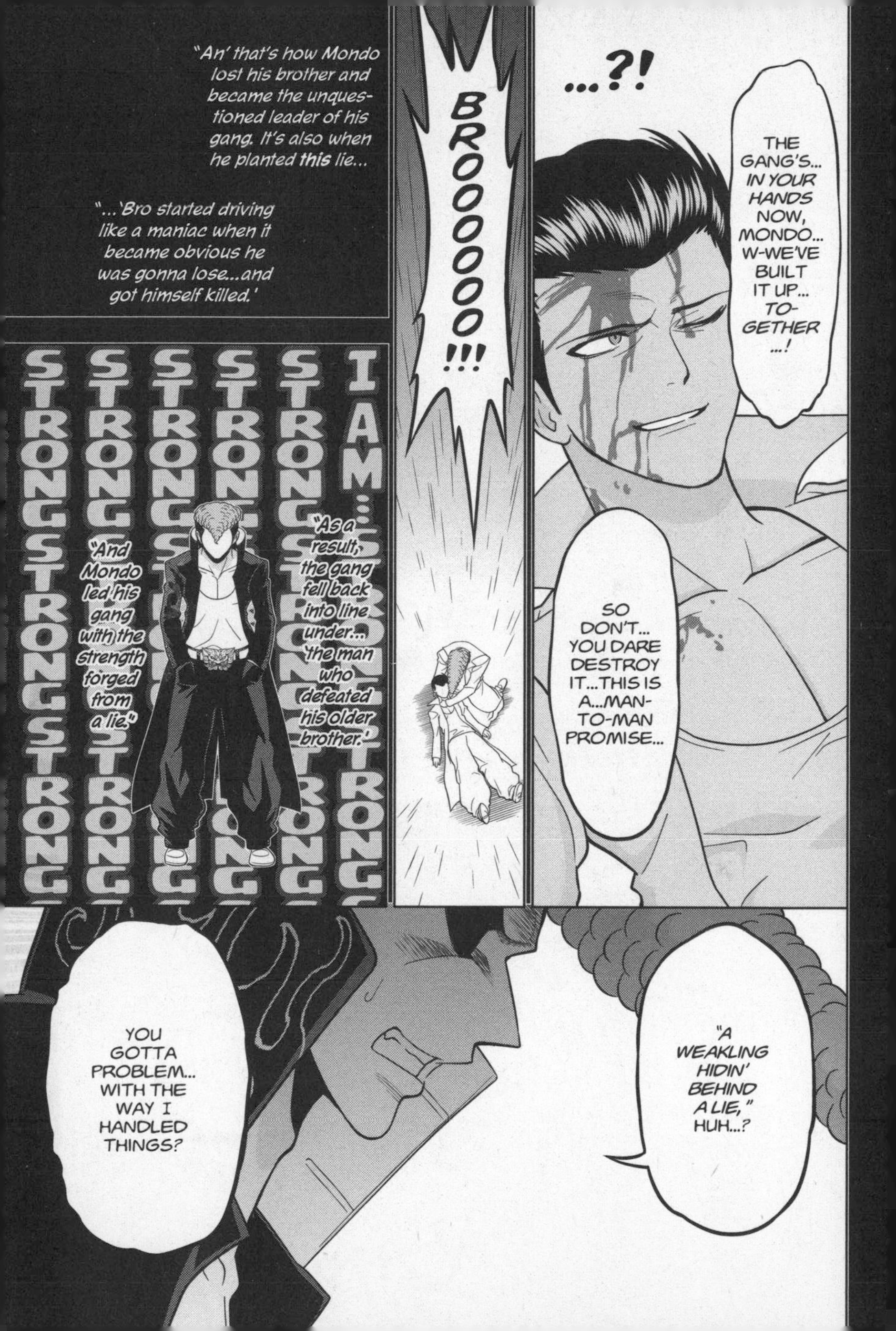
...?!
THE GANG'S... IN YOUR HANDS NOW, MONDO... W-WE'VE BUILT IT UP... TO-GETHER ...!
SO DON'T... YOU DARE DESTROY IT...THIS IS A...MAN-TO-MAN PROMISE...
BROOOOOOOO!!!
"An' that's how Mondo lost his brother and became the unquestioned leader of his gang. It's also when he planted this lie...
"...'Bro started driving like a maniac when it became obvious he was gonna lose...and got himself killed.'
I AM... STRONG
STRONG STRONG STRONG STRONG STRONG
"As a result, the gang fell back into line under... the man who defeated his older brother.'
"And Mondo led his gang with the strength forged from a lie."
"A WEAKLING HIDIN' BEHIND A LIE," HUH...?
YOU GOTTA PROBLEM... WITH THE WAY I HANDLED THINGS?

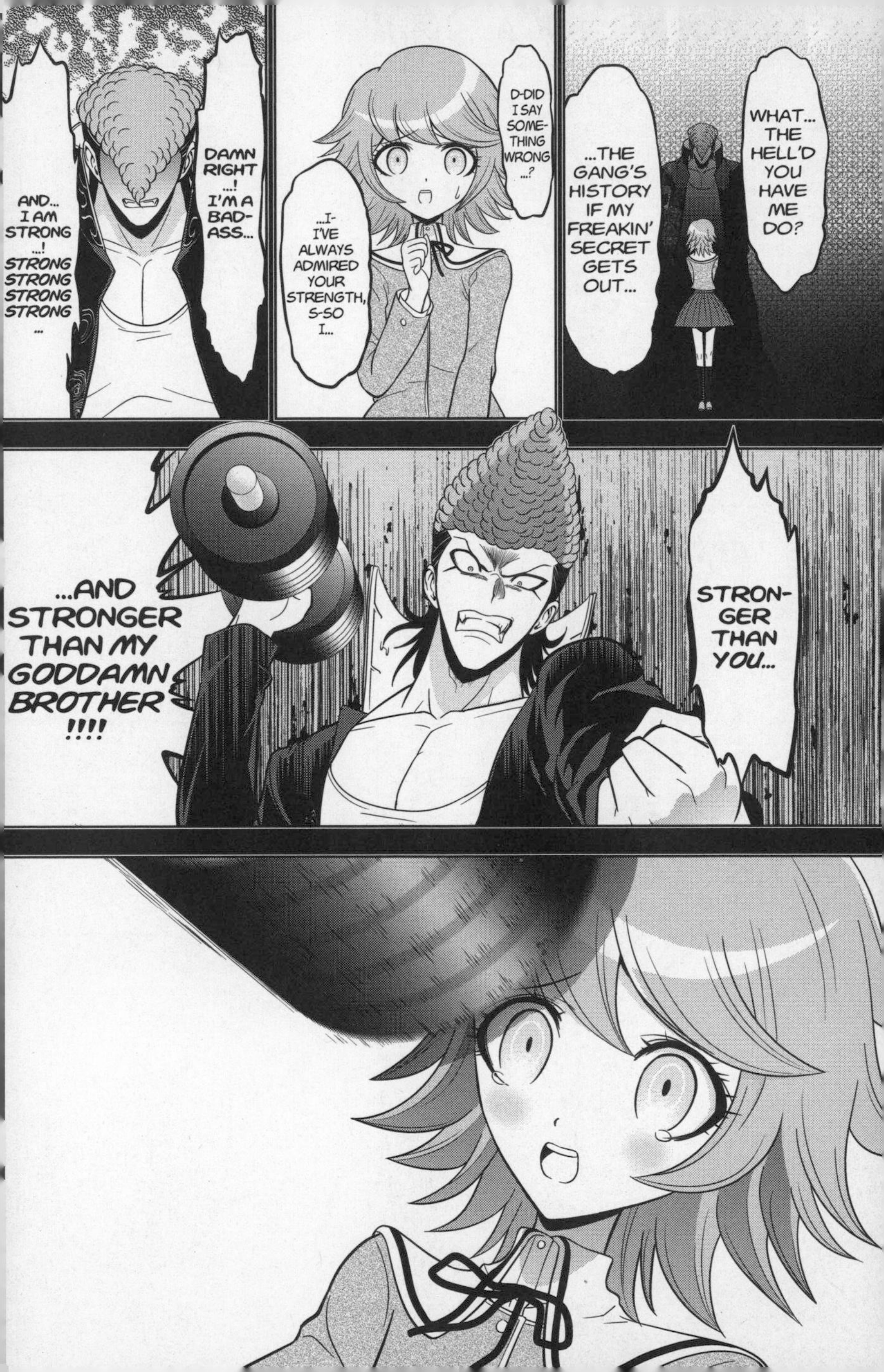
WHAT... THE HELL'D YOU HAVE ME DO?
...THE GANG'S HISTORY IF MY FREAKIN' SECRET GETS OUT...
D-DID I SAY SOME-THING WRONG ...?
...I- I'VE ALWAYS ADMIRED YOUR STRENGTH, S-SO I...
DAMN RIGHT ...! I'M A BAD-ASS...
AND... I AM STRONG ...! STRONG STRONG STRONG STRONG ...
STRON-GER THAN YOU...
...AND STRONGER THAN MY GODDAMN BROTHER !!!!

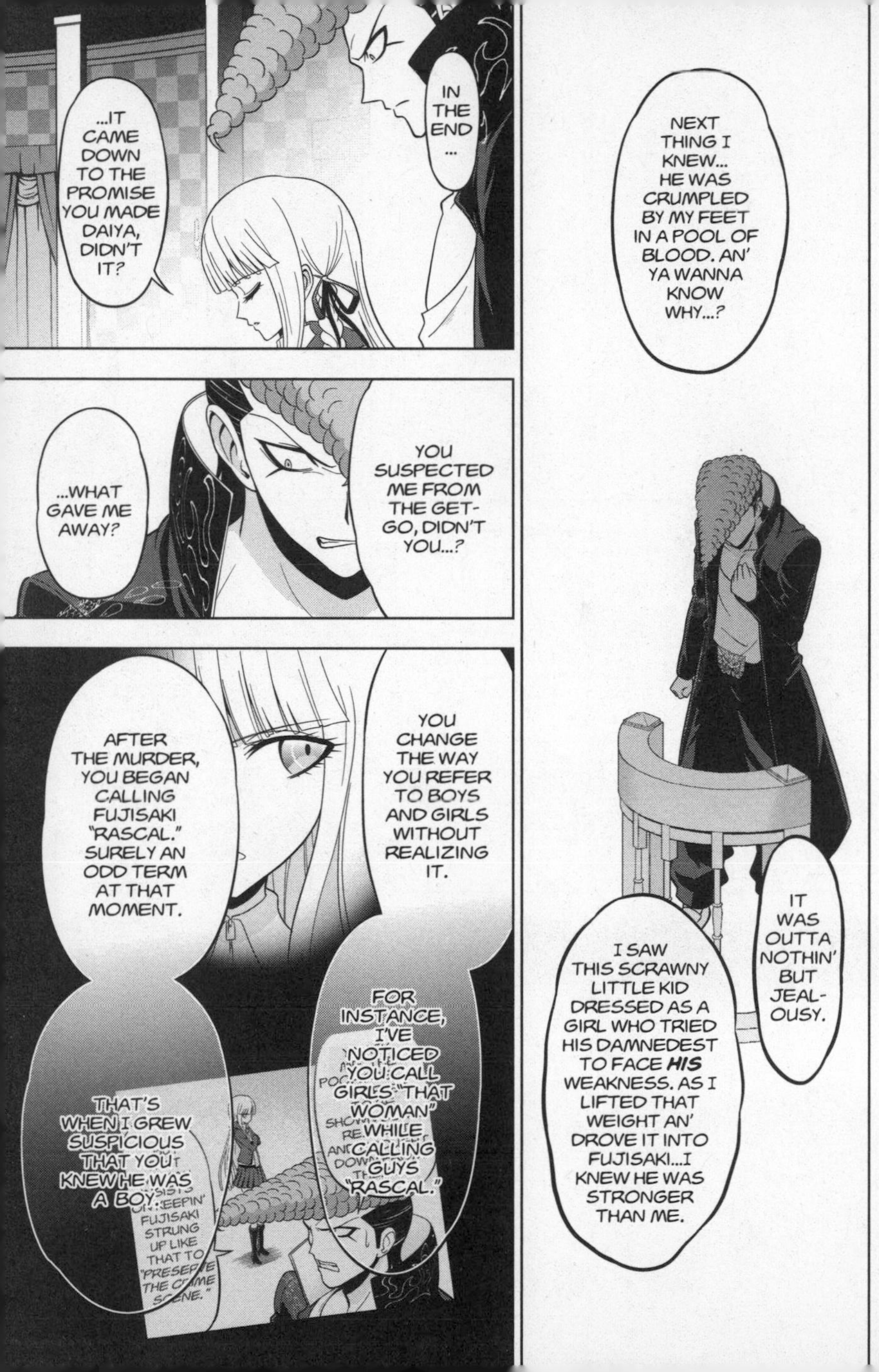
NEXT THING I KNEW... HE WAS CRUMPLED BY MY FEET IN A POOL OF BLOOD. AN' YA WANNA KNOW WHY...?
IT WAS OUTTA NOTHIN' BUT JEAL-OUSY.
I SAW THIS SCRAWNY LITTLE KID DRESSED AS A GIRL WHO TRIED HIS DAMNEDEST TO FACE ***HIS*** WEAKNESS. AS I LIFTED THAT WEIGHT AN' DROVE IT INTO FUJISAKI...I KNEW HE WAS STRONGER THAN ME.
IN THE END...
...IT CAME DOWN TO THE PROMISE YOU MADE DAIYA, DIDN'T IT?
YOU SUSPECTED ME FROM THE GET-GO, DIDN'T YOU...?
...WHAT GAVE ME AWAY?
YOU CHANGE THE WAY YOU REFER TO BOYS AND GIRLS WITHOUT REALIZING IT.
AFTER THE MURDER, YOU BEGAN CALLING FUJISAKI "RASCAL." SURELY AN ODD TERM AT THAT MOMENT.
FOR INSTANCE, I'VE NOTICED YOU CALL GIRLS "THAT WOMAN" WHILE CALLING GUYS "RASCAL."
THAT'S WHEN I GREW SUSPICIOUS THAT YOU KNEW HE WAS A BOY.

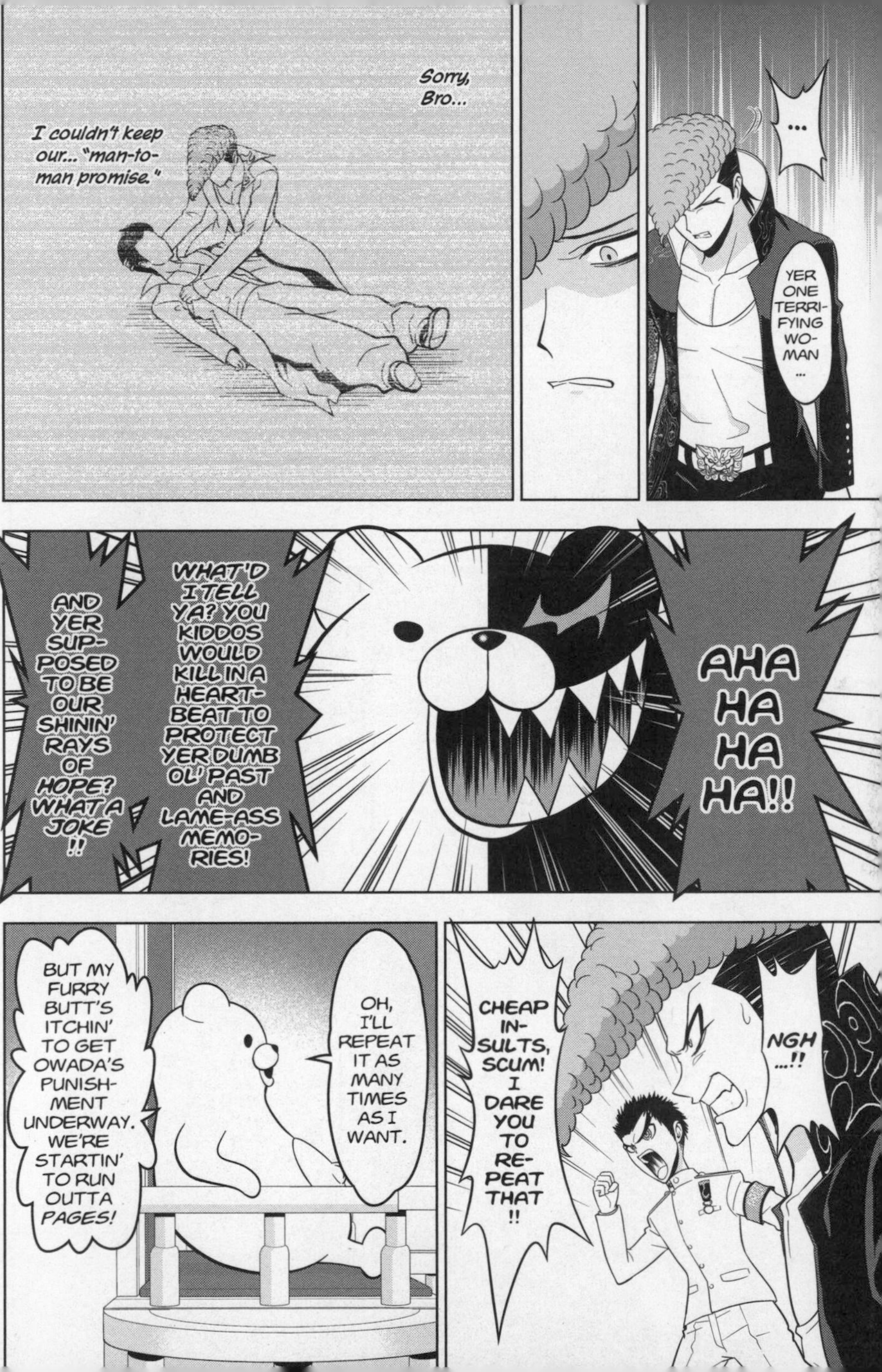
...
YER ONE TERRIFYING WOMAN ...
Sorry, Bro...
I couldn't keep our... "man-to-man promise."
AHA HA HA HA!!
WHAT'D I TELL YA? YOU KIDDOS WOULD KILL IN A HEARTBEAT TO PROTECT YER DUMB OL' PAST AND LAME-ASS MEMORIES!
AND YER SUPPOSED TO BE OUR SHININ' RAYS OF HOPE? WHAT A JOKE!!
NGH...!!
CHEAP INSULTS, SCUM! I DARE YOU TO REPEAT THAT!!
OH, I'LL REPEAT IT AS MANY TIMES AS I WANT.
BUT MY FURRY BUTT'S ITCHIN' TO GET OWADA'S PUNISHMENT UNDERWAY. WE'RE STARTIN' TO RUN OUTTA PAGES!

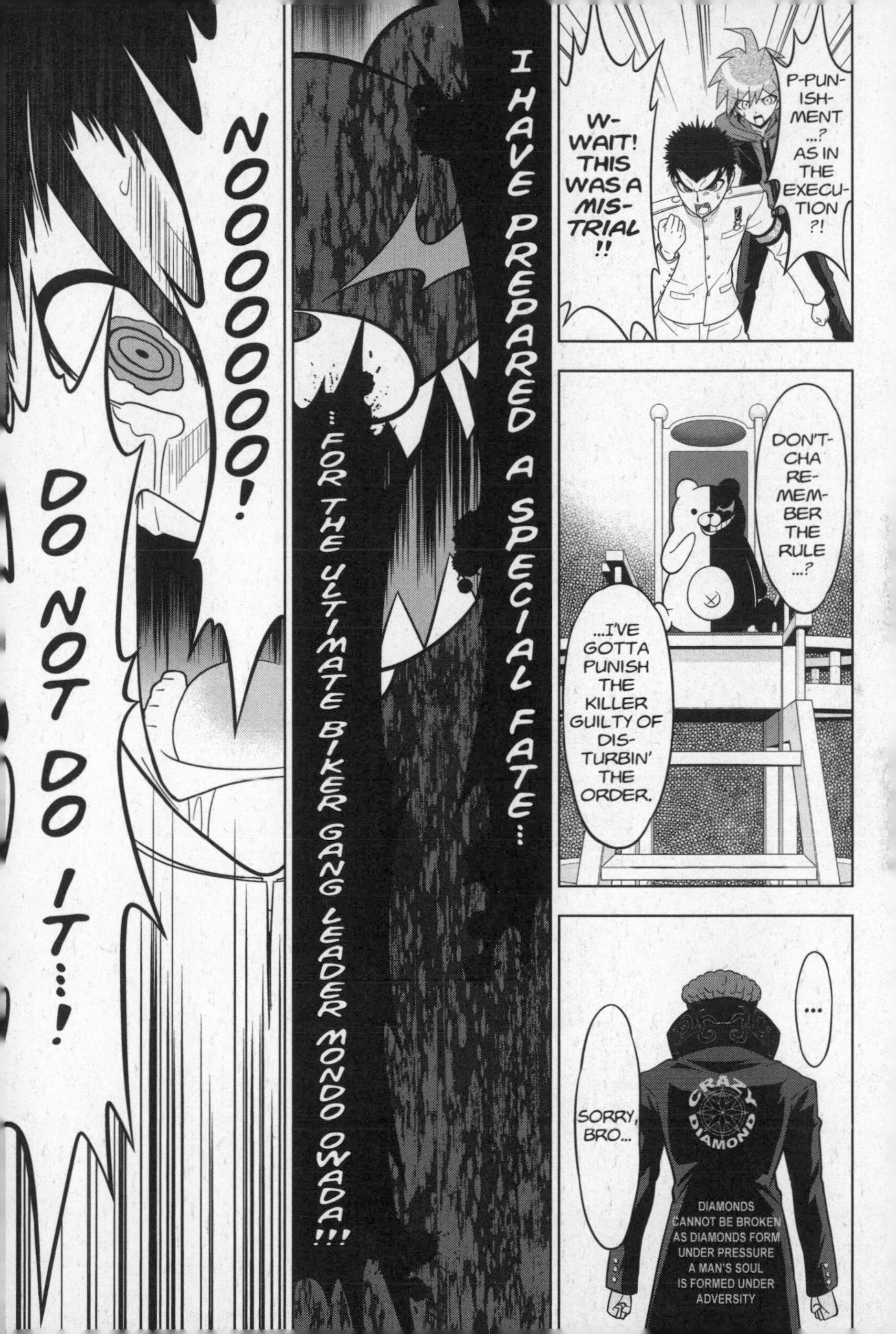
P-PUNISHMENT...? AS IN THE EXECUTION?!
W-WAIT! THIS WAS A MISTRIAL!!
DON'T-CHA REMEMBER THE RULE...?
...I'VE GOTTA PUNISH THE KILLER GUILTY OF DISTURBIN' THE ORDER.
...
SORRY, BRO...
CRAZY DIAMOND
DIAMONDS CANNOT BE BROKEN AS DIAMONDS FORM UNDER PRESSURE A MAN'S SOUL IS FORMED UNDER ADVERSITY
I HAVE PREPARED A SPECIAL FATE...
...FOR THE ULTIMATE BIKER GANG LEADER MONDO OWADA!!!
NOOOOOOOOO!
DO NOT DO IT...!

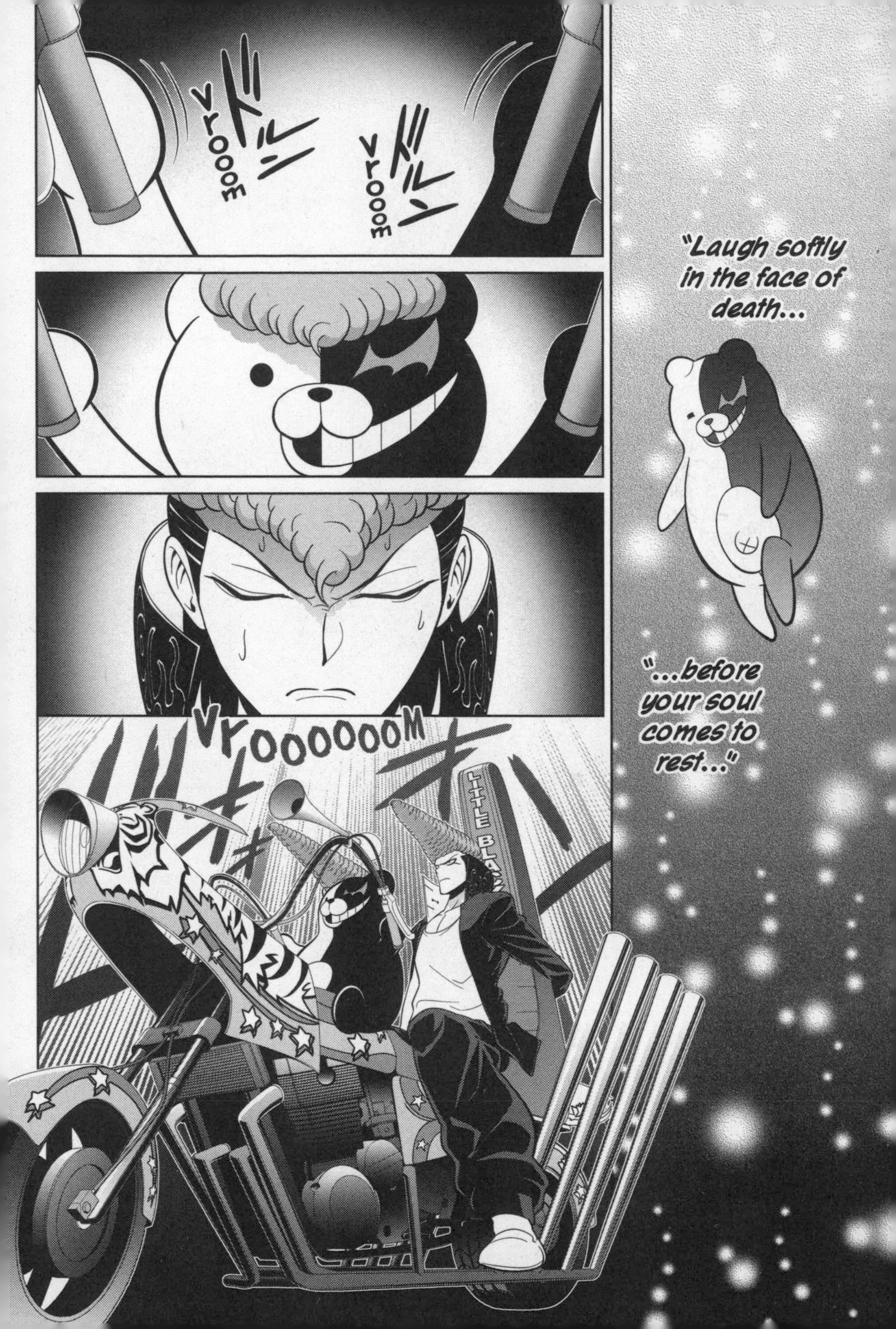
"Laugh softly in the face of death...
"...before your soul comes to rest..."
vrooom
vrooom
VROOOOOOM
LITTLE BLA

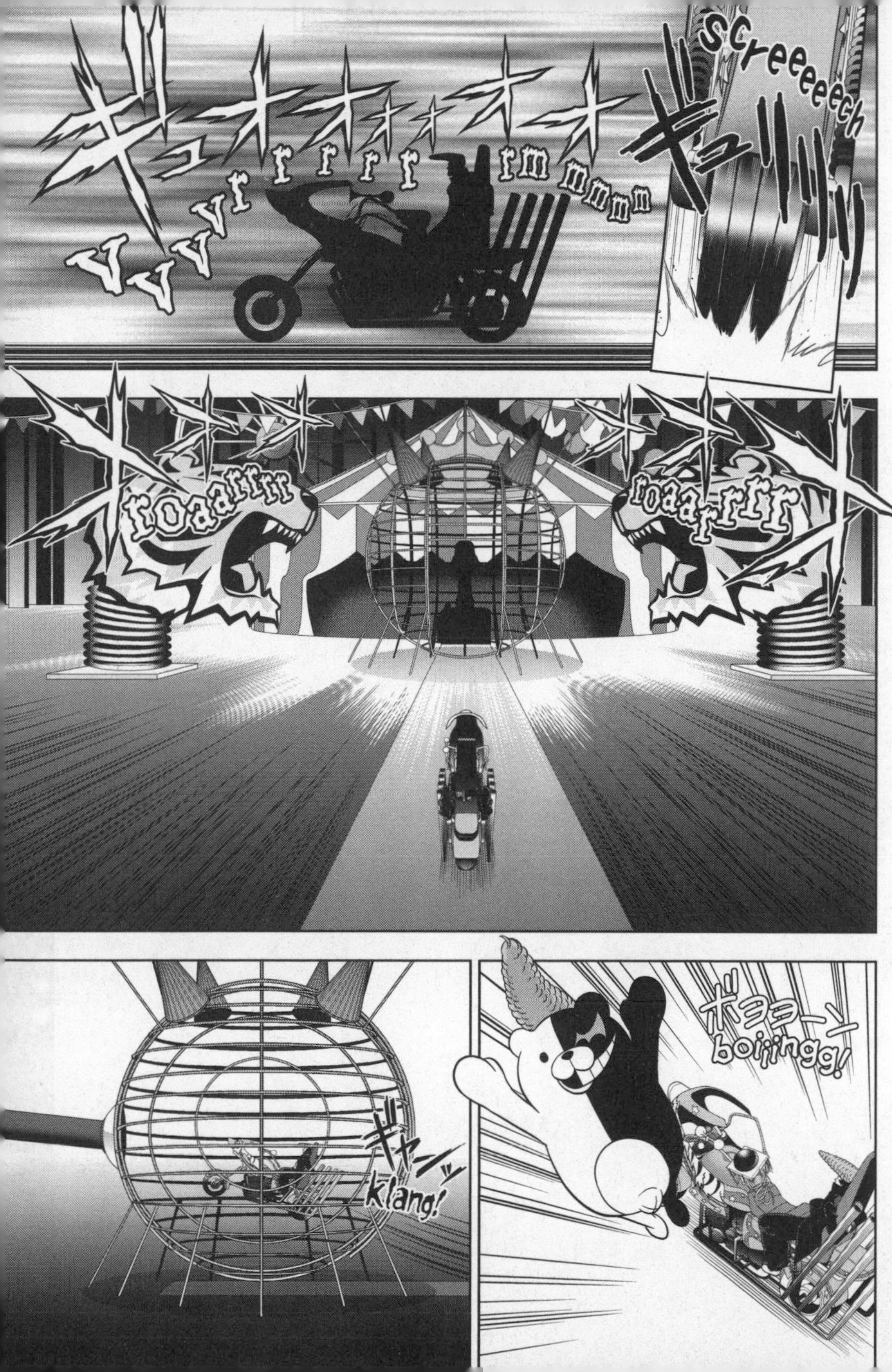
screeeeeech
vvvvrrrrrrrmmmmmn
roaarrrr
roaarrrr
boiiingg!
klang!

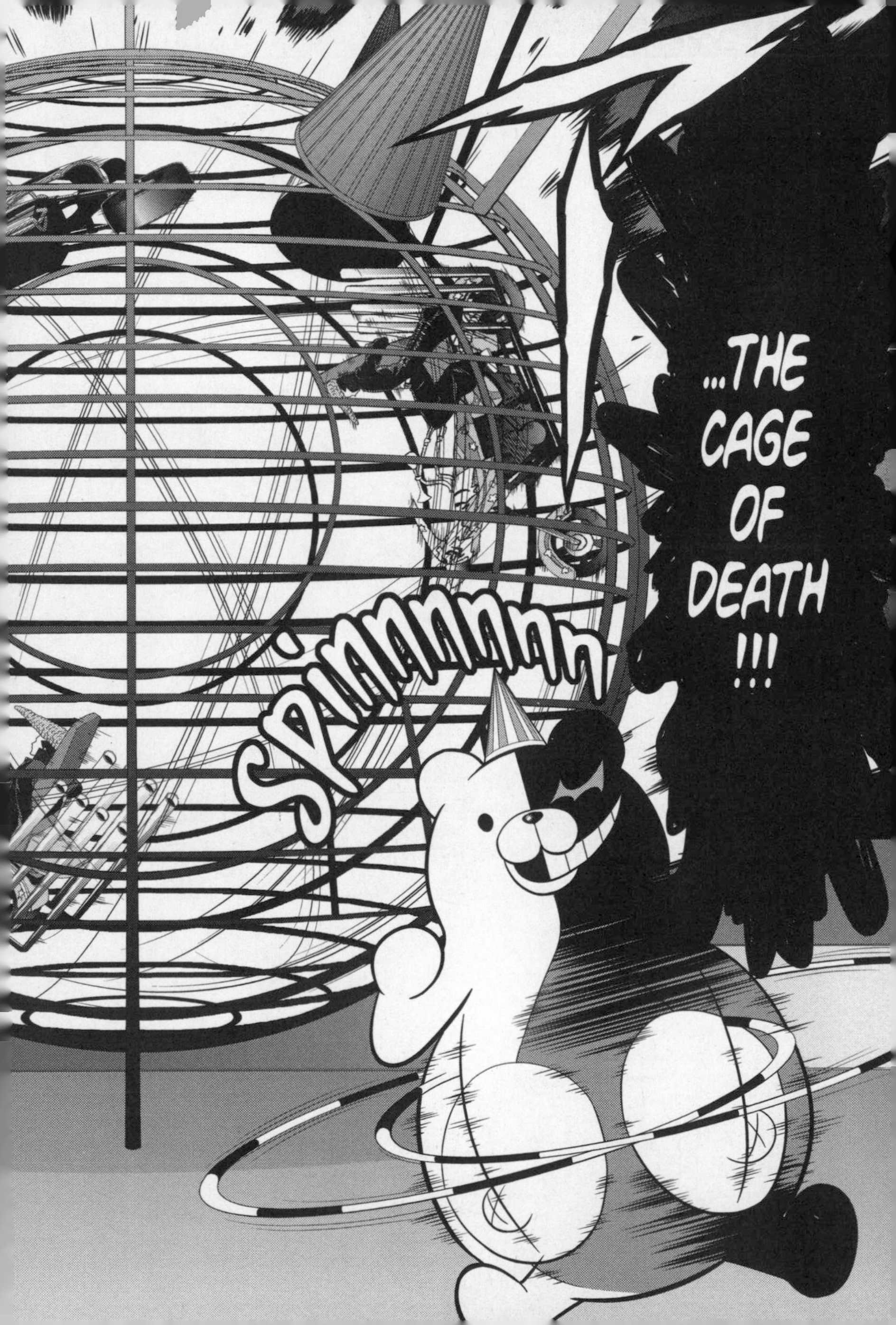
...THE CAGE OF DEATH !!!
SPINNNNNN

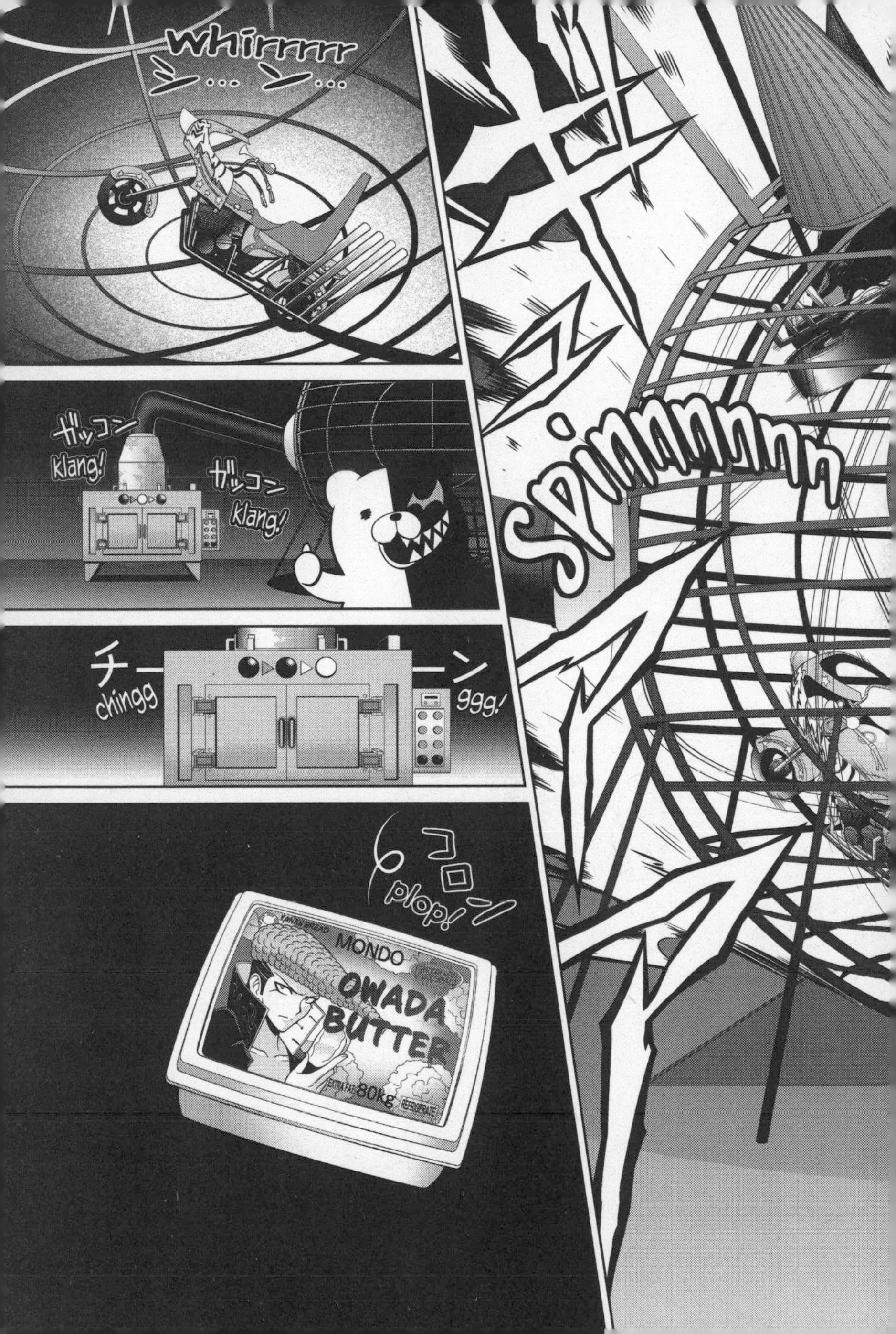
Spinnnnnnn
whirrrrr
ジ… ジ…
ガッコン
klang!
ガッコン
klang!
チーーン
chingg
ggg!
コローン
plop!
MONDO
OWADA BUTTER
EXTRA FAT 80kg
REFRIGERATE

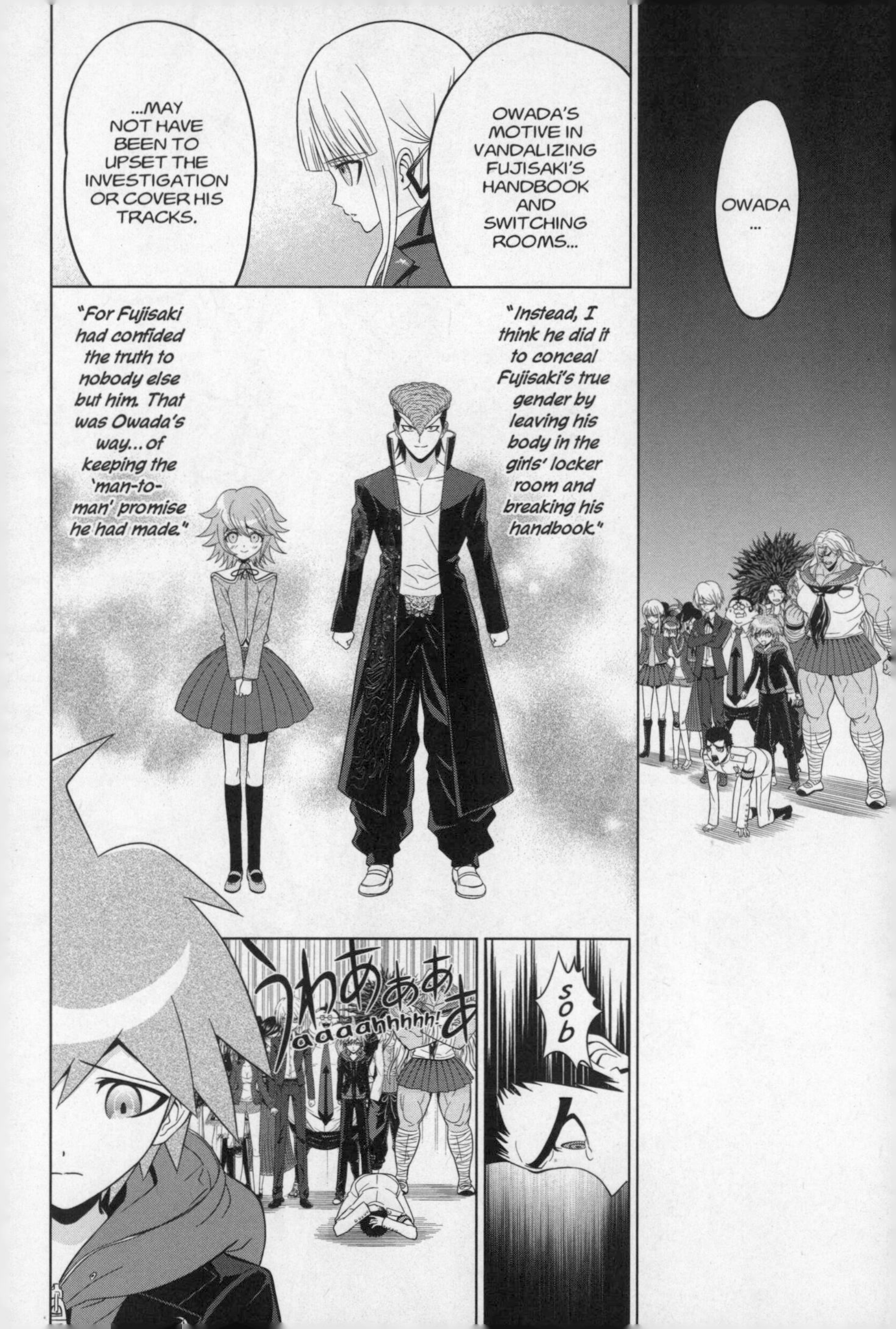
OWADA...
OWADA'S MOTIVE IN VANDALIZING FUJISAKI'S HANDBOOK AND SWITCHING ROOMS...
...MAY NOT HAVE BEEN TO UPSET THE INVESTIGATION OR COVER HIS TRACKS.
"Instead, I think he did it to conceal Fujisaki's true gender by leaving his body in the girls' locker room and breaking his handbook."
"For Fujisaki had confided the truth to nobody else but him. That was Owada's way... of keeping the 'man-to-man' promise he had made."
sob
うわああああ
aaaahhhhh!

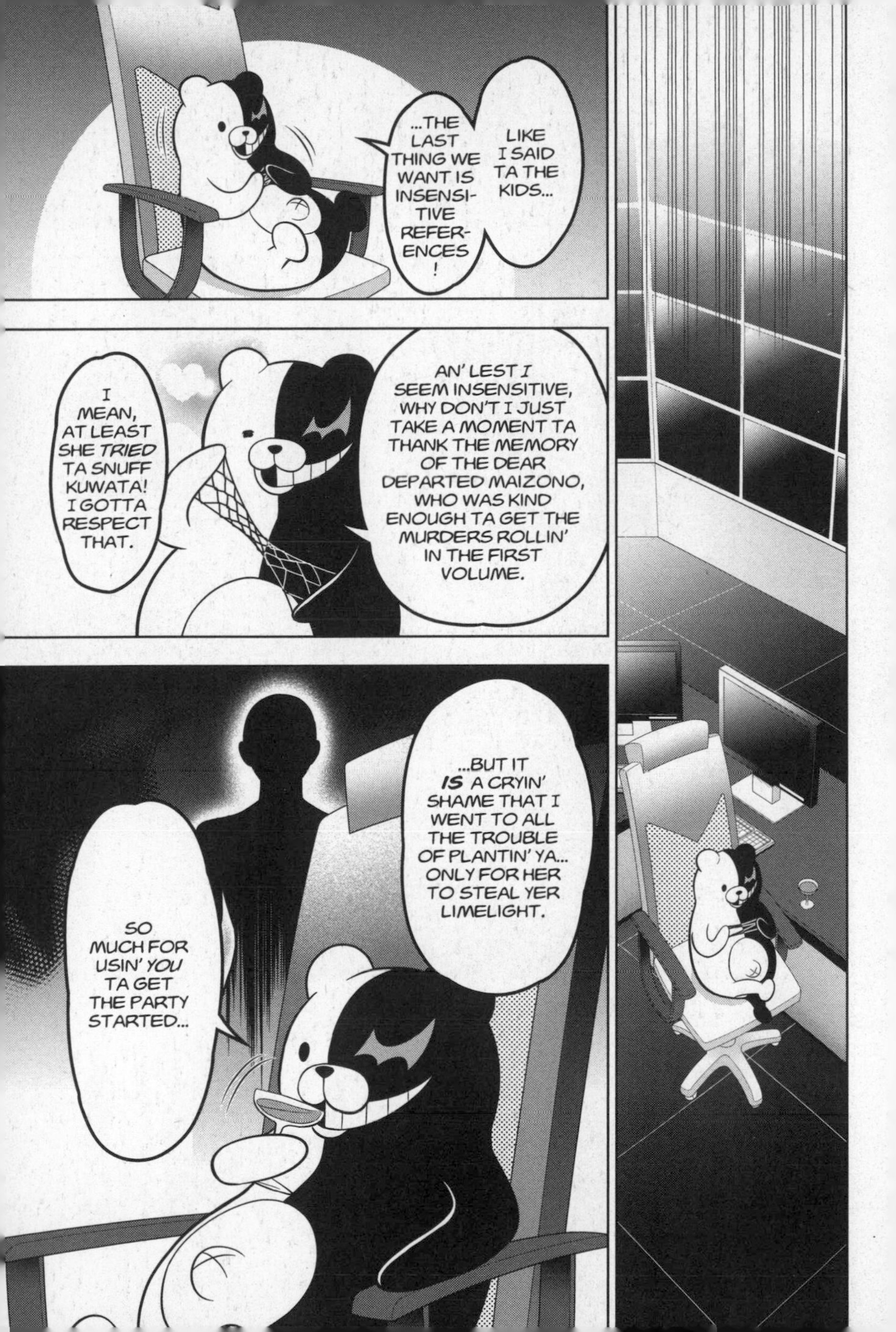
LIKE I SAID TA THE KIDS...
...THE LAST THING WE WANT IS INSENSI-TIVE REFER-ENCES!
AN' LEST *I* SEEM INSENSITIVE, WHY DON'T I JUST TAKE A MOMENT TA THANK THE MEMORY OF THE DEAR DEPARTED MAIZONO, WHO WAS KIND ENOUGH TA GET THE MURDERS ROLLIN' IN THE FIRST VOLUME.
I MEAN, AT LEAST SHE *TRIED* TA SNUFF KUWATA! I GOTTA RESPECT THAT.
...BUT IT ***IS*** A CRYIN' SHAME THAT I WENT TO ALL THE TROUBLE OF PLANTIN' YA... ONLY FOR HER TO STEAL YER LIMELIGHT.
SO MUCH FOR USIN' *YOU* TA GET THE PARTY STARTED...

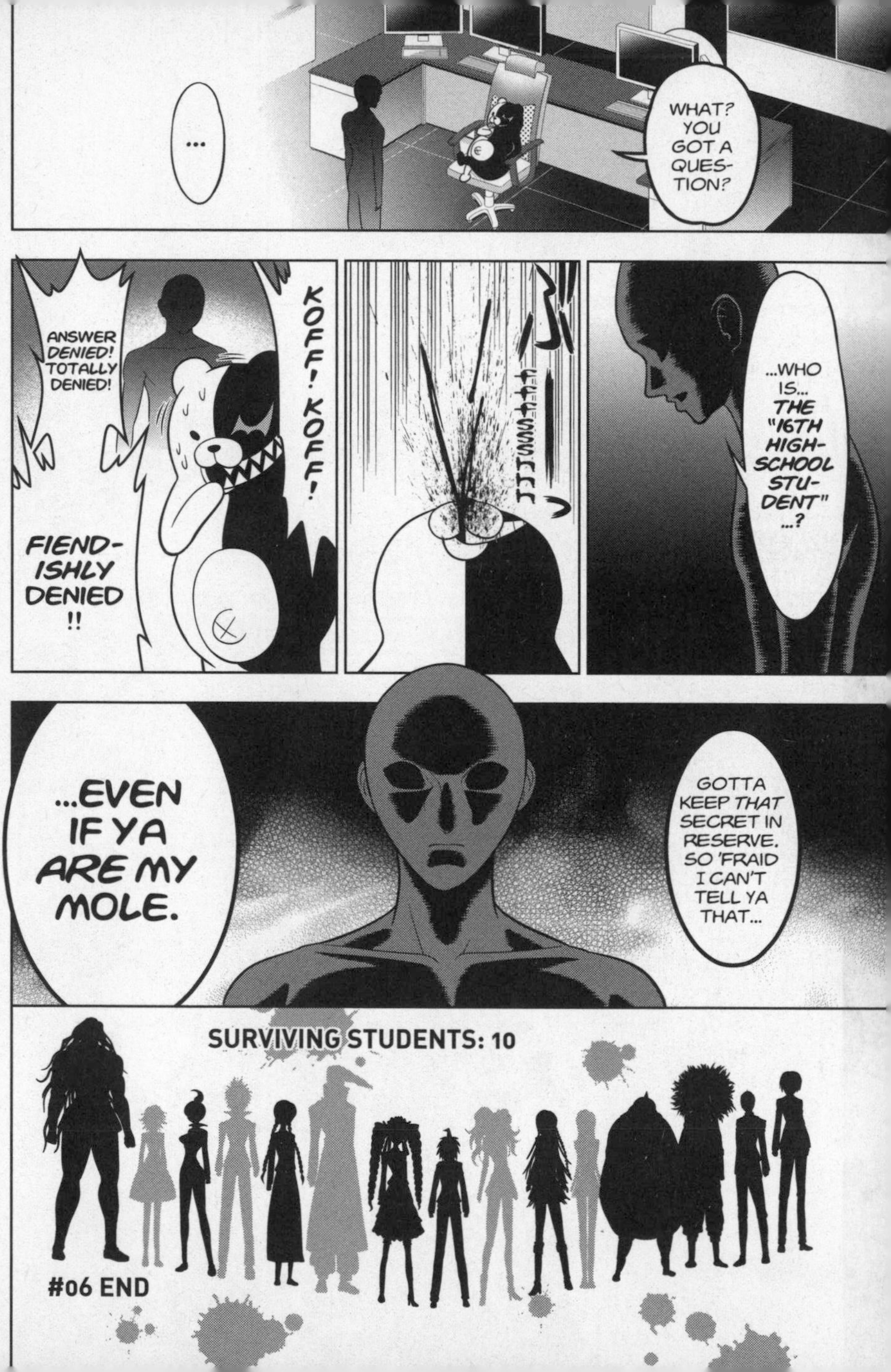

WHAT? YOU GOT A QUES-TION?
...
...WHO IS... *THE "16TH HIGH-SCHOOL STU-DENT"* ...?
KOFF! KOFF!
ANSWER DENIED! TOTALLY DENIED!
FIEND-ISHLY DENIED !!
GOTTA KEEP *THAT* SECRET IN RESERVE. SO 'FRAID I CAN'T TELL YA THAT...
...EVEN IF YA *ARE* MY MOLE.
SURVIVING STUDENTS: 10
#06 END

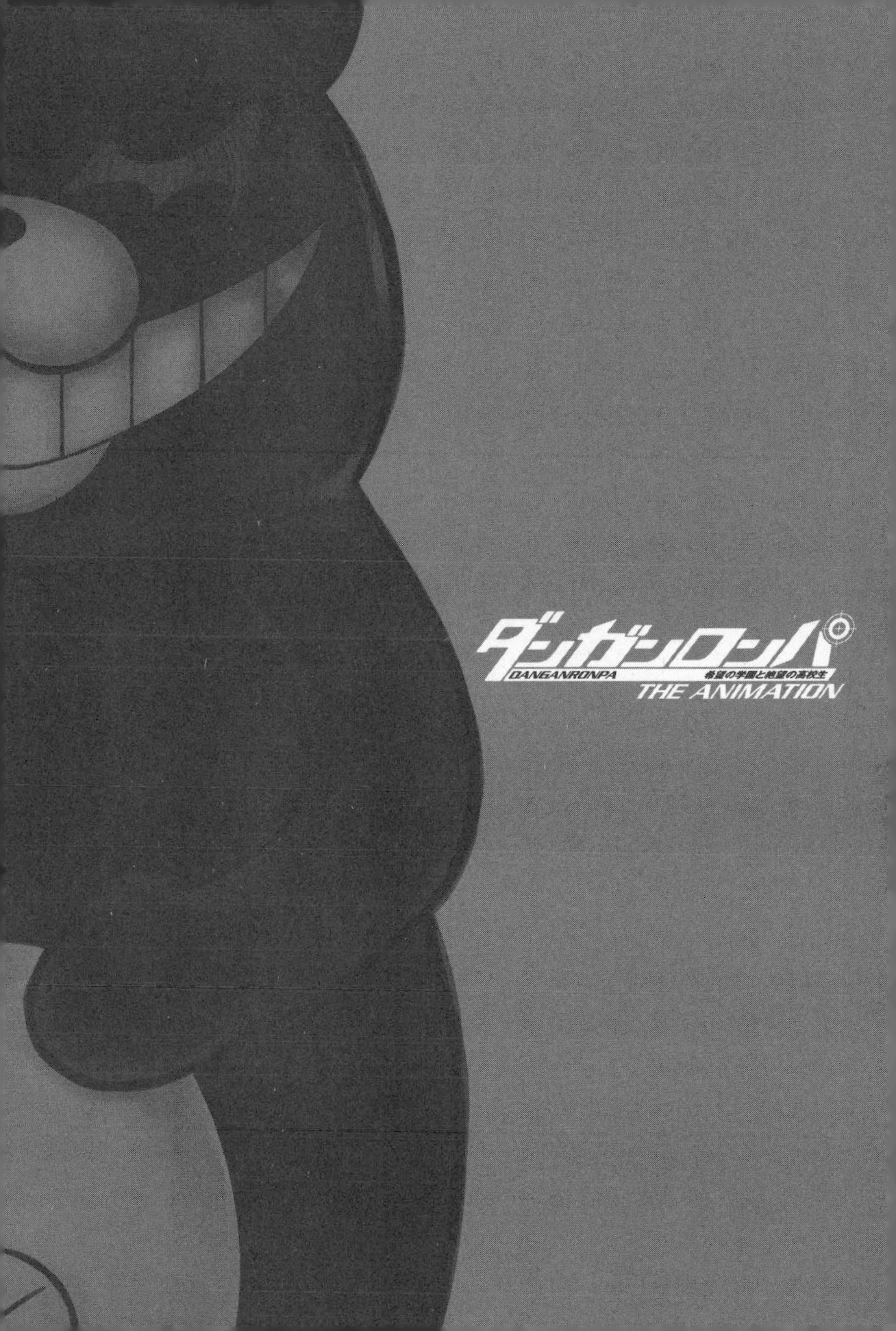
ダンガンロンパ
DANGANRONPA
希望の学園と絶望の高校生
THE ANIMATION

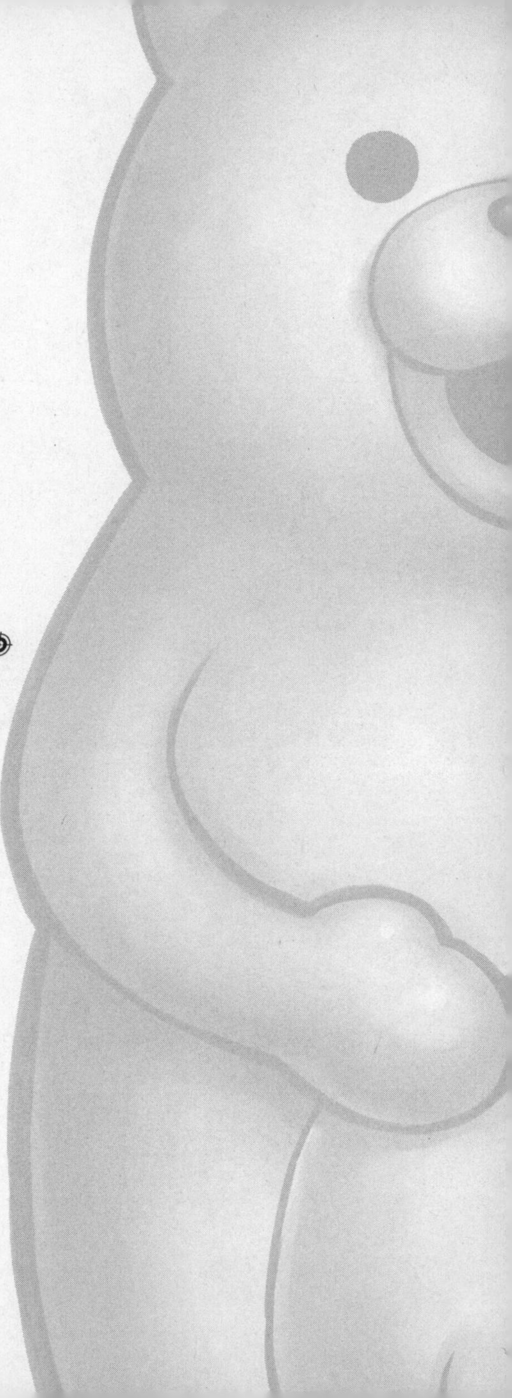

DANGANRONPA
A SCHOOL OF HOPE . . . WITH STUDENTS OF DESPAIR!
THE ANIMATION

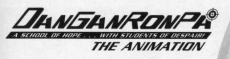

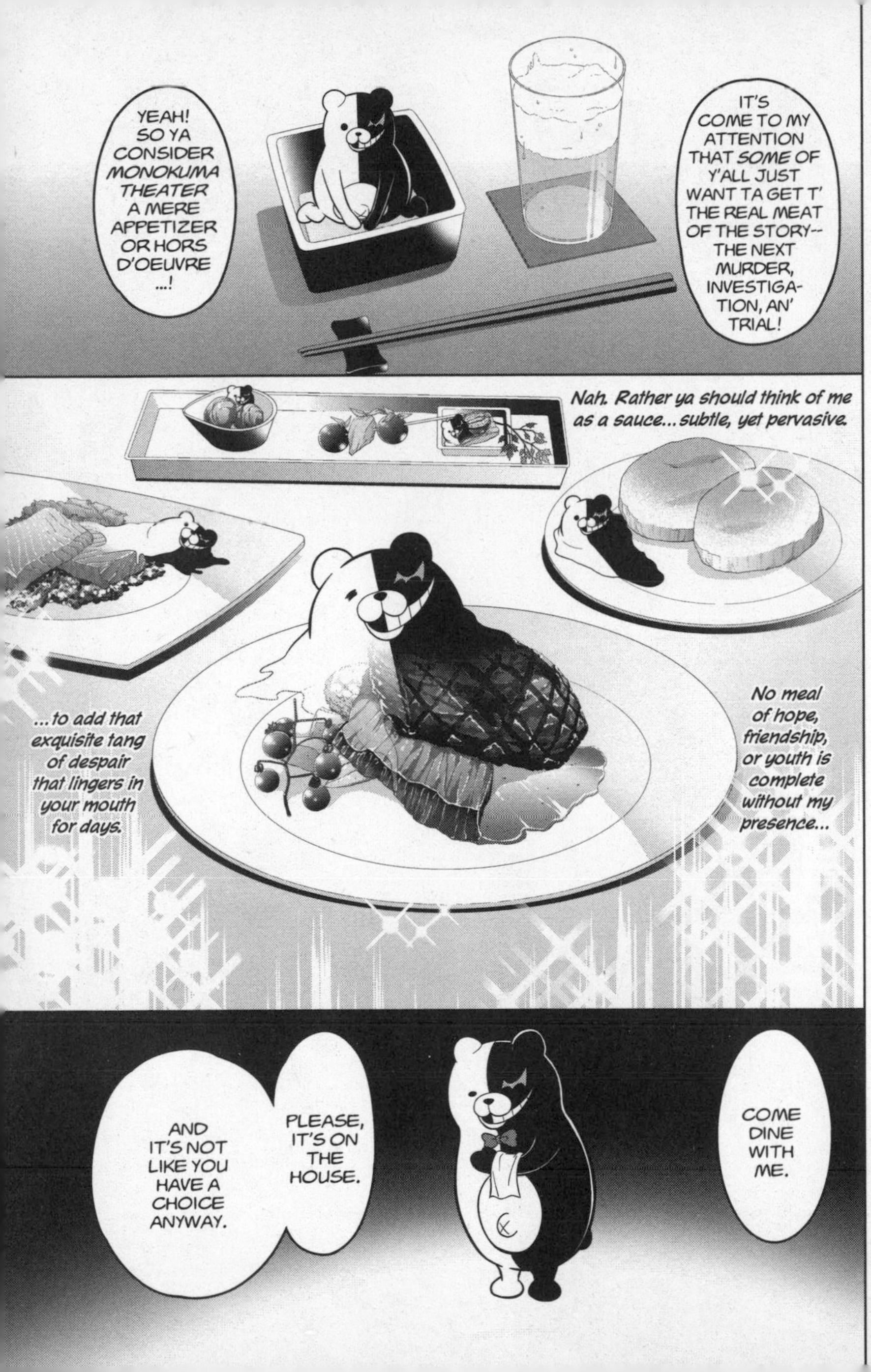
IT'S COME TO MY ATTENTION THAT *SOME* OF Y'ALL JUST WANT TA GET T' THE REAL MEAT OF THE STORY-- THE NEXT MURDER, INVESTIGATION, AN' TRIAL!
YEAH! SO YA CONSIDER *MONOKUMA THEATER* A MERE APPETIZER OR HORS D'OEUVRE ...!
Nah. Rather ya should think of me as a sauce... subtle, yet pervasive.
No meal of hope, friendship, or youth is complete without my presence...
...to add that exquisite tang of despair that lingers in your mouth for days.
COME DINE WITH ME.
PLEASE, IT'S ON THE HOUSE.
AND IT'S NOT LIKE YOU HAVE A CHOICE ANYWAY.

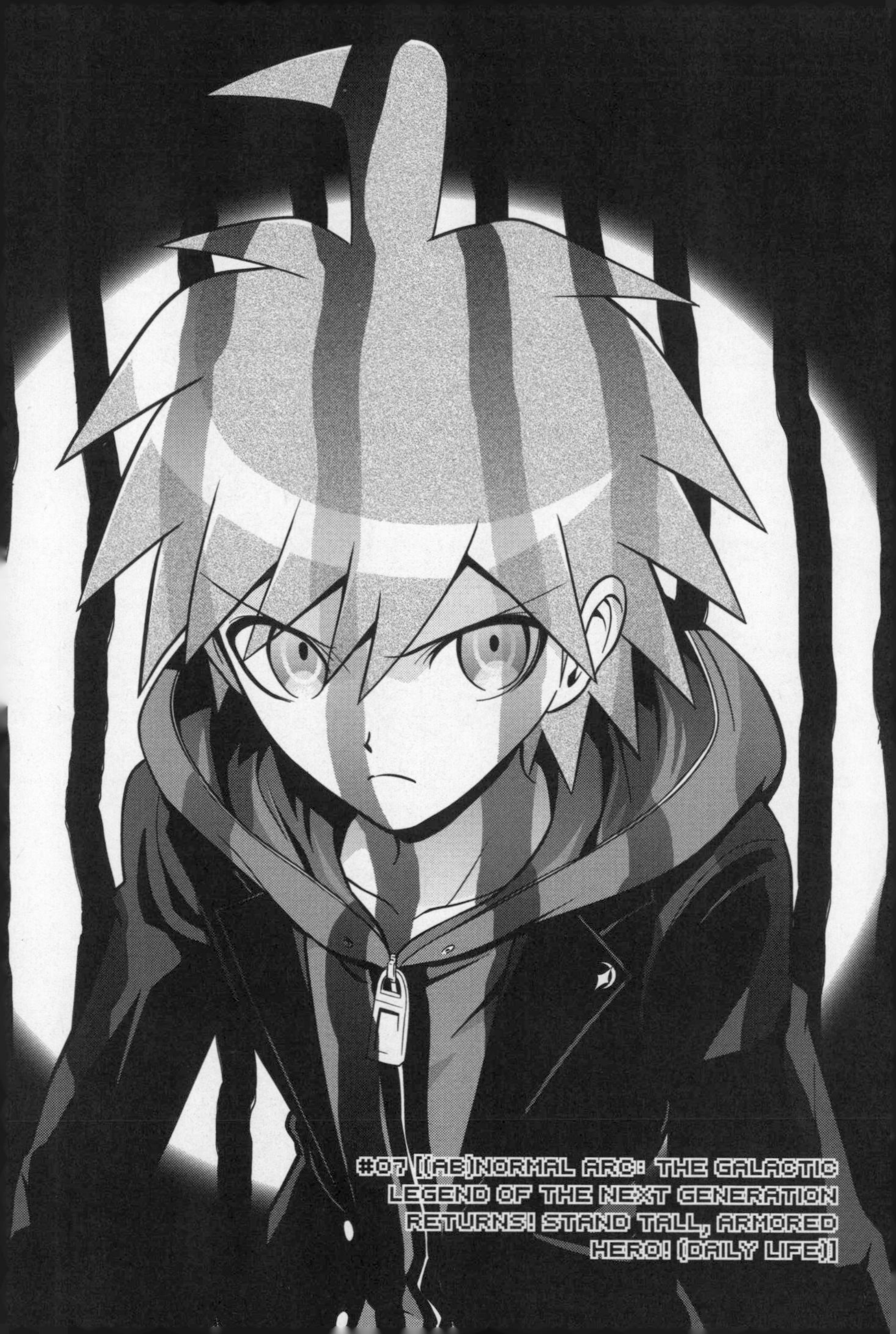
#07 [(AB)NORMAL ARC: THE GALACTIC
LEGEND OF THE NEXT GENERATION
RETURNS! STAND TALL, ARMORED
HERO! (DAILY LIFE)]

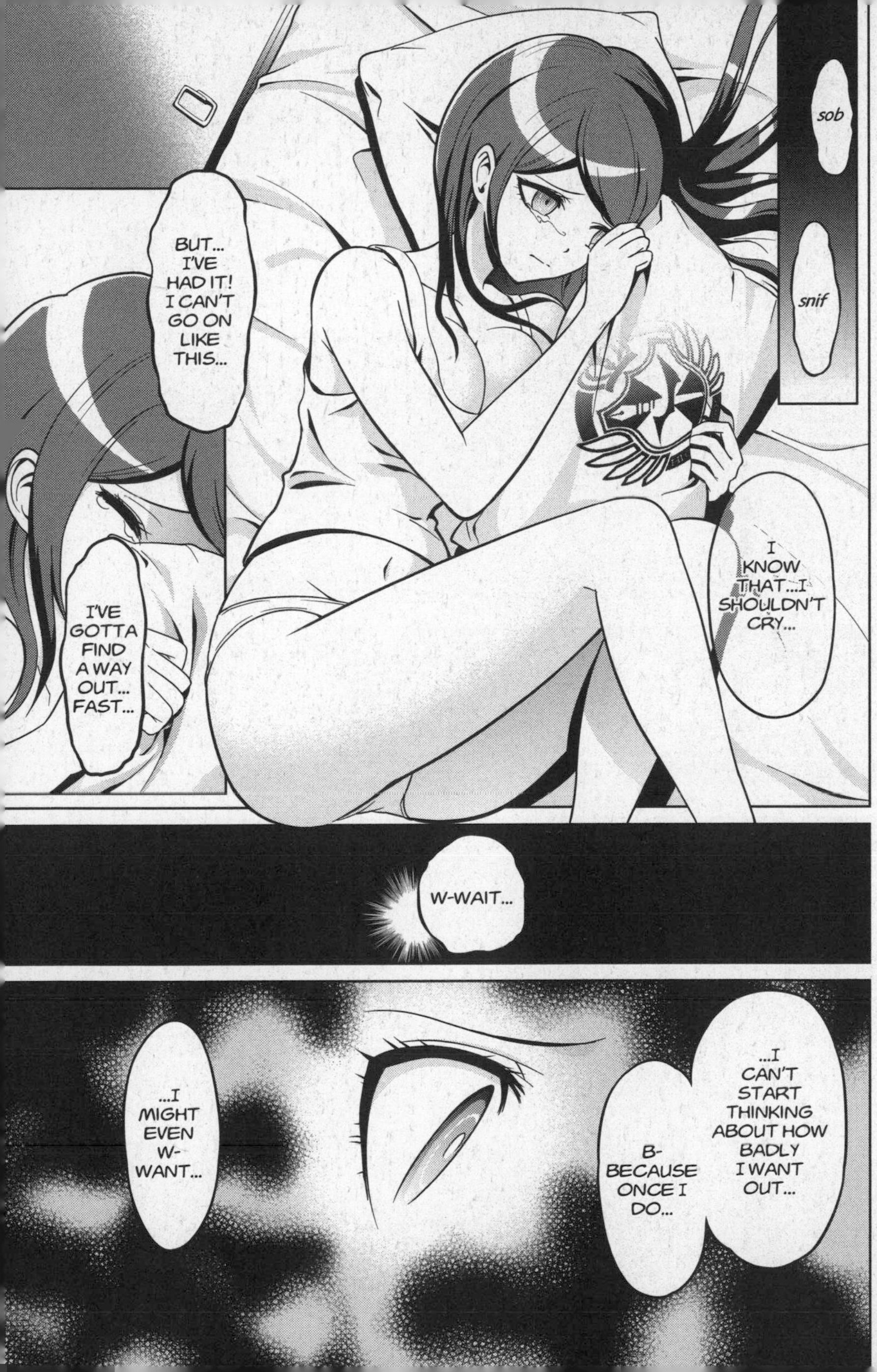
sob
snif
I KNOW THAT...I SHOULDN'T CRY...
BUT... I'VE HAD IT! I CAN'T GO ON LIKE THIS...
I'VE GOTTA FIND A WAY OUT... FAST...
W-WAIT...
...I CAN'T START THINKING ABOUT HOW BADLY I WANT OUT...
B-BECAUSE ONCE I DO...
...I MIGHT EVEN W-WANT...

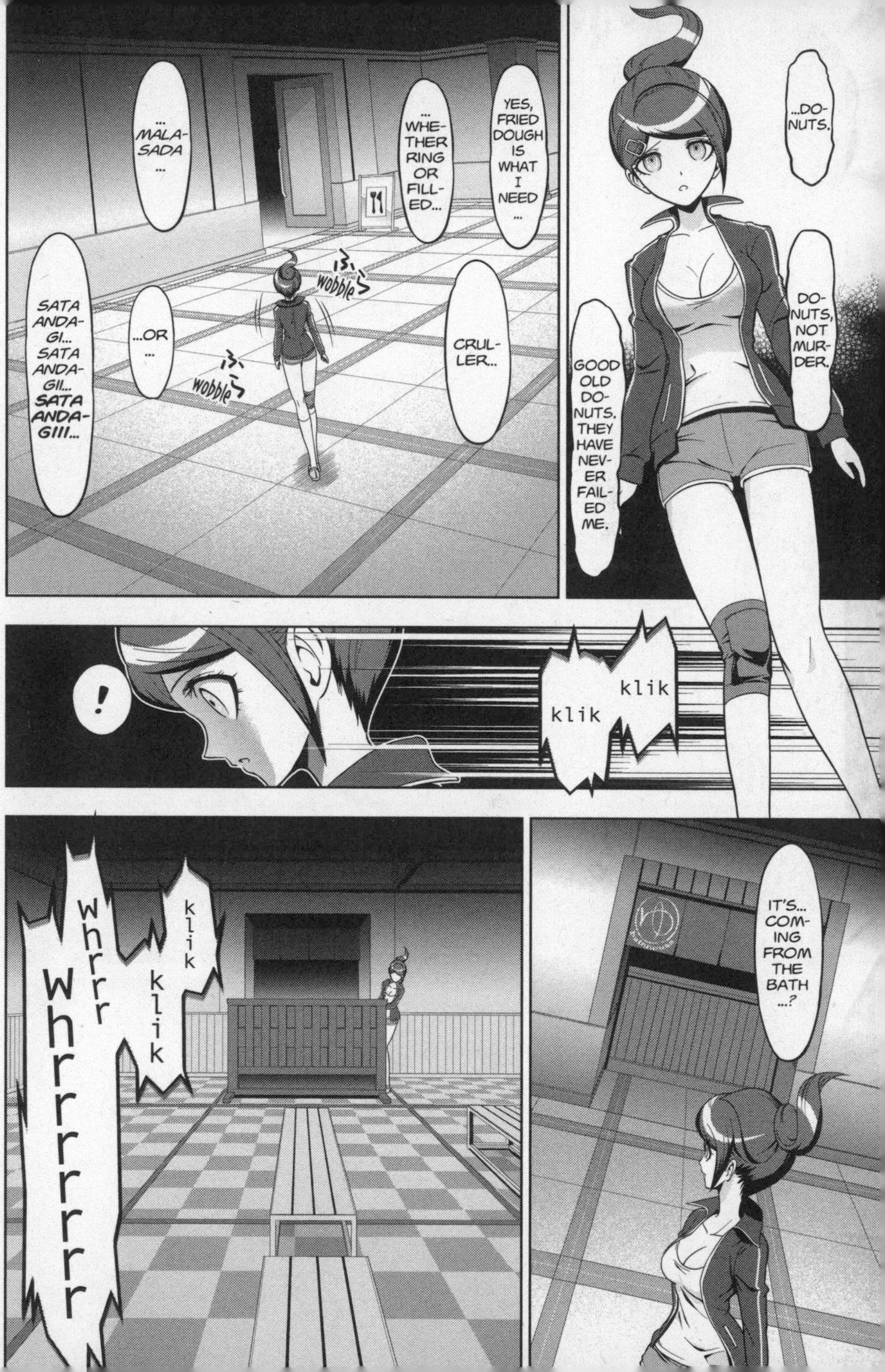
...DONUTS.
DONUTS, NOT MURDER.
GOOD OLD DONUTS. THEY HAVE NEVER FAILED ME.
YES, FRIED DOUGH IS WHAT I NEED...
...WHETHER RING OR FILLED...
...MALASADA...
CRULLER...
wobble
wobble
...OR...
SATA ANDAGI... SATA ANDAGI... **SATA ANDAGIII...**
klik
klik
!
IT'S... COMING FROM THE BATH...?
klik
klik
Whrrr
Whrrrrrrr

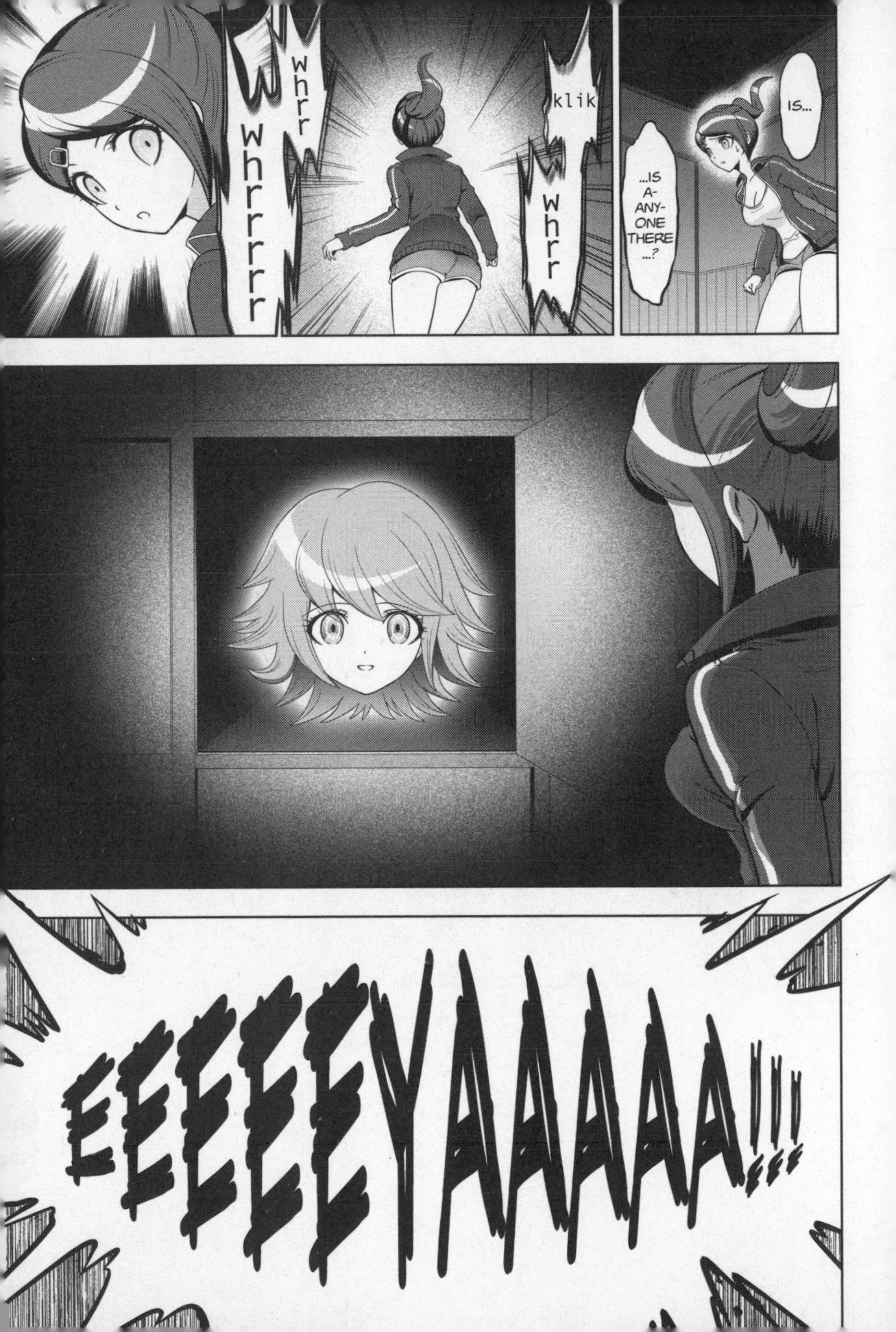
IS...
...IS A-ANYONE THERE ...?
klik
whrr
whrr
whrrrrr
EEEEEYAAAAA!!!

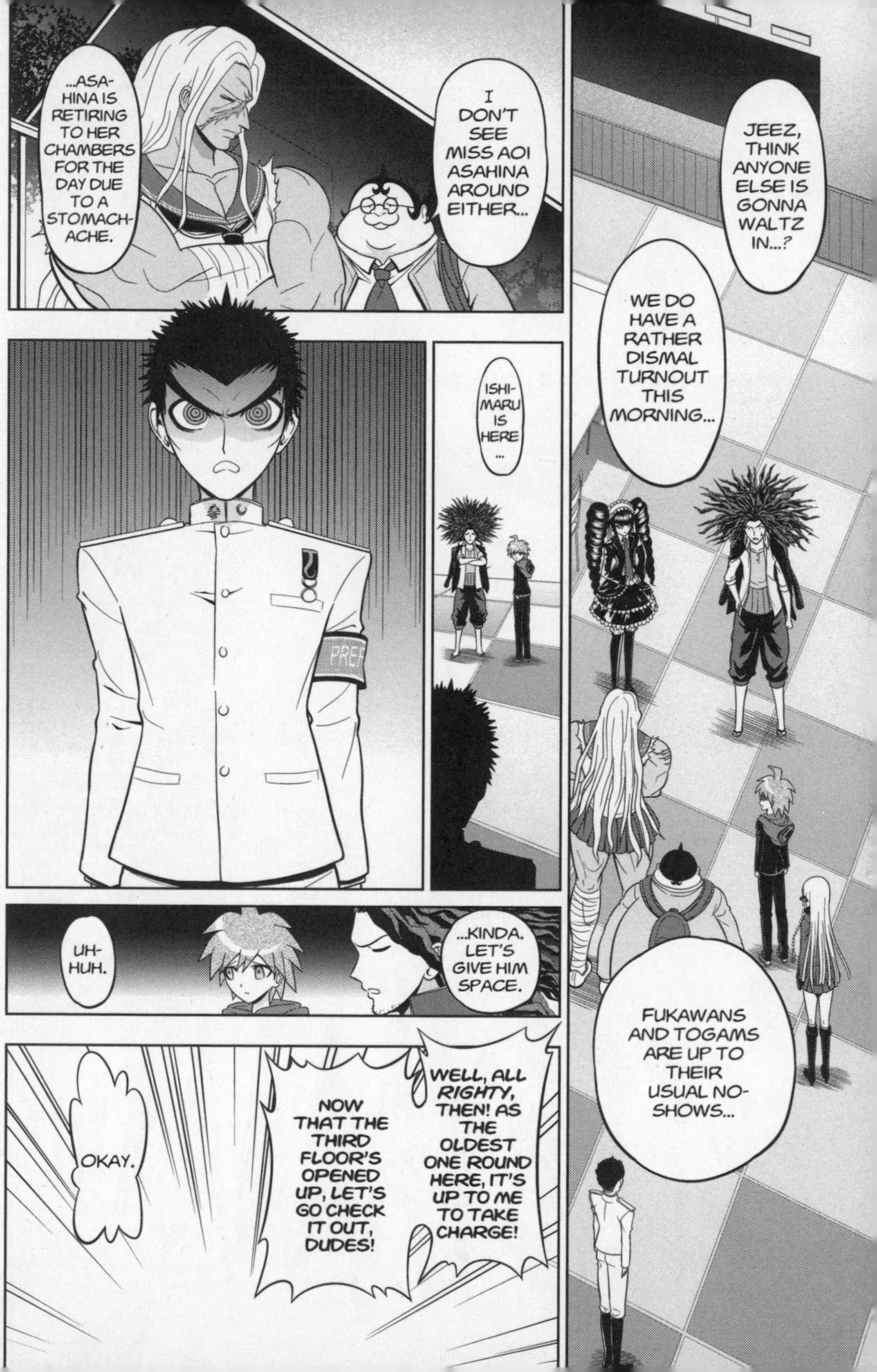
JEEZ, THINK ANYONE ELSE IS GONNA WALTZ IN...?
WE DO HAVE A RATHER DISMAL TURNOUT THIS MORNING...
FUKAWANS AND TOGAMS ARE UP TO THEIR USUAL NO-SHOWS...
I DON'T SEE MISS AOI ASAHINA AROUND EITHER...
...ASAHINA IS RETIRING TO HER CHAMBERS FOR THE DAY DUE TO A STOMACHACHE.
ISHIMARU IS HERE...
...KINDA. LET'S GIVE HIM SPACE.
UH-HUH.
WELL, ALL RIGHTY, THEN! AS THE OLDEST ONE ROUND HERE, IT'S UP TO ME TO TAKE CHARGE!
NOW THAT THE THIRD FLOOR'S OPENED UP, LET'S GO CHECK IT OUT, DUDES!
OKAY.

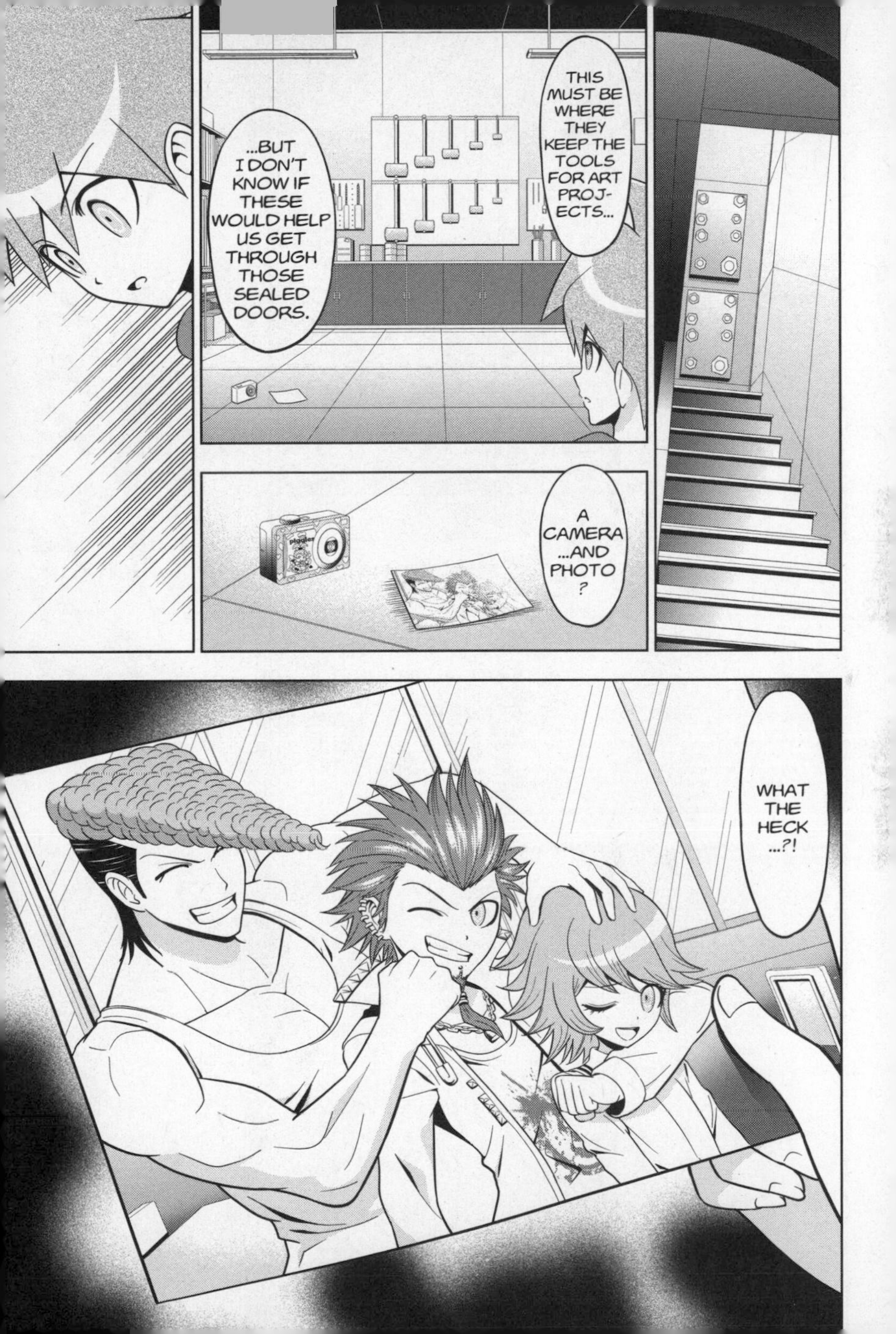
THIS MUST BE WHERE THEY KEEP THE TOOLS FOR ART PROJ-ECTS...
...BUT I DON'T KNOW IF THESE WOULD HELP US GET THROUGH THOSE SEALED DOORS.
A CAMERA ...AND PHOTO ?
WHAT THE HECK ...?!

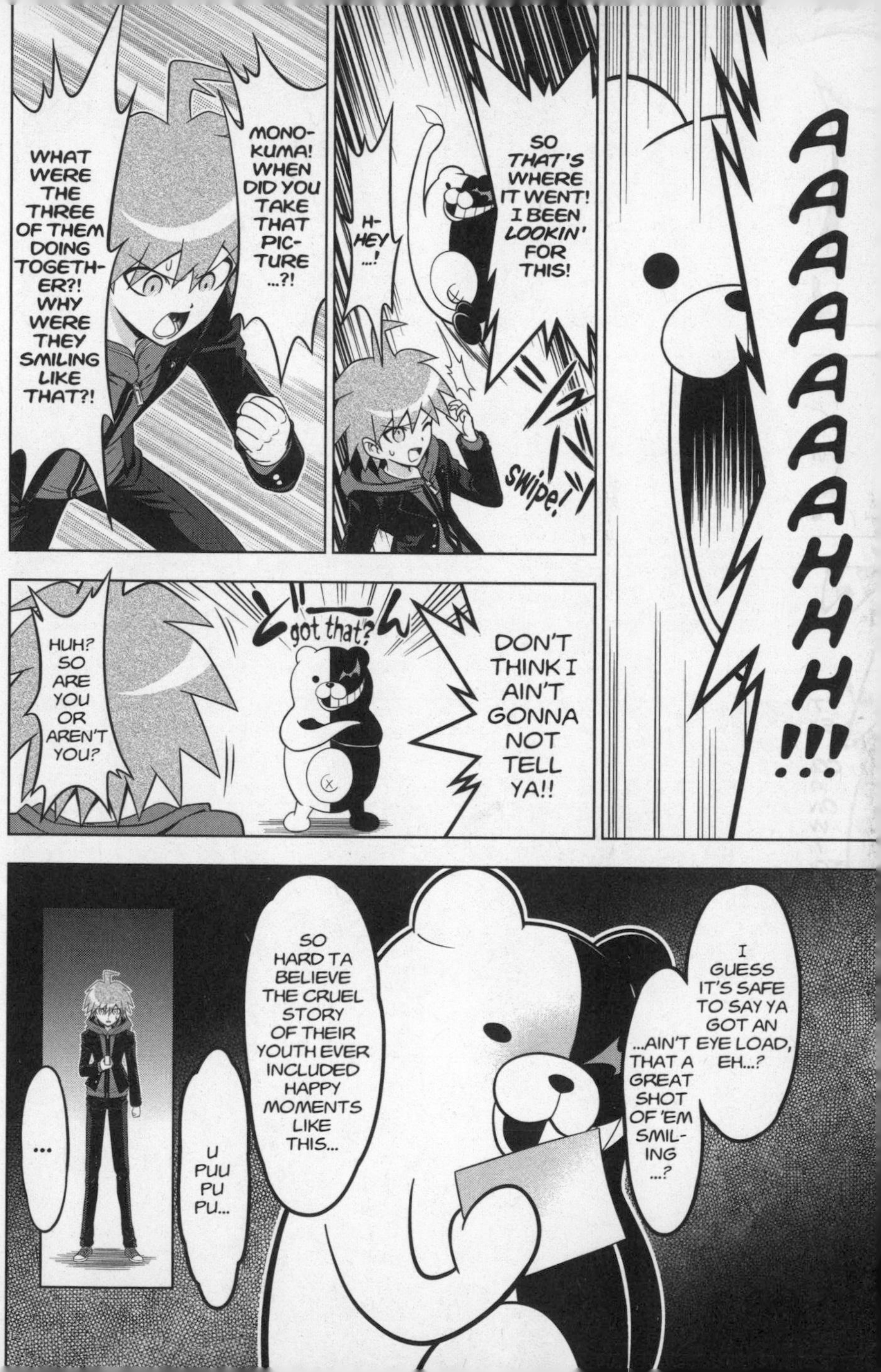

AAAAAAAAH!!!
SO THAT'S WHERE IT WENT! I BEEN LOOKIN' FOR THIS!
H-HEY ...!
swipe!
MONOKUMA! WHEN DID YOU TAKE THAT PICTURE ...?!
WHAT WERE THE THREE OF THEM DOING TOGETHER?! WHY WERE THEY SMILING LIKE THAT?!
DON'T THINK I AIN'T GONNA NOT TELL YA!!
got that?
HUH? SO ARE YOU OR AREN'T YOU?
I GUESS IT'S SAFE TO SAY YA GOT AN EYE LOAD, EH...?
...AIN'T THAT A GREAT SHOT OF 'EM SMILING ...?
SO HARD TA BELIEVE THE CRUEL STORY OF THEIR YOUTH EVER INCLUDED HAPPY MOMENTS LIKE THIS...
U PUU PU PU...
...

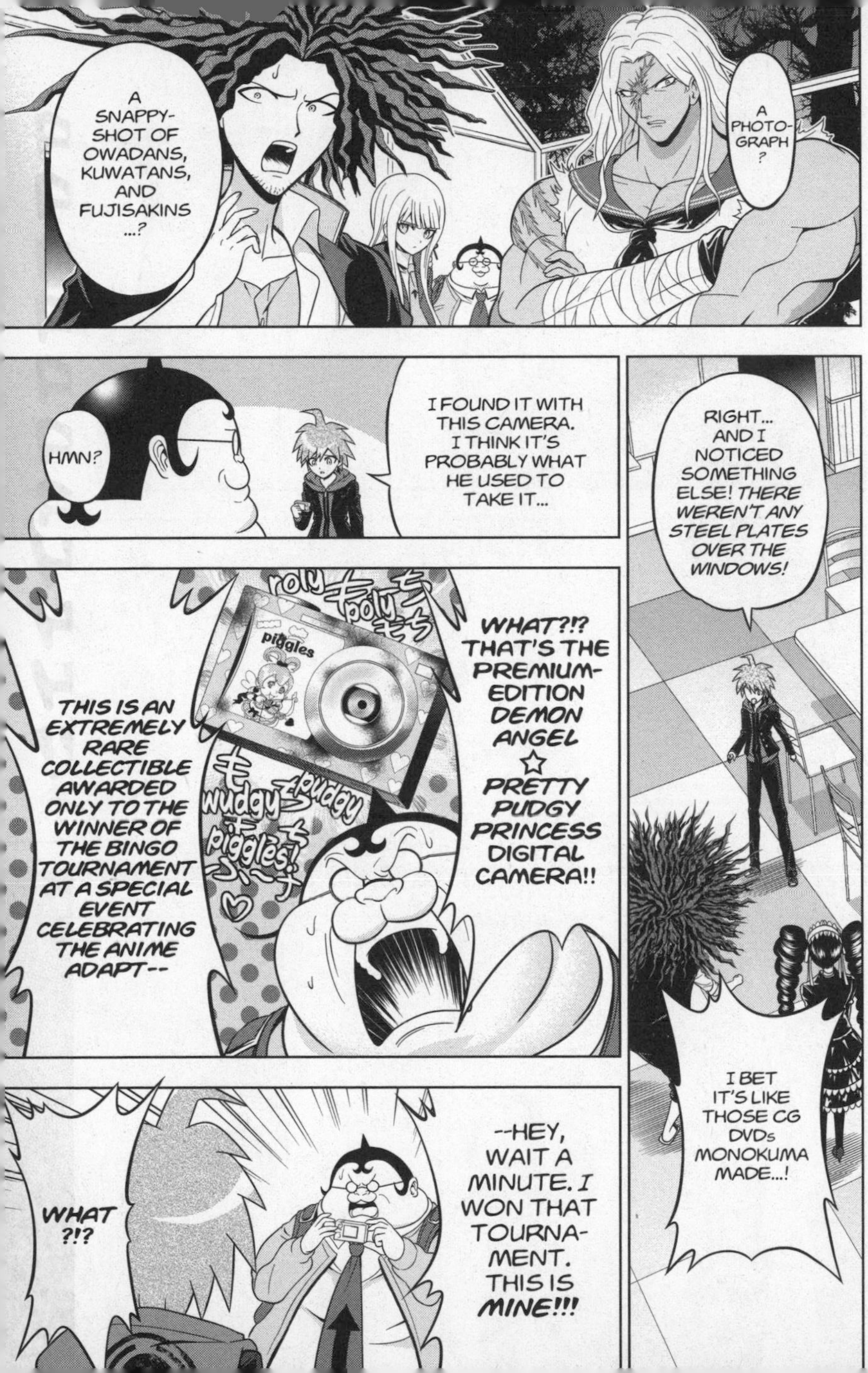

A PHOTOGRAPH?
A SNAPPY-SHOT OF OWADANS, KUWATANS, AND FUJISAKINS ...?
RIGHT... AND I NOTICED SOMETHING ELSE! THERE WEREN'T ANY STEEL PLATES OVER THE WINDOWS!
I BET IT'S LIKE THOSE CG DVDs MONOKUMA MADE...!
I FOUND IT WITH THIS CAMERA. I THINK IT'S PROBABLY WHAT HE USED TO TAKE IT...
HMN?
roly poly
piggles
WHAT?!? THAT'S THE PREMIUM-EDITION DEMON ANGEL ☆ PRETTY PUDGY PRINCESS DIGITAL CAMERA!!
THIS IS AN EXTREMELY RARE COLLECTIBLE AWARDED ONLY TO THE WINNER OF THE BINGO TOURNAMENT AT A SPECIAL EVENT CELEBRATING THE ANIME ADAPT--
wudgy pudgy piggles!
--HEY, WAIT A MINUTE. I WON THAT TOURNAMENT. THIS IS MINE!!!
WHAT?!?

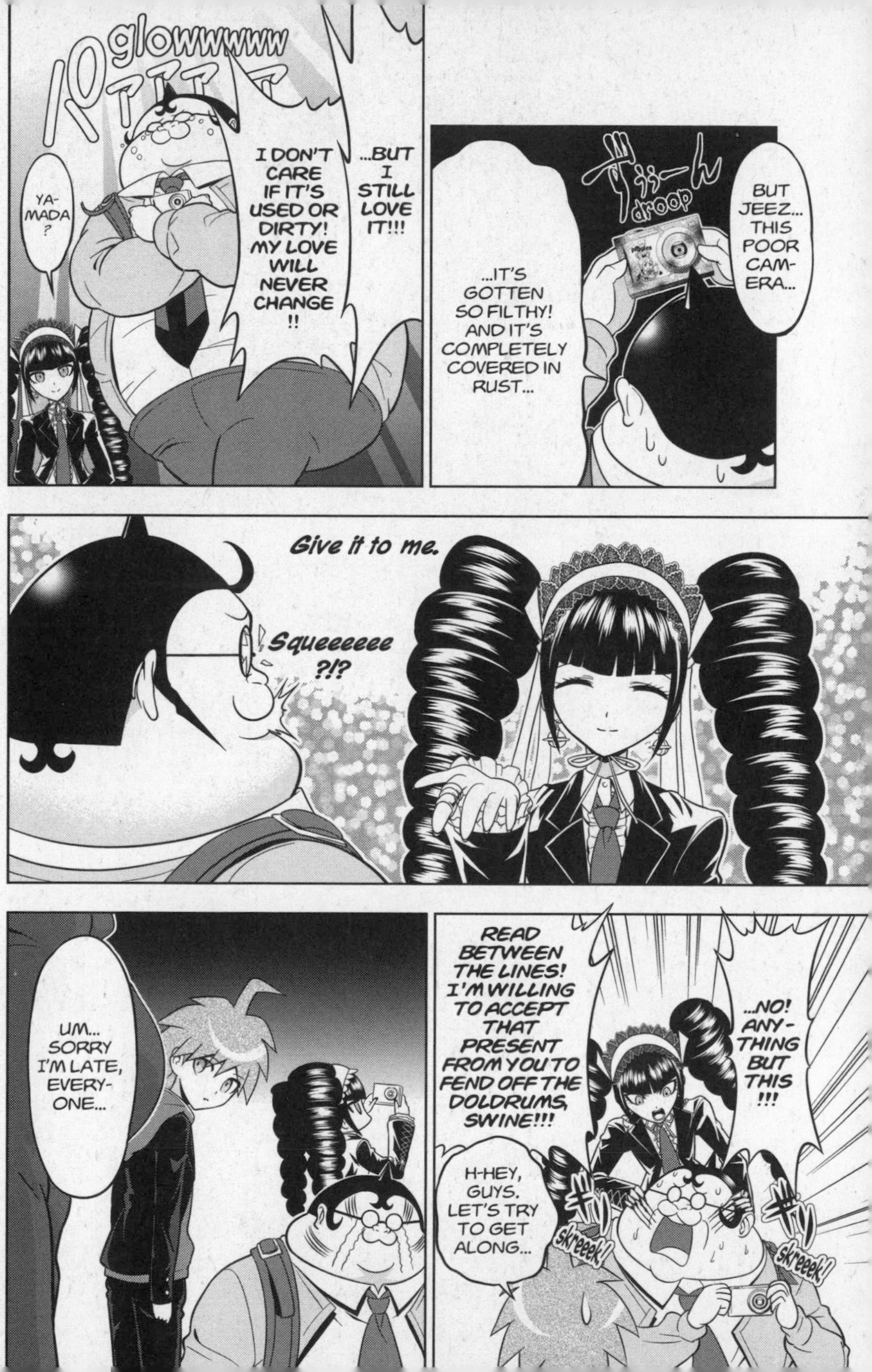

droop
BUT JEEZ... THIS POOR CAMERA...
...IT'S GOTTEN SO FILTHY! AND IT'S COMPLETELY COVERED IN RUST...
glowwwww
...BUT I STILL LOVE IT!!!
I DON'T CARE IF IT'S USED OR DIRTY! MY LOVE WILL NEVER CHANGE !!
YA-MADA ?
Give it to me.
Squeeeeee ?!?
...NO! ANYTHING BUT THIS !!!
READ BETWEEN THE LINES! I'M WILLING TO ACCEPT THAT PRESENT FROM YOU TO FEND OFF THE DOLDRUMS, SWINE!!!
skreeek!
skreeek!
H-HEY, GUYS. LET'S TRY TO GET ALONG...
UM... SORRY I'M LATE, EVERY-ONE...

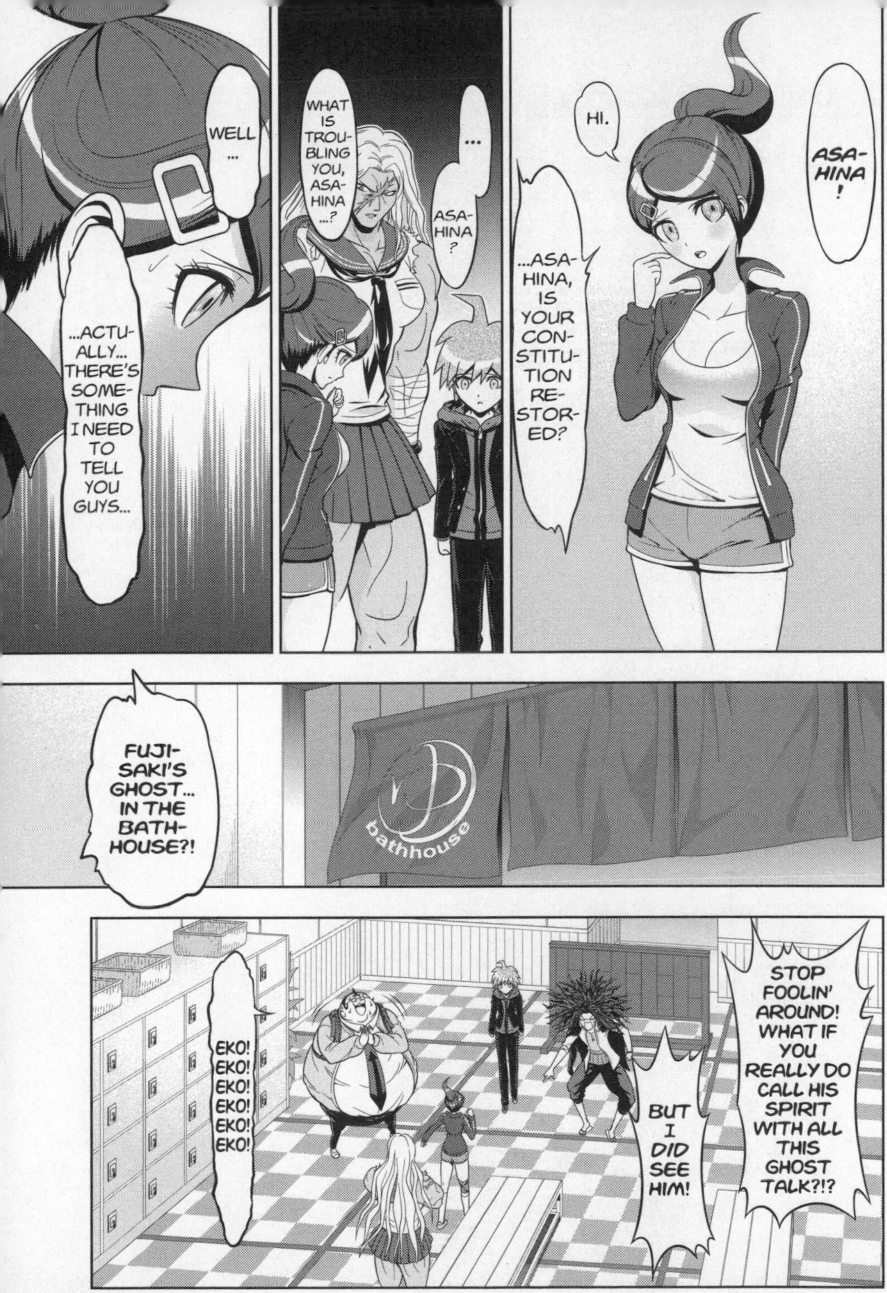
ASA-HINA!
HI.
...ASA-HINA, IS YOUR CON-STITU-TION RE-STOR-ED?
...
ASA-HINA?
WHAT IS TROU-BLING YOU, ASA-HINA...?
WELL...
...ACTU-ALLY... THERE'S SOME-THING I NEED TO TELL YOU GUYS...
FUJI-SAKI'S GHOST... IN THE BATH-HOUSE?!
bathhouse
STOP FOOLIN' AROUND! WHAT IF YOU REALLY DO CALL HIS SPIRIT WITH ALL THIS GHOST TALK?!?
BUT I DID SEE HIM!
EKO! EKO! EKO! EKO! EKO! EKO!

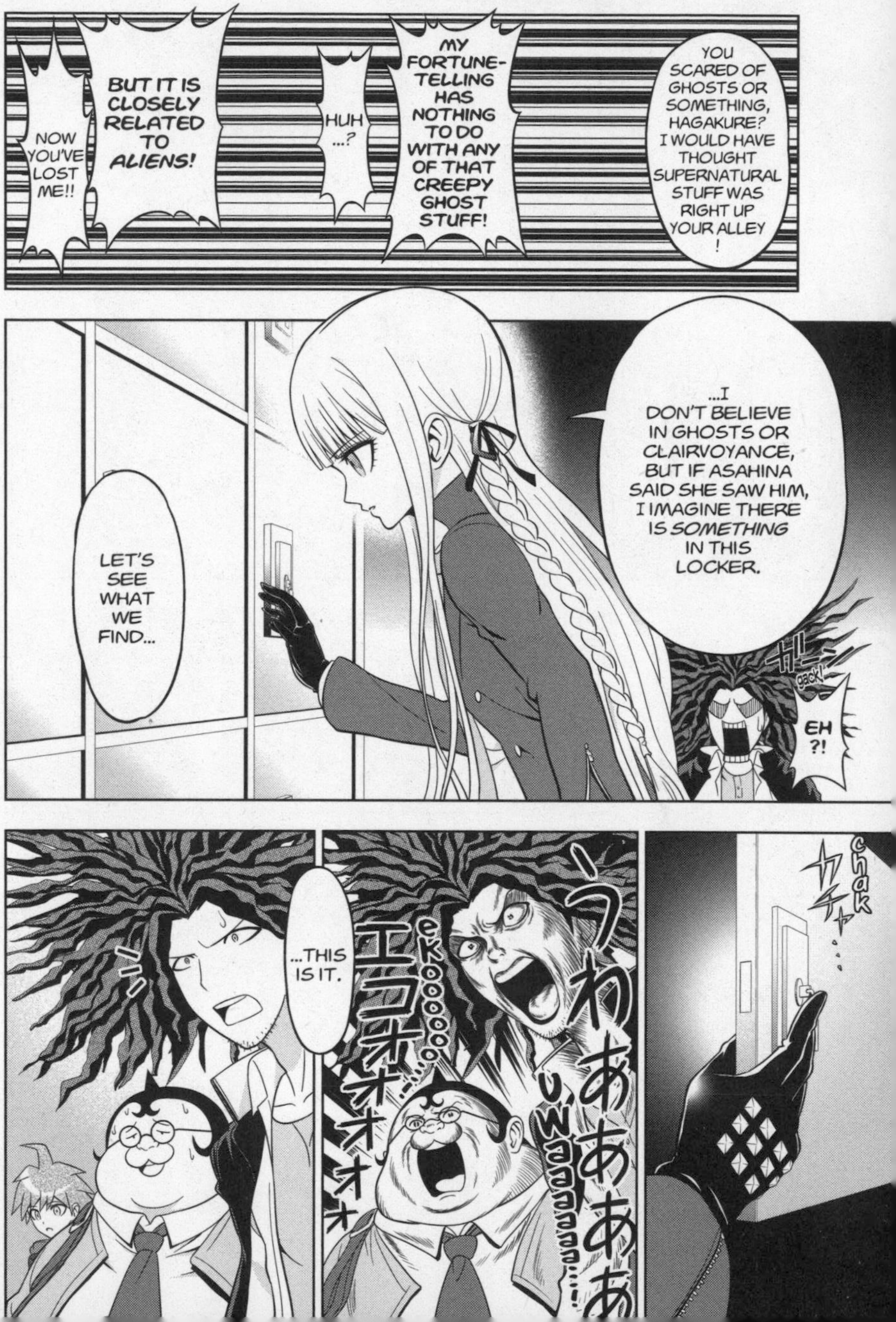
YOU SCARED OF GHOSTS OR SOMETHING, HAGAKURE? I WOULD HAVE THOUGHT SUPERNATURAL STUFF WAS RIGHT UP YOUR ALLEY!
MY FORTUNE-TELLING HAS NOTHING TO DO WITH ANY OF THAT CREEPY GHOST STUFF!
HUH ...?
BUT IT IS CLOSELY RELATED TO ALIENS!
NOW YOU'VE LOST ME!!
...I DON'T BELIEVE IN GHOSTS OR CLAIRVOYANCE, BUT IF ASAHINA SAID SHE SAW HIM, I IMAGINE THERE IS SOMETHING IN THIS LOCKER.
gack!
EH ?!
LET'S SEE WHAT WE FIND...
chak
uwaaaaaa...!
ekoooooo...!
...THIS IS IT.

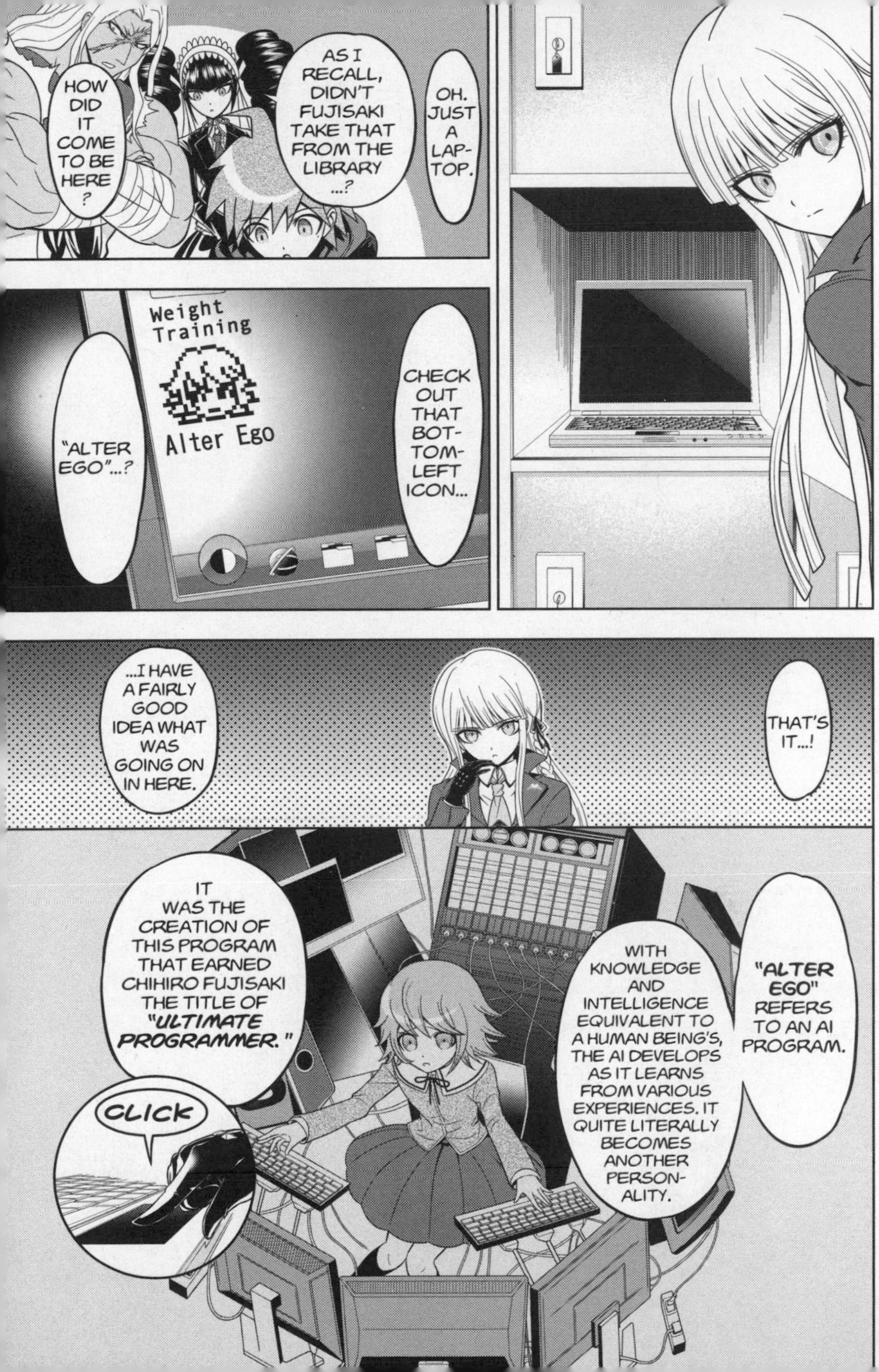
OH. JUST A LAPTOP.
AS I RECALL, DIDN'T FUJISAKI TAKE THAT FROM THE LIBRARY ...?
HOW DID IT COME TO BE HERE ?
CHECK OUT THAT BOTTOM-LEFT ICON...
Weight Training
Alter Ego
"ALTER EGO"...?
THAT'S IT...!
...I HAVE A FAIRLY GOOD IDEA WHAT WAS GOING ON IN HERE.
"ALTER EGO" REFERS TO AN AI PROGRAM.
WITH KNOWLEDGE AND INTELLIGENCE EQUIVALENT TO A HUMAN BEING'S, THE AI DEVELOPS AS IT LEARNS FROM VARIOUS EXPERIENCES. IT QUITE LITERALLY BECOMES ANOTHER PERSONALITY.
IT WAS THE CREATION OF THIS PROGRAM THAT EARNED CHIHIRO FUJISAKI THE TITLE OF "ULTIMATE PROGRAMMER."
CLICK

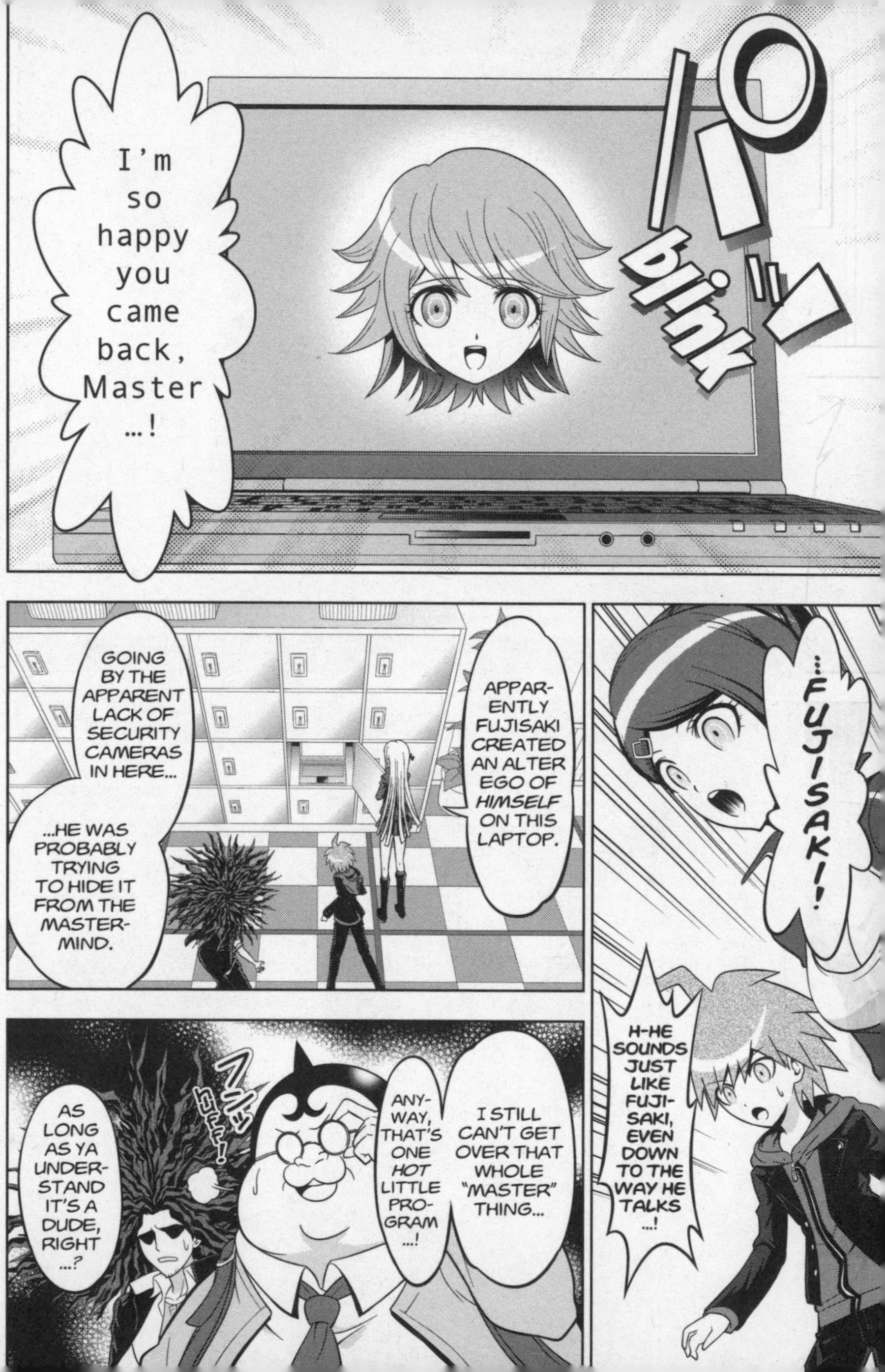
blink
I'm so happy you came back, Master...!
...FUJISAKI...!
H-HE SOUNDS JUST LIKE FUJISAKI, EVEN DOWN TO THE WAY HE TALKS...!
APPARENTLY FUJISAKI CREATED AN ALTER EGO OF *HIMSELF* ON THIS LAPTOP.
GOING BY THE APPARENT LACK OF SECURITY CAMERAS IN HERE...
...HE WAS PROBABLY TRYING TO HIDE IT FROM THE MASTERMIND.
I STILL CAN'T GET OVER THAT WHOLE "MASTER" THING...
ANYWAY, THAT'S ONE *HOT* LITTLE PROGRAM...!
HUFF!
AS LONG AS YA UNDERSTAND IT'S A DUDE, RIGHT...?

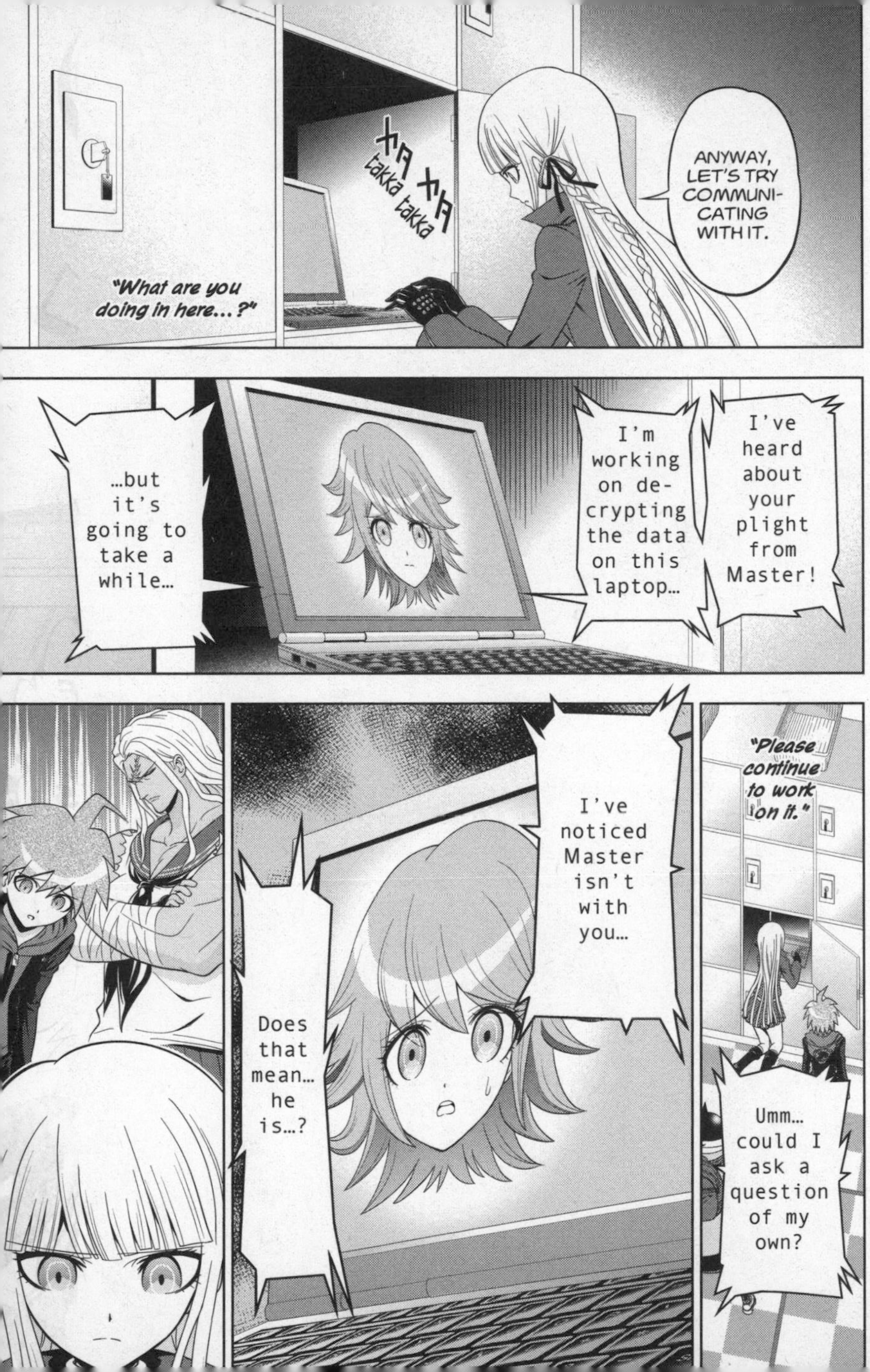
ANYWAY, LET'S TRY COMMUNICATING WITH IT.
カタ カタ takka takka
"What are you doing in here...?"
I've heard about your plight from Master!
I'm working on decrypting the data on this laptop...
...but it's going to take a while...
"Please continue to work on it."
Umm... could I ask a question of my own?
I've noticed Master isn't with you...
Does that mean... he is...?

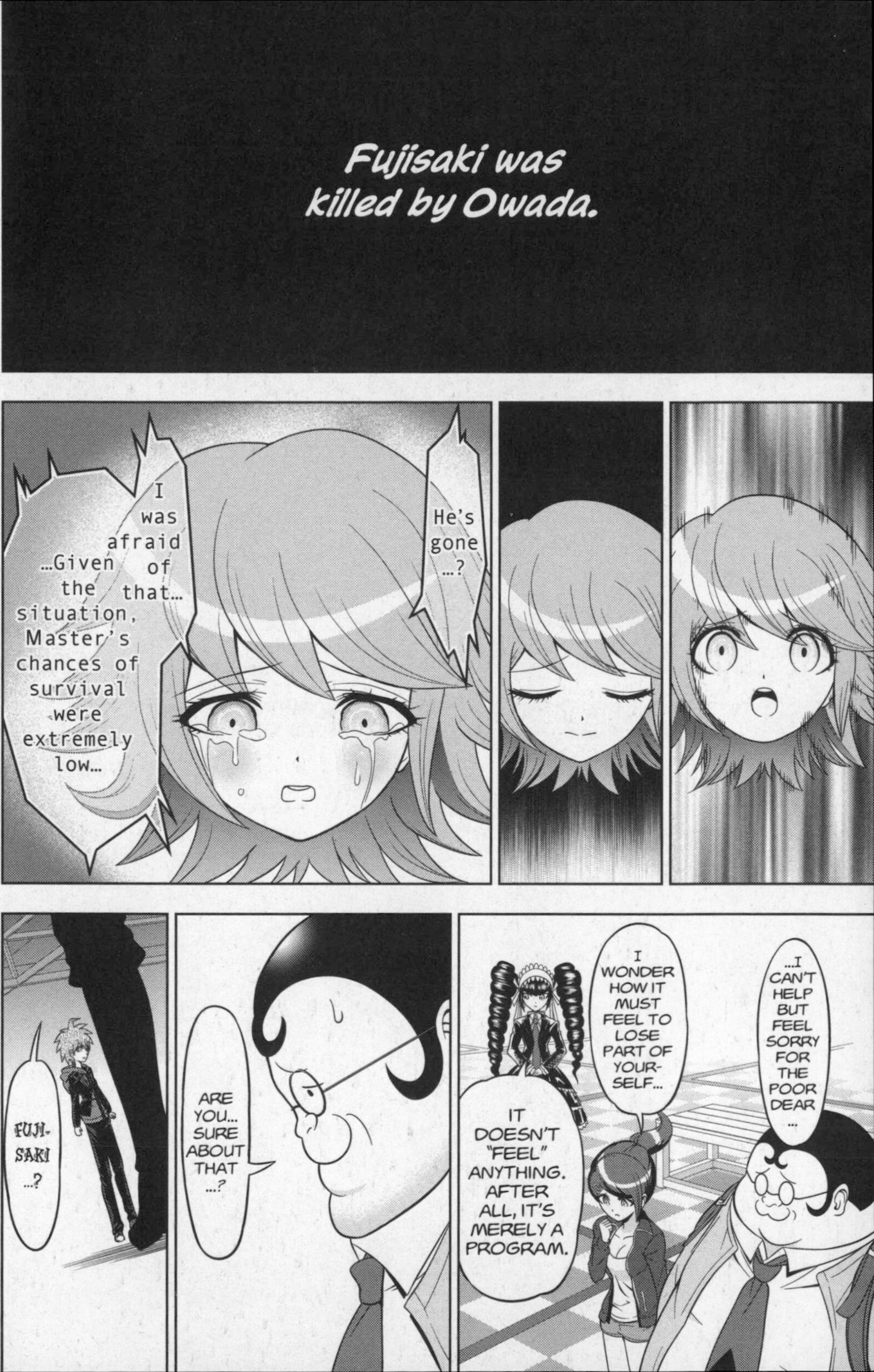

Fujisaki was killed by Owada.
He's gone ...?
I was afraid of that...
...Given the situation, Master's chances of survival were extremely low...
...I CAN'T HELP BUT FEEL SORRY FOR THE POOR DEAR ...
I WONDER HOW IT MUST FEEL TO LOSE PART OF YOUR-SELF...
IT DOESN'T "FEEL" ANYTHING. AFTER ALL, IT'S MERELY A PROGRAM.
ARE YOU... SURE ABOUT THAT ...?
FUJI-SAKI ...?

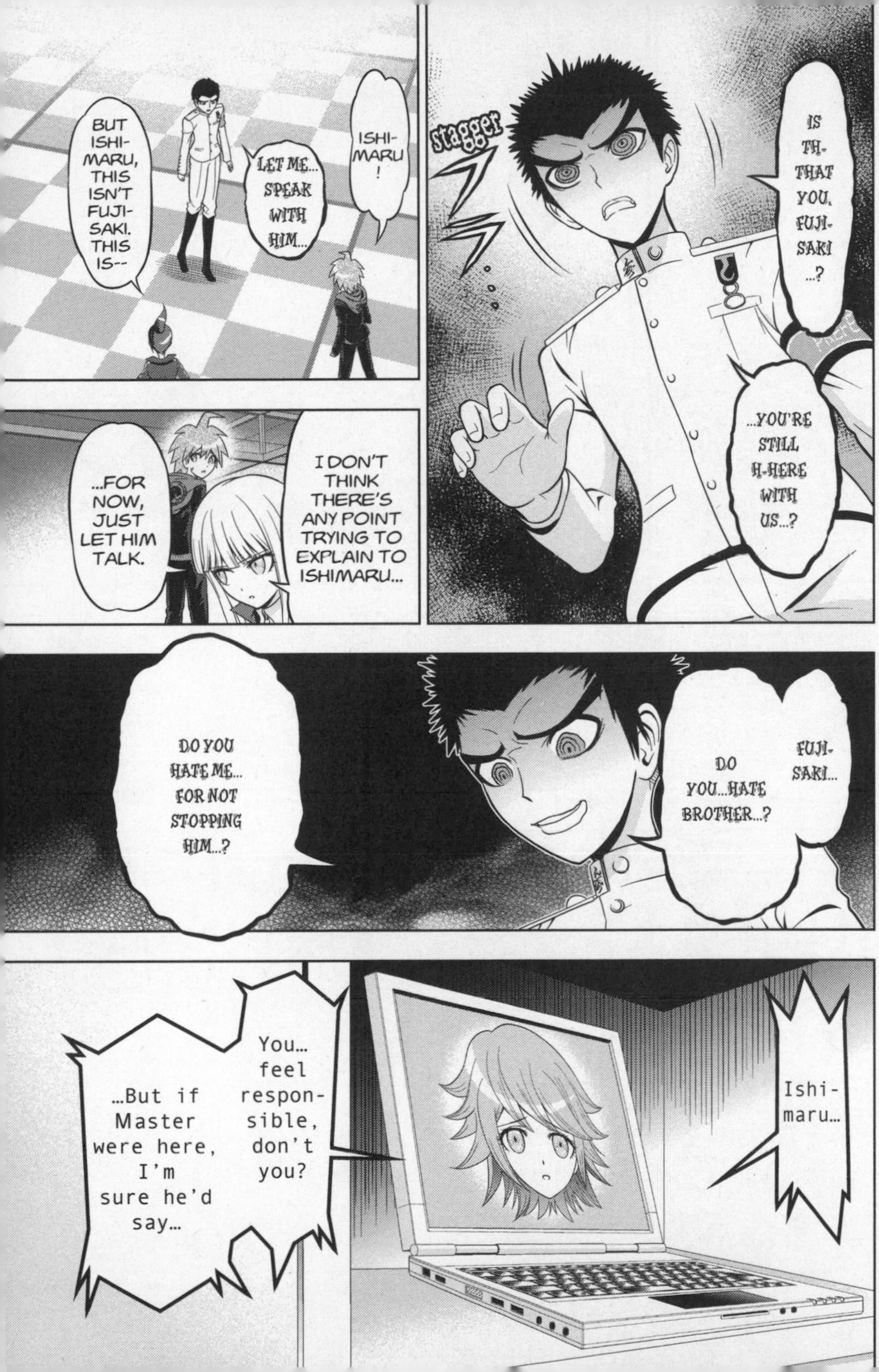
stagger
IS TH-THAT YOU, FUJI-SAKI...?
...YOU'RE STILL H-HERE WITH US...?
ISHI-MARU!
LET ME... SPEAK WITH HIM...
BUT ISHI-MARU, THIS ISN'T FUJI-SAKI. THIS IS--
I DON'T THINK THERE'S ANY POINT TRYING TO EXPLAIN TO ISHIMARU...
...FOR NOW, JUST LET HIM TALK.
FUJI-SAKI...
DO YOU...HATE BROTHER...?
DO YOU HATE ME... FOR NOT STOPPING HIM...?
Ishi-maru...
You... feel respon-sible, don't you?
...But if Master were here, I'm sure he'd say...

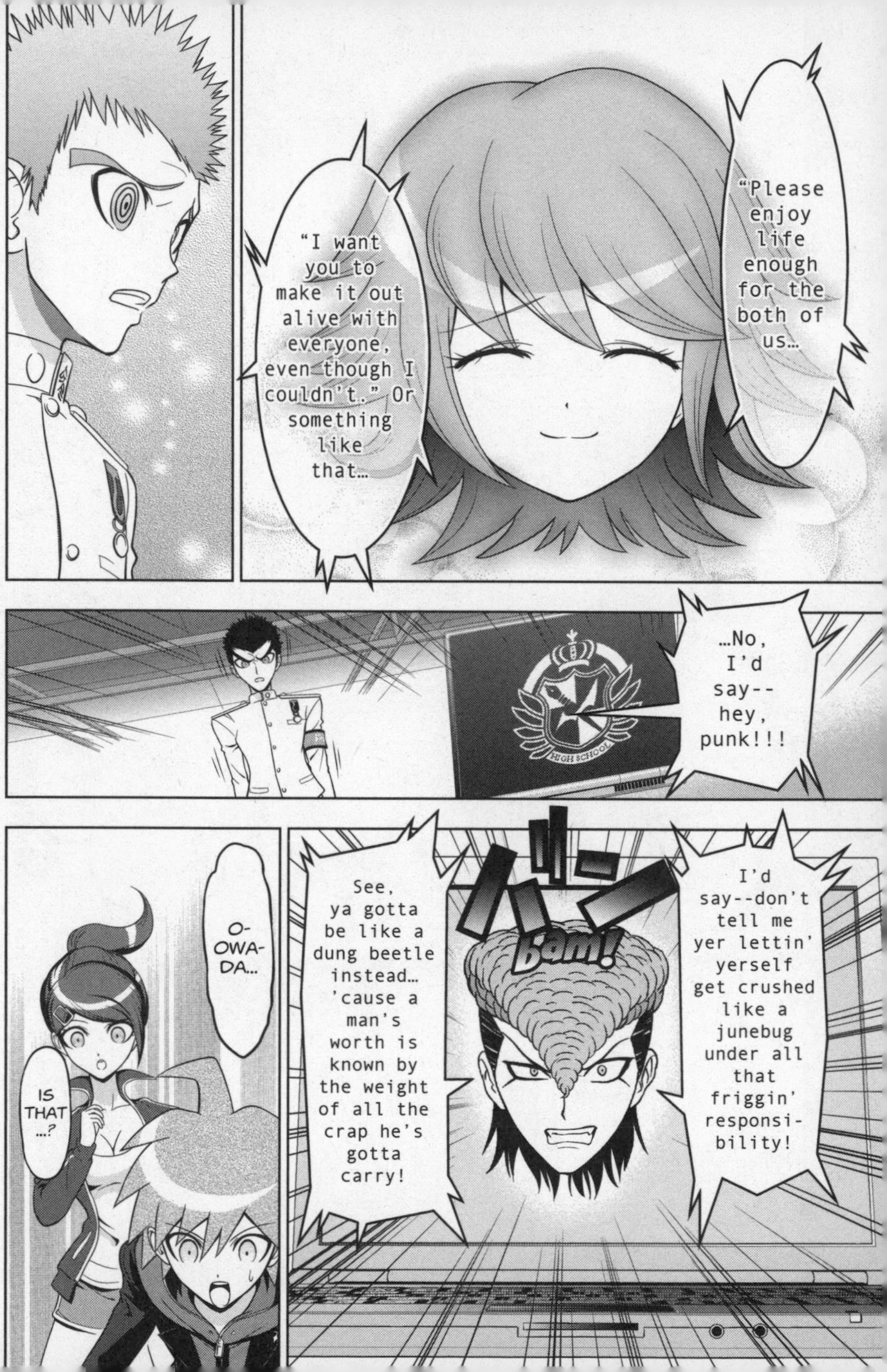
"Please enjoy life enough for the both of us…
"I want you to make it out alive with everyone, even though I couldn't." Or something like that…
…No, I'd say-- hey, punk!!!
HIGH SCHOOL
I'd say--don't tell me yer lettin' yerself get crushed like a junebug under all that friggin' responsi-bility!
BAM!
See, ya gotta be like a dung beetle instead… 'cause a man's worth is known by the weight of all the crap he's gotta carry!
O-OWADA…
IS THAT …?

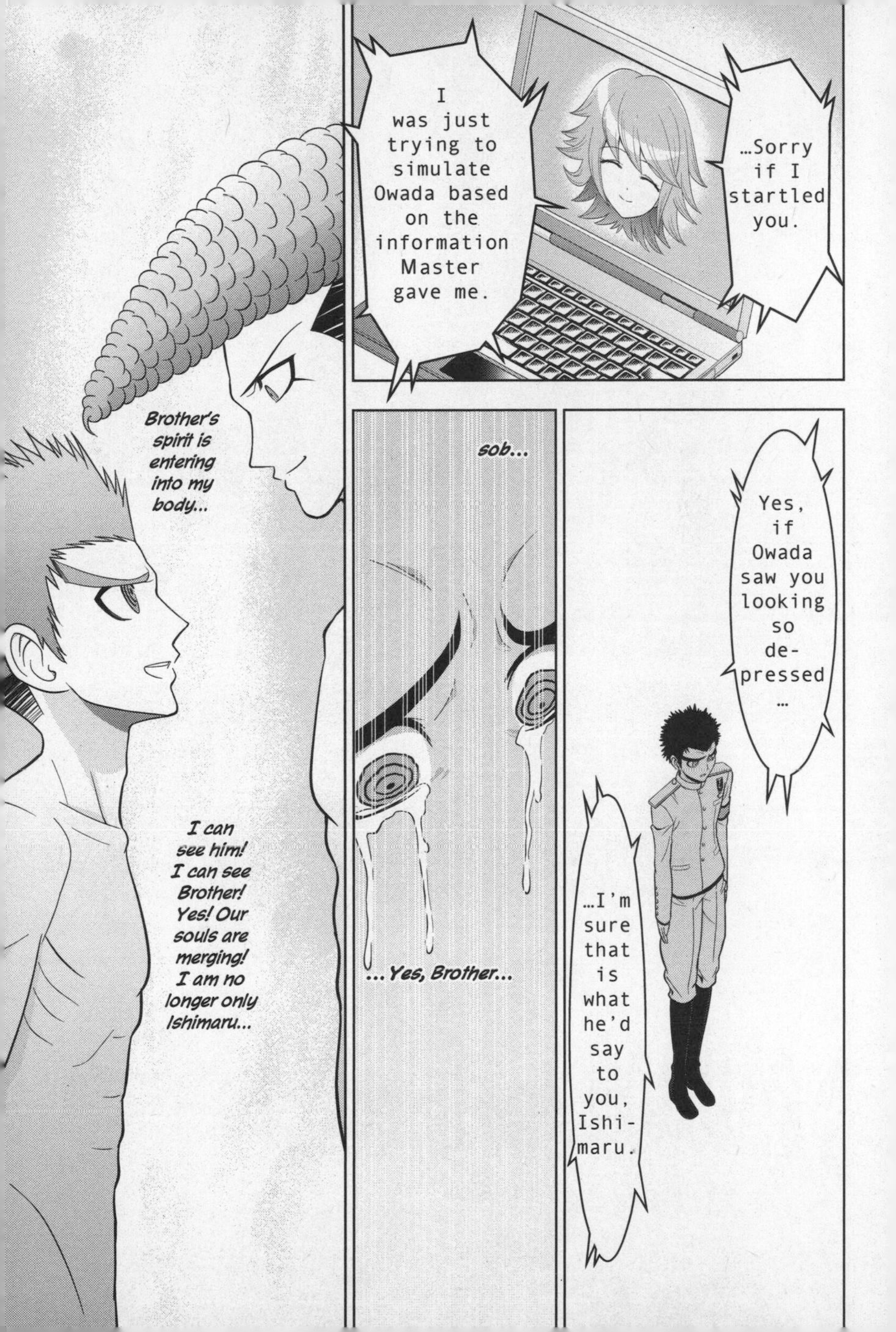

…Sorry if I startled you.
I was just trying to simulate Owada based on the information Master gave me.
Yes, if Owada saw you looking so de-pressed…
…I'm sure that is what he'd say to you, Ishi-maru.
sob…
…Yes, Brother…
Brother's spirit is entering into my body…
I can see him! I can see Brother! Yes! Our souls are merging! I am no longer only Ishimaru…

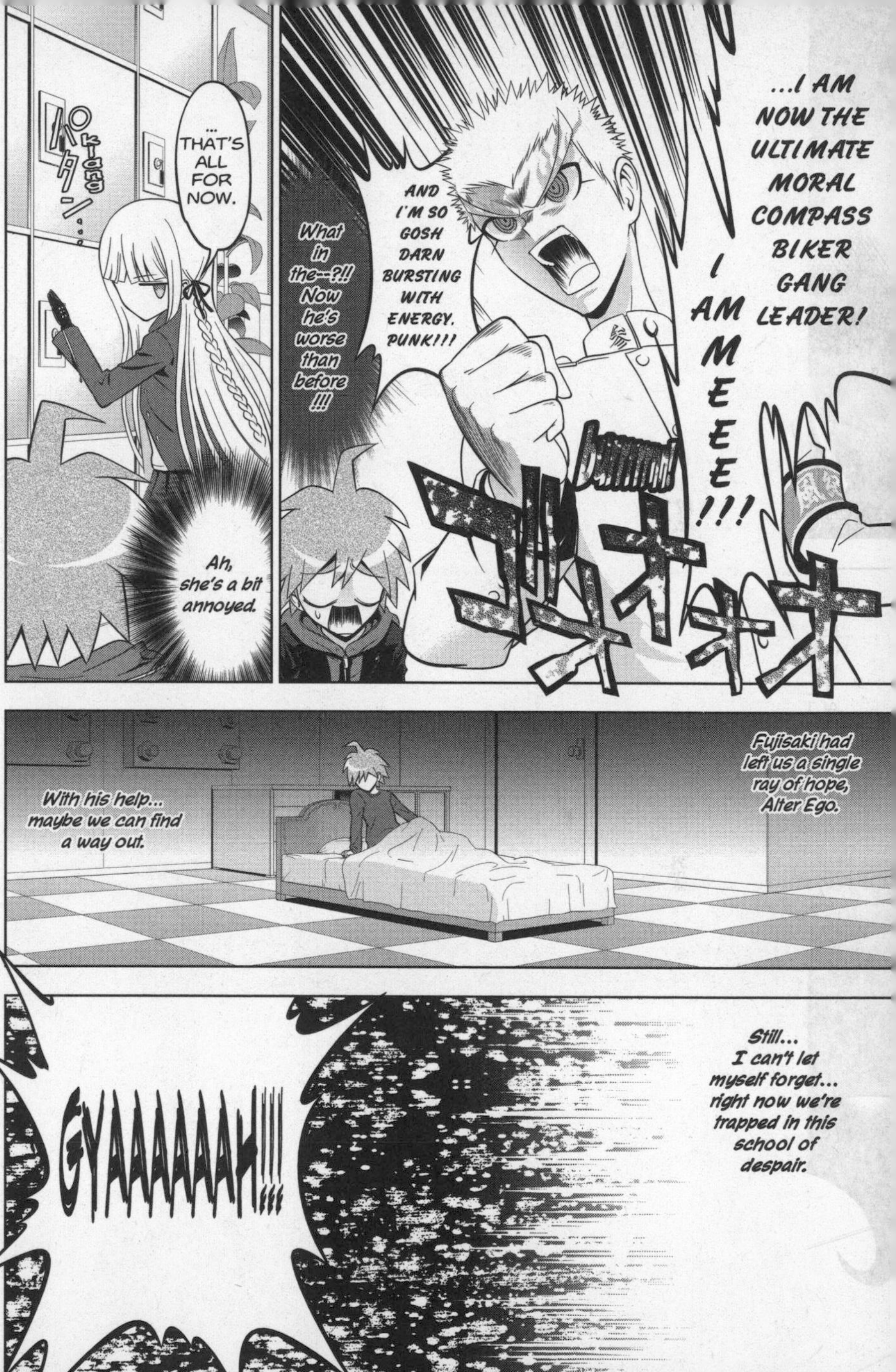
...I AM NOW THE ULTIMATE MORAL COMPASS BIKER GANG LEADER!
I AM MEEEE!!!
AND I'M SO GOSH DARN BURSTING WITH ENERGY, PUNK!!!
What in the--?!! Now he's worse than before!!!
... THAT'S ALL FOR NOW.
Ah, she's a bit annoyed.
Fujisaki had left us a single ray of hope, Alter Ego.
With his help... maybe we can find a way out.
Still... I can't let myself forget... right now we're trapped in this school of despair.
GYAAAAAH!!!

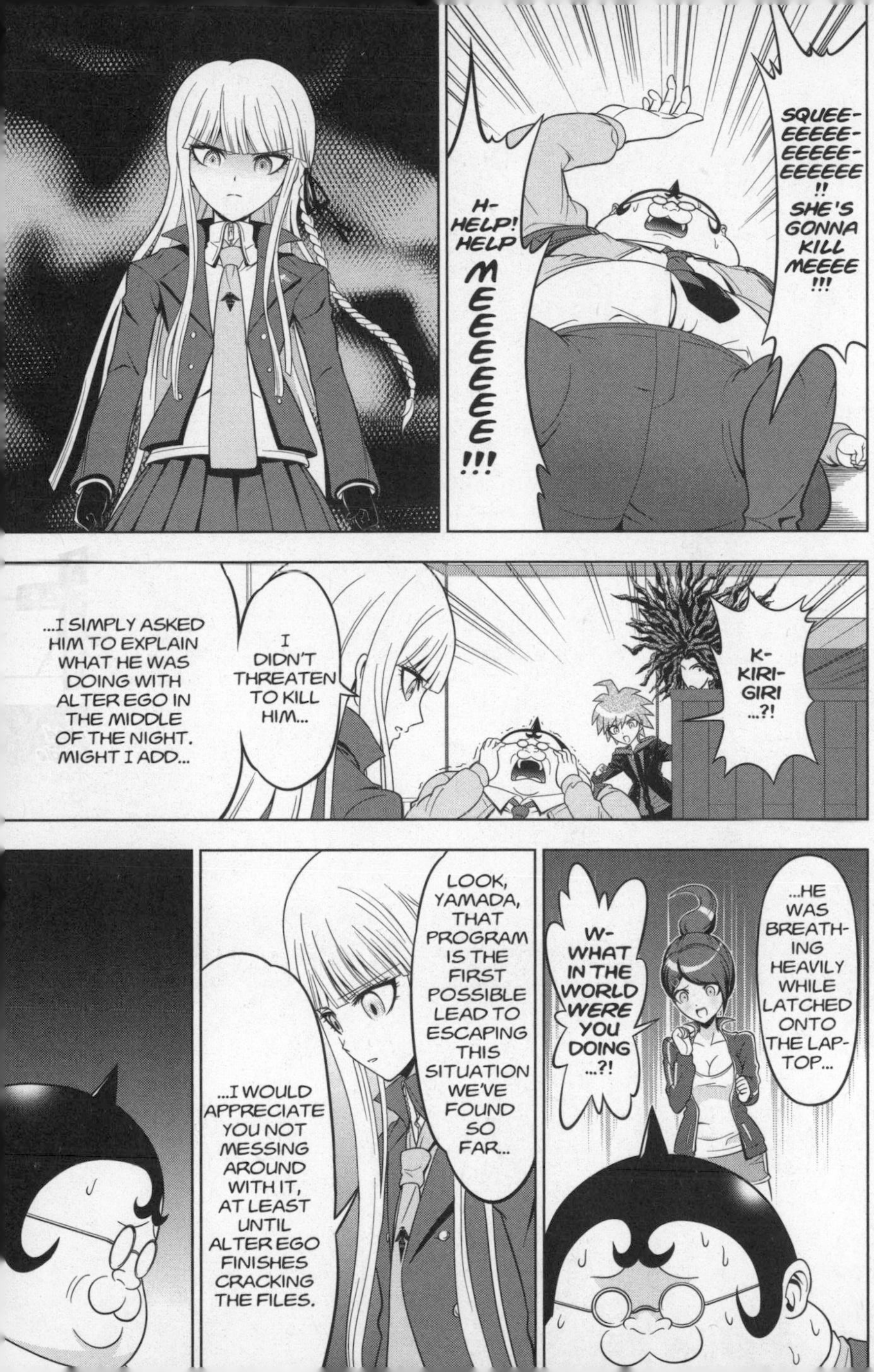
SQUEEE-EEEEE-EEEEE-EEEEEE!! SHE'S GONNA KILL MEEEE!!!
H-HELP! HELP MEEEEEEE!!!
K-KIRIGIRI...?!
I DIDN'T THREATEN TO KILL HIM...
...I SIMPLY ASKED HIM TO EXPLAIN WHAT HE WAS DOING WITH ALTER EGO IN THE MIDDLE OF THE NIGHT. MIGHT I ADD...
...HE WAS BREATHING HEAVILY WHILE LATCHED ONTO THE LAPTOP...
W-WHAT IN THE WORLD WERE YOU DOING...?!
LOOK, YAMADA, THAT PROGRAM IS THE FIRST POSSIBLE LEAD TO ESCAPING THIS SITUATION WE'VE FOUND SO FAR...
...I WOULD APPRECIATE YOU NOT MESSING AROUND WITH IT, AT LEAST UNTIL ALTER EGO FINISHES CRACKING THE FILES.

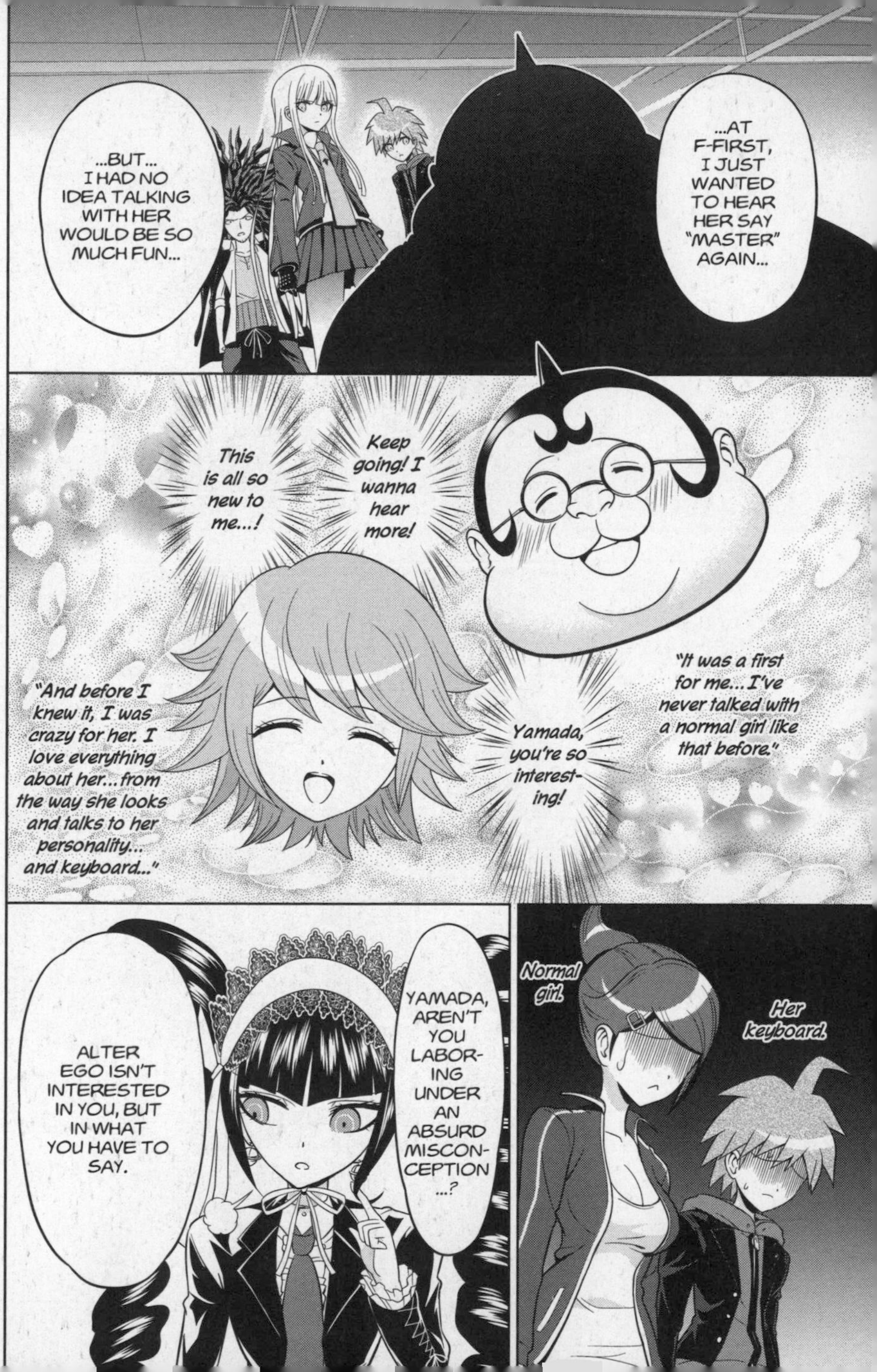
...AT F-FIRST, I JUST WANTED TO HEAR HER SAY "MASTER" AGAIN...
...BUT... I HAD NO IDEA TALKING WITH HER WOULD BE SO MUCH FUN...
Keep going! I wanna hear more!
This is all so new to me...!
"It was a first for me... I've never talked with a normal girl like that before."
Yamada, you're so interest-ing!
"And before I knew it, I was crazy for her. I love everything about her... from the way she looks and talks to her personality... and keyboard..."
Her keyboard.
Normal girl.
YAMADA, AREN'T YOU LABOR-ING UNDER AN ABSURD MISCON-CEPTION ...?
ALTER EGO ISN'T INTERESTED IN YOU, BUT IN WHAT YOU HAVE TO SAY.

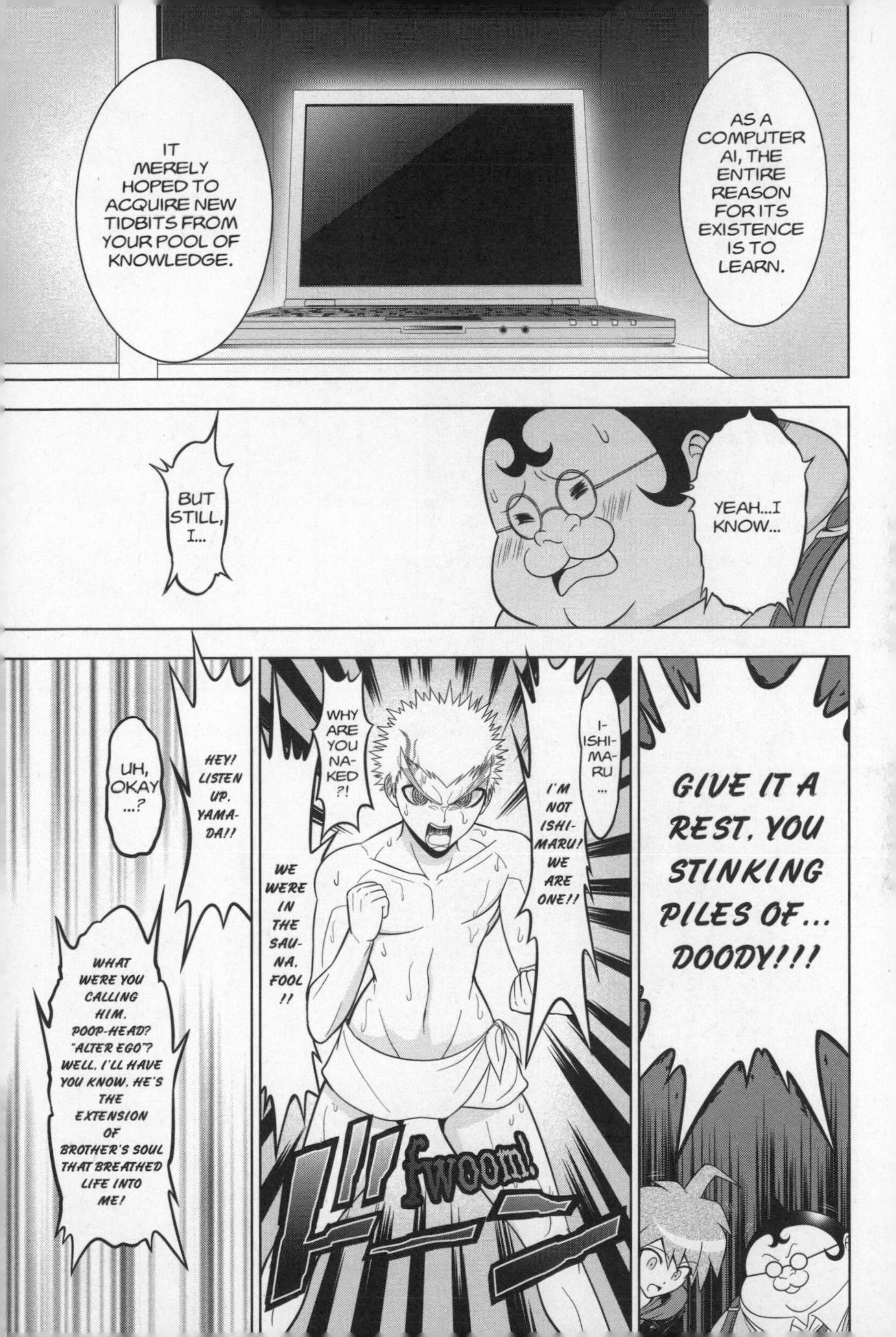
AS A COMPUTER AI, THE ENTIRE REASON FOR ITS EXISTENCE IS TO LEARN.
IT MERELY HOPED TO ACQUIRE NEW TIDBITS FROM YOUR POOL OF KNOWLEDGE.
YEAH...I KNOW...
BUT STILL, I...
GIVE IT A REST, YOU STINKING PILES OF... DOODY!!!
I-ISHI-MARU...
I'M NOT ISHI-MARU! WE ARE ONE!!
WHY ARE YOU NA-KED?!
WE WERE IN THE SAU-NA, FOOL!!
fwoom!
HEY! LISTEN UP, YAMA-DA!!
UH, OKAY...?
WHAT WERE YOU CALLING HIM, POOP-HEAD? "ALTER EGO"? WELL, I'LL HAVE YOU KNOW, HE'S THE EXTENSION OF BROTHER'S SOUL THAT BREATHED LIFE INTO ME!

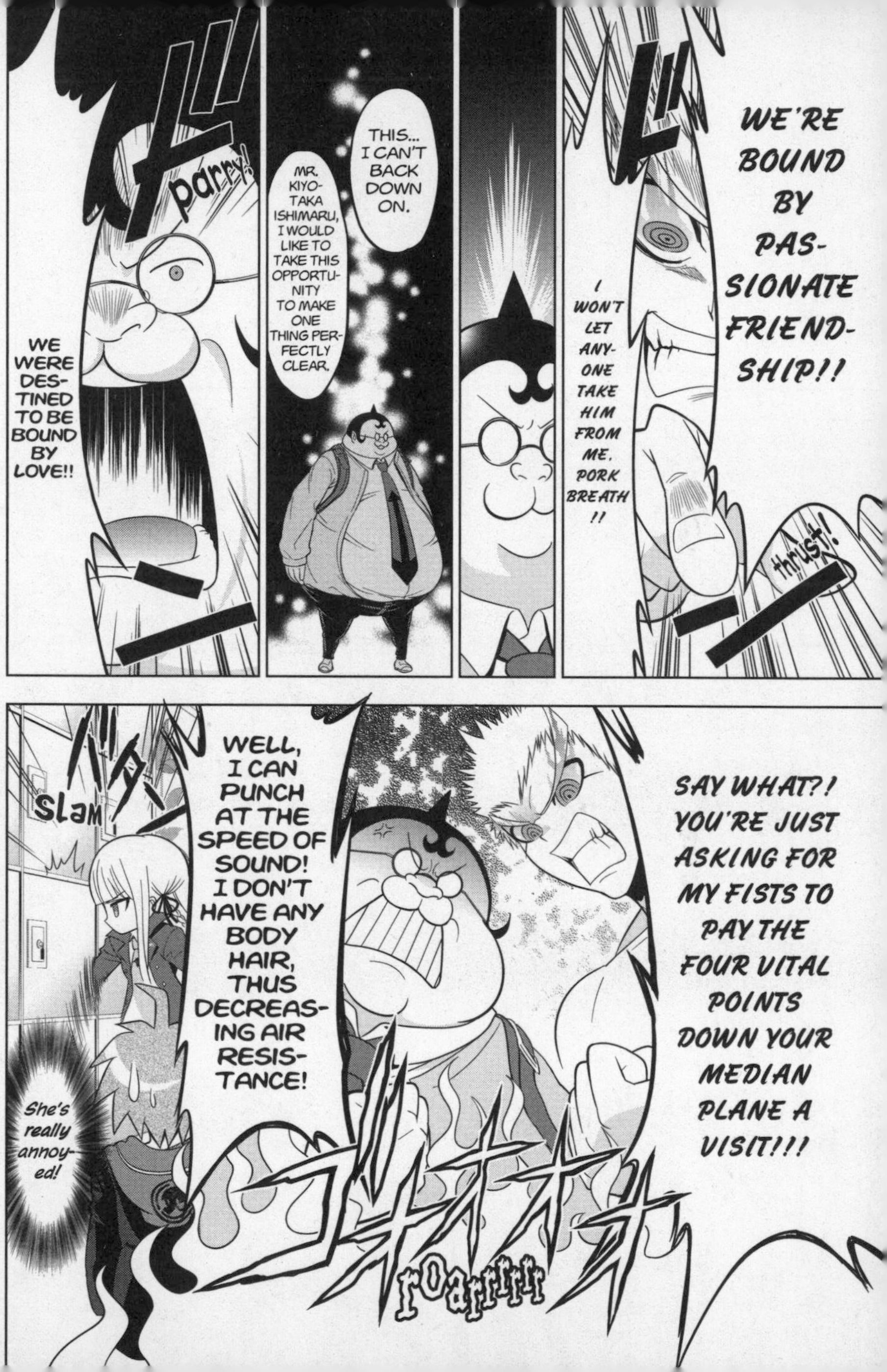
WE'RE BOUND BY PAS-SIONATE FRIEND-SHIP!!
I WON'T LET ANY-ONE TAKE HIM FROM ME, PORK BREATH!!
thrust!
THIS... I CAN'T BACK DOWN ON.
MR. KIYO-TAKA ISHIMARU, I WOULD LIKE TO TAKE THIS OPPORTU-NITY TO MAKE ONE THING PER-FECTLY CLEAR.
parry!
WE WERE DES-TINED TO BE BOUND BY LOVE!!
SAY WHAT?! YOU'RE JUST ASKING FOR MY FISTS TO PAY THE FOUR VITAL POINTS DOWN YOUR MEDIAN PLANE A VISIT!!!
WELL, I CAN PUNCH AT THE SPEED OF SOUND! I DON'T HAVE ANY BODY HAIR, THUS DECREAS-ING AIR RESIS-TANCE!
roarrrr
slam
She's really annoy-ed!

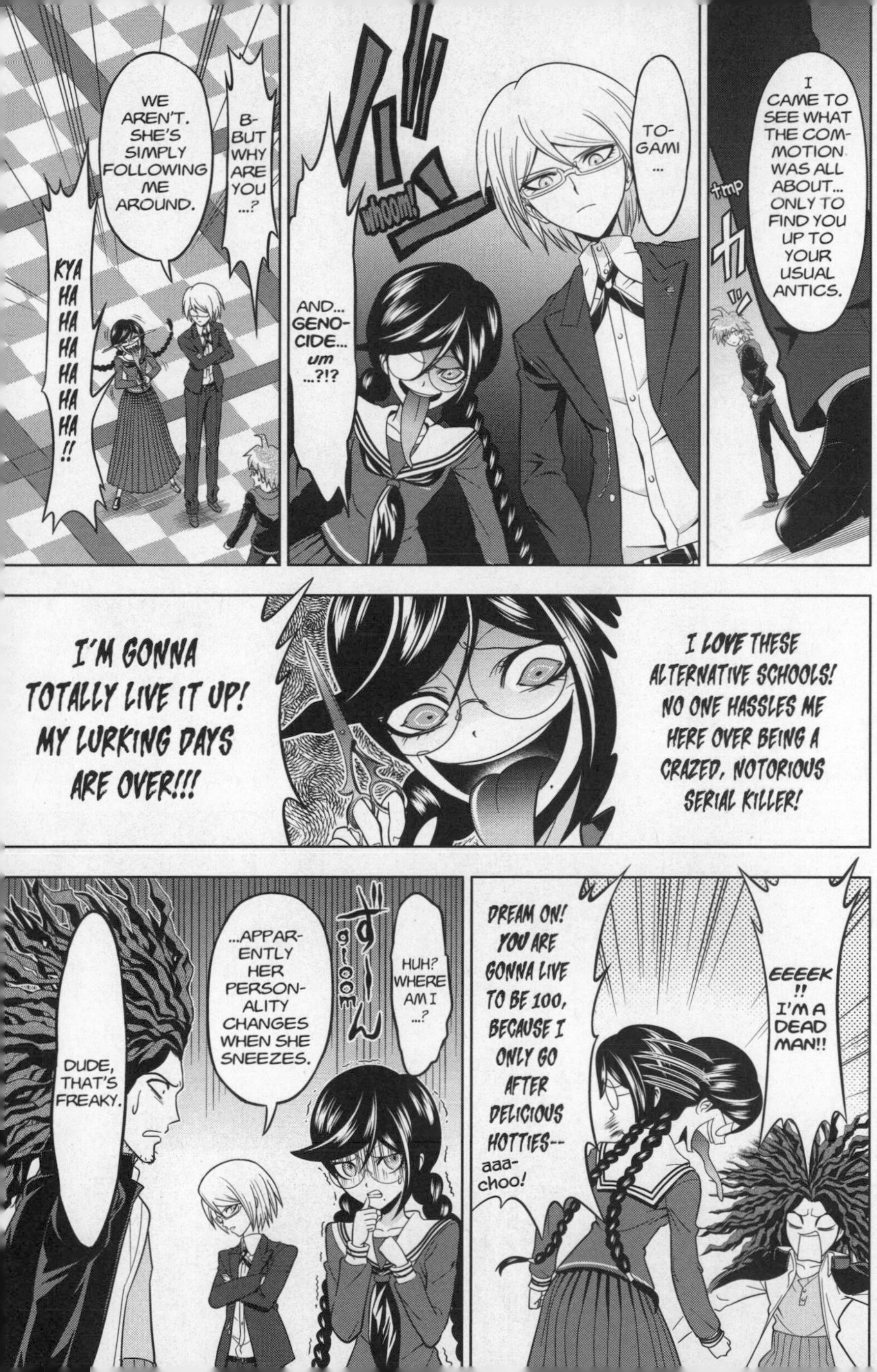
I CAME TO SEE WHAT THE COMMOTION WAS ALL ABOUT... ONLY TO FIND YOU UP TO YOUR USUAL ANTICS.
tmp
TO-GAMI ...
whoom!
AND... GENO-CIDE... um ...?!?
B-BUT WHY ARE YOU ...?
WE AREN'T. SHE'S SIMPLY FOLLOWING ME AROUND.
KYA HA HA HA HA HA HA HA HA!!
I LOVE THESE ALTERNATIVE SCHOOLS! NO ONE HASSLES ME HERE OVER BEING A CRAZED, NOTORIOUS SERIAL KILLER!
I'M GONNA TOTALLY LIVE IT UP! MY LURKING DAYS ARE OVER!!!
EEEEK!! I'M A DEAD MAN!!
DREAM ON! YOU ARE GONNA LIVE TO BE 100, BECAUSE I ONLY GO AFTER DELICIOUS HOTTIES--
aaa-choo!
HUH? WHERE AM I ...?
gloom
...APPARENTLY HER PERSONALITY CHANGES WHEN SHE SNEEZES.
DUDE, THAT'S FREAKY.

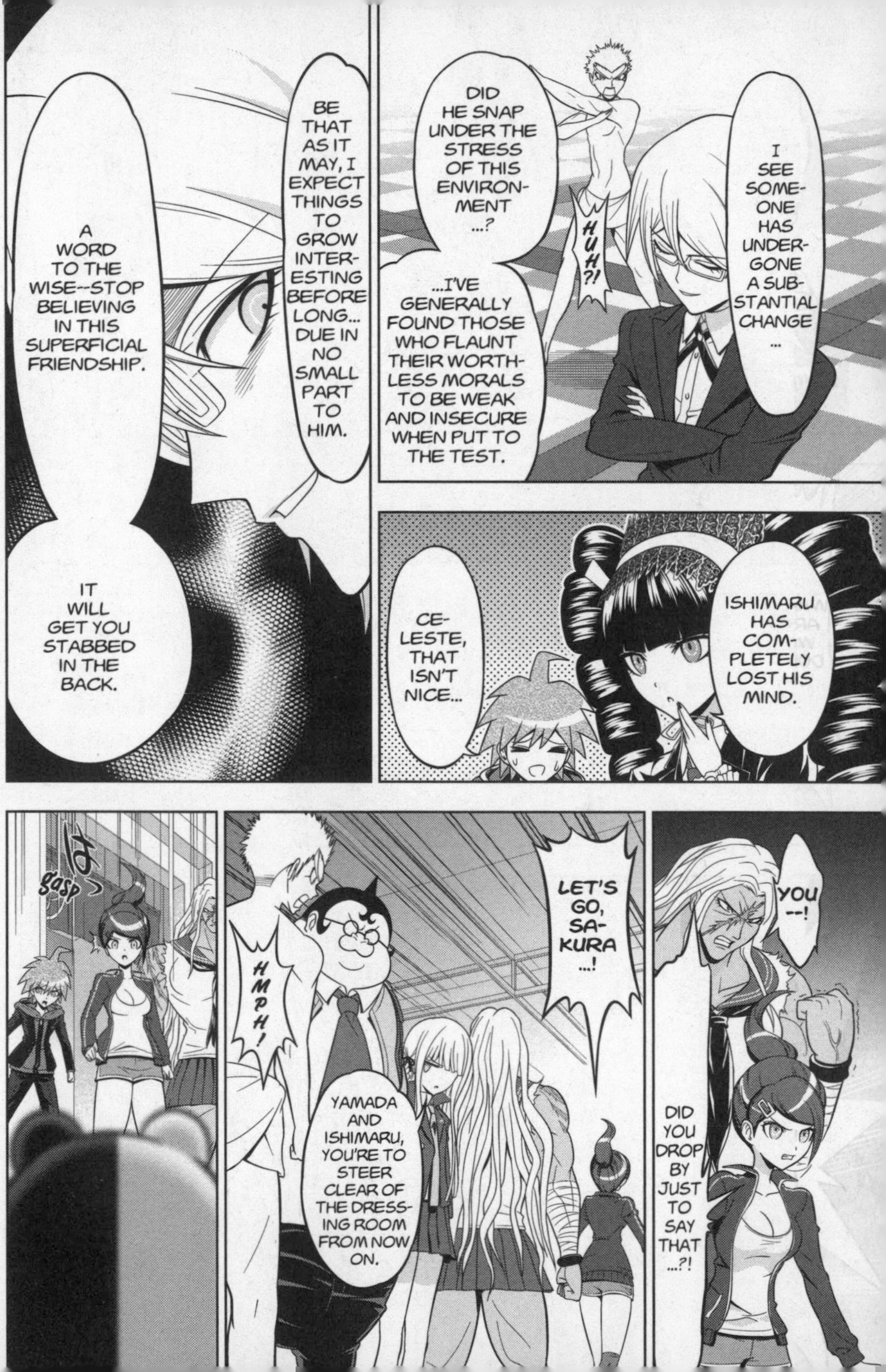
I SEE SOMEONE HAS UNDERGONE A SUBSTANTIAL CHANGE ...
HUH?!
DID HE SNAP UNDER THE STRESS OF THIS ENVIRONMENT ...?
...I'VE GENERALLY FOUND THOSE WHO FLAUNT THEIR WORTHLESS MORALS TO BE WEAK AND INSECURE WHEN PUT TO THE TEST.
ISHIMARU HAS COMPLETELY LOST HIS MIND.
CELESTE, THAT ISN'T NICE...
BE THAT AS IT MAY, I EXPECT THINGS TO GROW INTERESTING BEFORE LONG... DUE IN NO SMALL PART TO HIM.
A WORD TO THE WISE--STOP BELIEVING IN THIS SUPERFICIAL FRIENDSHIP.
IT WILL GET YOU STABBED IN THE BACK.
YOU--!
DID YOU DROP BY JUST TO SAY THAT...?!
LET'S GO, SAKURA...!
HMPH!
YAMADA AND ISHIMARU, YOU'RE TO STEER CLEAR OF THE DRESSING ROOM FROM NOW ON.
は
gasp

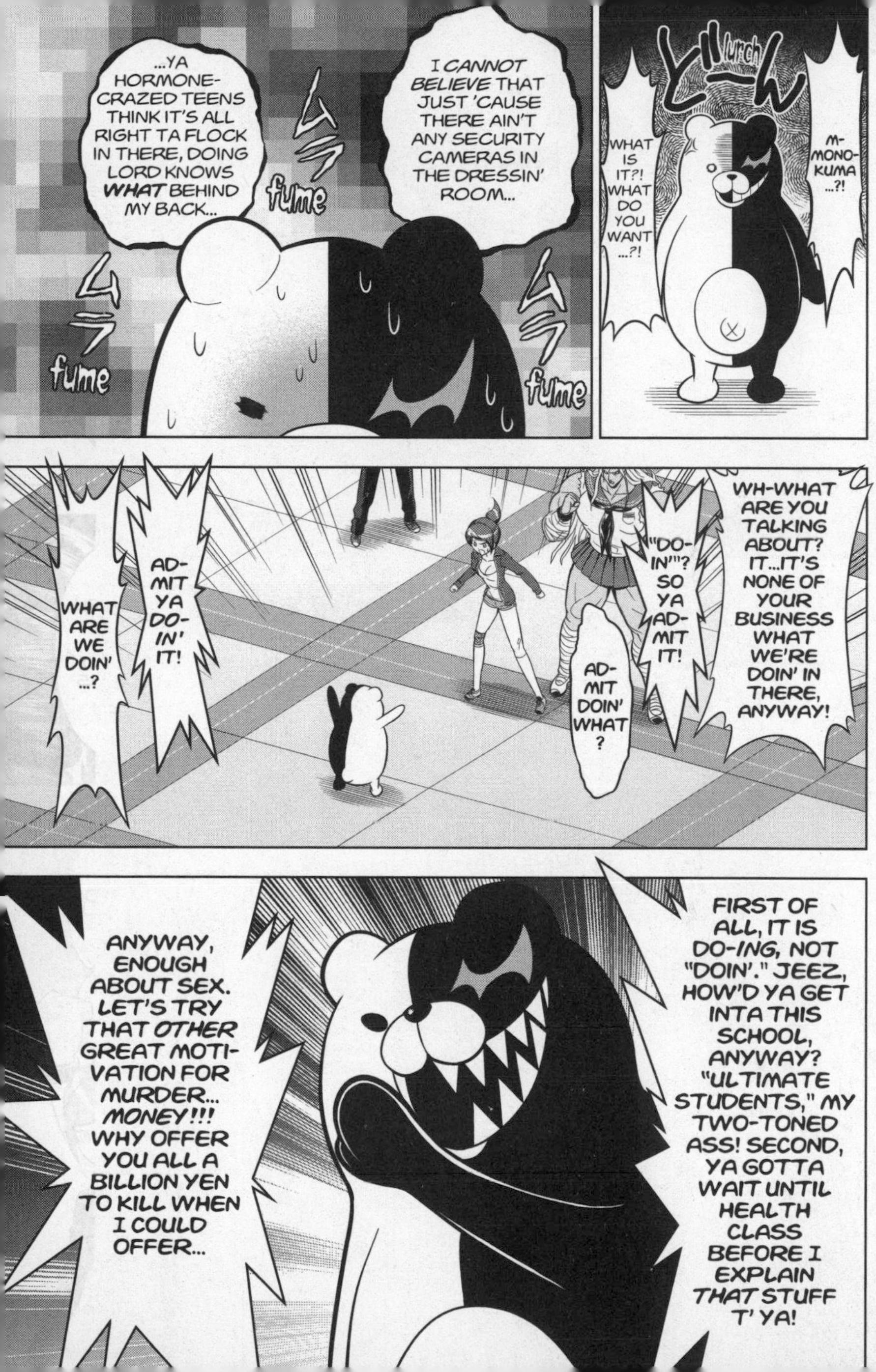
lurch
M-MONOKUMA...?!
WHAT IS IT?! WHAT DO YOU WANT...?!
I CANNOT BELIEVE THAT JUST 'CAUSE THERE AIN'T ANY SECURITY CAMERAS IN THE DRESSIN' ROOM...
...YA HORMONE-CRAZED TEENS THINK IT'S ALL RIGHT TA FLOCK IN THERE, DOING LORD KNOWS WHAT BEHIND MY BACK...
ムラ fume
ムラ fume
ムラ fume
WH-WHAT ARE YOU TALKING ABOUT? IT...IT'S NONE OF YOUR BUSINESS WHAT WE'RE DOIN' IN THERE, ANYWAY!
"DO-IN'"? SO YA ADMIT IT!
ADMIT DOIN' WHAT?
ADMIT YA DO-IN' IT!
WHAT ARE WE DOIN'...?
FIRST OF ALL, IT IS DO-ING, NOT "DOIN'." JEEZ, HOW'D YA GET INTA THIS SCHOOL, ANYWAY? "ULTIMATE STUDENTS," MY TWO-TONED ASS! SECOND, YA GOTTA WAIT UNTIL HEALTH CLASS BEFORE I EXPLAIN THAT STUFF T' YA!
ANYWAY, ENOUGH ABOUT SEX. LET'S TRY THAT OTHER GREAT MOTI-VATION FOR MURDER... MONEY!!! WHY OFFER YOU ALL A BILLION YEN TO KILL WHEN I COULD OFFER...

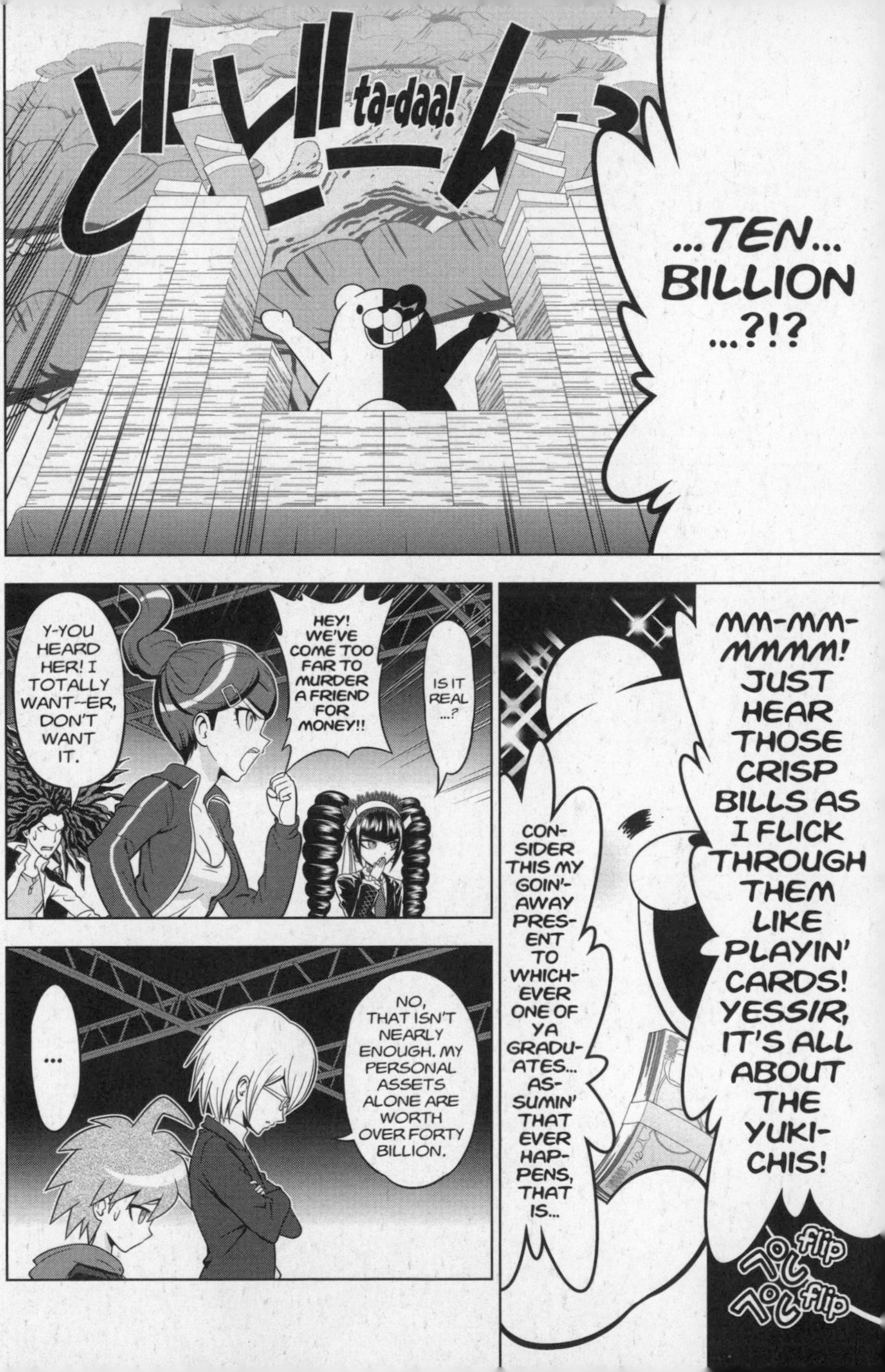
どどーん
ta-daa!
...TEN... BILLION ...?!?
MM-MM-MMMM! JUST HEAR THOSE CRISP BILLS AS I FLICK THROUGH THEM LIKE PLAYIN' CARDS! YESSIR, IT'S ALL ABOUT THE YUKI-CHIS!
CON-SIDER THIS MY GOIN'-AWAY PRES-ENT TO WHICH-EVER ONE OF YA GRADU-ATES... AS-SUMIN' THAT EVER HAP-PENS, THAT IS...
ぺしぺし flip flip
IS IT REAL ...?
HEY! WE'VE COME TOO FAR TO MURDER A FRIEND FOR MONEY!!
Y-YOU HEARD HER! I TOTALLY WANT--ER, DON'T WANT IT.
NO, THAT ISN'T NEARLY ENOUGH. MY PERSONAL ASSETS ALONE ARE WORTH OVER FORTY BILLION.
...

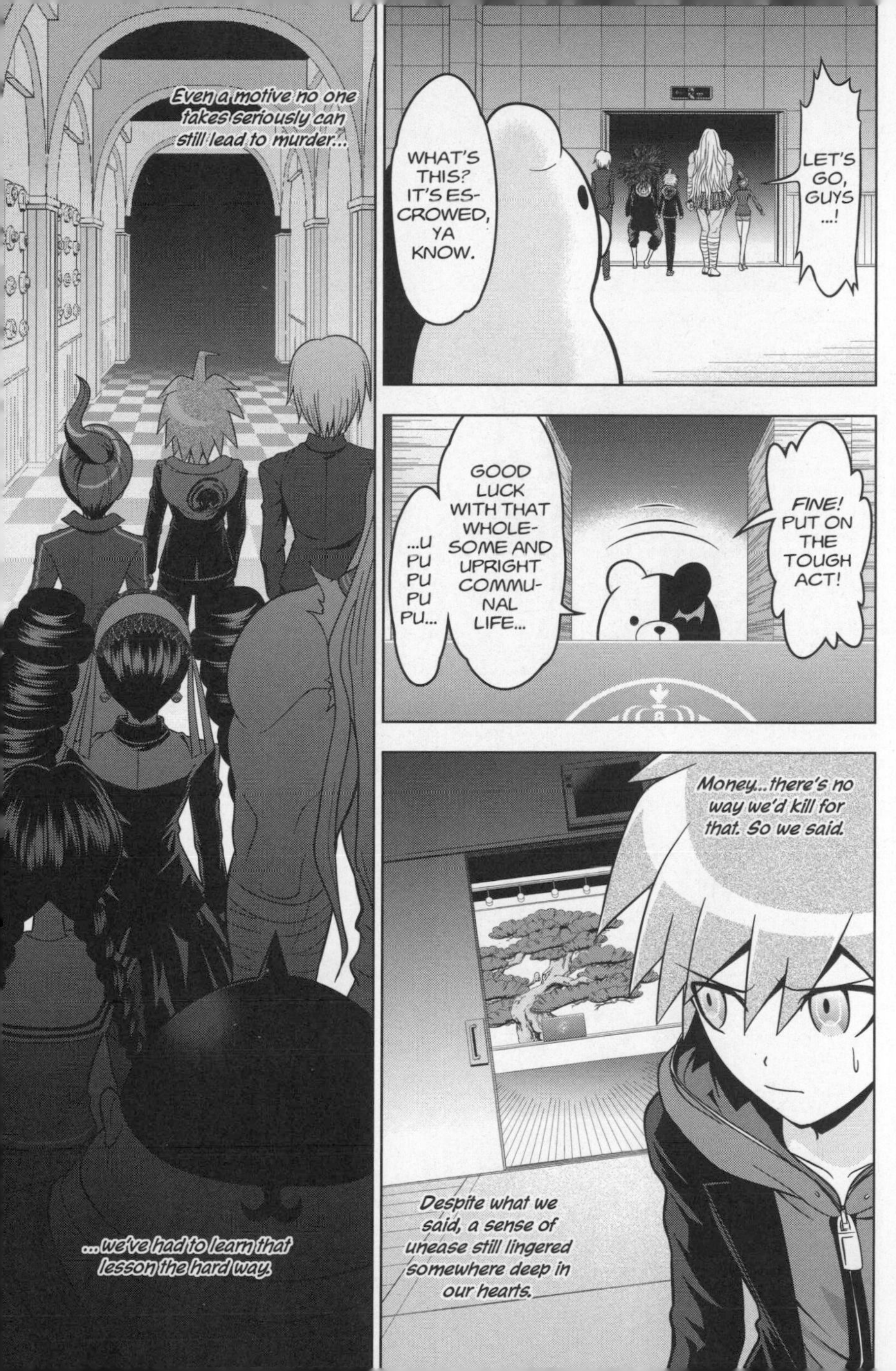
LET'S GO, GUYS ...!
WHAT'S THIS? IT'S ES-CROWED, YA KNOW.
FINE! PUT ON THE TOUGH ACT!
GOOD LUCK WITH THAT WHOLE-SOME AND UPRIGHT COMMU-NAL LIFE...
...U PU PU PU PU...
Money...there's no way we'd kill for that. So we said.
Despite what we said, a sense of unease still lingered somewhere deep in our hearts.
Even a motive no one takes seriously can still lead to murder...
...we've had to learn that lesson the hard way.

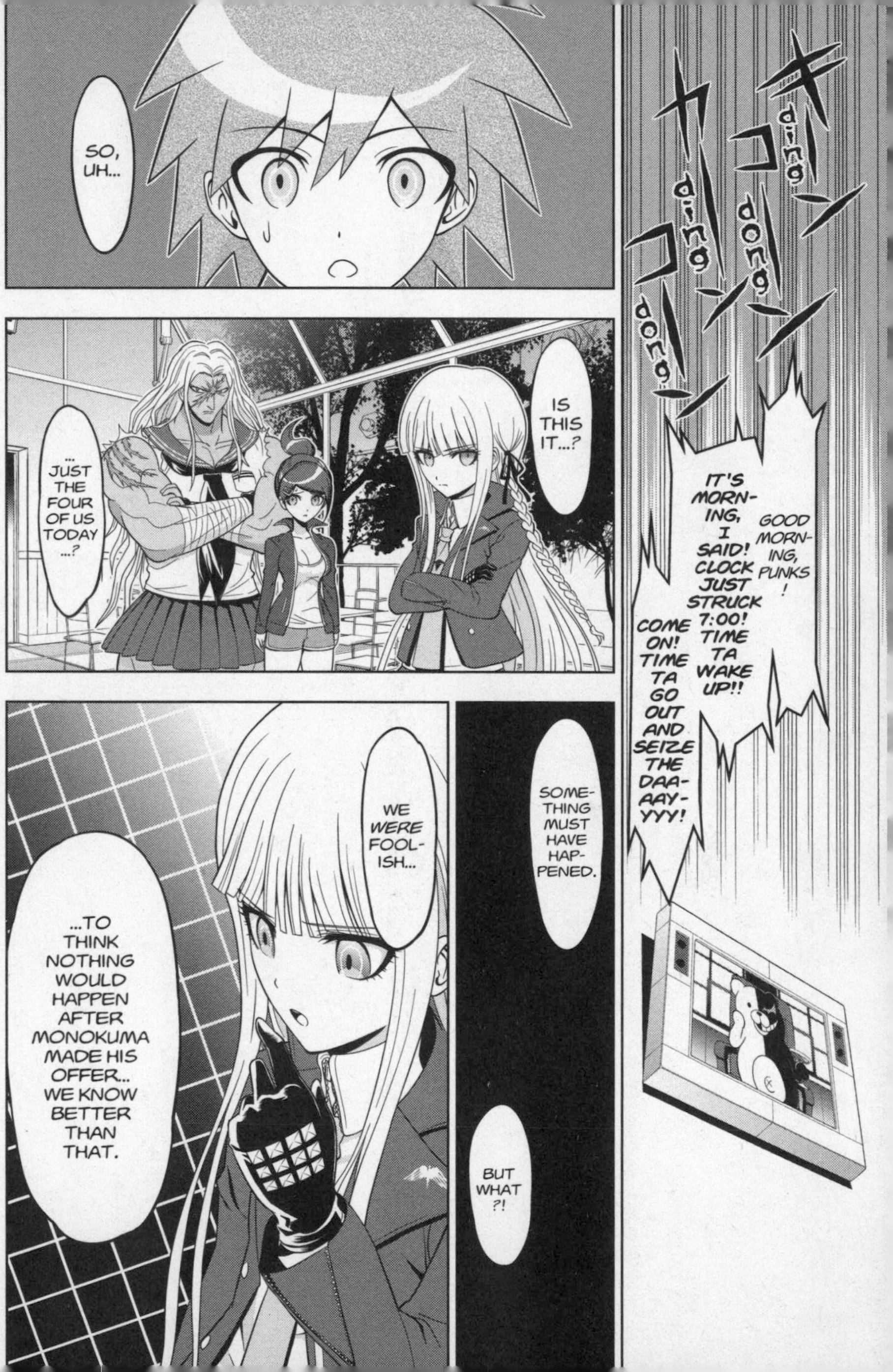

ding dong
ding dong
GOOD MORNING, PUNKS!
IT'S MORNING, I SAID! CLOCK JUST STRUCK 7:00! TIME TA WAKE UP!!
COME ON! TIME TA GO OUT AND SEIZE THE DAAAAYYYY!
SO, UH...
IS THIS IT...?
...JUST THE FOUR OF US TODAY...?
SOMETHING MUST HAVE HAPPENED.
BUT WHAT?!
WE WERE FOOLISH...
...TO THINK NOTHING WOULD HAPPEN AFTER MONOKUMA MADE HIS OFFER... WE KNOW BETTER THAN THAT.

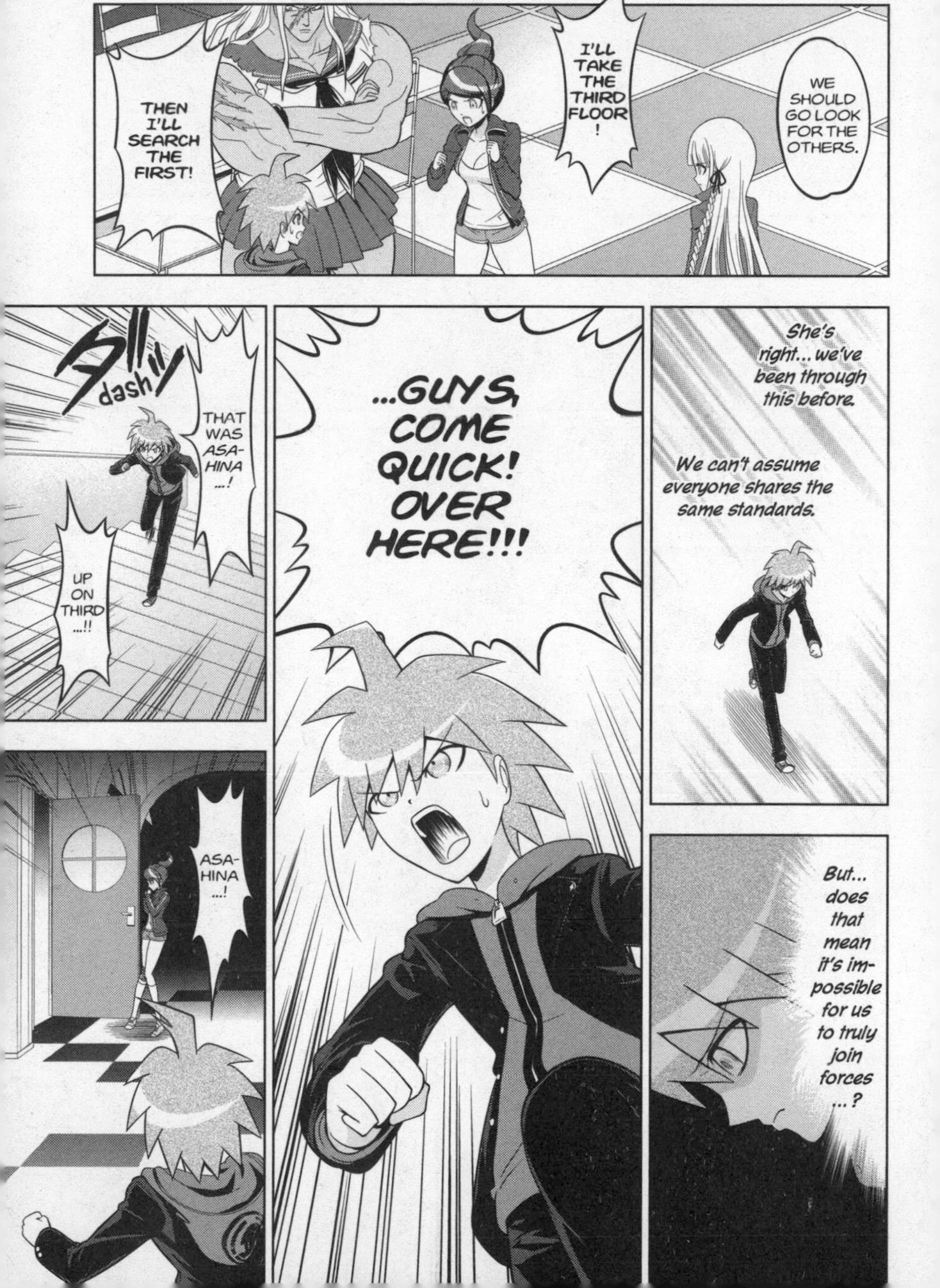
WE SHOULD GO LOOK FOR THE OTHERS.
I'LL TAKE THE THIRD FLOOR!
THEN I'LL SEARCH THE FIRST!
She's right... we've been through this before.
We can't assume everyone shares the same standards.
But... does that mean it's impossible for us to truly join forces...?
...GUYS, COME QUICK! OVER HERE!!!
dash
THAT WAS ASAHINA...!
UP ON THIRD...!!
ASAHINA...!

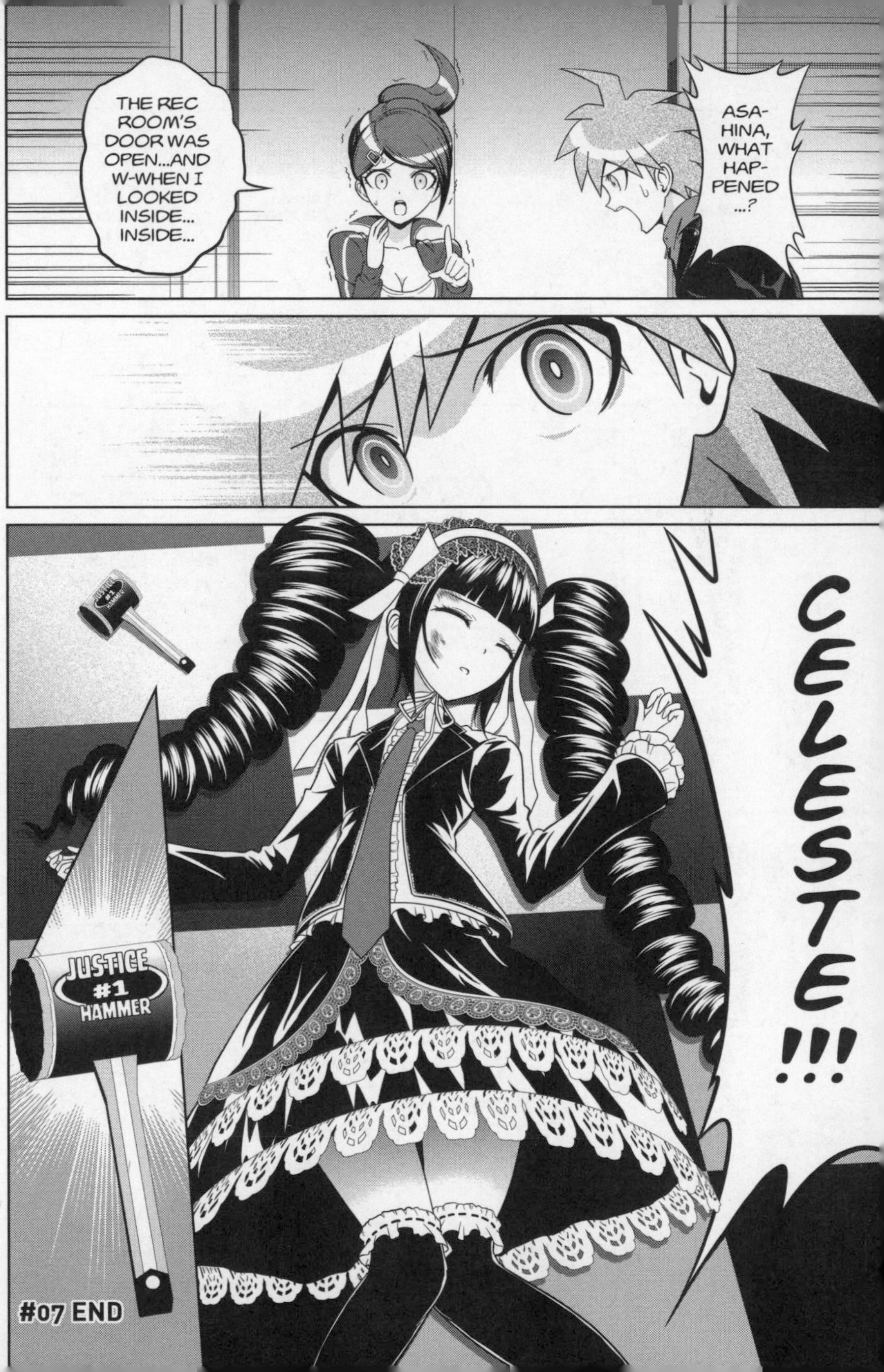
ASA-HINA, WHAT HAP-PENED ...?
THE REC ROOM'S DOOR WAS OPEN...AND W-WHEN I LOOKED INSIDE... INSIDE...
CELESTE!!!
JUSTICE #1 HAMMER
#07 END

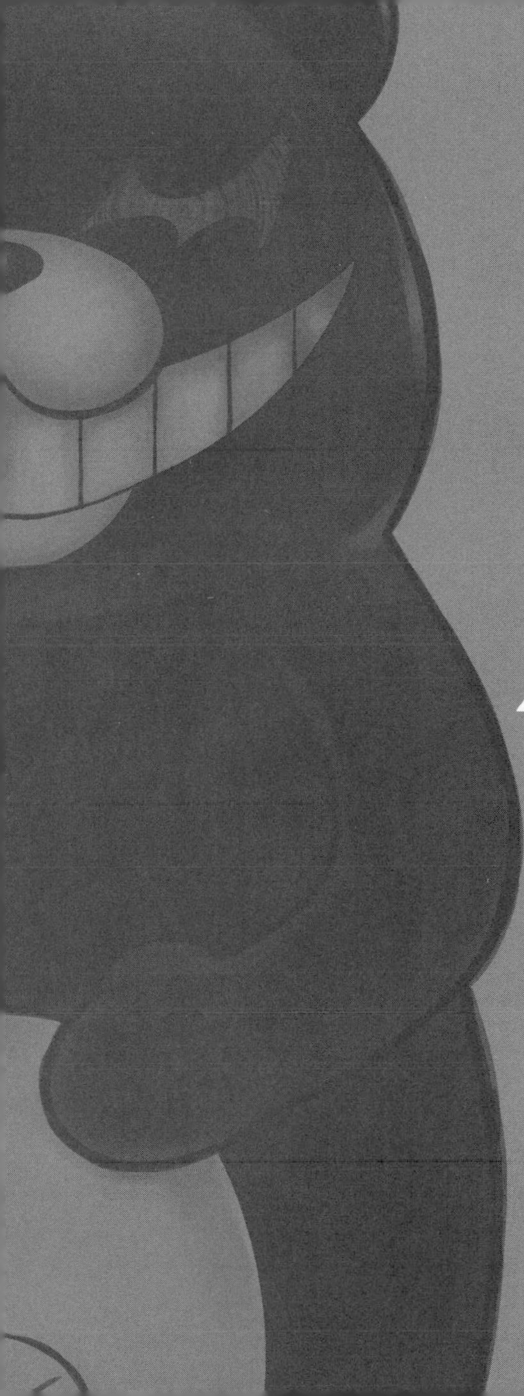

ダンガンロンパ

DANGANRONPA 希望の学園と絶望の高校生

THE ANIMATION

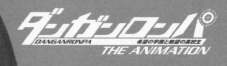

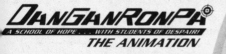

DANGANRONPA

A SCHOOL OF HOPE . . . WITH STUDENTS OF DESPAIR!

THE ANIMATION

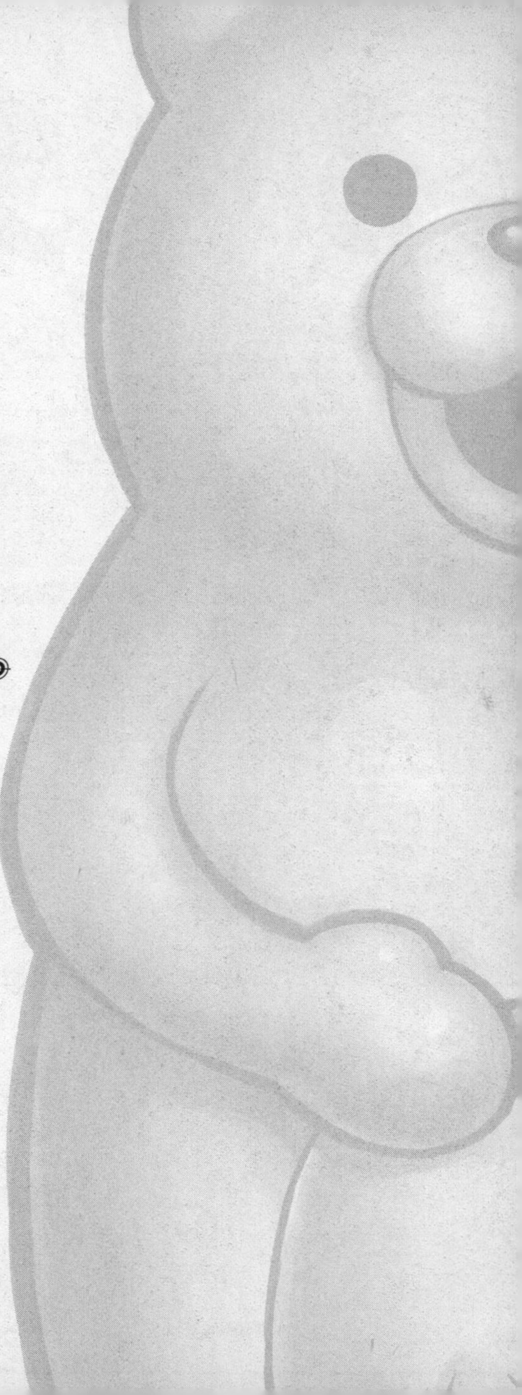

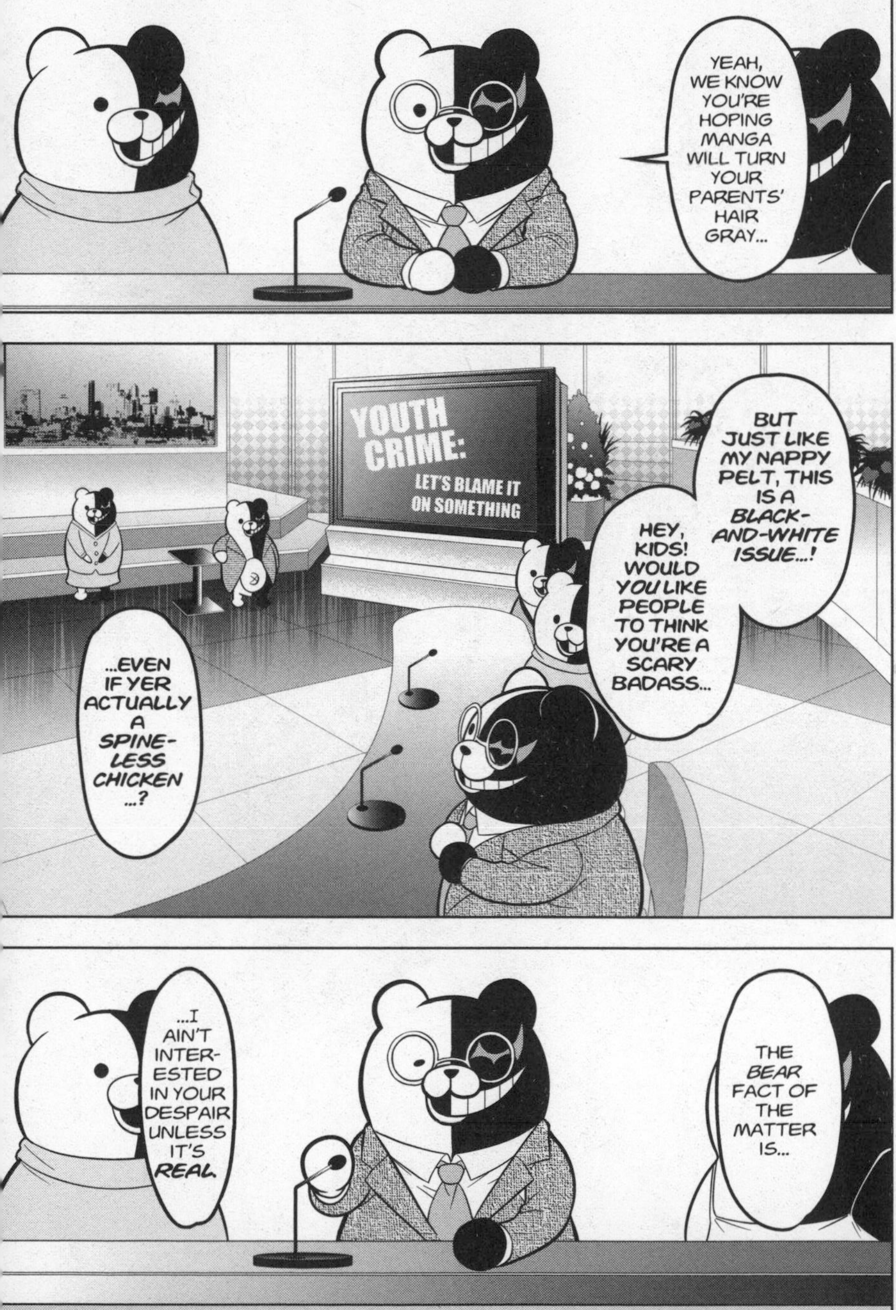
YEAH, WE KNOW YOU'RE HOPING MANGA WILL TURN YOUR PARENTS' HAIR GRAY...
YOUTH CRIME:
LET'S BLAME IT ON SOMETHING
BUT JUST LIKE MY NAPPY PELT, THIS IS A *BLACK-AND-WHITE ISSUE*...!
HEY, KIDS! WOULD *YOU* LIKE PEOPLE TO THINK YOU'RE A SCARY BADASS...
...EVEN IF YER ACTUALLY A *SPINE-LESS* CHICKEN...?
THE *BEAR* FACT OF THE MATTER IS...
...I AIN'T INTER-ESTED IN YOUR DESPAIR UNLESS IT'S ***REAL.***

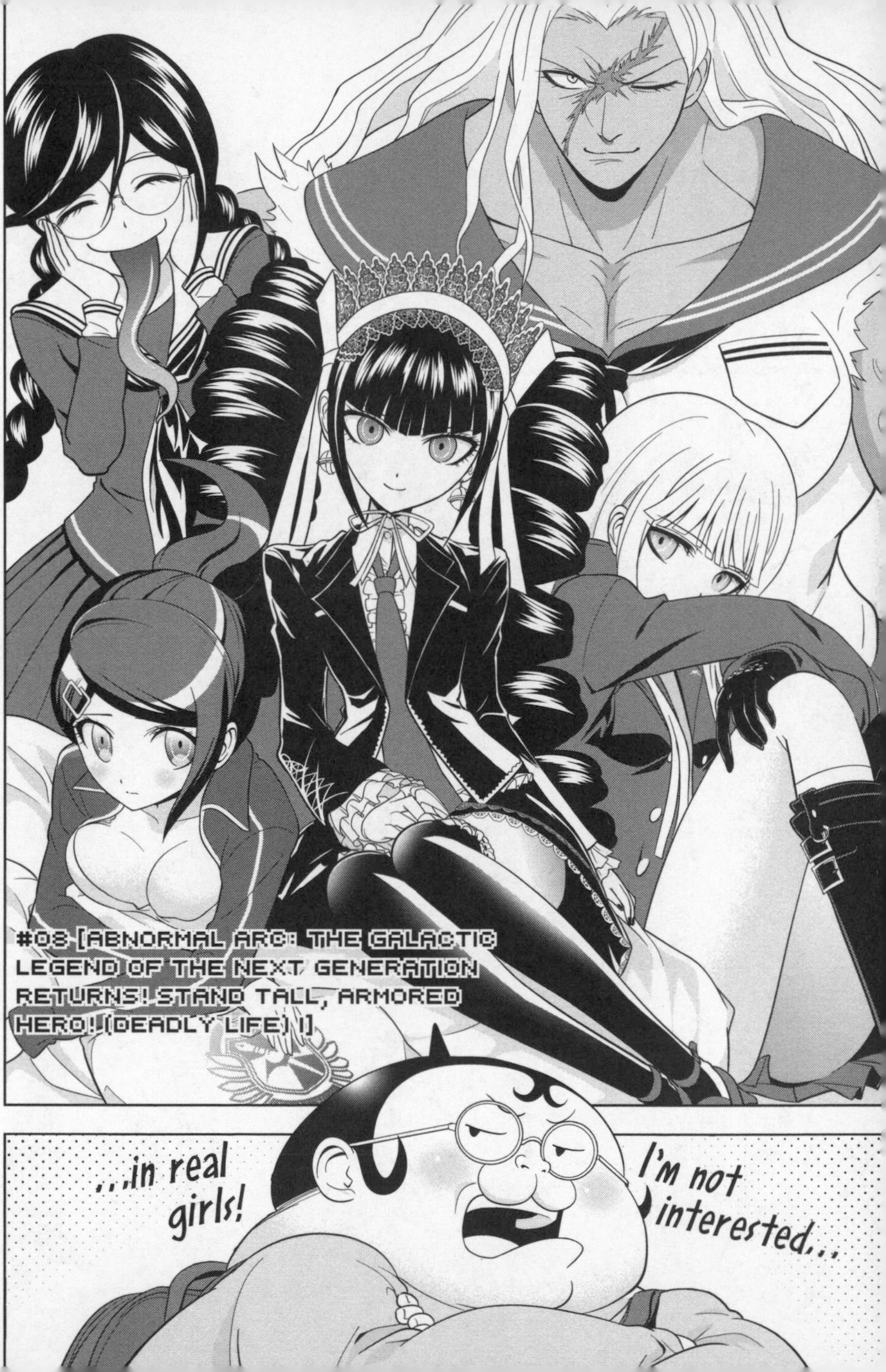
#08 [ABNORMAL ARC: THE GALACTIC LEGEND OF THE NEXT GENERATION RETURNS! STAND TALL, ARMORED HERO! (DEADLY LIFE) I]
I'm not interested...
...in real girls!

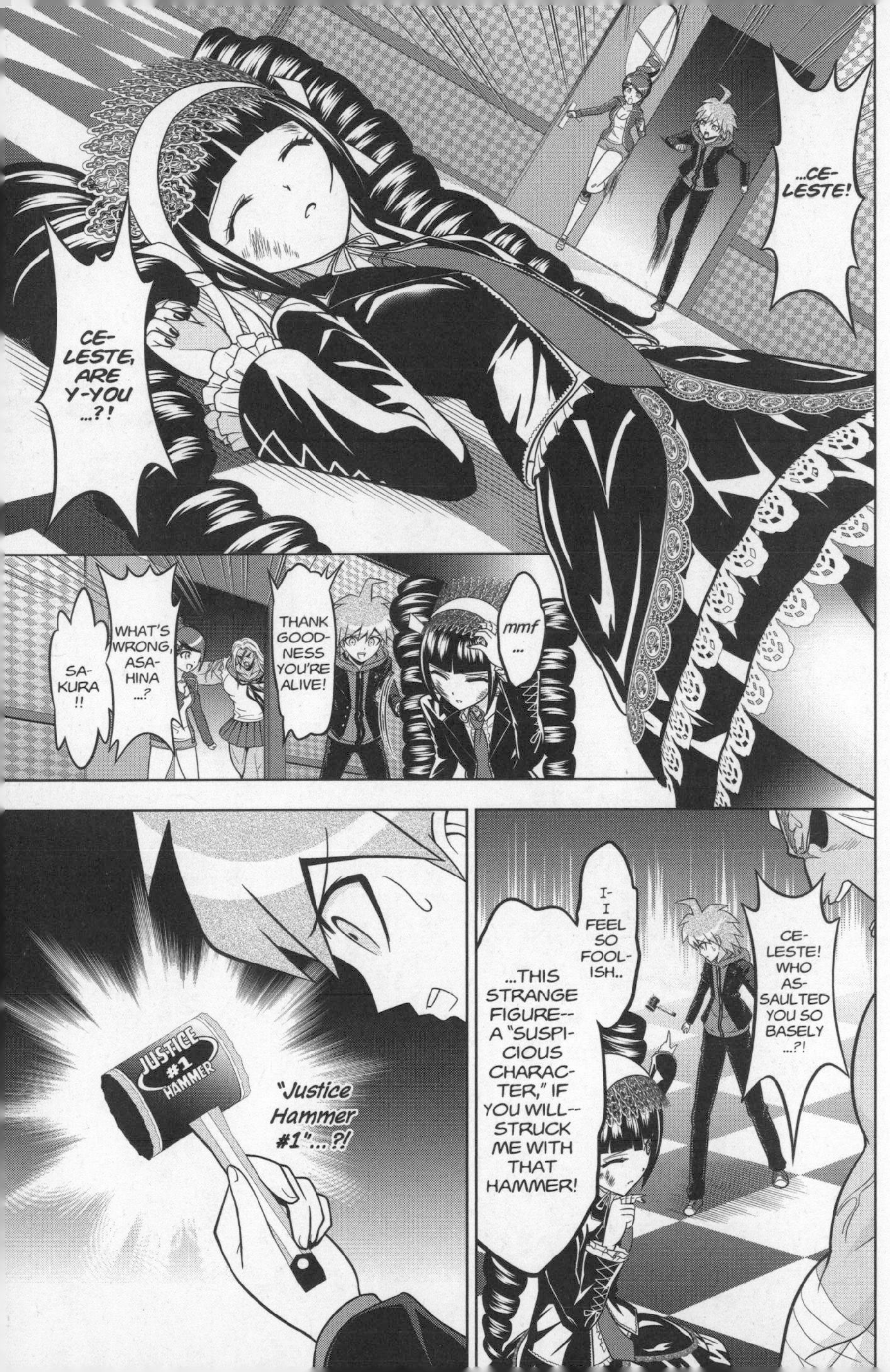
...CE-LESTE!
CE-LESTE, ARE Y-YOU ...?!
mmf ...
THANK GOODNESS YOU'RE ALIVE!
WHAT'S WRONG, ASAHINA ...?
SA-KURA !!
CE-LESTE! WHO AS-SAULTED YOU SO BASELY ...?!
I-I FEEL SO FOOL-ISH..
...THIS STRANGE FIGURE-- A "SUSPICIOUS CHARACTER," IF YOU WILL-- STRUCK ME WITH THAT HAMMER!
"Justice Hammer #1"...?!
JUSTICE #1 HAMMER

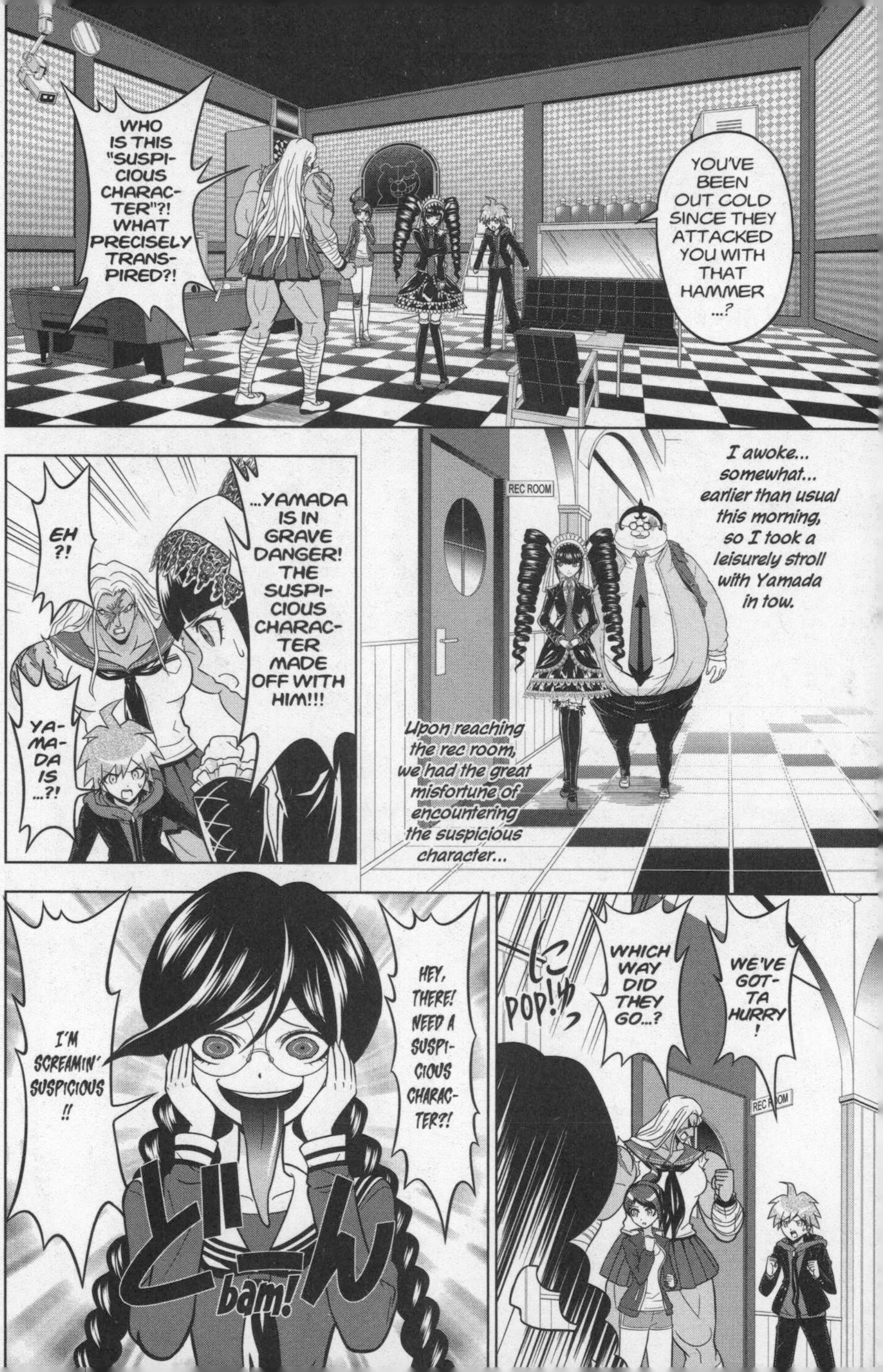
YOU'VE BEEN OUT COLD SINCE THEY ATTACKED YOU WITH THAT HAMMER ...?
WHO IS THIS "SUSPICIOUS CHARACTER"?! WHAT PRECISELY TRANSPIRED?!
I awoke... somewhat... earlier than usual this morning, so I took a leisurely stroll with Yamada in tow.
REC ROOM
Upon reaching the rec room, we had the great misfortune of encountering the suspicious character...
...YAMADA IS IN GRAVE DANGER! THE SUSPICIOUS CHARACTER MADE OFF WITH HIM!!!
EH?!
YAMADA IS ...?!
WE'VE GOTTA HURRY!
WHICH WAY DID THEY GO...?
POP!
REC ROOM
HEY, THERE! NEED A SUSPICIOUS CHARACTER?!
I'M SCREAMIN' SUSPICIOUS!!
bam!

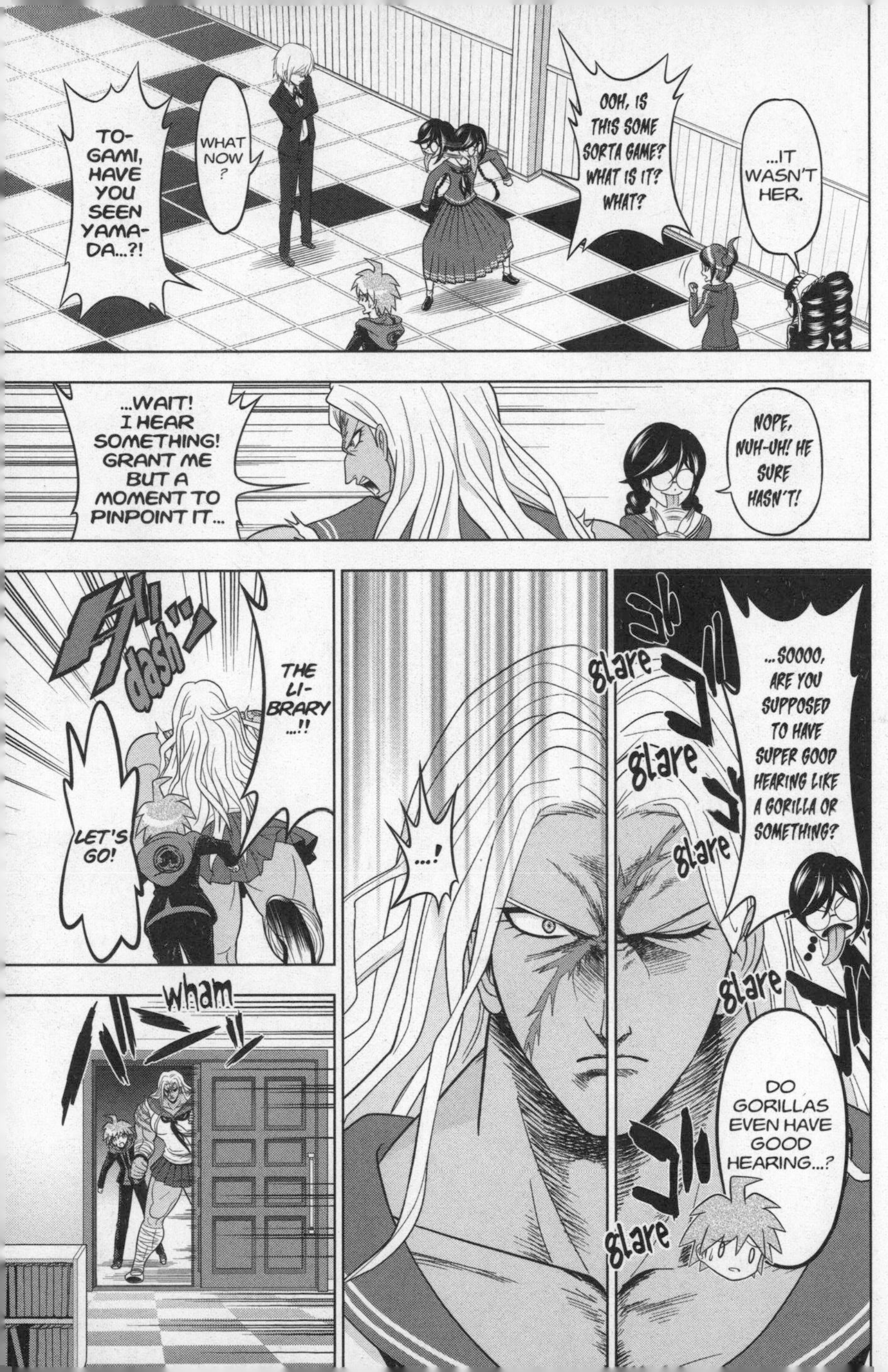
...IT WASN'T HER.
OOH, IS THIS SOME SORTA GAME? WHAT IS IT? WHAT?
WHAT NOW?
TO-GAMI, HAVE YOU SEEN YAMA-DA...?!
NOPE, NUH-UH! HE SURE HASN'T!
...WAIT! I HEAR SOMETHING! GRANT ME BUT A MOMENT TO PINPOINT IT...
glare
...SOOOO, ARE YOU SUPPOSED TO HAVE SUPER GOOD HEARING LIKE A GORILLA OR SOMETHING?
glare
glare
glare
DO GORILLAS EVEN HAVE GOOD HEARING...?
glare
...!
dash
THE LI-BRARY...!!
LET'S GO!
wham

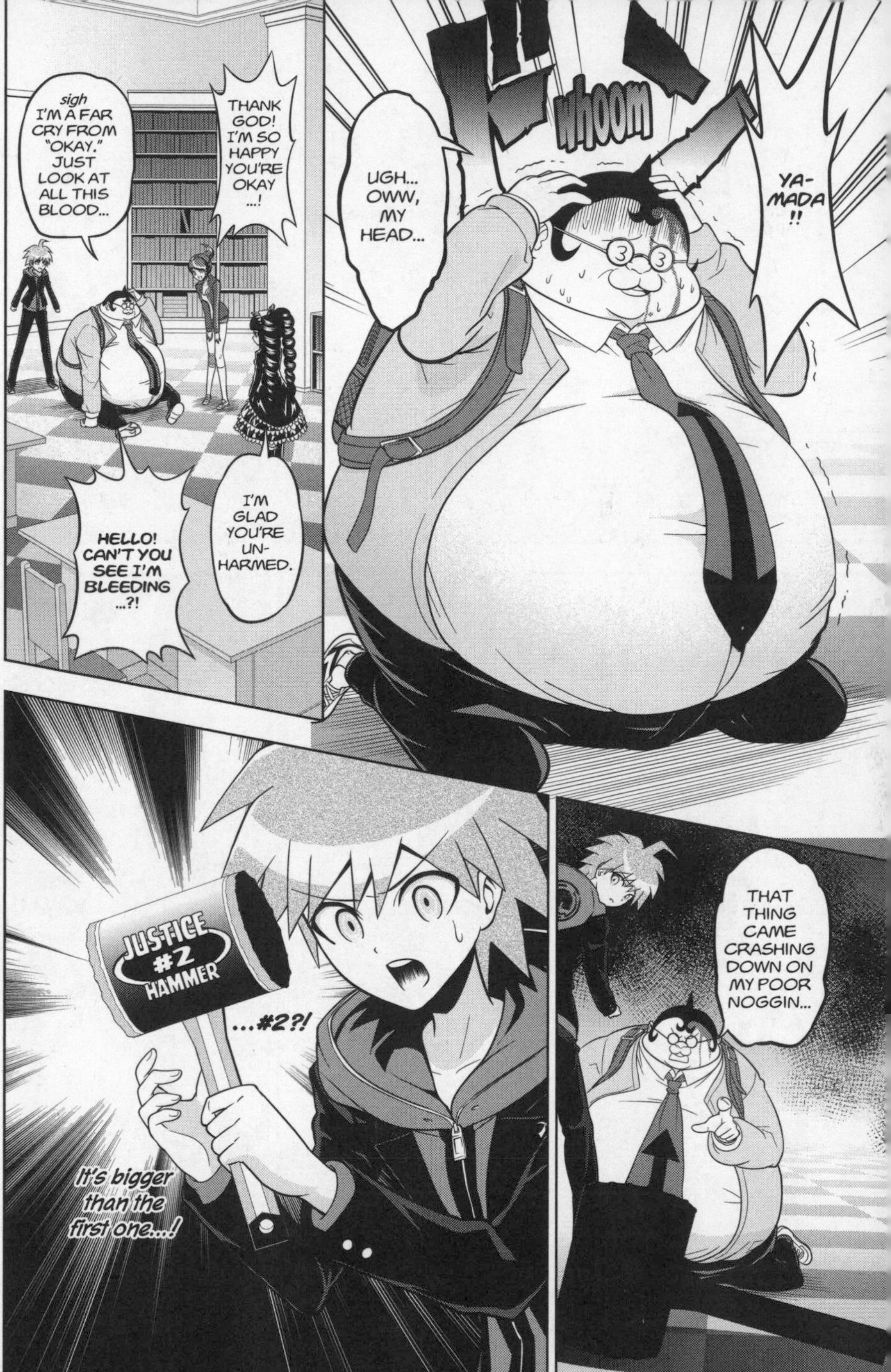
YA-MADA!!
whoom
UGH... OWW, MY HEAD...
THANK GOD! I'M SO HAPPY YOU'RE OKAY ...!
sigh I'M A FAR CRY FROM "OKAY." JUST LOOK AT ALL THIS BLOOD...
I'M GLAD YOU'RE UN-HARMED.
HELLO! CAN'T YOU SEE I'M BLEEDING ...?!
THAT THING CAME CRASHING DOWN ON MY POOR NOGGIN...
JUSTICE #2 HAMMER
...#2?!
It's bigger than the first one...!

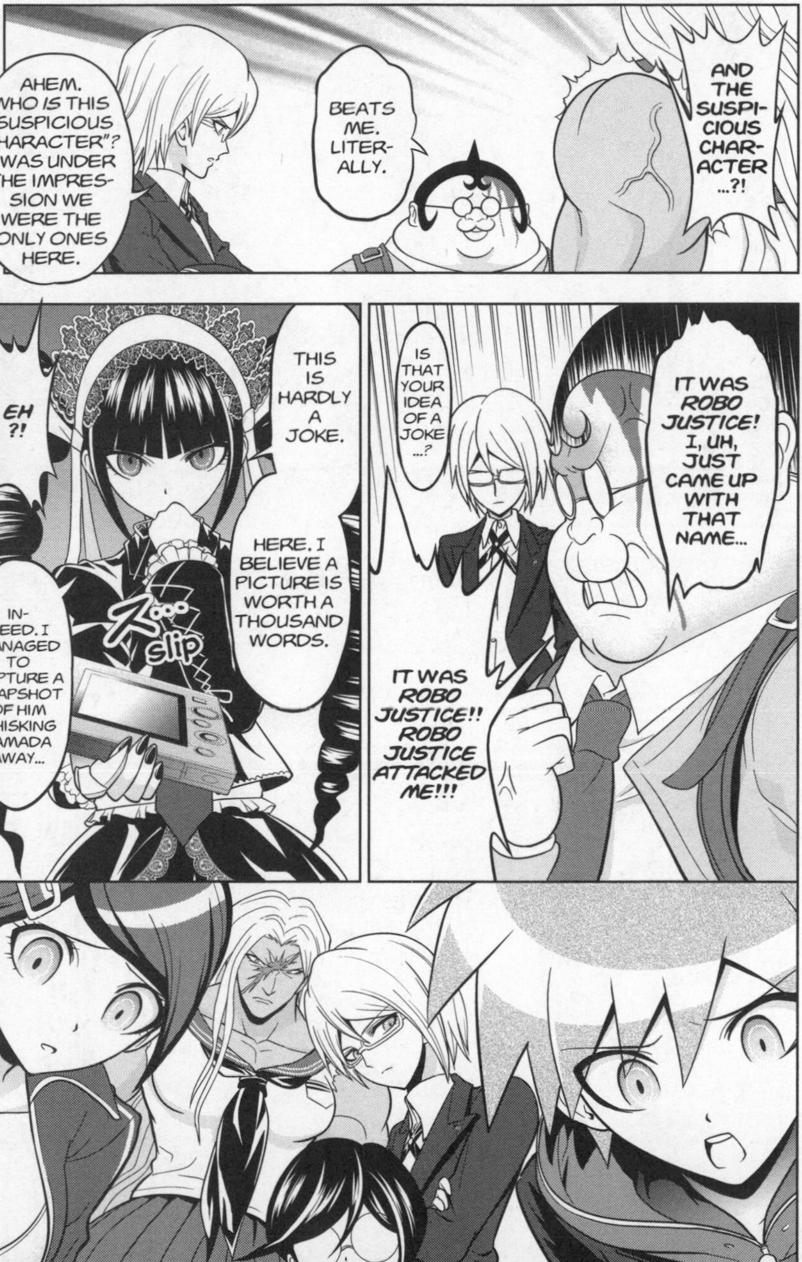
AND THE SUSPICIOUS CHARACTER ...?!
BEATS ME. LITERALLY.
AHEM. WHO IS THIS "SUSPICIOUS CHARACTER"? I WAS UNDER THE IMPRESSION WE WERE THE ONLY ONES HERE.
IT WAS ROBO JUSTICE! I, UH, JUST CAME UP WITH THAT NAME...
IS THAT YOUR IDEA OF A JOKE ...?
IT WAS ROBO JUSTICE!! ROBO JUSTICE ATTACKED ME!!!
THIS IS HARDLY A JOKE.
EH ?!
HERE. I BELIEVE A PICTURE IS WORTH A THOUSAND WORDS.
slip
IN-DEED. I MANAGED TO CAPTURE A SNAPSHOT OF HIM WHISKING YAMADA AWAY...

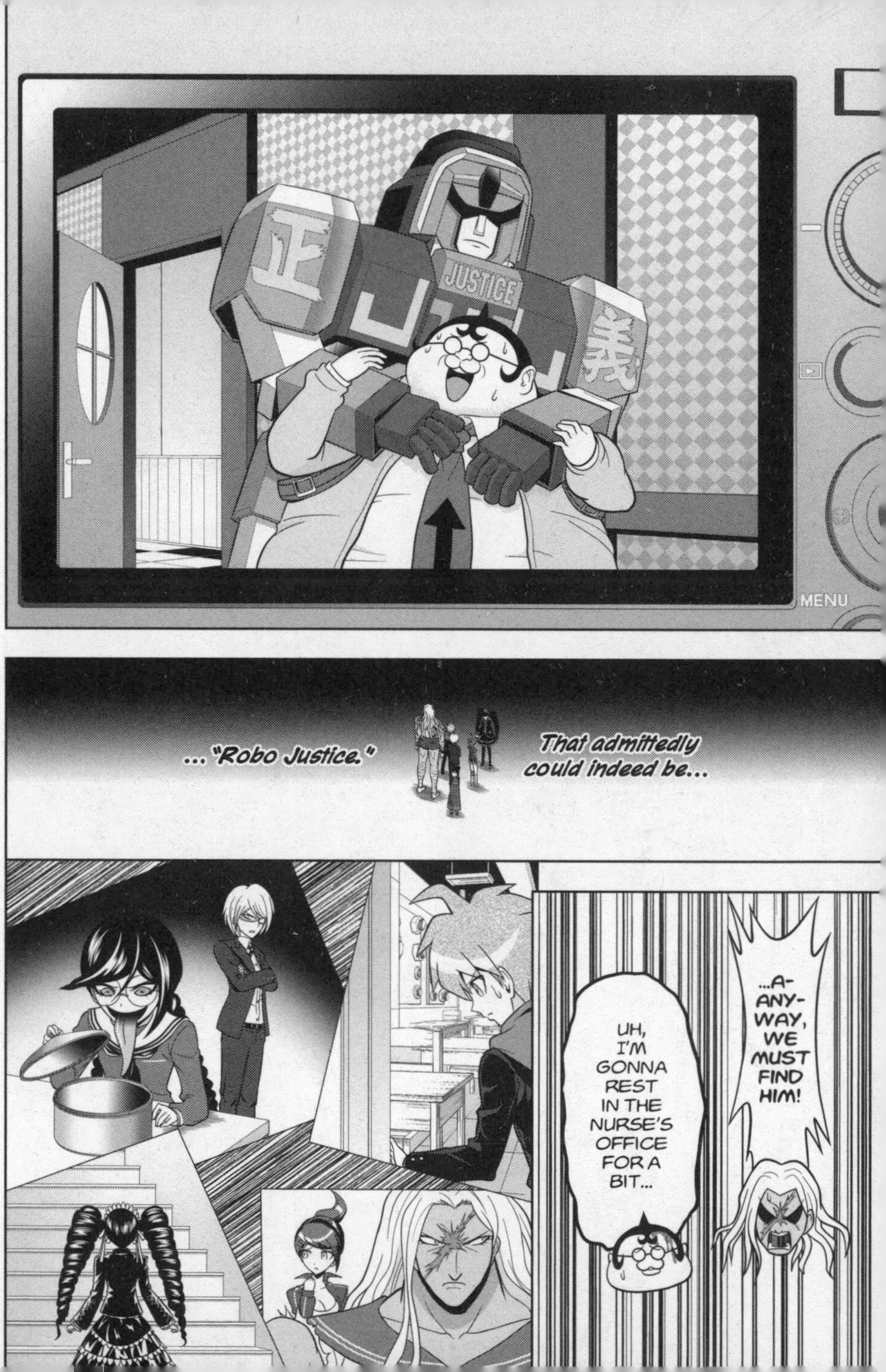

正
JUSTICE
義
MENU
That admittedly could indeed be...
... "Robo Justice."
...A-ANYWAY, WE MUST FIND HIM!
UH, I'M GONNA REST IN THE NURSE'S OFFICE FOR A BIT...

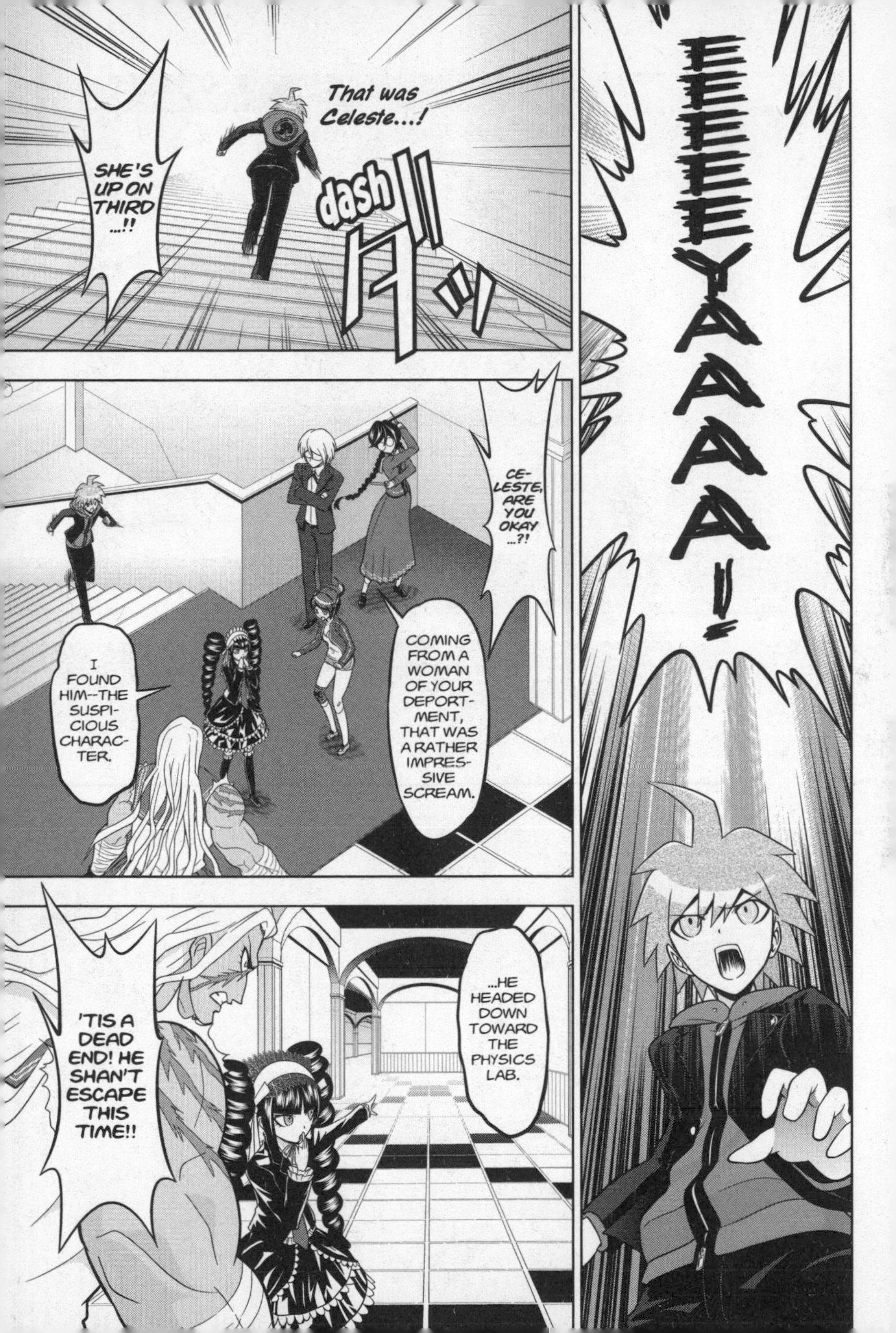
EEEEEYAAAA!!
That was Celeste...!
SHE'S UP ON THIRD ...!!
dash
CE-LESTE, ARE YOU OKAY ...?!
COMING FROM A WOMAN OF YOUR DEPORT-MENT, THAT WAS A RATHER IMPRES-SIVE SCREAM.
I FOUND HIM--THE SUSPI-CIOUS CHARAC-TER.
...HE HEADED DOWN TOWARD THE PHYSICS LAB.
'TIS A DEAD END! HE SHAN'T ESCAPE THIS TIME!!

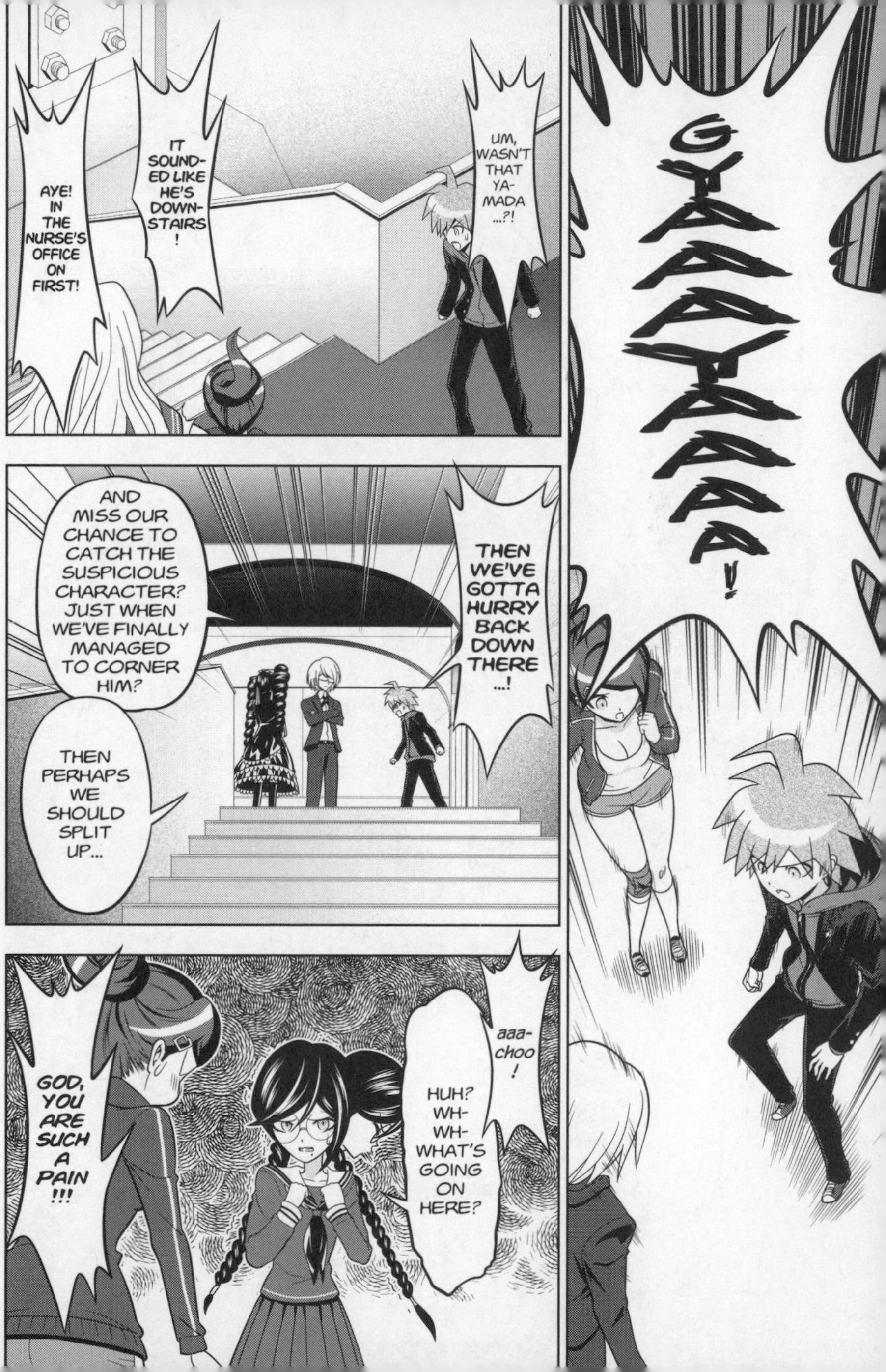
GYAAAYAAAA!
UM, WASN'T THAT YA-MADA ...?!
IT SOUND-ED LIKE HE'S DOWN-STAIRS!
AYE! IN THE NURSE'S OFFICE ON FIRST!
THEN WE'VE GOTTA HURRY BACK DOWN THERE ...!
AND MISS OUR CHANCE TO CATCH THE SUSPICIOUS CHARACTER? JUST WHEN WE'VE FINALLY MANAGED TO CORNER HIM?
THEN PERHAPS WE SHOULD SPLIT UP...
aaa-choo!
HUH? WH-WH-WHAT'S GOING ON HERE?
GOD, YOU ARE SUCH A PAIN!!!

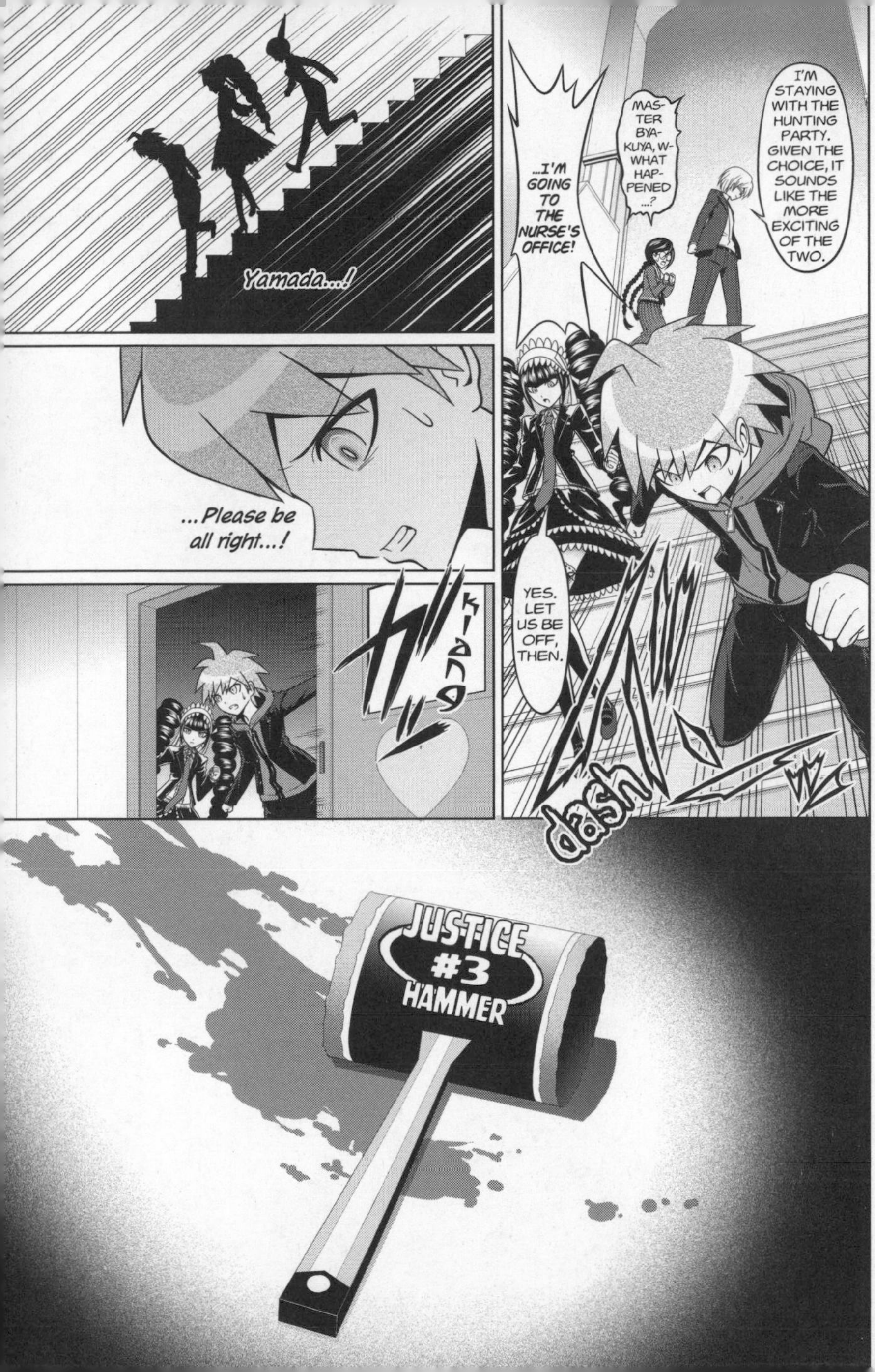
I'M STAYING WITH THE HUNTING PARTY. GIVEN THE CHOICE, IT SOUNDS LIKE THE MORE EXCITING OF THE TWO.
MASTER BYAKUYA, W-WHAT HAPPENED...?
...I'M GOING TO THE NURSE'S OFFICE!
YES. LET US BE OFF, THEN.
dash
Yamada...!
...Please be all right...!
klang
JUSTICE #3 HAMMER

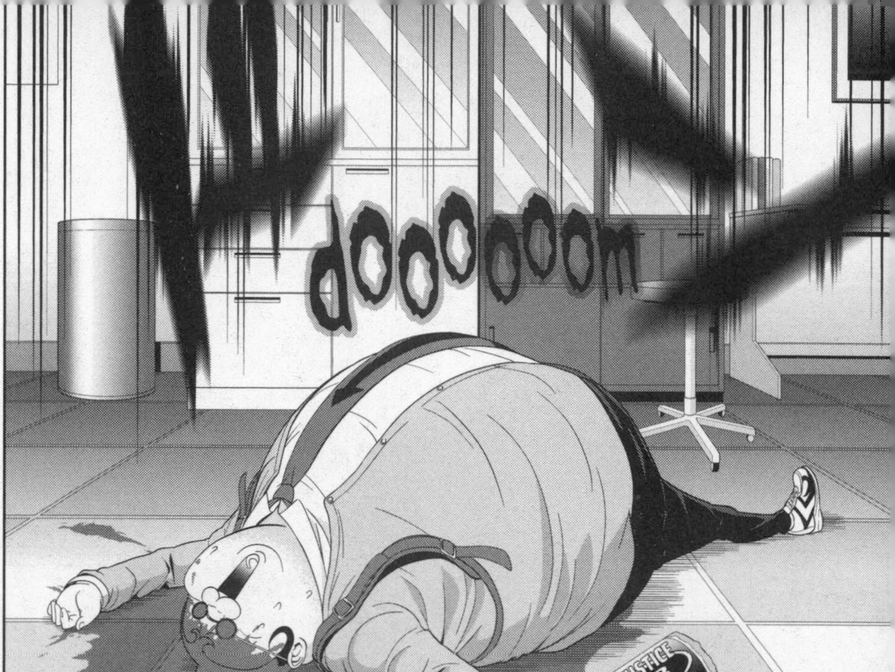
doooooom
JUSTICE #3 HAMMER

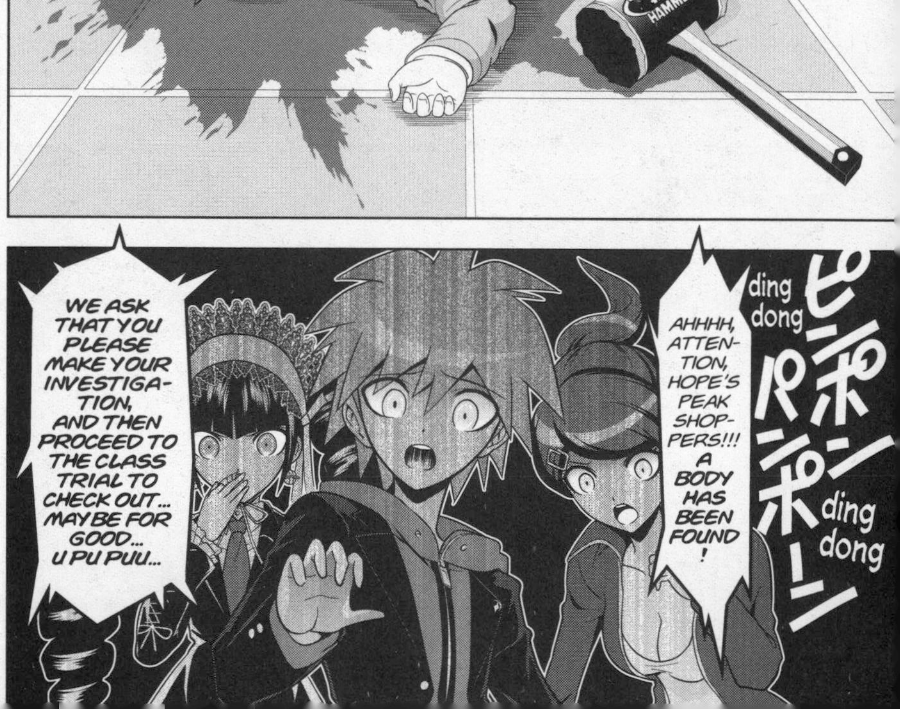
ピンポンパンポーン
ding dong ding dong
AHHHH, ATTENTION, HOPE'S PEAK SHOPPERS!!! A BODY HAS BEEN FOUND!
WE ASK THAT YOU PLEASE MAKE YOUR INVESTIGATION, AND THEN PROCEED TO THE CLASS TRIAL TO CHECK OUT... MAYBE FOR GOOD... UPU PUU...

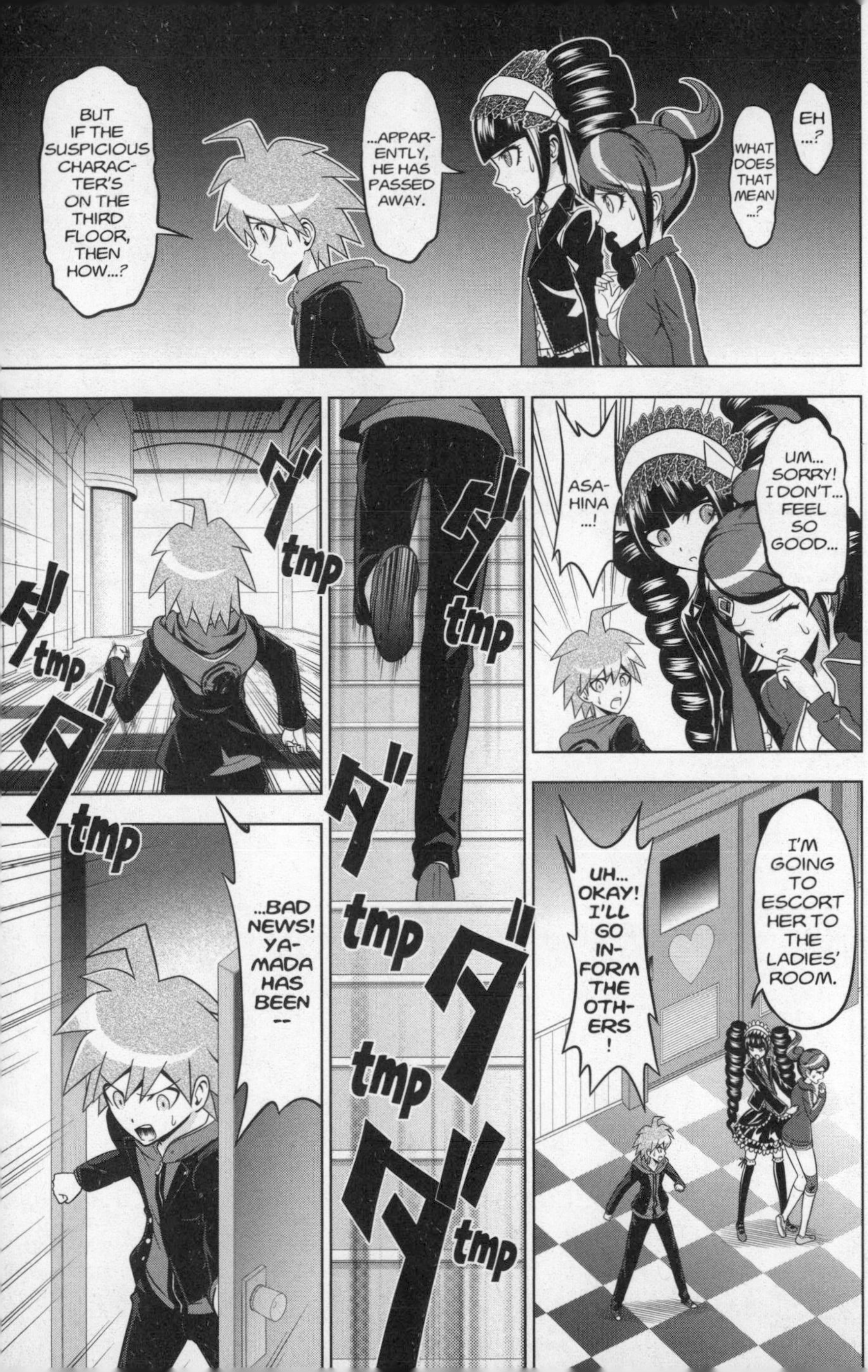
EH ...?
WHAT DOES THAT MEAN ...?
...APPARENTLY, HE HAS PASSED AWAY.
BUT IF THE SUSPICIOUS CHARACTER'S ON THE THIRD FLOOR, THEN HOW...?
UM... SORRY! I DON'T... FEEL SO GOOD...
ASAHINA ...!
I'M GOING TO ESCORT HER TO THE LADIES' ROOM.
UH... OKAY! I'LL GO INFORM THE OTHERS!
ダ tmp
ダ tmp
ダ tmp
ダ tmp
ダ tmp
ダ tmp
ダ tmp
ダ tmp
...BAD NEWS! YAMADA HAS BEEN --

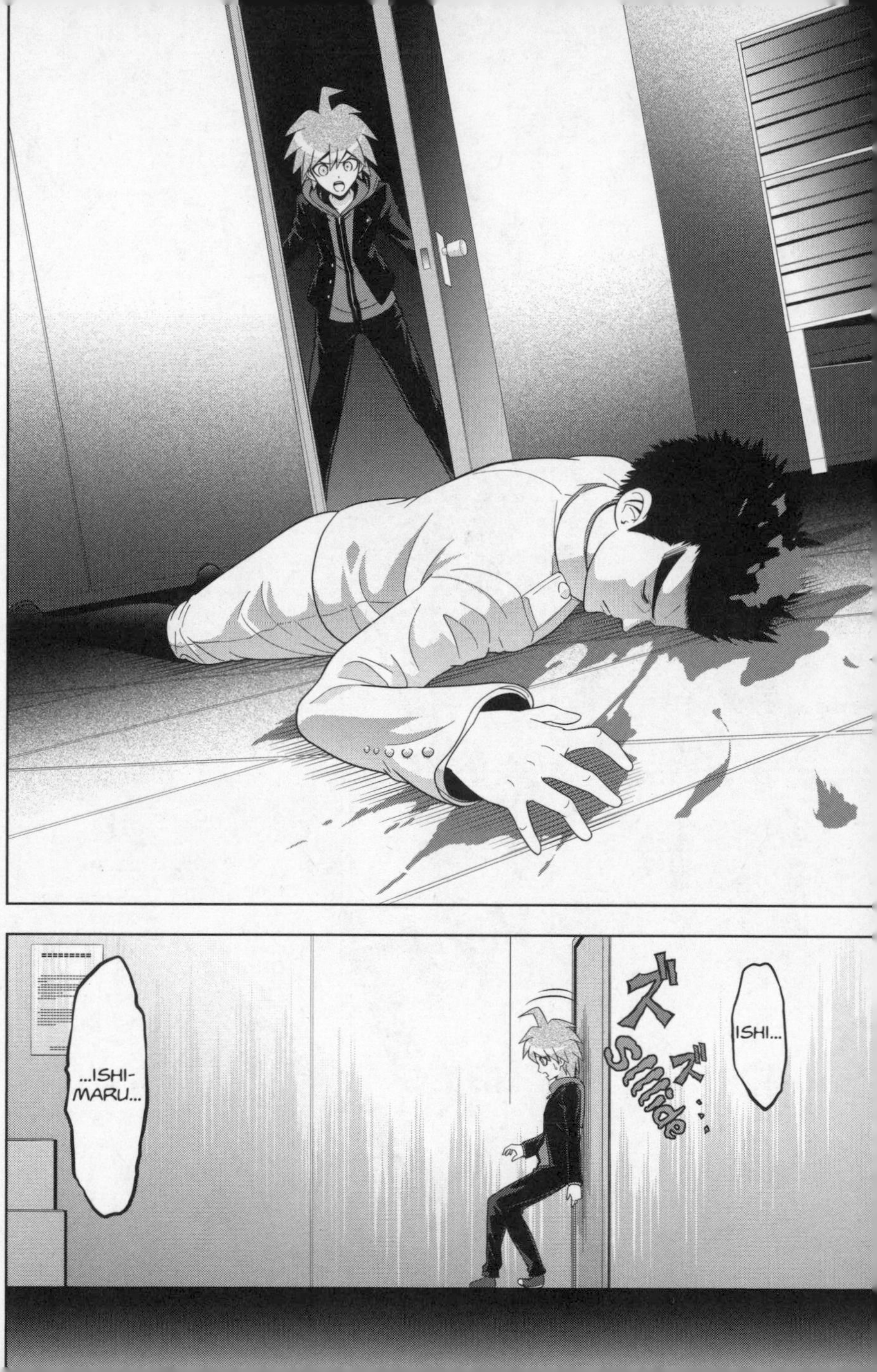
ISHI...
ズズ...
Sliiide
...ISHI-MARU...

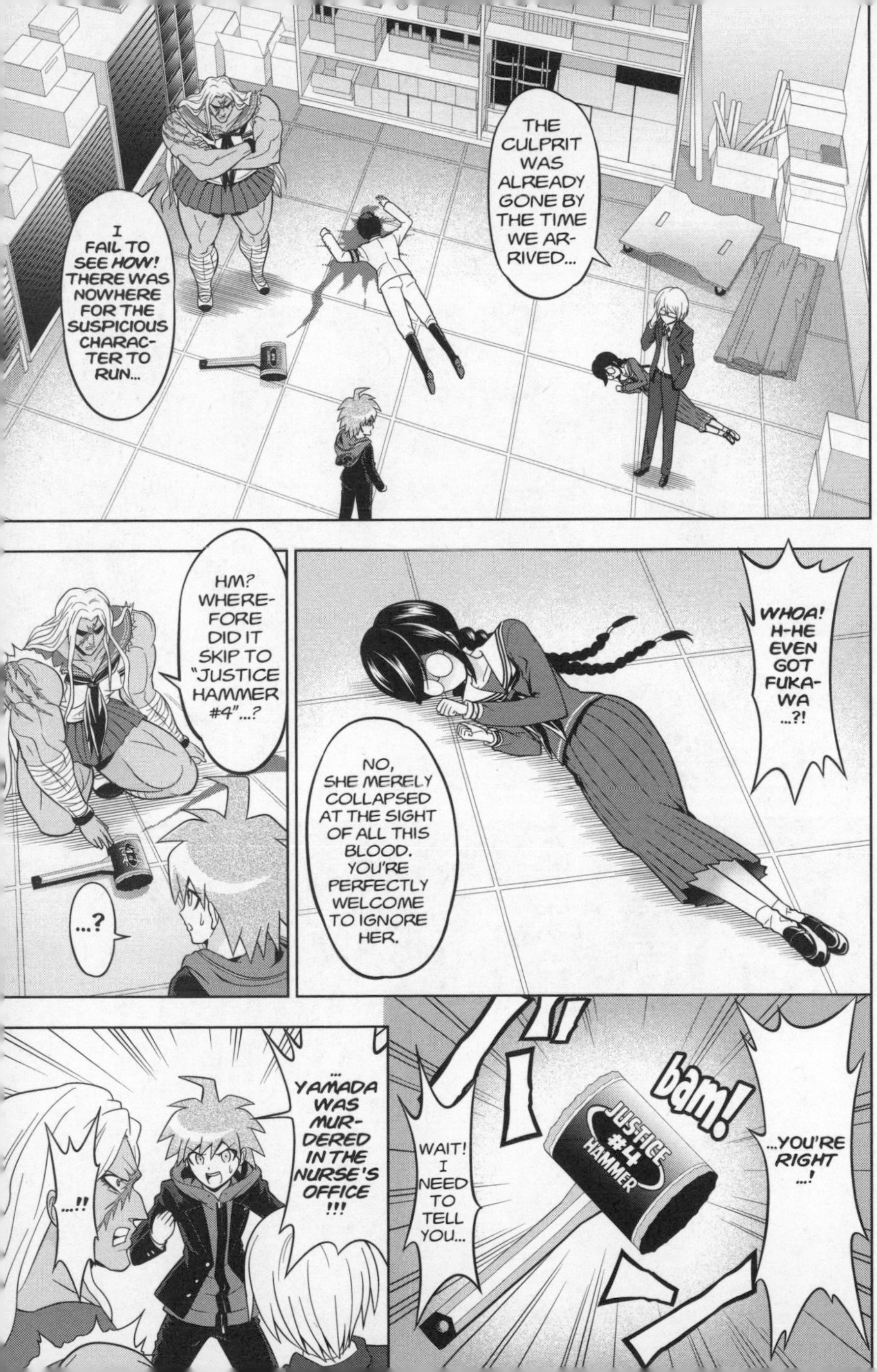
THE CULPRIT WAS ALREADY GONE BY THE TIME WE ARRIVED...
I FAIL TO SEE *HOW*! THERE WAS NOWHERE FOR THE SUSPICIOUS CHARACTER TO RUN...
WHOA! H-HE EVEN GOT FUKAWA...?!
NO, SHE MERELY COLLAPSED AT THE SIGHT OF ALL THIS BLOOD. YOU'RE PERFECTLY WELCOME TO IGNORE HER.
HM? WHEREFORE DID IT SKIP TO "JUSTICE HAMMER #4"...?
...?
...YOU'RE RIGHT...!
bam!
JUSTICE #4 HAMMER
WAIT! I NEED TO TELL YOU...
...YAMADA WAS MURDERED IN THE NURSE'S OFFICE!!!
...!!

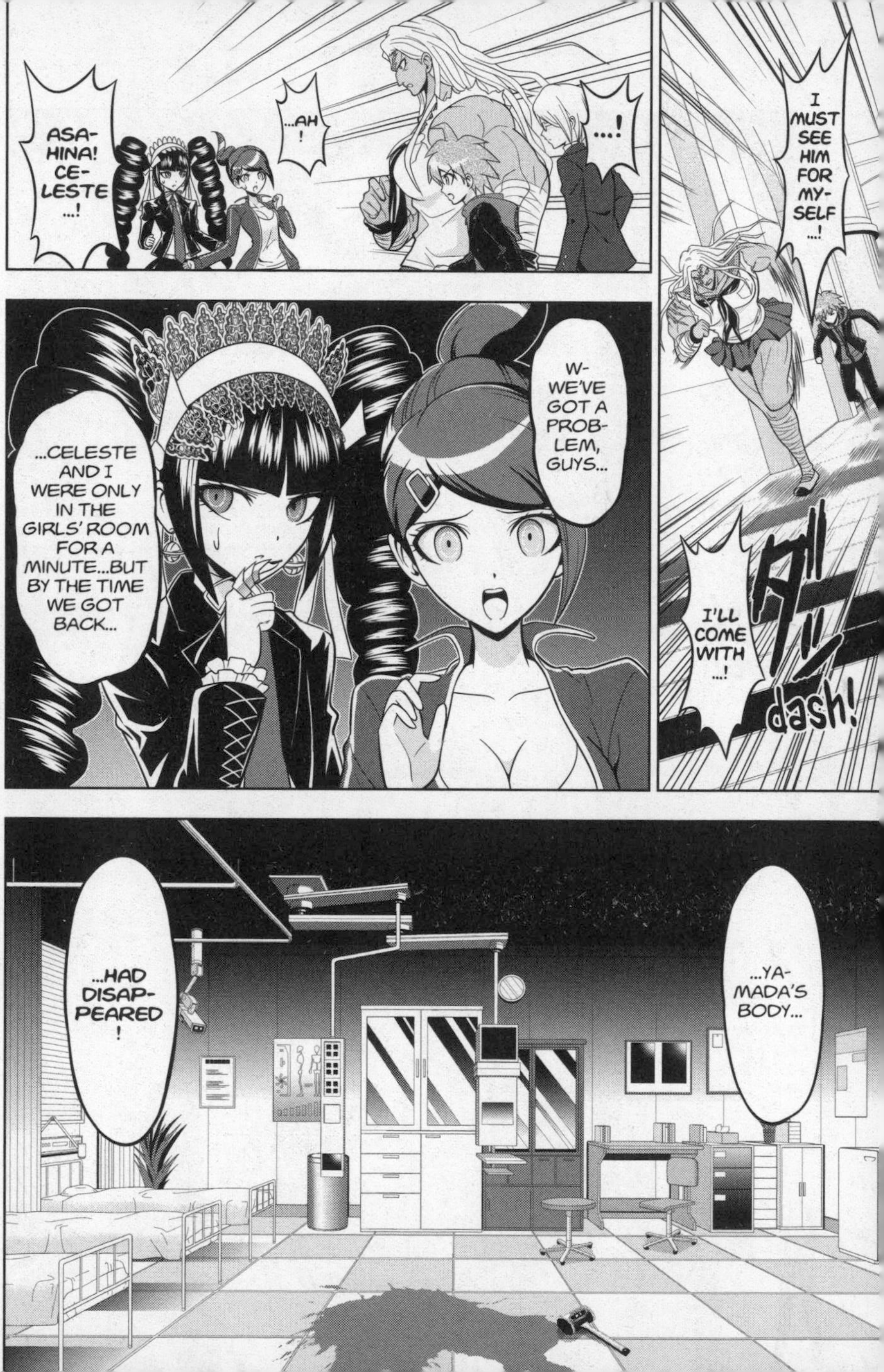
I MUST SEE HIM FOR MYSELF ...!
I'LL COME WITH ...!
ダッ
dash!
...!
...AH !
ASAHINA! CELESTE ...!
W-WE'VE GOT A PROBLEM, GUYS...
...CELESTE AND I WERE ONLY IN THE GIRLS' ROOM FOR A MINUTE...BUT BY THE TIME WE GOT BACK...
...YAMADA'S BODY...
...HAD DISAPPEARED !

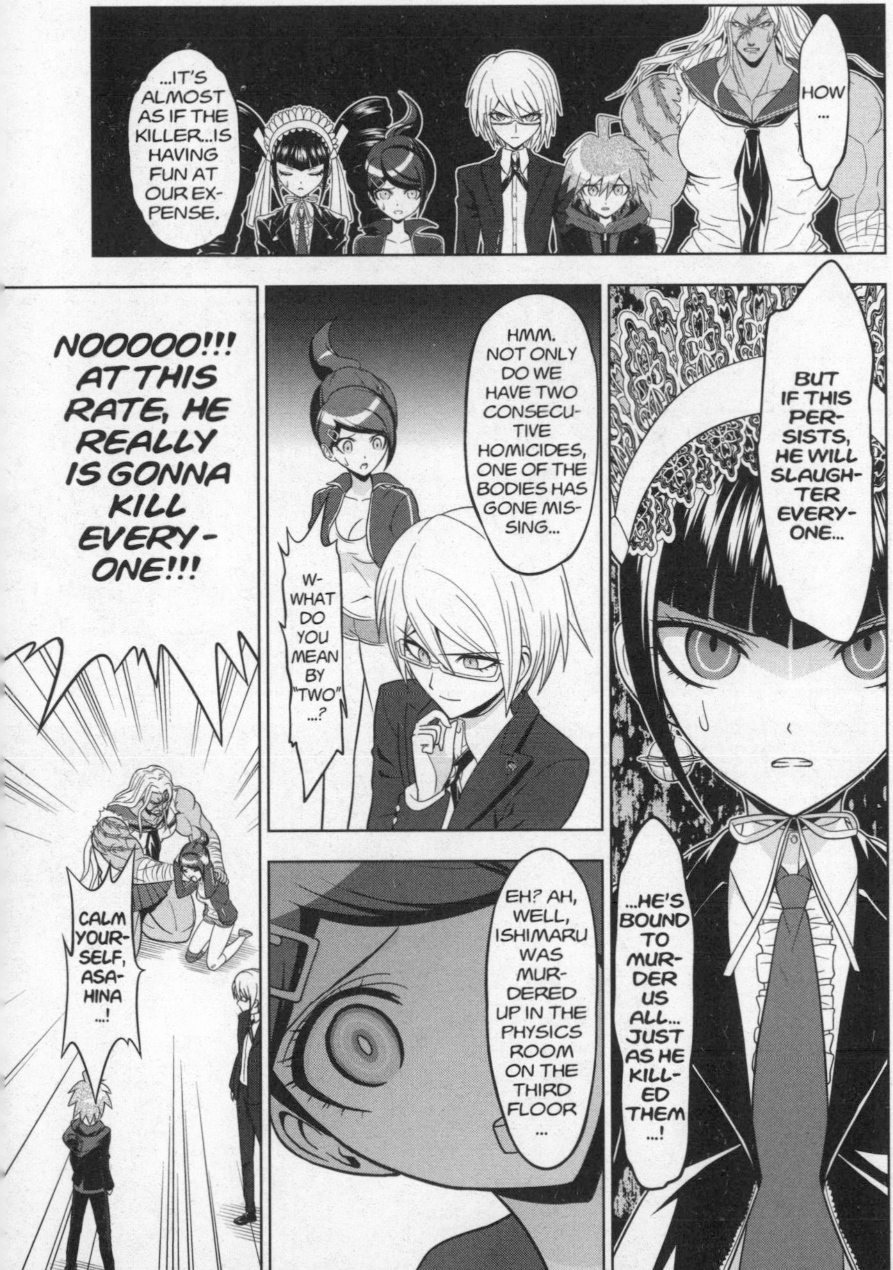

HOW ...
...IT'S ALMOST AS IF THE KILLER...IS HAVING FUN AT OUR EXPENSE.
BUT IF THIS PERSISTS, HE WILL SLAUGHTER EVERYONE...
...HE'S BOUND TO MURDER US ALL... JUST AS HE KILLED THEM ...!
HMM. NOT ONLY DO WE HAVE TWO CONSECUTIVE HOMICIDES, ONE OF THE BODIES HAS GONE MISSING...
W-WHAT DO YOU MEAN BY "TWO" ...?
EH? AH, WELL, ISHIMARU WAS MURDERED UP IN THE PHYSICS ROOM ON THE THIRD FLOOR ...
NOOOOO!!! AT THIS RATE, HE REALLY IS GONNA KILL EVERYONE!!!
CALM YOURSELF, ASAHINA ...!

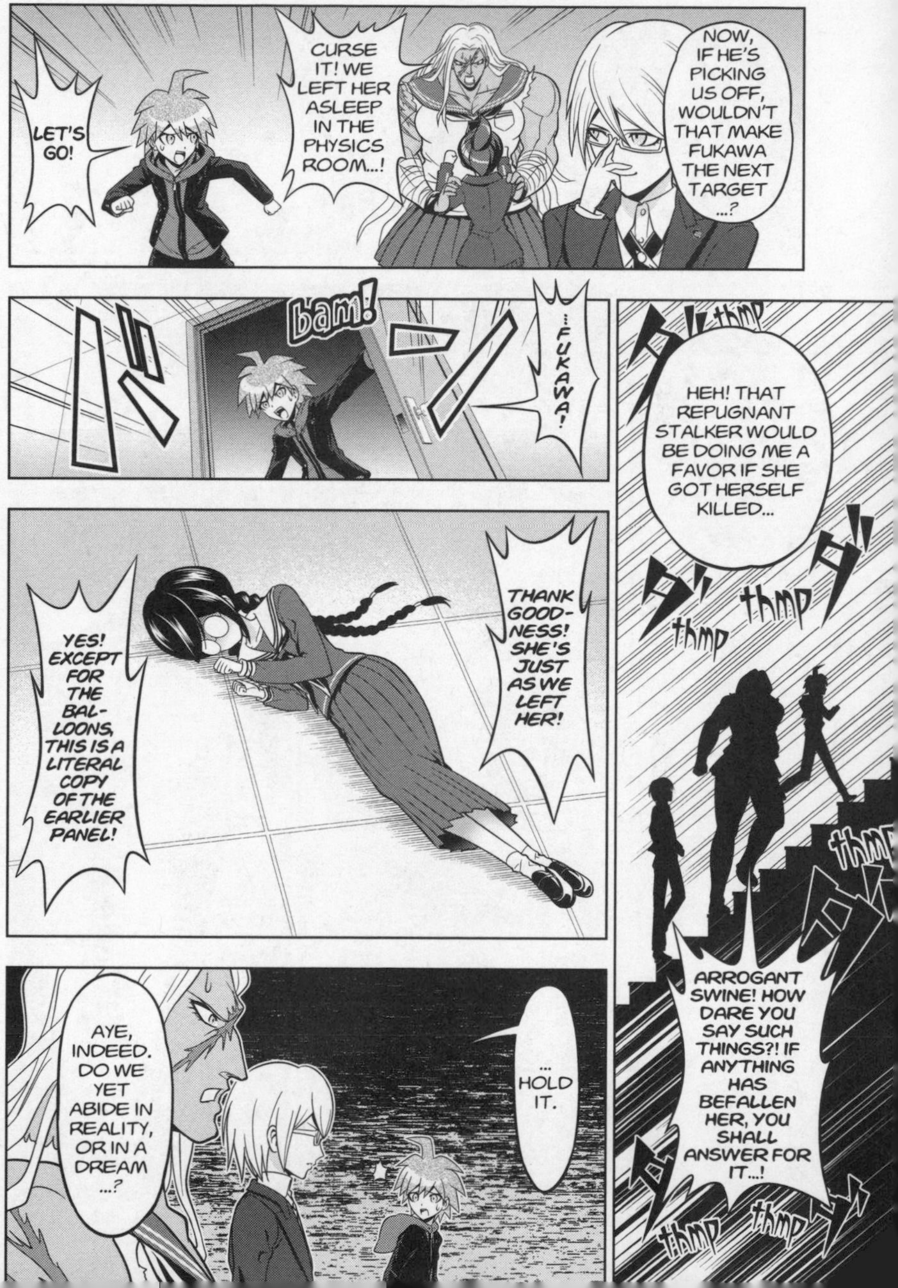
NOW, IF HE'S PICKING US OFF, WOULDN'T THAT MAKE FUKAWA THE NEXT TARGET ...?
CURSE IT! WE LEFT HER ASLEEP IN THE PHYSICS ROOM...!
LET'S GO!
thmp
HEH! THAT REPUGNANT STALKER WOULD BE DOING ME A FAVOR IF SHE GOT HERSELF KILLED...
thmp
thmp
thmp
ARROGANT SWINE! HOW DARE YOU SAY SUCH THINGS?! IF ANYTHING HAS BEFALLEN HER, YOU SHALL ANSWER FOR IT...!
thmp
thmp
...FUKAWA!
bam!
THANK GOODNESS! SHE'S JUST AS WE LEFT HER!
YES! EXCEPT FOR THE BALLOONS, THIS IS A LITERAL COPY OF THE EARLIER PANEL!
...HOLD IT.
AYE, INDEED. DO WE YET ABIDE IN REALITY, OR IN A DREAM ...?

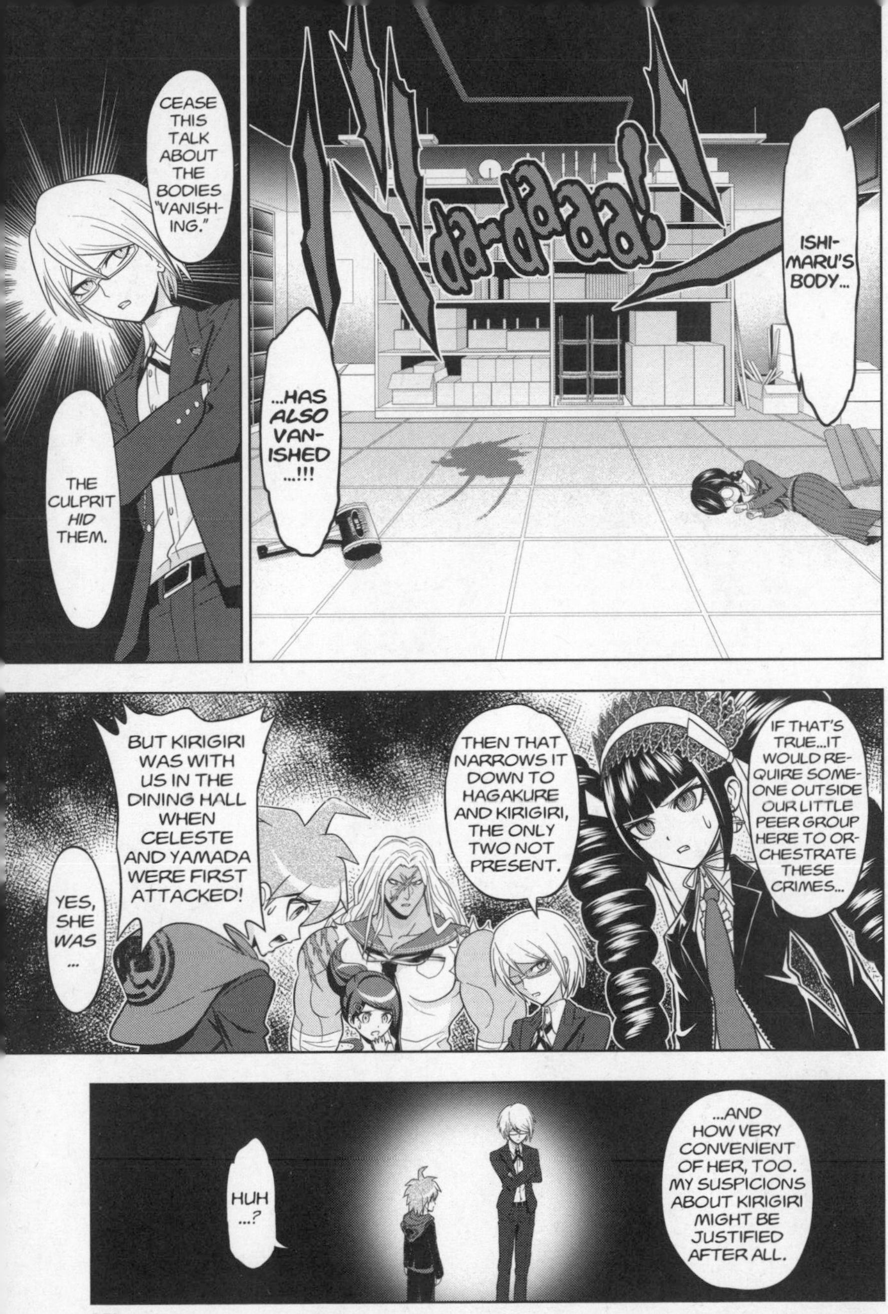
ISHI-MARU'S BODY...
da-daaa!
...HAS ALSO VAN-ISHED ...!!!
CEASE THIS TALK ABOUT THE BODIES "VANISH-ING."
THE CULPRIT HID THEM.
IF THAT'S TRUE...IT WOULD RE-QUIRE SOME-ONE OUTSIDE OUR LITTLE PEER GROUP HERE TO OR-CHESTRATE THESE CRIMES...
THEN THAT NARROWS IT DOWN TO HAGAKURE AND KIRIGIRI, THE ONLY TWO NOT PRESENT.
BUT KIRIGIRI WAS WITH US IN THE DINING HALL WHEN CELESTE AND YAMADA WERE FIRST ATTACKED!
YES, SHE WAS ...
...AND HOW VERY CONVENIENT OF HER, TOO. MY SUSPICIONS ABOUT KIRIGIRI MIGHT BE JUSTIFIED AFTER ALL.
HUH ...?

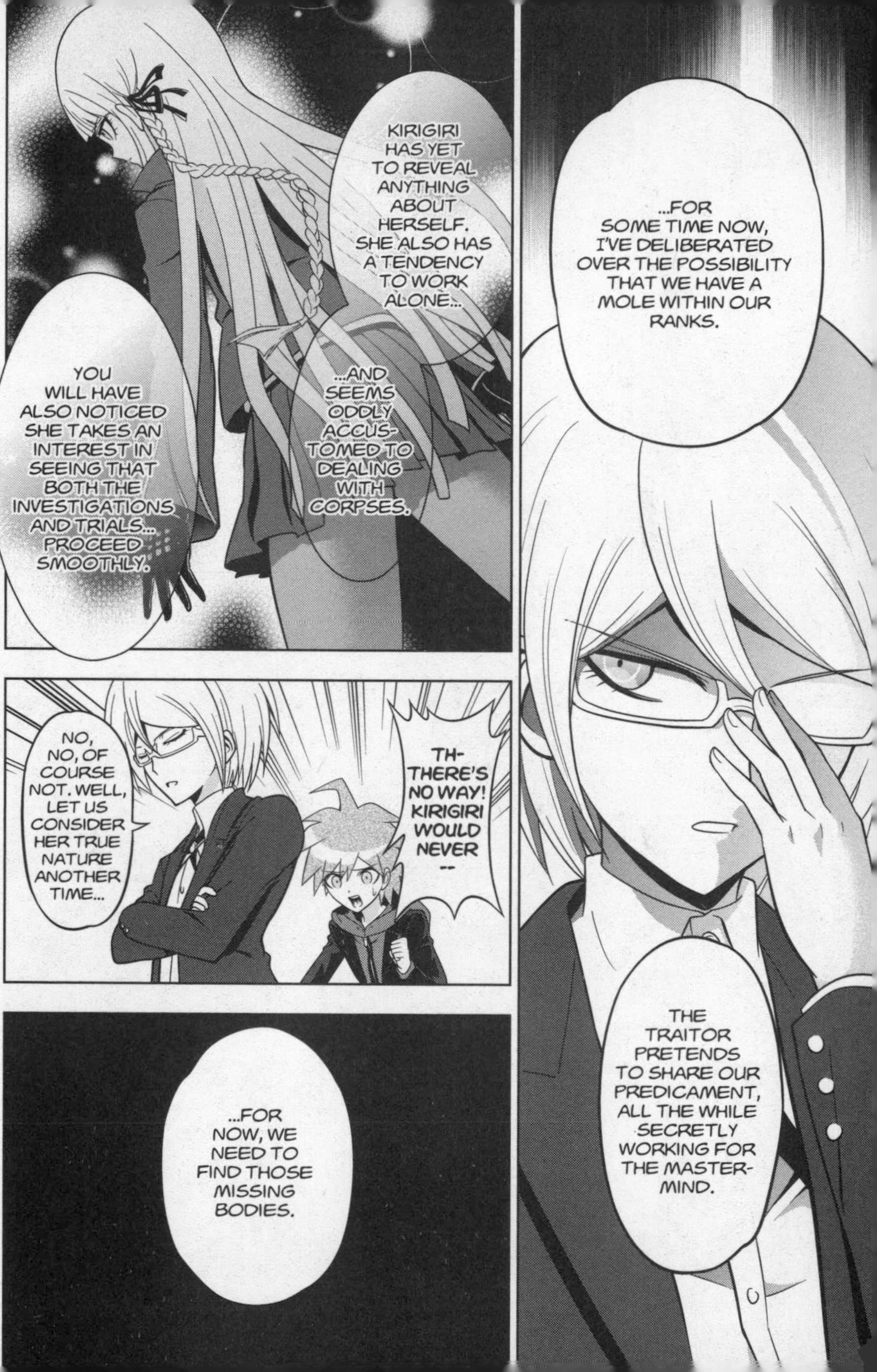
...FOR SOME TIME NOW, I'VE DELIBERATED OVER THE POSSIBILITY THAT WE HAVE A MOLE WITHIN OUR RANKS.
THE TRAITOR PRETENDS TO SHARE OUR PREDICAMENT, ALL THE WHILE SECRETLY WORKING FOR THE MASTER-MIND.
KIRIGIRI HAS YET TO REVEAL ANYTHING ABOUT HERSELF. SHE ALSO HAS A TENDENCY TO WORK ALONE...
...AND SEEMS ODDLY ACCUS-TOMED TO DEALING WITH CORPSES.
YOU WILL HAVE ALSO NOTICED SHE TAKES AN INTEREST IN SEEING THAT BOTH THE INVESTIGATIONS AND TRIALS... PROCEED SMOOTHLY.
TH-THERE'S NO WAY! KIRIGIRI WOULD NEVER --
NO, NO, OF COURSE NOT. WELL, LET US CONSIDER HER TRUE NATURE ANOTHER TIME...
...FOR NOW, WE NEED TO FIND THOSE MISSING BODIES.

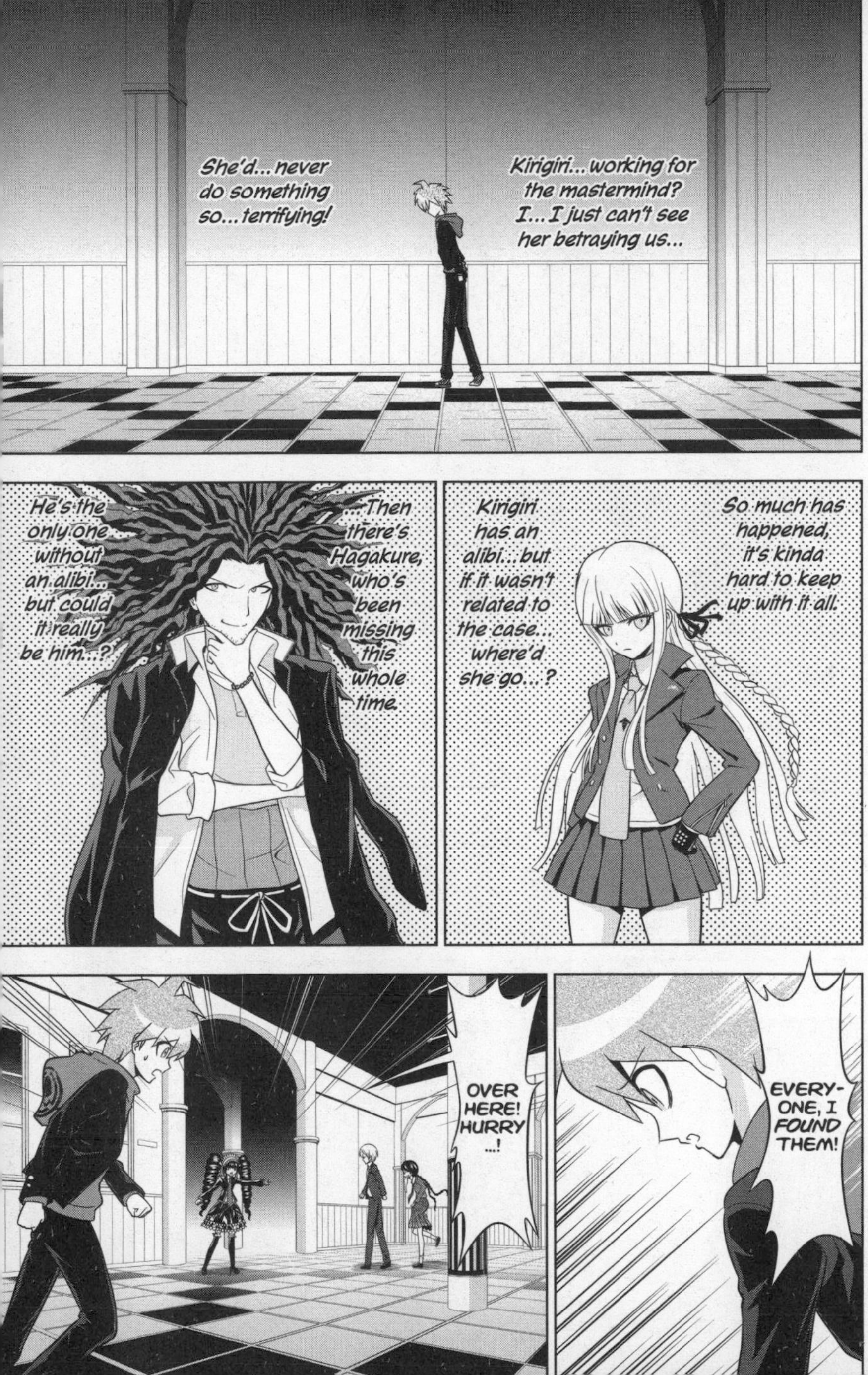
Kirigiri... working for the mastermind? I... I just can't see her betraying us...
She'd... never do something so... terrifying!
So much has happened, it's kinda hard to keep up with it all.
Kirigiri has an alibi... but if it wasn't related to the case... where'd she go...?
...Then there's Hagakure, who's been missing this whole time.
He's the only one without an alibi... but could it really be him...?
EVERY-ONE, I FOUND THEM!
OVER HERE! HURRY ...!

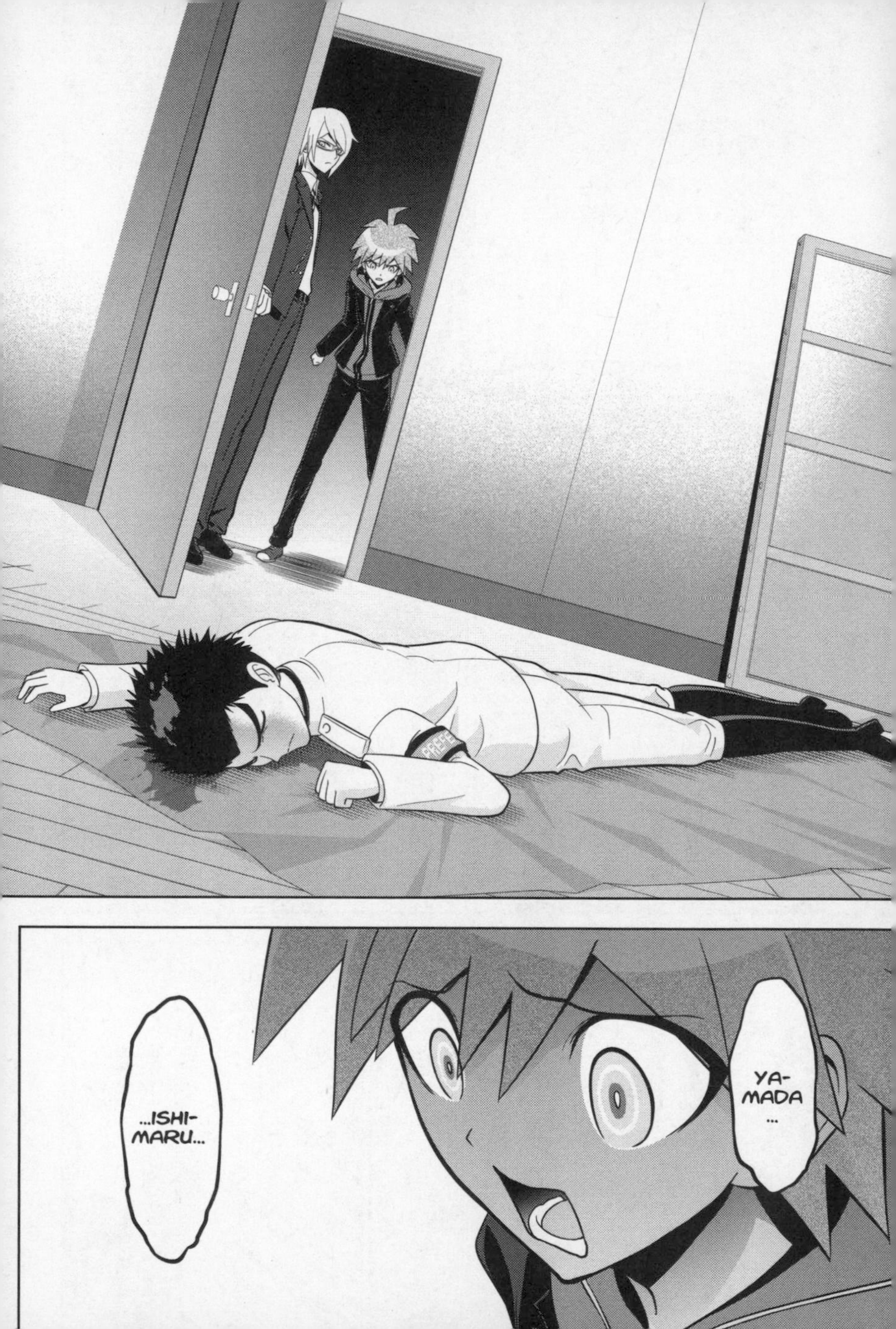
YA-MADA...
...ISHI-MARU...

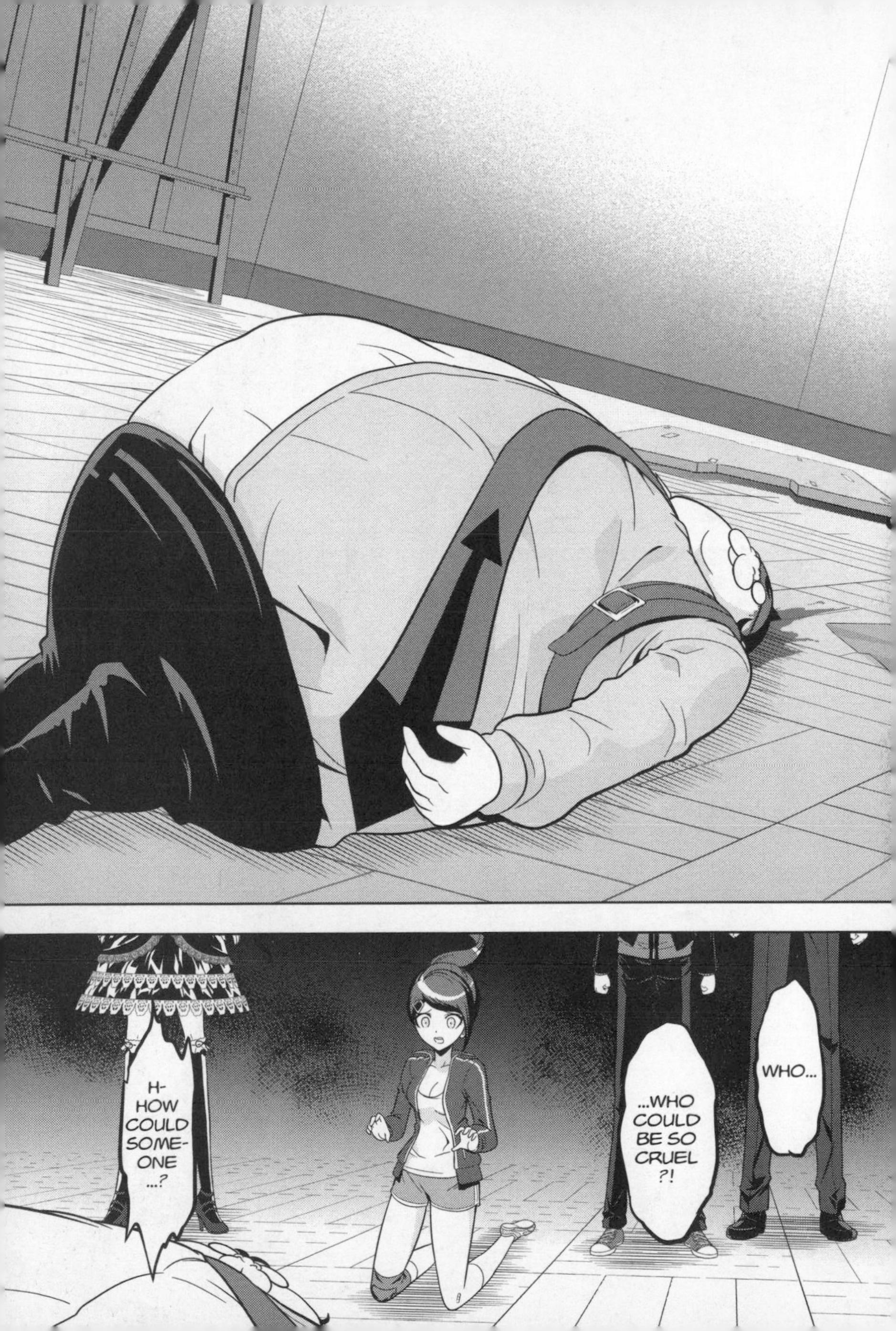
WHO...
...WHO COULD BE SO CRUEL?!
H-HOW COULD SOME-ONE...?

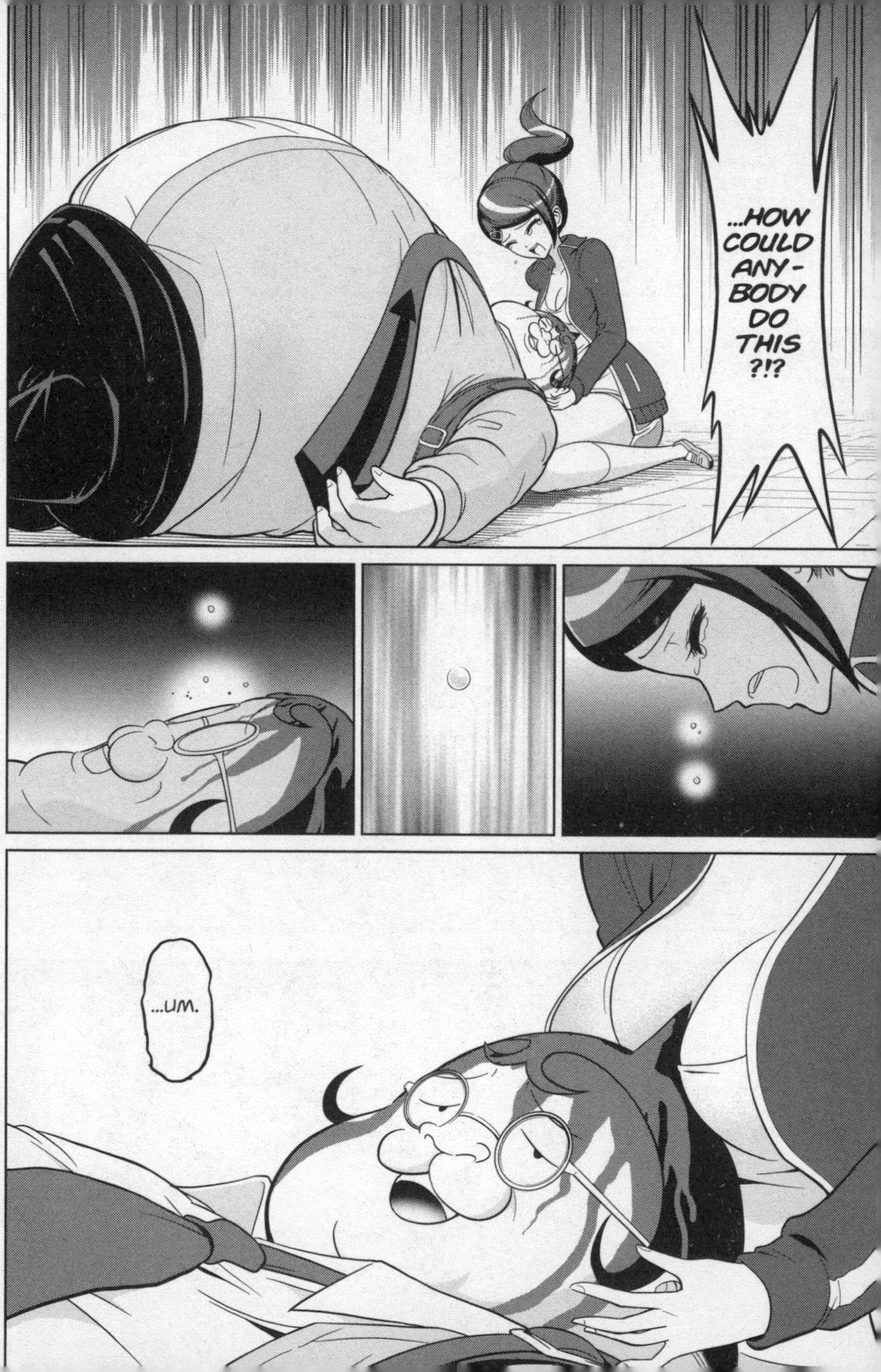
...HOW COULD ANY-BODY DO THIS ?!?
...UM.

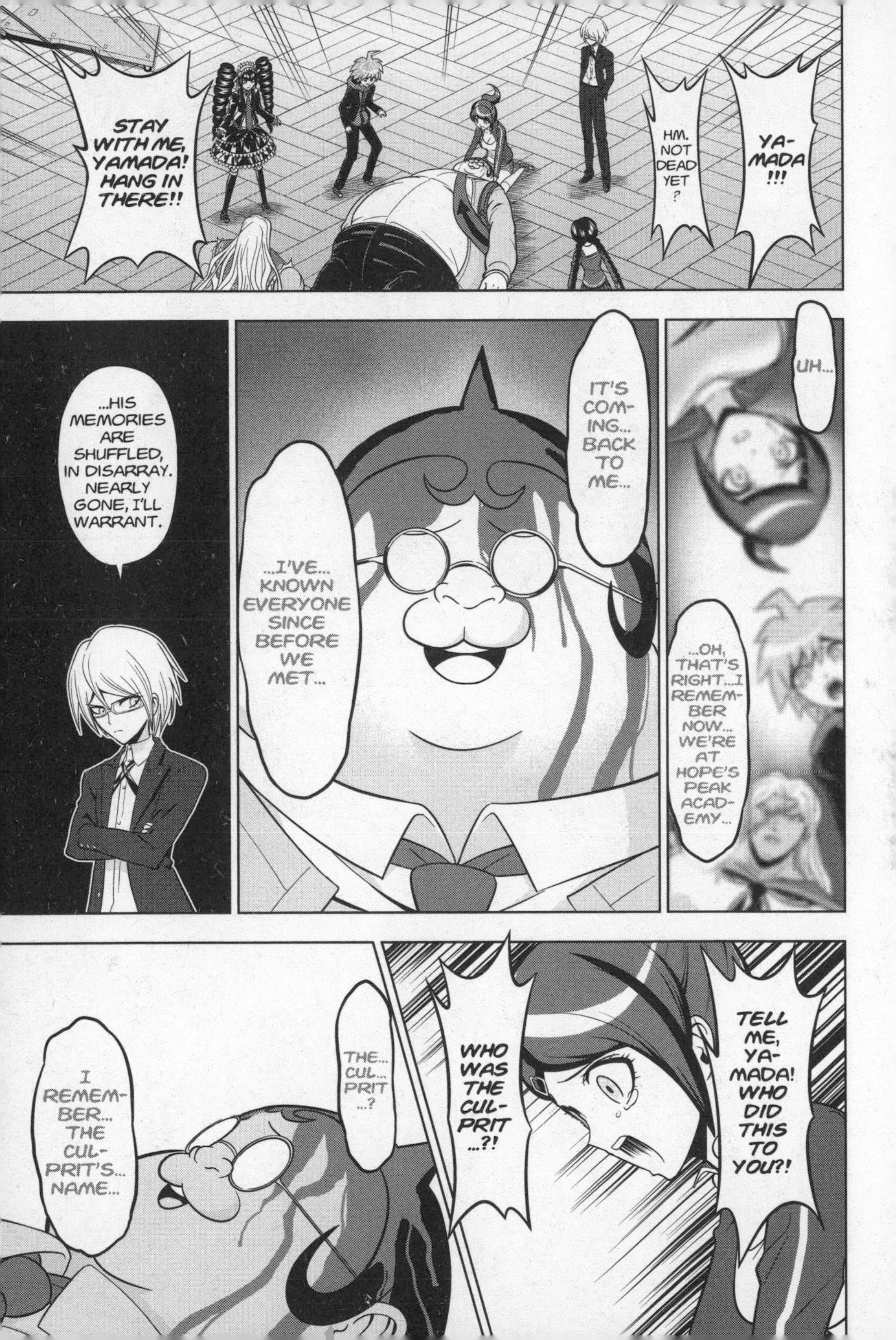
YAMADA!!!
HM. NOT DEAD YET?
STAY WITH ME, YAMADA! HANG IN THERE!!
UH...
...OH, THAT'S RIGHT...I REMEMBER NOW... WE'RE AT HOPE'S PEAK ACADEMY...
IT'S COMING... BACK TO ME...
...I'VE... KNOWN EVERYONE SINCE BEFORE WE MET...
...HIS MEMORIES ARE SHUFFLED, IN DISARRAY. NEARLY GONE, I'LL WARRANT.
TELL ME, YAMADA! WHO DID THIS TO YOU?!
WHO WAS THE CULPRIT...?!
THE... CULPRIT...?
I REMEMBER... THE CULPRIT'S... NAME...

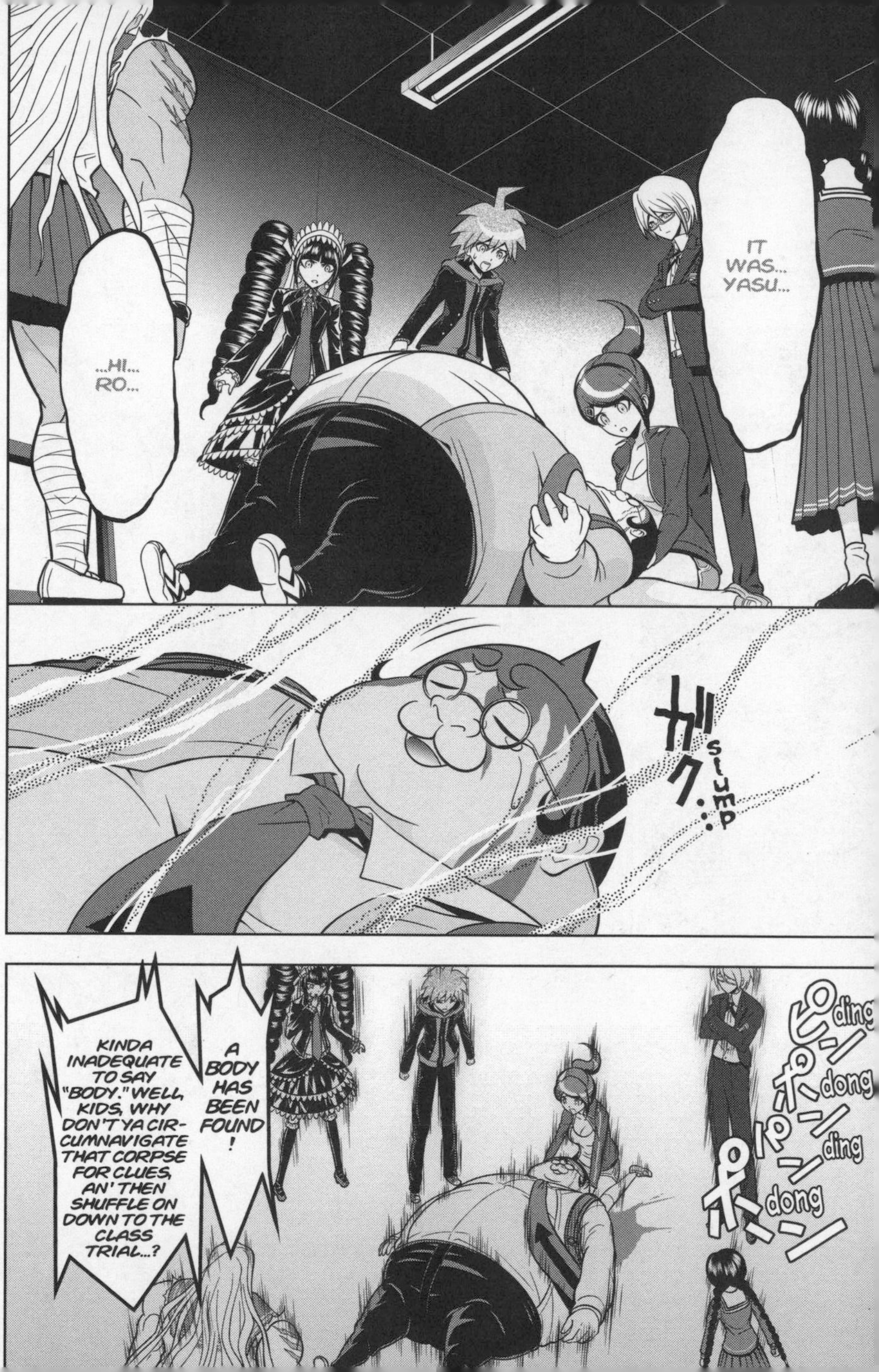
IT WAS... YASU...
...HI... RO...
ガク slump
ピンポンパンポーン ding dong ding dong
A BODY HAS BEEN FOUND!
KINDA INADEQUATE TO SAY "BODY." WELL, KIDS, WHY DON'T YA CIRCUMNAVIGATE THAT CORPSE FOR CLUES, AN' THEN SHUFFLE ON DOWN TO THE CLASS TRIAL...?

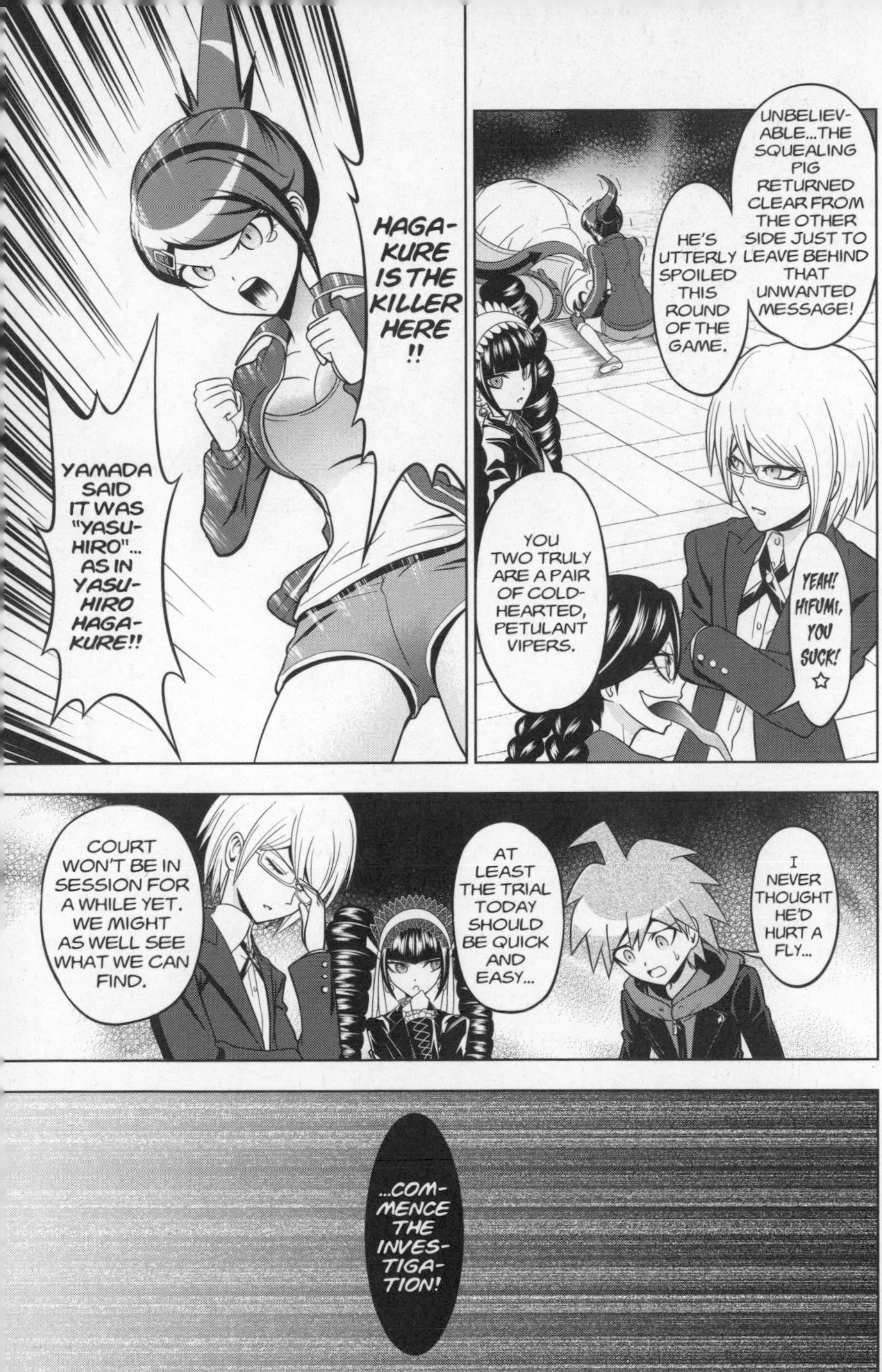
UNBELIEVABLE...THE SQUEALING PIG RETURNED CLEAR FROM THE OTHER SIDE JUST TO LEAVE BEHIND THAT UNWANTED MESSAGE!
HE'S UTTERLY SPOILED THIS ROUND OF THE GAME.
YEAH! HIFUMI, YOU SUCK! ☆
YOU TWO TRULY ARE A PAIR OF COLD-HEARTED, PETULANT VIPERS.
HAGAKURE IS THE KILLER HERE!!
YAMADA SAID IT WAS "YASUHIRO"... AS IN YASUHIRO HAGAKURE!!
I NEVER THOUGHT HE'D HURT A FLY...
AT LEAST THE TRIAL TODAY SHOULD BE QUICK AND EASY...
COURT WON'T BE IN SESSION FOR A WHILE YET. WE MIGHT AS WELL SEE WHAT WE CAN FIND.
...COMMENCE THE INVESTIGATION!

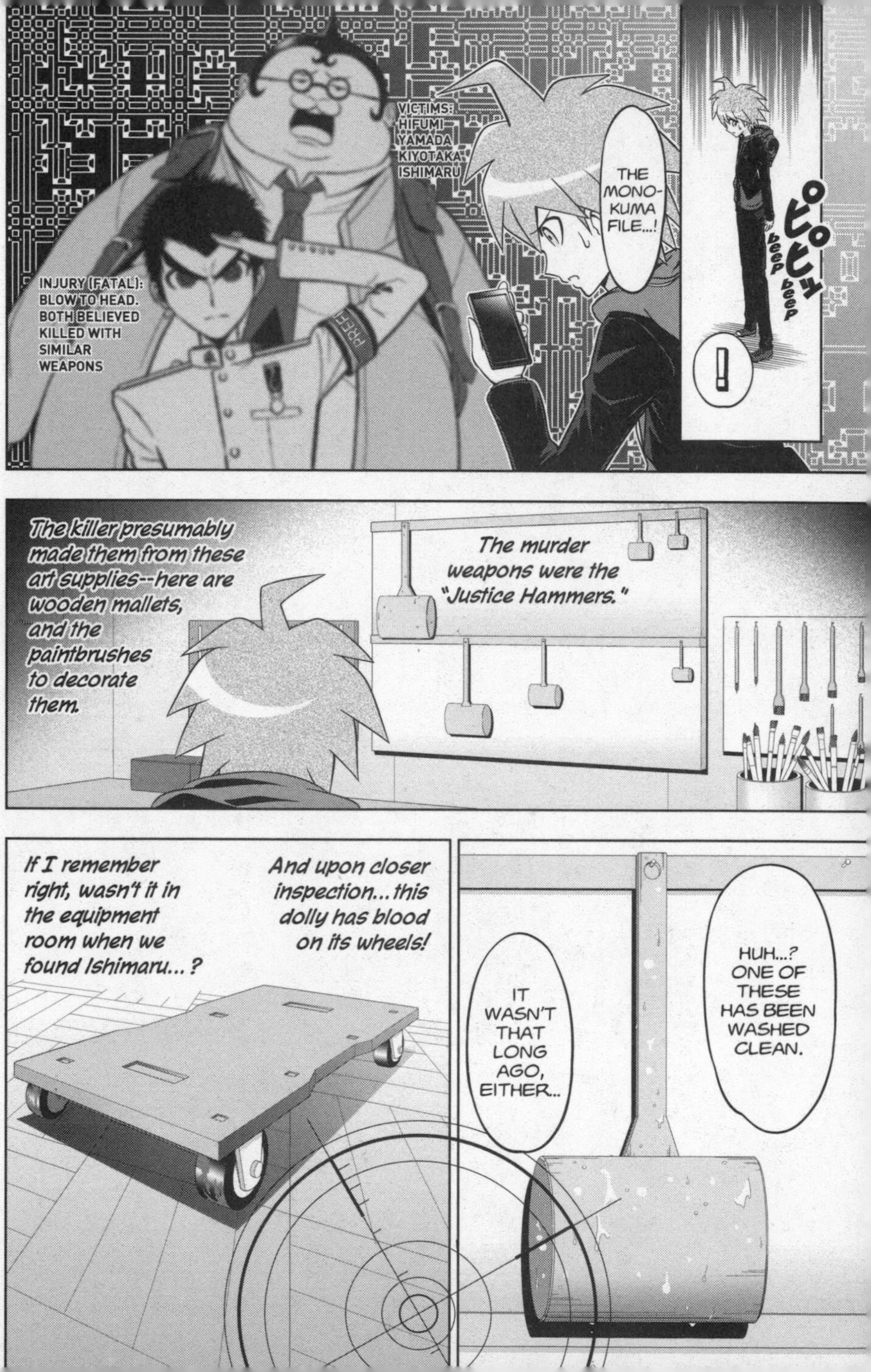
ピロピッ
beep beep
!
THE MONO-KUMA FILE...!
VICTIMS: HIFUMI YAMADA KIYOTAKA ISHIMARU
INJURY (FATAL): BLOW TO HEAD. BOTH BELIEVED KILLED WITH SIMILAR WEAPONS
The murder weapons were the "Justice Hammers."
The killer presumably made them from these art supplies--here are wooden mallets, and the paintbrushes to decorate them.
HUH...? ONE OF THESE HAS BEEN WASHED CLEAN.
IT WASN'T THAT LONG AGO, EITHER...
And upon closer inspection... this dolly has blood on its wheels!
If I remember right, wasn't it in the equipment room when we found Ishimaru...?

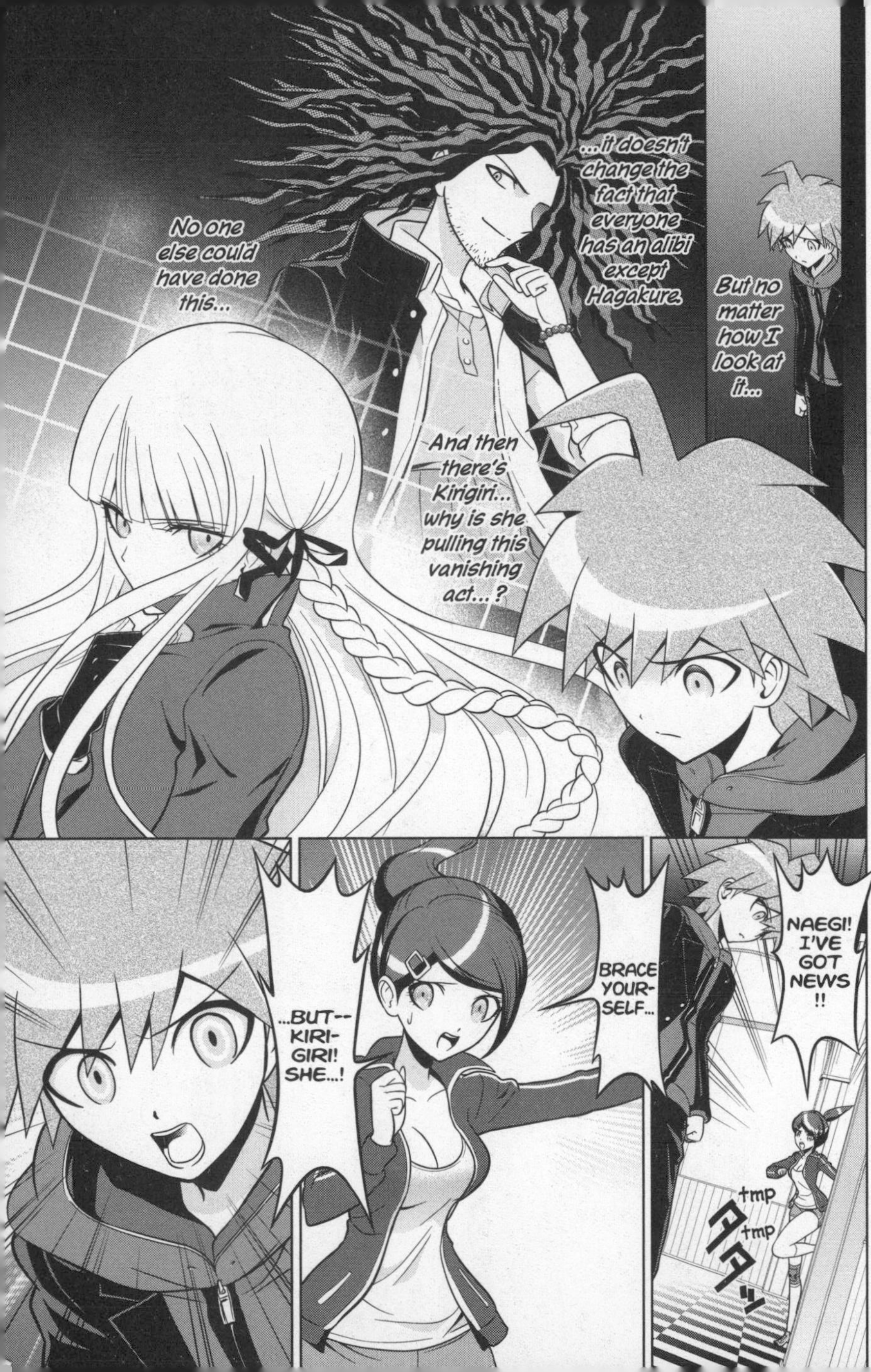
But no matter how I look at it...
...it doesn't change the fact that everyone has an alibi except Hagakure.
No one else could have done this...
And then there's Kirigiri... why is she pulling this vanishing act...?
NAEGI! I'VE GOT NEWS !!
tmp
タタッ
tmp
BRACE YOUR-SELF...
...BUT-- KIRI-GIRI! SHE...!

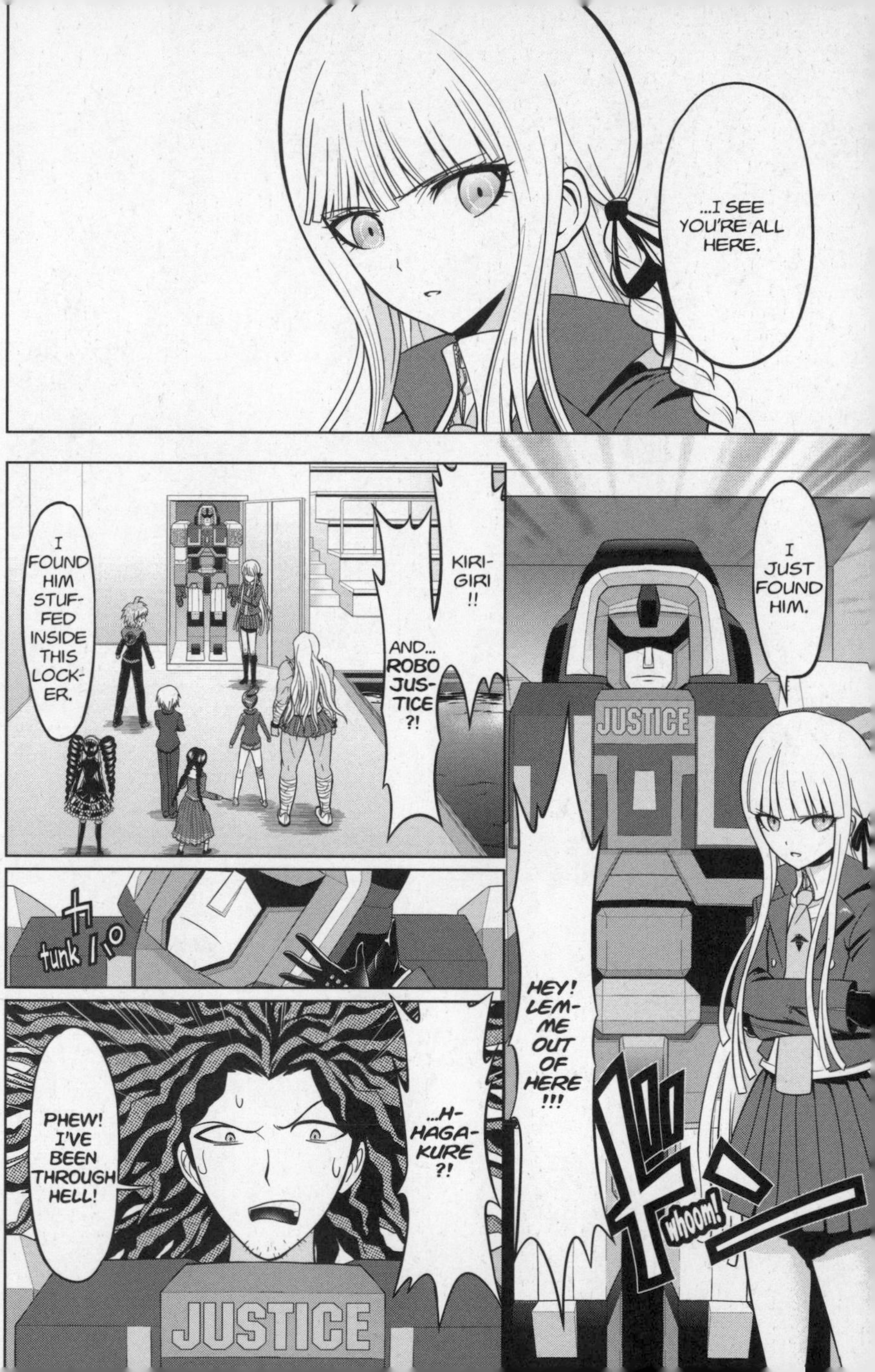
...I SEE YOU'RE ALL HERE.
I JUST FOUND HIM.
JUSTICE
HEY! LEMME OUT OF HERE!!!
whoom!
KIRI-GIRI!!
AND... ROBO JUSTICE?!
I FOUND HIM STUFFED INSIDE THIS LOCKER.
tunk
...H-HAGAKURE?!
PHEW! I'VE BEEN THROUGH HELL!
JUSTICE

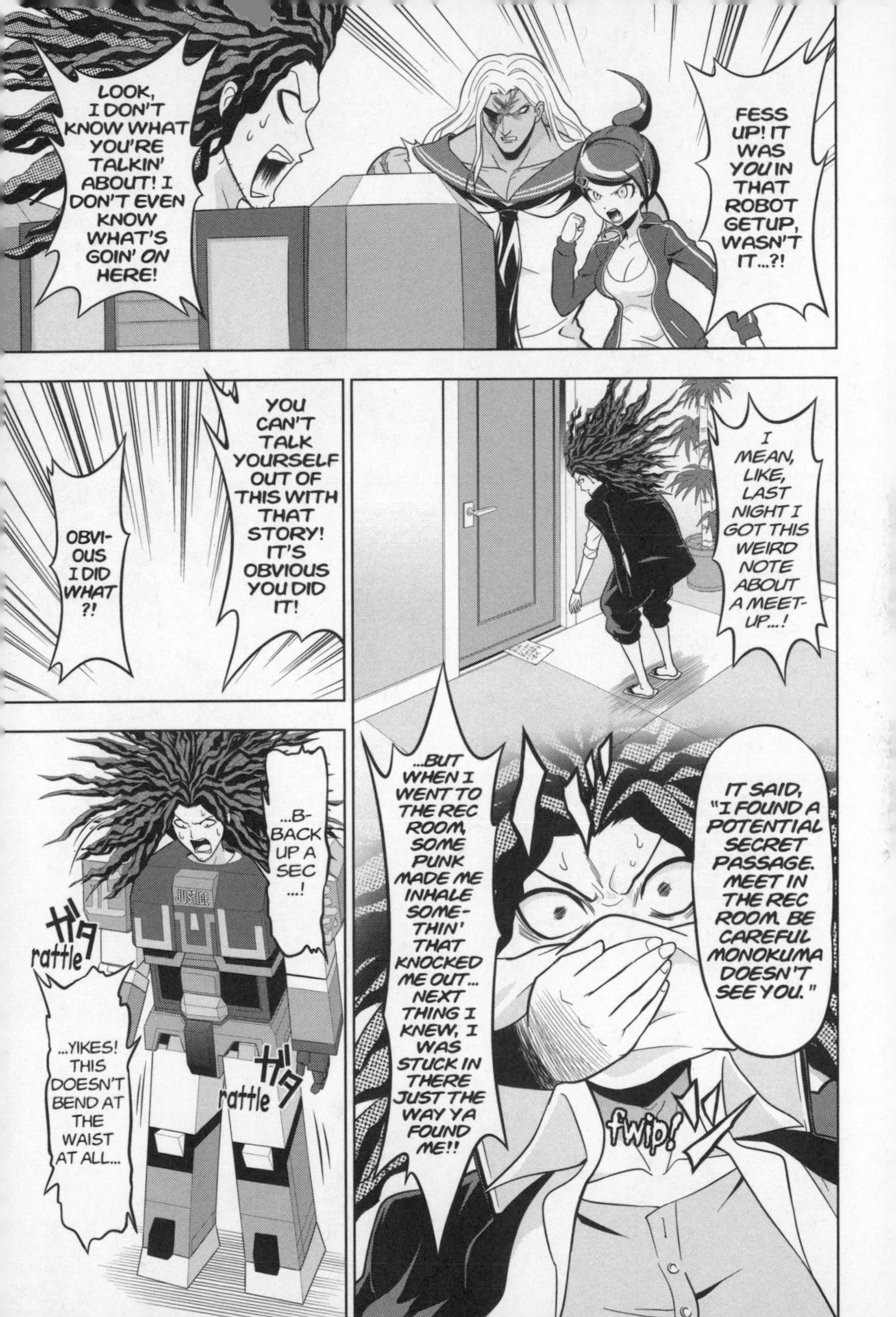
FESS UP! IT WAS YOU IN THAT ROBOT GETUP, WASN'T IT...?!
LOOK, I DON'T KNOW WHAT YOU'RE TALKIN' ABOUT! I DON'T EVEN KNOW WHAT'S GOIN' ON HERE!
I MEAN, LIKE, LAST NIGHT I GOT THIS WEIRD NOTE ABOUT A MEET-UP...!
YOU CAN'T TALK YOURSELF OUT OF THIS WITH THAT STORY! IT'S OBVIOUS YOU DID IT!
OBVI-OUS I DID WHAT?!
IT SAID, "I FOUND A POTENTIAL SECRET PASSAGE. MEET IN THE REC ROOM. BE CAREFUL MONOKUMA DOESN'T SEE YOU."
...BUT WHEN I WENT TO THE REC ROOM, SOME PUNK MADE ME INHALE SOME-THIN' THAT KNOCKED ME OUT... NEXT THING I KNEW, I WAS STUCK IN THERE JUST THE WAY YA FOUND ME!!
fwip!
...B-BACK UP A SEC...!
JUSTICE
ガタ
rattle
ガタ
rattle
...YIKES! THIS DOESN'T BEND AT THE WAIST AT ALL...

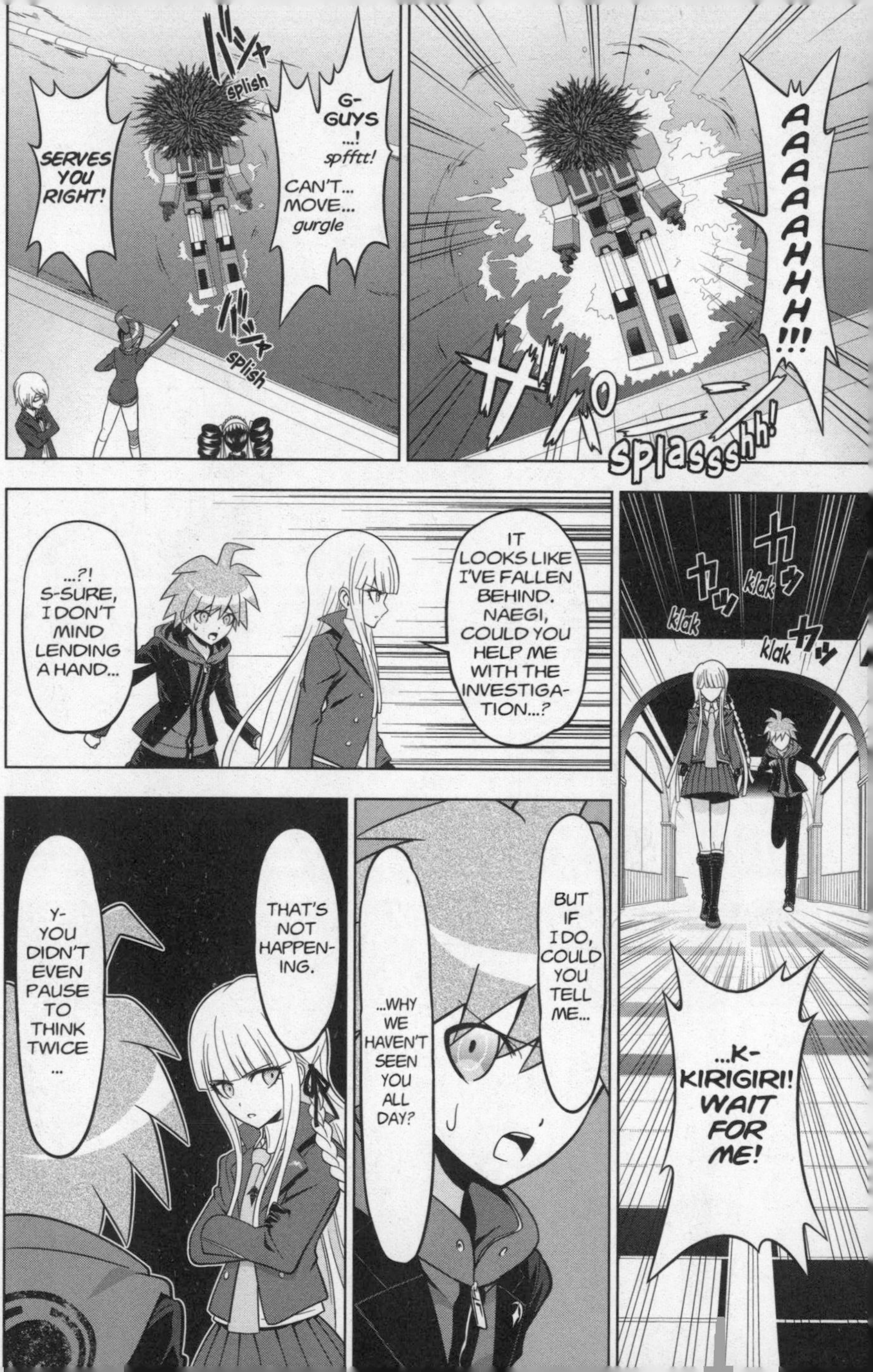
AAAAAHHH!!!
splasssshh!
G-GUYS ...! spfftt! CAN'T... MOVE... gurgle
splish
SERVES YOU RIGHT!
splish
klak
klak
klak
...K-KIRIGIRI! WAIT FOR ME!
IT LOOKS LIKE I'VE FALLEN BEHIND. NAEGI, COULD YOU HELP ME WITH THE INVESTIGA-TION...?
...?! S-SURE, I DON'T MIND LENDING A HAND...
BUT IF I DO, COULD YOU TELL ME...
...WHY WE HAVEN'T SEEN YOU ALL DAY?
THAT'S NOT HAPPEN-ING.
Y-YOU DIDN'T EVEN PAUSE TO THINK TWICE ...

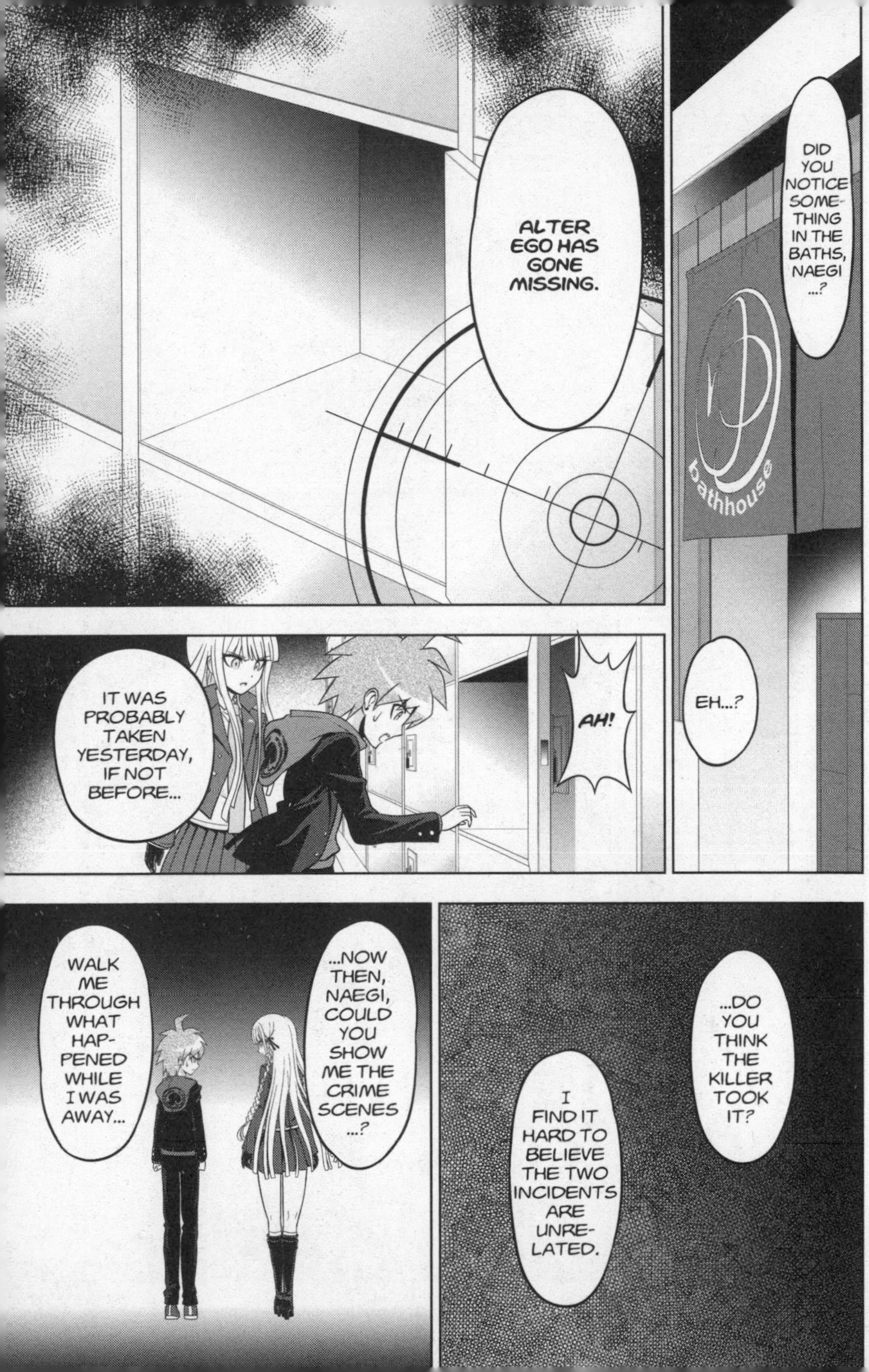
DID YOU NOTICE SOMETHING IN THE BATHS, NAEGI ...?
bathhouse
EH...?
ALTER EGO HAS GONE MISSING.
AH!
IT WAS PROBABLY TAKEN YESTERDAY, IF NOT BEFORE...
...DO YOU THINK THE KILLER TOOK IT?
I FIND IT HARD TO BELIEVE THE TWO INCIDENTS ARE UNRELATED.
...NOW THEN, NAEGI, COULD YOU SHOW ME THE CRIME SCENES ...?
WALK ME THROUGH WHAT HAPPENED WHILE I WAS AWAY...

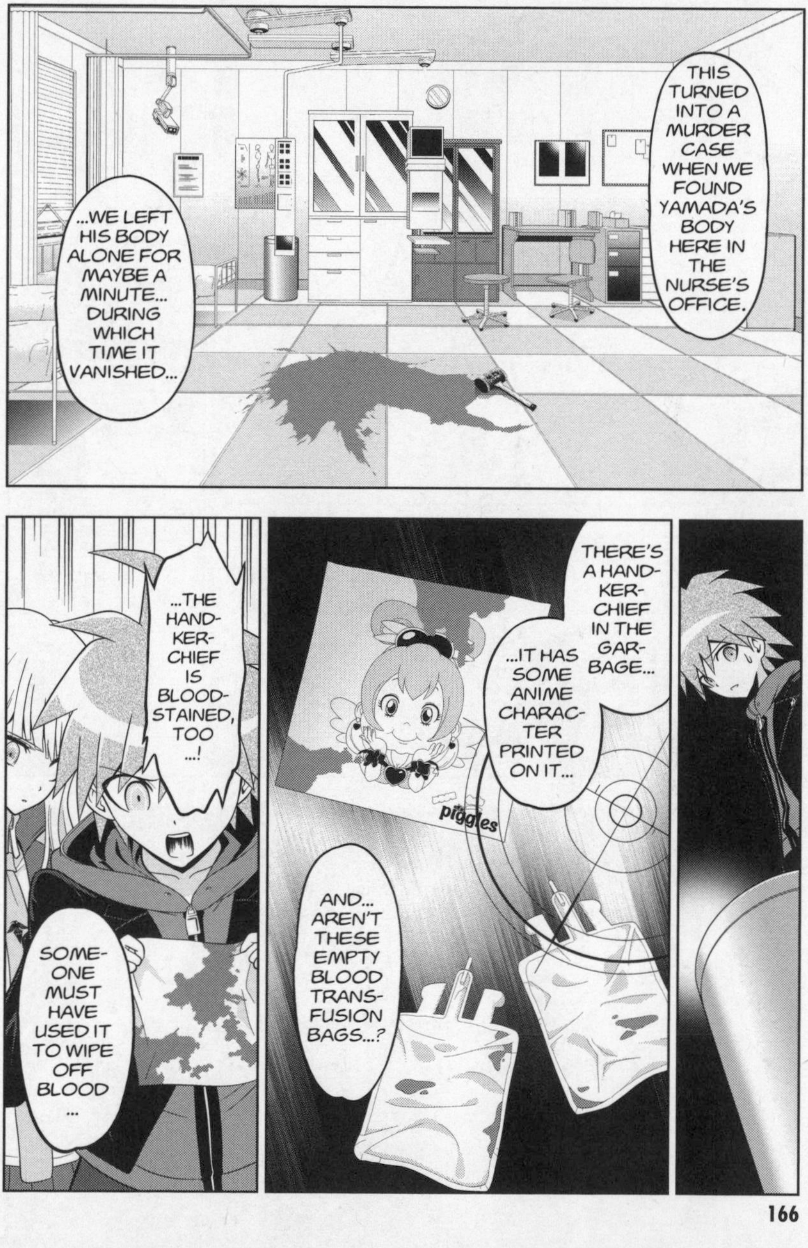
THIS TURNED INTO A MURDER CASE WHEN WE FOUND YAMADA'S BODY HERE IN THE NURSE'S OFFICE.
...WE LEFT HIS BODY ALONE FOR MAYBE A MINUTE... DURING WHICH TIME IT VANISHED...
THERE'S A HANDKERCHIEF IN THE GARBAGE...
...IT HAS SOME ANIME CHARACTER PRINTED ON IT...
piggles
AND... AREN'T THESE EMPTY BLOOD TRANSFUSION BAGS...?
...THE HANDKERCHIEF IS BLOOD-STAINED, TOO...!
SOMEONE MUST HAVE USED IT TO WIPE OFF BLOOD...

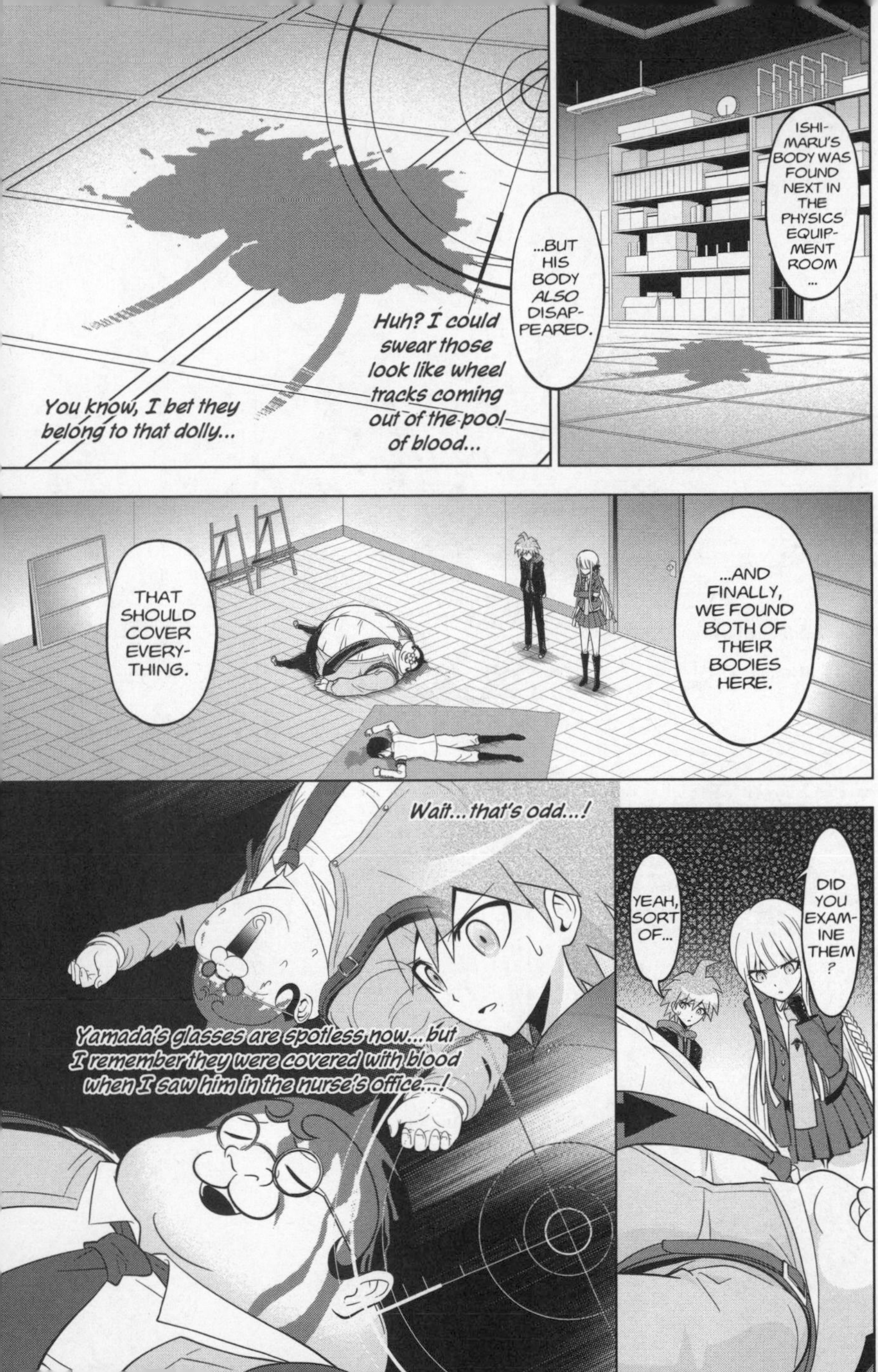
ISHI-MARU'S BODY WAS FOUND NEXT IN THE PHYSICS EQUIP-MENT ROOM ...
...BUT HIS BODY ALSO DISAP-PEARED.
Huh? I could swear those look like wheel tracks coming out of the pool of blood...
You know, I bet they belong to that dolly...
...AND FINALLY, WE FOUND BOTH OF THEIR BODIES HERE.
THAT SHOULD COVER EVERY-THING.
DID YOU EXAM-INE THEM ?
YEAH, SORT OF...
Wait...that's odd...!
Yamada's glasses are spotless now...but I remember they were covered with blood when I saw him in the nurse's office...!

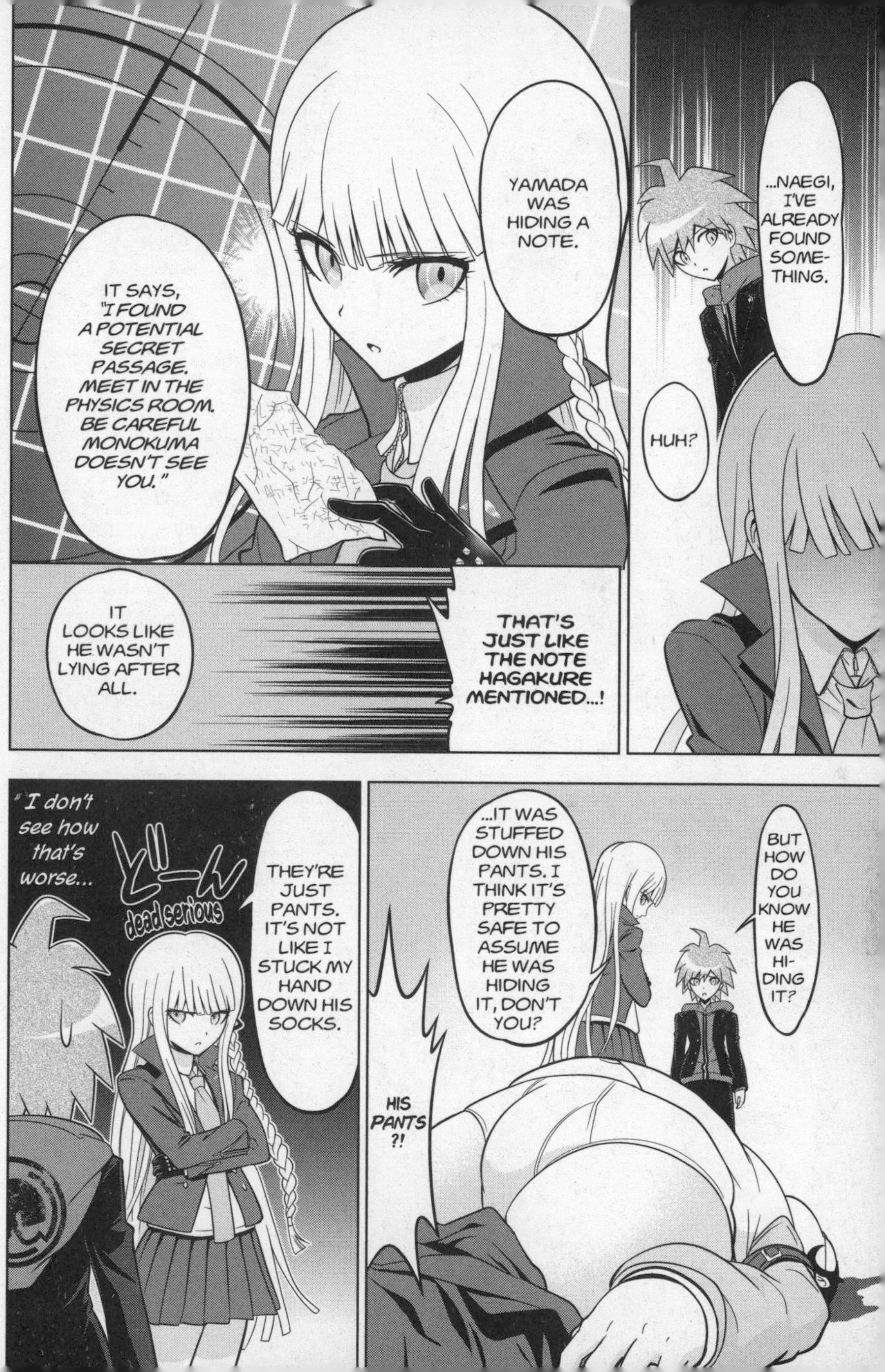

...NAEGI, I'VE ALREADY FOUND SOME-THING.
HUH?
YAMADA WAS HIDING A NOTE.
IT SAYS, "I FOUND A POTENTIAL SECRET PASSAGE. MEET IN THE PHYSICS ROOM. BE CAREFUL MONOKUMA DOESN'T SEE YOU."
THAT'S JUST LIKE THE NOTE HAGAKURE MENTIONED...!
IT LOOKS LIKE HE WASN'T LYING AFTER ALL.
BUT HOW DO YOU KNOW HE WAS HI-DING IT?
...IT WAS STUFFED DOWN HIS PANTS. I THINK IT'S PRETTY SAFE TO ASSUME HE WAS HIDING IT, DON'T YOU?
HIS PANTS?!
THEY'RE JUST PANTS. IT'S NOT LIKE I STUCK MY HAND DOWN HIS SOCKS.
どーん
dead serious
I don't see how that's worse...

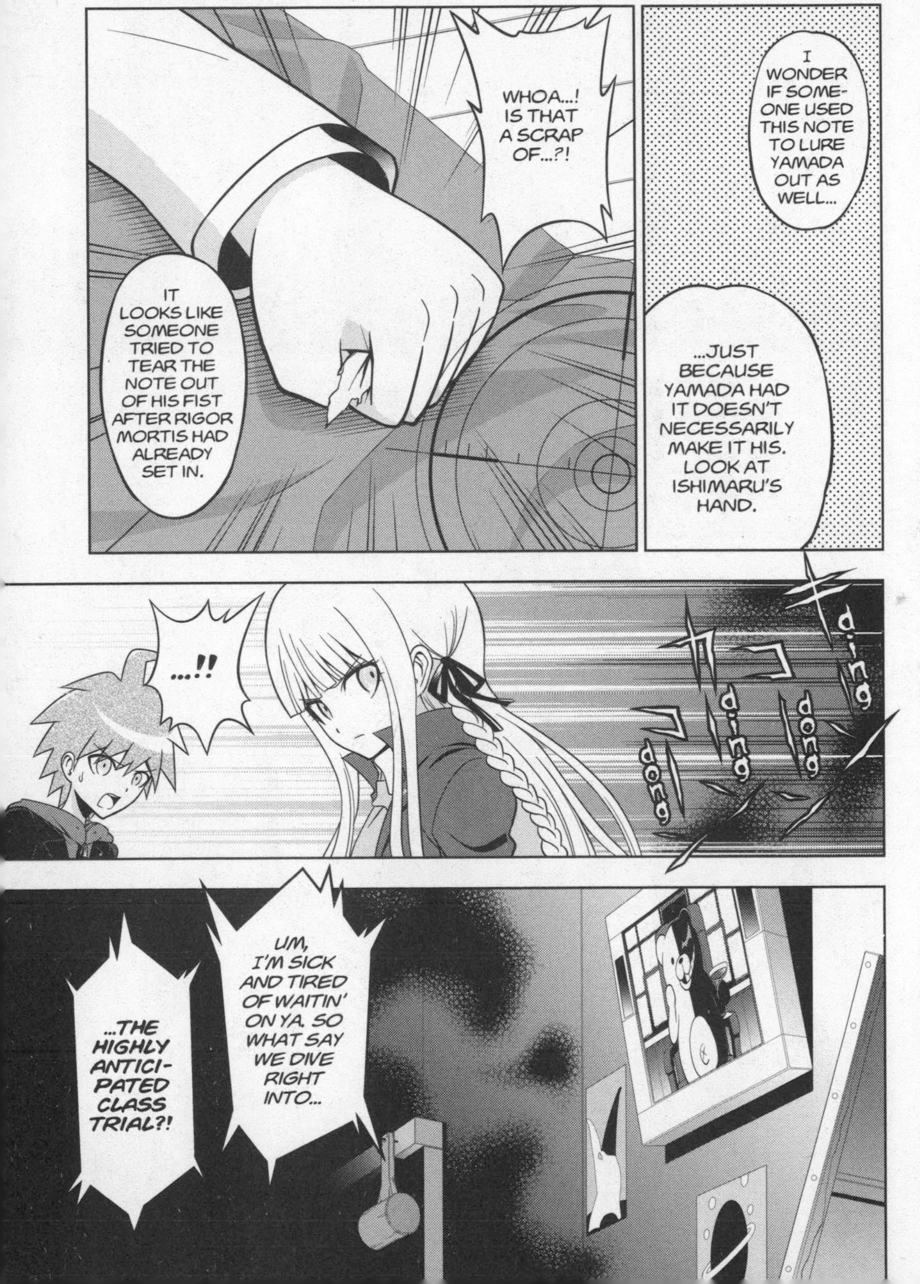
I WONDER IF SOME-ONE USED THIS NOTE TO LURE YAMADA OUT AS WELL...
...JUST BECAUSE YAMADA HAD IT DOESN'T NECESSARILY MAKE IT HIS. LOOK AT ISHIMARU'S HAND.
WHOA...! IS THAT A SCRAP OF...?!
IT LOOKS LIKE SOMEONE TRIED TO TEAR THE NOTE OUT OF HIS FIST AFTER RIGOR MORTIS HAD ALREADY SET IN.
ding dong ding dong
...!!
UM, I'M SICK AND TIRED OF WAITIN' ON YA. SO WHAT SAY WE DIVE RIGHT INTO...
...THE HIGHLY ANTICI-PATED CLASS TRIAL?!

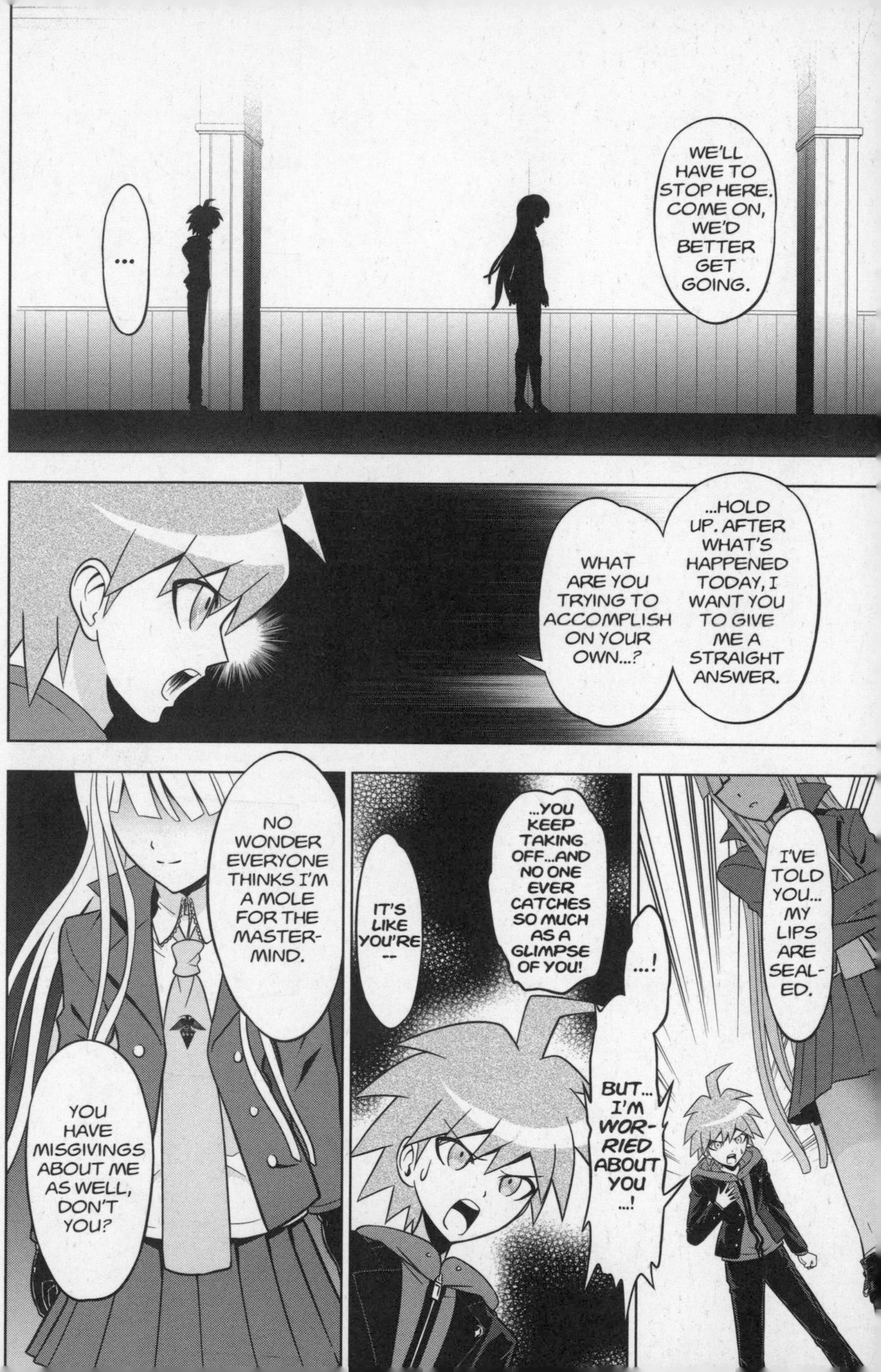
WE'LL HAVE TO STOP HERE. COME ON, WE'D BETTER GET GOING.
...
...HOLD UP. AFTER WHAT'S HAPPENED TODAY, I WANT YOU TO GIVE ME A STRAIGHT ANSWER.
WHAT ARE YOU TRYING TO ACCOMPLISH ON YOUR OWN...?
I'VE TOLD YOU... MY LIPS ARE SEAL-ED.
...!
BUT... I'M WOR-RIED ABOUT YOU ...!
...YOU KEEP TAKING OFF...AND NO ONE EVER CATCHES SO MUCH AS A GLIMPSE OF YOU!
IT'S LIKE YOU'RE --
NO WONDER EVERYONE THINKS I'M A MOLE FOR THE MASTER-MIND.
YOU HAVE MISGIVINGS ABOUT ME AS WELL, DON'T YOU?

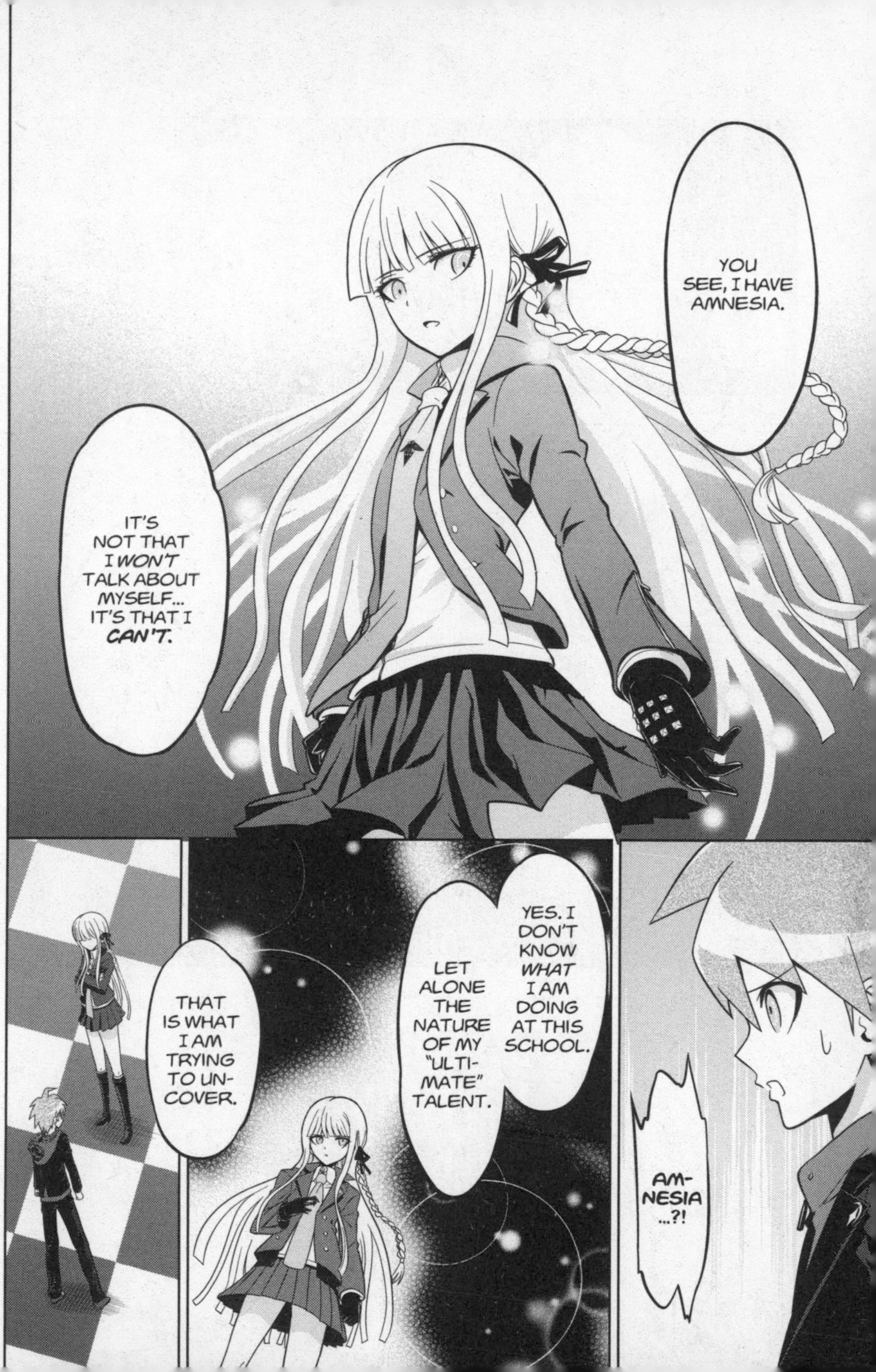
YOU SEE, I HAVE AMNESIA.
IT'S NOT THAT I *WON'T* TALK ABOUT MYSELF... IT'S THAT I ***CAN'T***.
AM-NESIA ...?!
YES. I DON'T KNOW *WHAT* I AM DOING AT THIS SCHOOL.
LET ALONE THE NATURE OF MY "ULTI-MATE" TALENT.
THAT IS WHAT I AM TRYING TO UN-COVER.

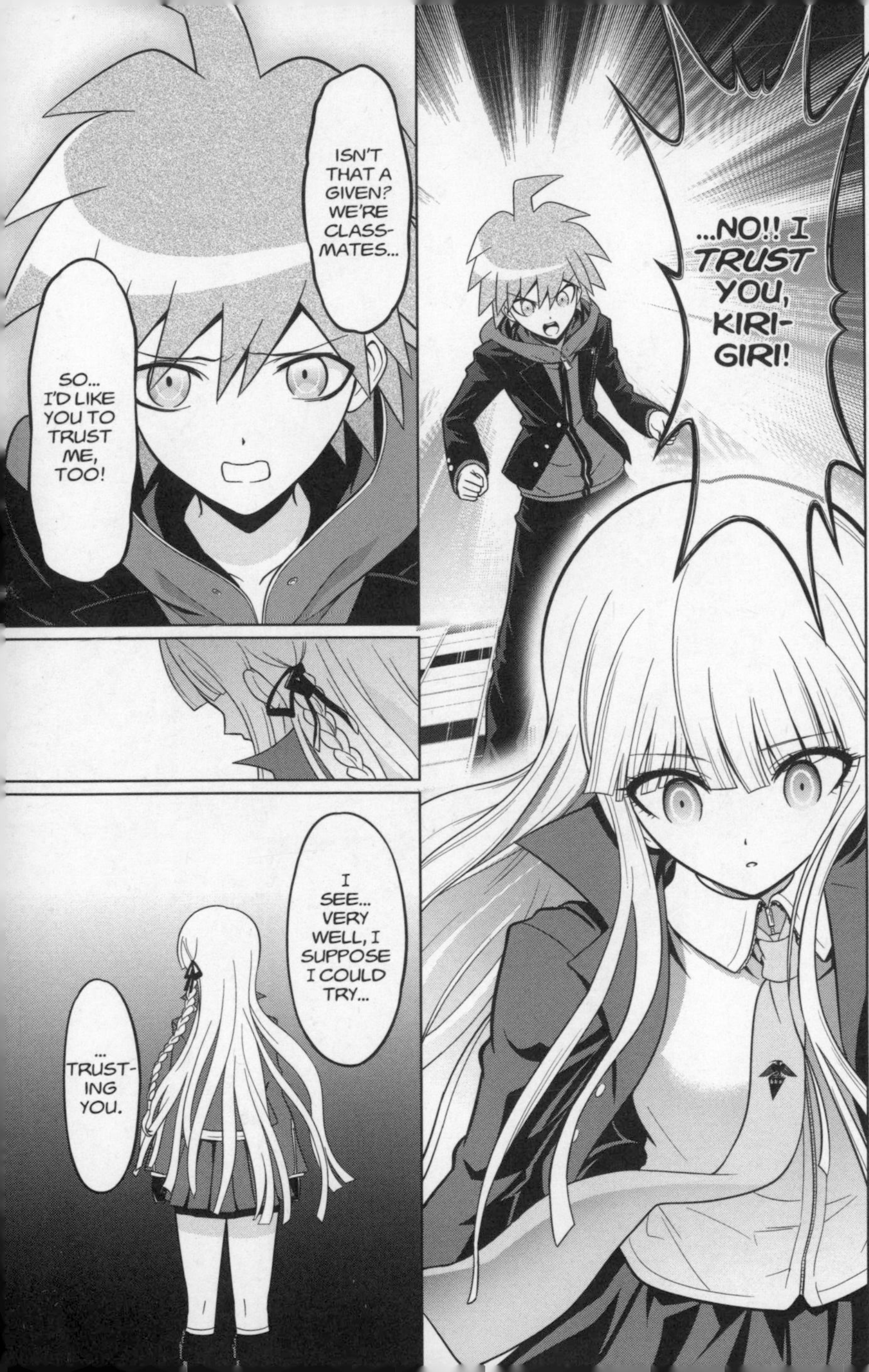
...NO!! I TRUST YOU, KIRI-GIRI!
ISN'T THAT A GIVEN? WE'RE CLASS-MATES...
SO... I'D LIKE YOU TO TRUST ME, TOO!
I SEE... VERY WELL, I SUPPOSE I COULD TRY...
... TRUST-ING YOU.

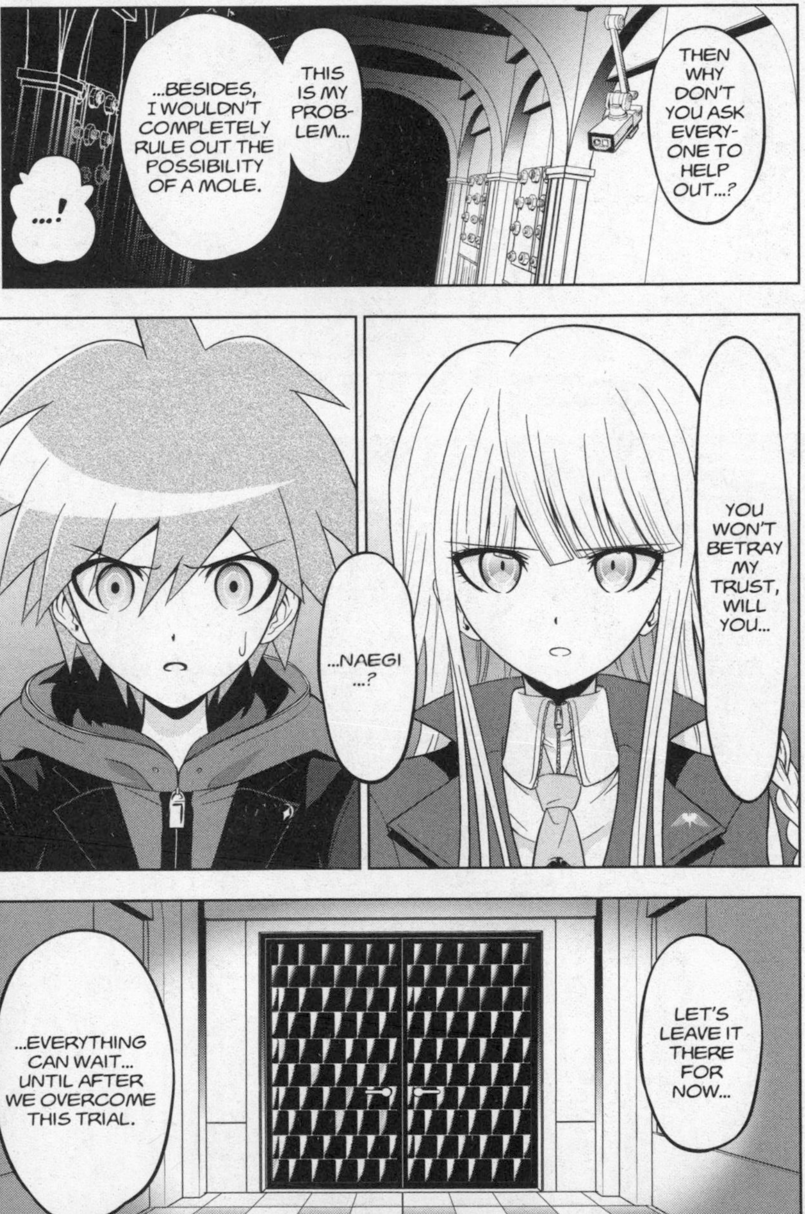
THEN WHY DON'T YOU ASK EVERY-ONE TO HELP OUT...?
THIS IS MY PROB-LEM...
...BESIDES, I WOULDN'T COMPLETELY RULE OUT THE POSSIBILITY OF A MOLE.
...!
YOU WON'T BETRAY MY TRUST, WILL YOU...
...NAEGI ...?
LET'S LEAVE IT THERE FOR NOW...
...EVERYTHING CAN WAIT... UNTIL AFTER WE OVERCOME THIS TRIAL.

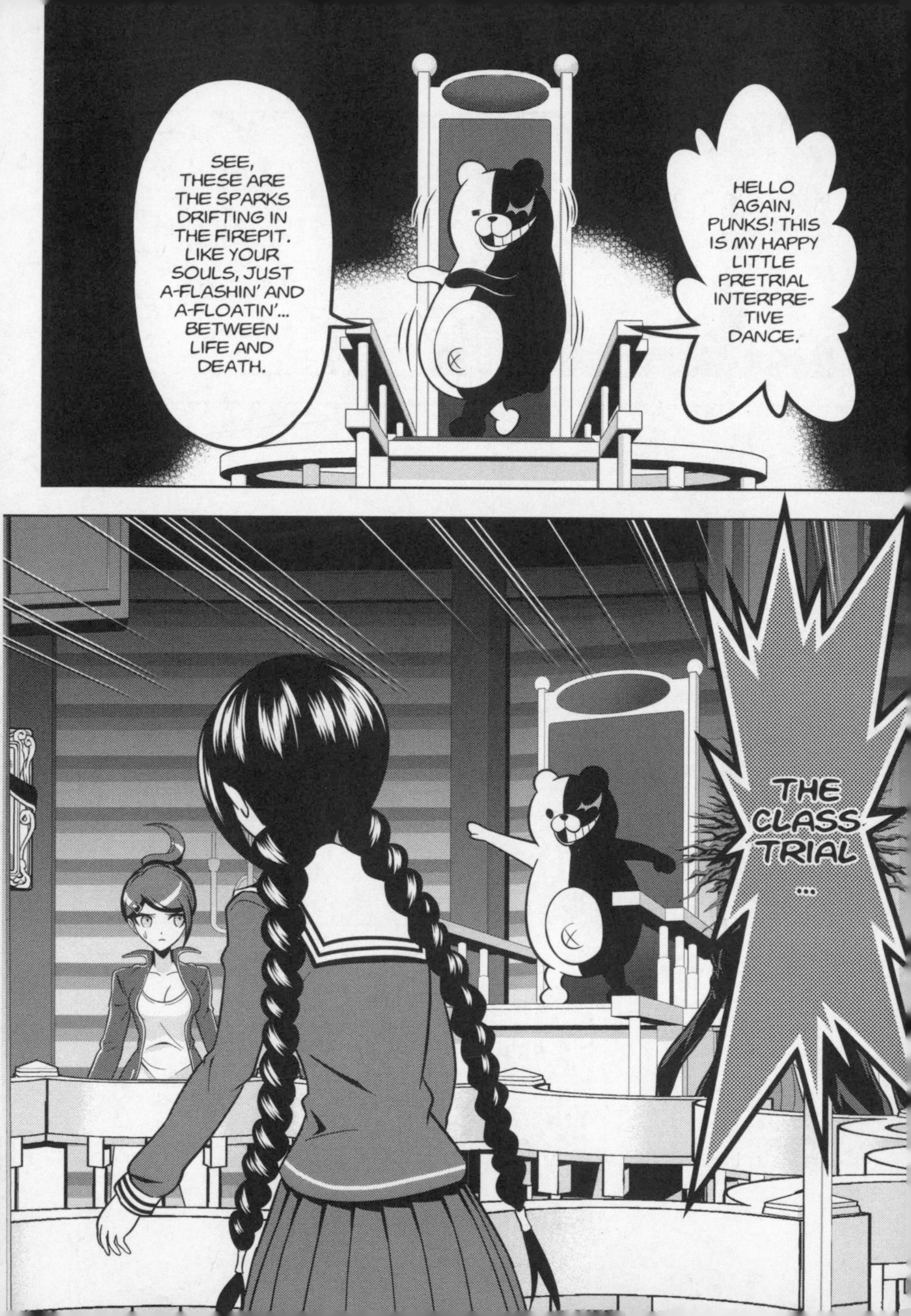
HELLO AGAIN, PUNKS! THIS IS MY HAPPY LITTLE PRETRIAL INTERPRE-TIVE DANCE.
SEE, THESE ARE THE SPARKS DRIFTING IN THE FIREPIT. LIKE YOUR SOULS, JUST A-FLASHIN' AND A-FLOATIN'... BETWEEN LIFE AND DEATH.
THE CLASS TRIAL ...

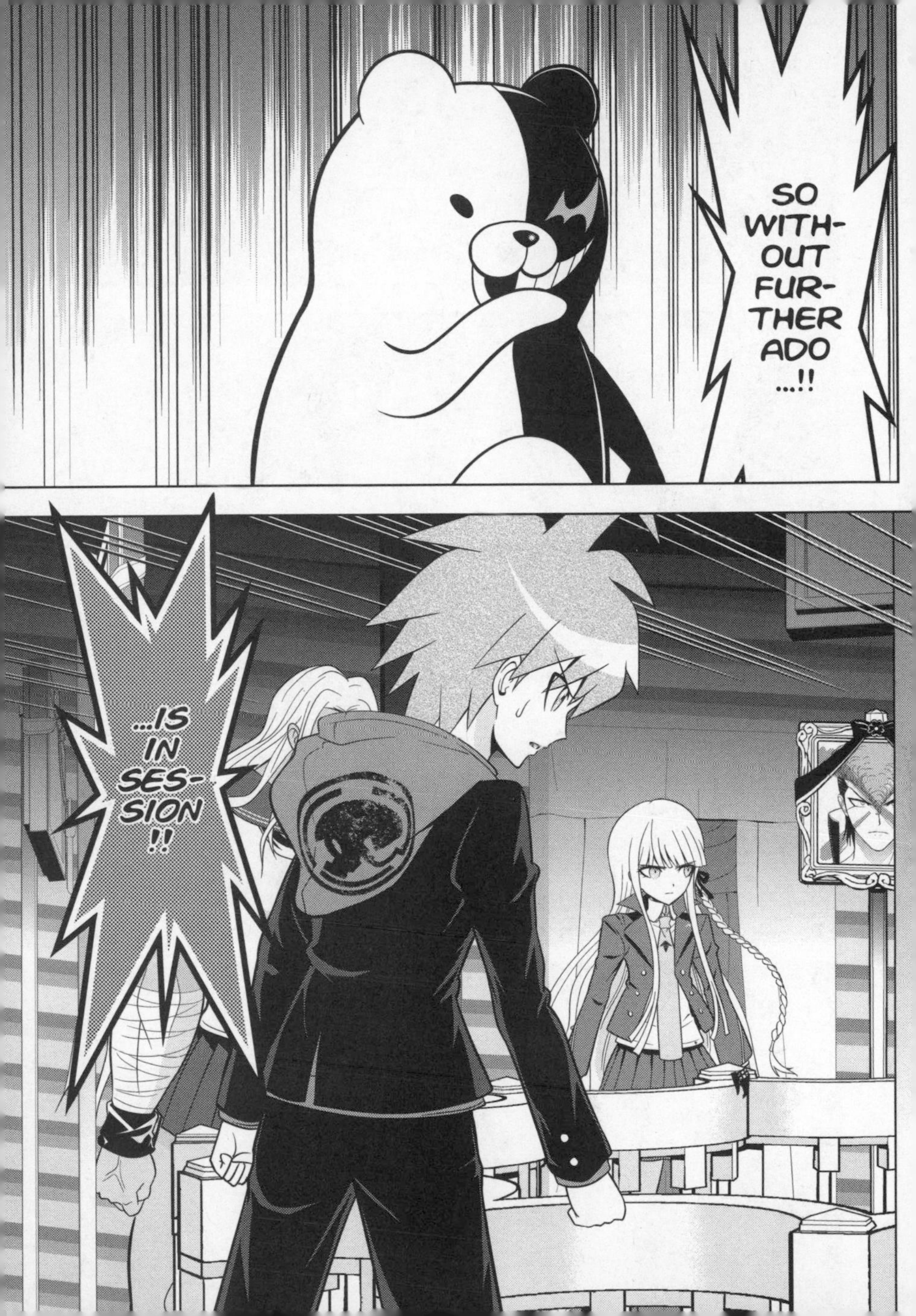
SO WITH-OUT FUR-THER ADO ...!!
...IS IN SES-SION !!

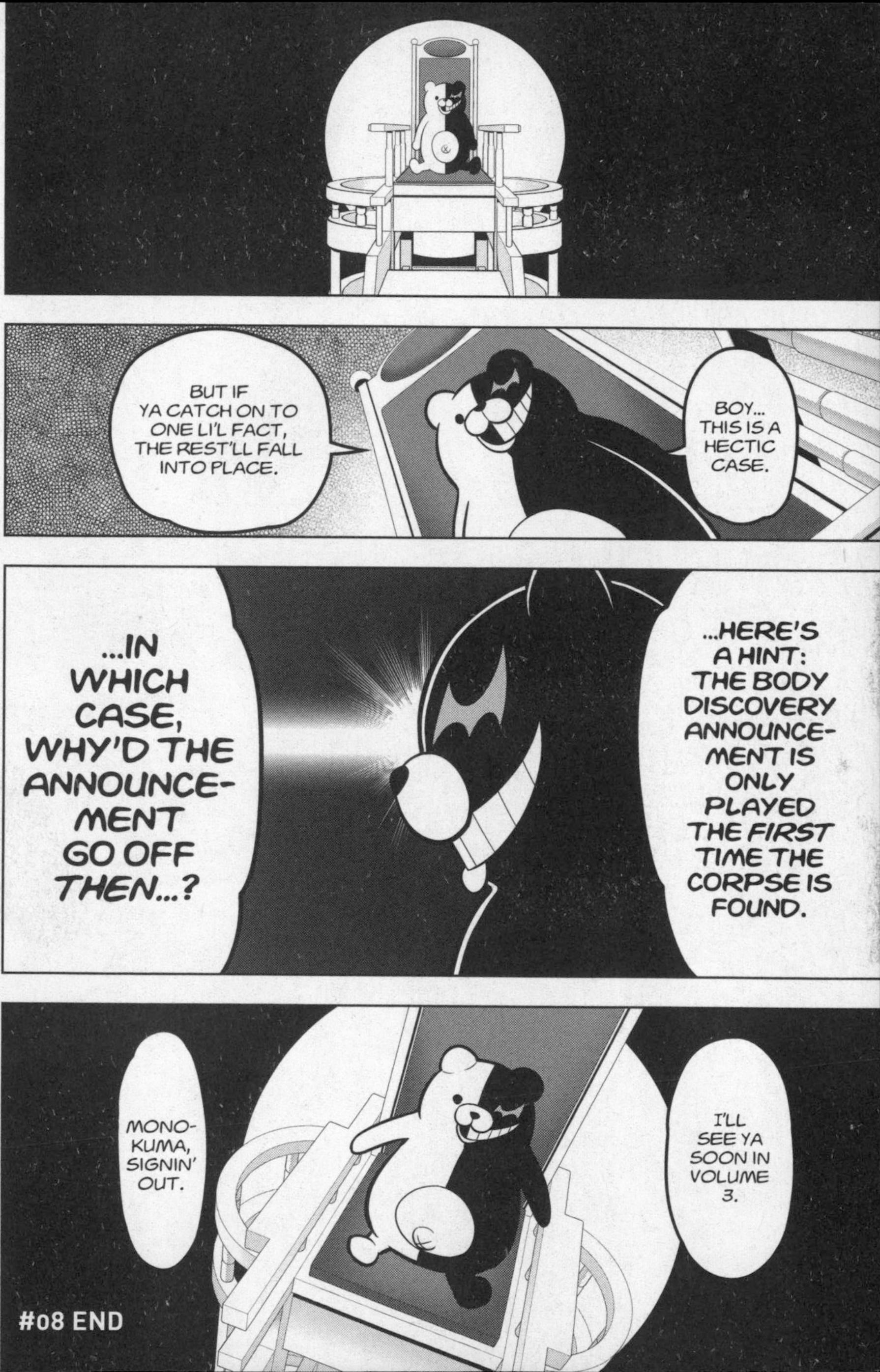
BOY... THIS IS A HECTIC CASE.
BUT IF YA CATCH ON TO ONE LI'L FACT, THE REST'LL FALL INTO PLACE.
...HERE'S A HINT: THE BODY DISCOVERY ANNOUNCEMENT IS ONLY PLAYED THE *FIRST* TIME THE CORPSE IS FOUND.
...IN WHICH CASE, WHY'D THE ANNOUNCEMENT GO OFF *THEN*...?
I'LL SEE YA SOON IN VOLUME 3.
MONOKUMA, SIGNIN' OUT.
#08 END

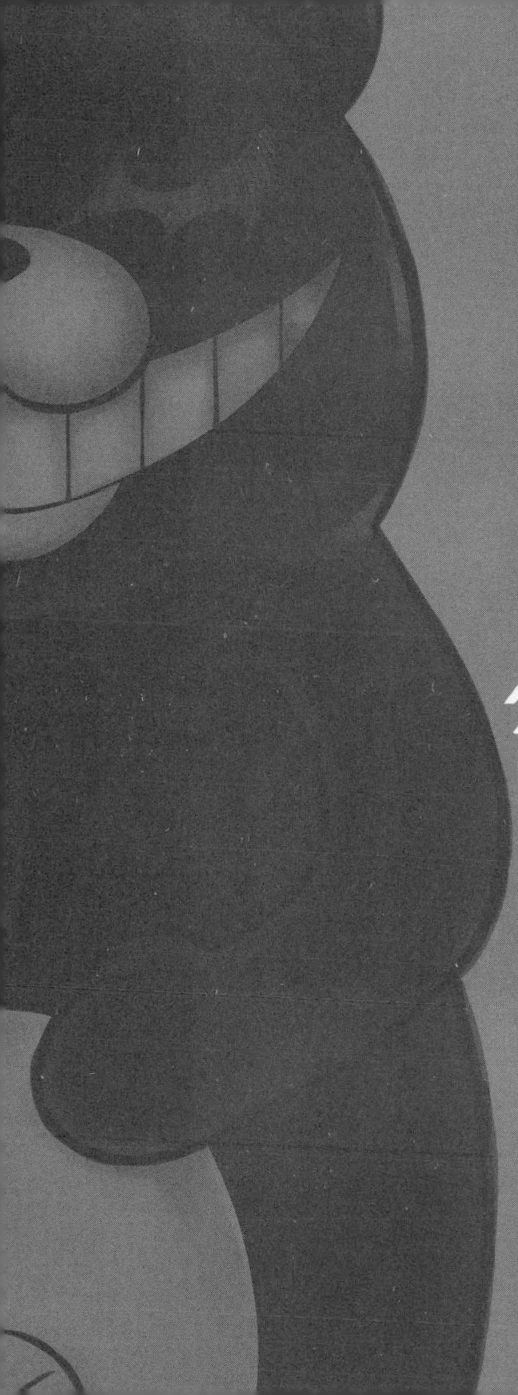

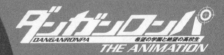

ダンガンロンパ
DANGANRONPA
希望の学園と絶望の高校生
THE ANIMATION

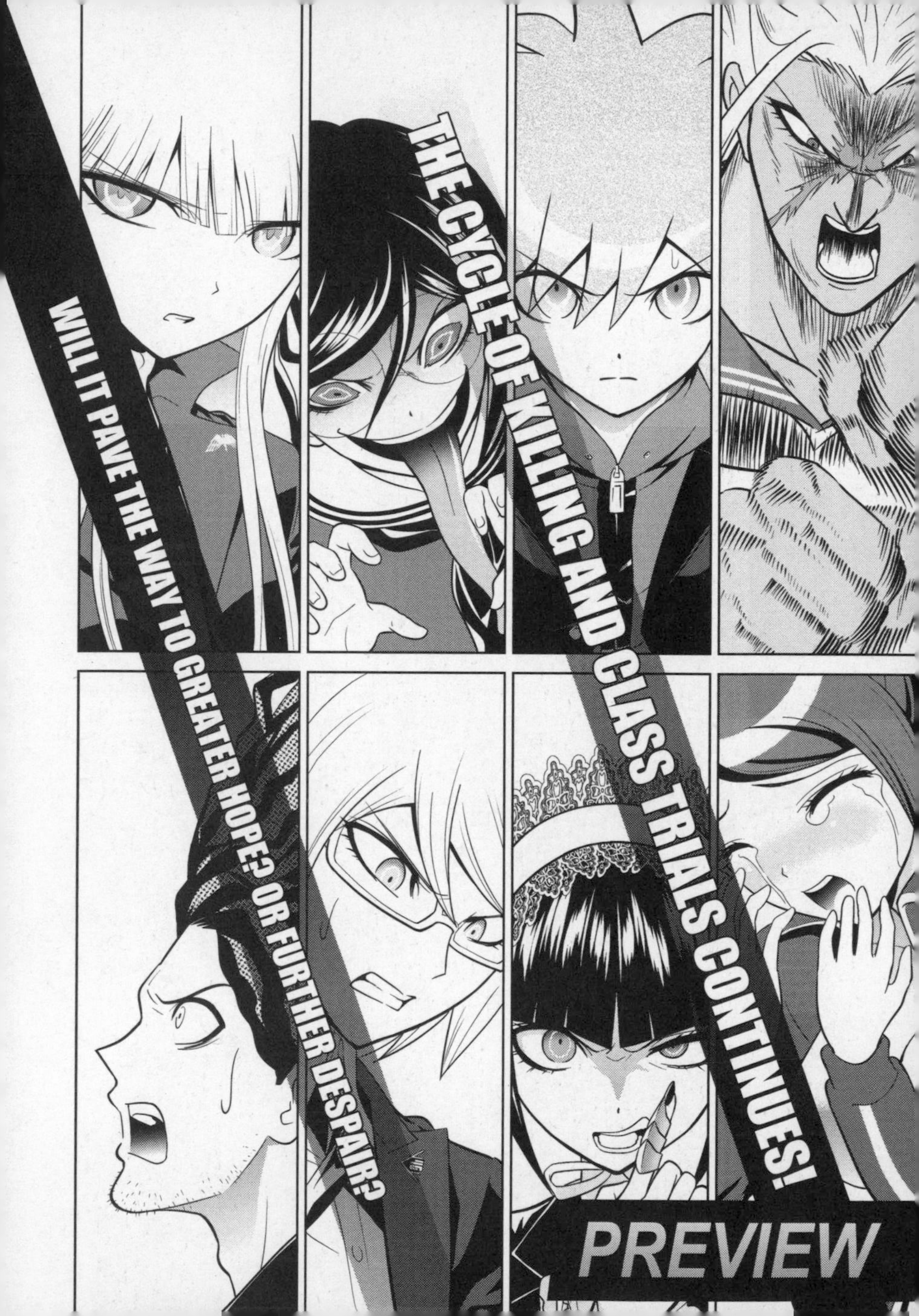
THE CYCLE OF KILLING AND CLASS TRIALS CONTINUES!
WILL IT PAVE THE WAY TO GREATER HOPE? OR FURTHER DESPAIR?
PREVIEW

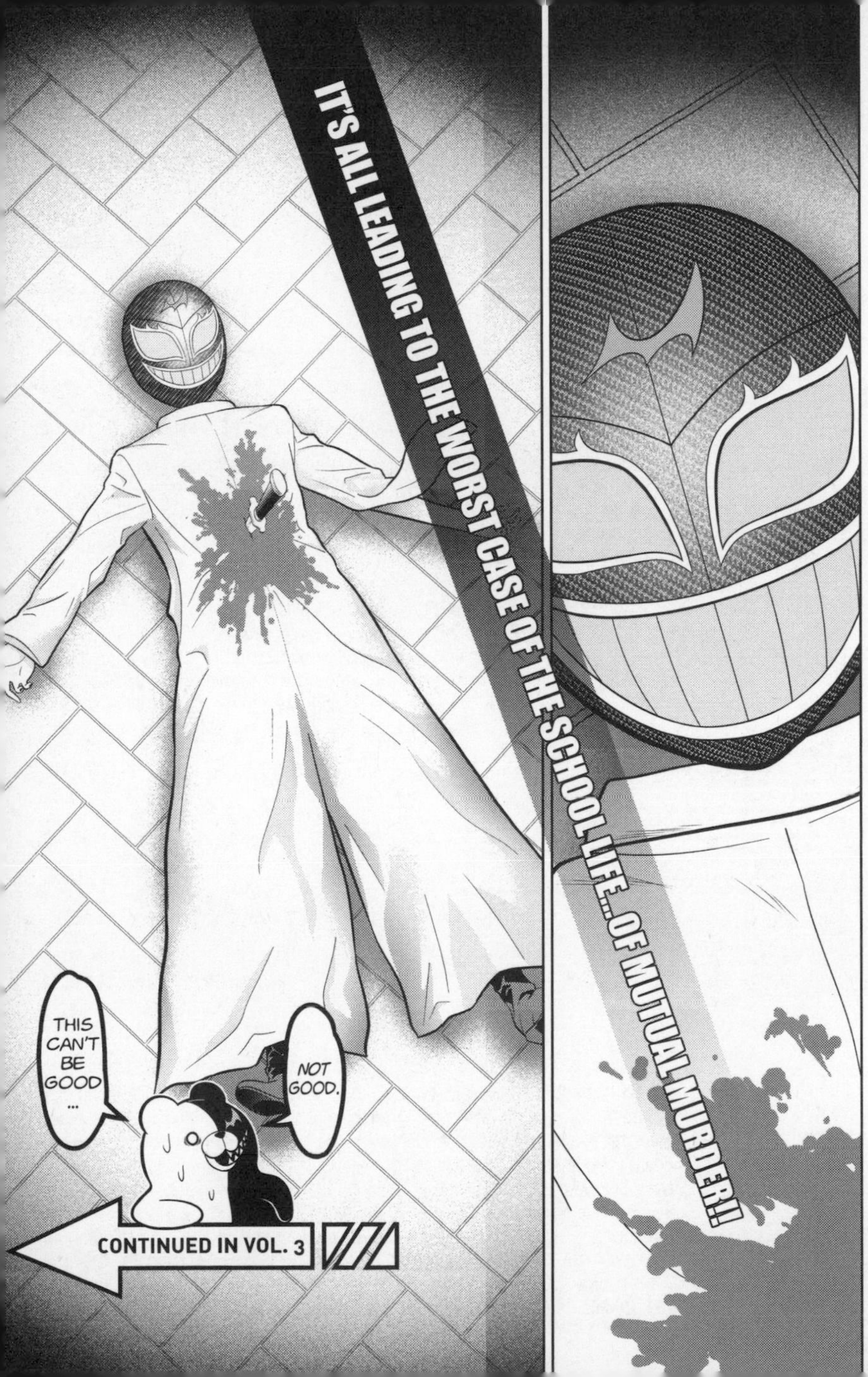
IT'S ALL LEADING TO THE WORST CASE OF THE SCHOOL LIFE...OF MUTUAL MURDER!!
NOT GOOD.
THIS CAN'T BE GOOD ...
CONTINUED IN VOL. 3

president and publisher
MIKE RICHARDSON

designer
SARAH TERRY

ultimate digital art technician
CHRISTINA McKENZIE

English-language version produced by Dark Horse Comics

DANGANRONPA: THE ANIMATION VOLUME 2

Published by
Dark Horse Manga
A division of Dark Horse Comics LLC
10956 SE Main Street I Milwaukie, OR 97222

DarkHorse.com

To find a comics shop in your area, visit comicshoplocator.com

First edition: July 2016
ISBN 978-1-61655-963-2

8 9 10

Printed in the United States of America

DESPAIR MAIL

c/o Dark Horse Comics | 10956 SE Main St. | Milwaukie, OR 97222 | danganronpa@darkhorse.com

Welcome back to Despair Mail, the place for Ultimate Danganronpa Fans! If you'd like to share your thoughts or comments on Danganronpa . . . pictures of your Danganronpa cosplay . . . or your Danganronpa fan art—this is the place for you! Send it to the address or email at the top of the page, and remember to use high resolution (300 dpi or better) for your photos or images, so it'll look good in print!

This time, we've got contributions from another eight fans to feature, including our first cosplay photos!

In the photo, Irelza is portraying Byakuya Togami and Stellaenowa is portraying Toko Fukawa. You can find them on Facebook under irelza.lowell and nowacosplay, and on DeviantArt under irelza and nowii. Thank you both very much for sharing your photos with Despair Mail, and we hope to see you all in volume 3 . . . if you SURVIVE, that is!

This fan art is from Rhiannon Ayres, who comments, "The only thing is that it's a drawing for a character from the second game, so I wasn't sure if it would count or not, but I'm sending it in anyway! I just wanted to say that I'm extremely happy that you guys created Despair Mail—as far as I've known, there hasn't been much of a chance within Danganronpa to be able to turn in fan-made creations, so the fact that you guys are doing this is so amazing!! Thank you all so much!! I will make sure to buy every volume!"

Well, thank YOU, Rhiannon. This, of course, is a depiction of Gundham Tanaka, and it's fine to send in contributions to Despair Mail from any part of the Danganronpa series. In fact, it was seeing a screencap of just a single quote from the second game that originally got me into Danganronpa, but I'm not going to say which character it was. (Naegi stabs his finger at me: "It was Akane Owari . . . wasn't it . . .?!" Yes. Yes, it was.)

This photo is from fan Lauren Barton, who says, "A selfie is completely appropriate for an Ultimate Fashionista, I'd think! I'm a really big fan of Danganronpa, and when I saw you guys asking for submissions, I knew I had to send something right away! I can't wait to see what you guys include in the manga—it's super exciting." Thank you very much for sharing your photo with Despair Mail!

Next is Ashley's cosplay of the Ultimate Gambler, Celestia "Celeste" Ludenberg. I really feel they should let Celeste be a character in a James Bond movie, playing baccarat against 007 at some elegant European casino. Ashley writes: *"I'm super excited for the manga and I know you guys will do a great job with it. There are so many of us fans out here ready to support you! I'm going to preorder my copy this week. Take care! :)"* Thank you very much for all your encouragement, and I think the many responses we have received for Despair Mail definitely demonstrate that support!

Naegi has a tough job in Danganronpa, so I'm glad to see him represented in Despair Mail too! Here are Juliane and her friend cosplaying Junko Enoshima and Makoto Naegi. "Thank you for allowing us fans the opportunity to have a part in the manga!" writes Juliane. Well, it wouldn't work without everyone's contributions, so thank you all for wanting to be a part of the manga, too! We have to send these books to the printer some time before it shows up in your store. So if you don't see your contribution here, we'll do our best to include it next time!

—CGH